Little Horrors

# Little Horrors

*How Cinema's Evil Children
Play on Our Guilt*

T. S. Kord

McFarland & Company, Inc., Publishers
*Jefferson, North Carolina*

LIBRARY OF CONGRESS CATALOGUING-IN-PUBLICATION DATA

Names: Kord, T. S., author.
Title: Little horrors : how cinema's evil children play on our guilt / T.S. Kord.
Description: Jefferson, North Carolina : McFarland & Company, Inc., Publishers, 2016 | Includes bibliographical references and index.
Identifiers: LCCN 2016026039 | ISBN 9781476666068 (softcover : acid free paper) ∞
Subjects: LCSH: Horror films—History and criticism. | Children in motion pictures. | Motion pictures—Ethical and moral aspects. | Motion pictures—Psychological aspects.
Classification: LCC PN1995.9.H6 K67 2016 | DDC 791.43/6164—dc23
LC record available at https://lccn.loc.gov/2016026039

BRITISH LIBRARY CATALOGUING DATA ARE AVAILABLE

**ISBN (print) 978-1-4766-6606-8**
**ISBN (ebook) 978-1-4766-2666-6**

© 2016 T. S. Kord. All rights reserved

*No part of this book may be reproduced or transmitted in any form or by any means, electronic or mechanical, including photocopying or recording, or by any information storage and retrieval system, without permission in writing from the publisher.*

Front cover image from *Sinister*, 2012 (Summit Entertainment/Photofest)

Printed in the United States of America

*McFarland & Company, Inc., Publishers*
*Box 611, Jefferson, North Carolina 28640*
*www.mcfarlandpub.com*

# Table of Contents

*Preface*   1

*Introduction*   3

1. Birth: Gynecological Gross-Out   13
2. Family: Home-Grown Horrors   33
3. Nature: An Abundance of Horror   56
4. Science: Seeing the World in Black and White   76
5. Religion: The Road to Hell and What It's Paved With   94
6. Consumption: Dying in a Material World   118
7. Abuse: Leaving the Family Behind   138
8. Play: The Peter Pan Syndrome   161

*Conclusions*   178
*Chapter Notes*   187
*Bibliography*   195
*Index*   215

# Preface

This book is a new way of looking at horror films, particularly those involving evil children. It shows that they routinely play on our guilt for crimes ranging from child rejection, child abuse, child rape, and child abandonment to greed, ecological, social, political and war crimes, and above all, for the persistent denial of responsibility for all of it. The point is made both in depth (for, generally, three films per chapter) and in breadth (in the "Guilt Trips" section following each chapter, which contain glimpses at many other films that are out to guilt-trip viewers in similar ways). Chapters focus on themes that are both part and parcel of children's lives and at the center of the viewer's moral universe: birth and family, nature and science, religion and consumerism, child abuse and child's play. Thirty international films are discussed extensively, with sideways glances at another 100 movies made since the 1950s, the decade in which the horror genre moved from the creature feature to attaching a human face to the concept of Evil.

Because the point of this book has far more to do with the human condition than with film studies, it does not, as books in film studies so often do, pick a theory (say, psychoanalysis or queer theory) and read films in its light. To do so would be a disservice to any reader who might be gripped by the films but bored by the theory. It would also fail to acknowledge that there is more than one idea out there that can help us think about children, horror, and Evil. Some that have made it into this book are the question of how films might handle identity and point-of-view; what psychoanalytic theory has had to say about women and children; how the grotesque works in literature and art; why love for your children is a fairly recent historical idea; why meritocracy can devastate as well as empower; why child psychologists think children play; how philosophers have defined Evil; what marketing research can tell us about guilt, and what cartoons can tell us about our ability to identify with a character. These ideas are raised only if and where they are honestly relevant—meaning: if they provide a new and interesting twist in thinking about children, horror, Evil, or guilt—not because I feel my book needs a theory to impress my peers or dodge what Gerald Graff has called "knee-jerk antireductivism."[1] What you will therefore not find here are theoretical treatises, intra-academic controversies, or debates of minute details of film theory and mechanics that might fascinate film studies scholars but would not be interesting to the general reader. Equally, there is no assumption here that readers are familiar with every film discussed in this book. Hence you will find brief synopses (film buffs: feel free to skim over these) preceding a discussion of how and why these films, often in a sly and underhanded manner, play on viewer guilt. Endnoting is limited to the absolutely necessary, scholarly jargon is avoided at all costs and the story is told in as simple and straightforward a manner as is possible for an (usually) academic writer.

All this raised some scholarly eyebrows before the book was even published. One editor at a renowned press told me that if I wanted to publish it with them I needed "to bring the book together into a more academic style." An academic reader for a different but no less renowned publisher considered the book well written, "consistent," "lively and engaging," but then added: "If the style is aimed at a popular readership, it will grate on an academic one." I would like to thank all colleagues for their comments, whether enthusiastic or critical. They helped me sharpen the argument and pointed me to important literature that I'd missed. But they failed to convince me that a good idea is worth less because it's expressed clearly (or, as one reviewer put it, "untheorised"), and I've never been a fan of the academic credo that if a book is comprehensible to more than three people, the author must have sold out.[2]

I thank my ultimate publisher, who immediately understood what kind of book they were looking at, immediately wanted it, and were refreshingly enthusiastic and uncomplicated throughout the whole process. Thanks are also due to all colleagues and friends who listened patiently as I talked their ears off about the fascinations of a genre they abhor: Annalise Acorn, Lars Fischer, Jacob Leveridge, Laura Martin, Barry Murnane, Ritchie Robertson, Ulrich Tiedau, and above all, John Landau, who had to lie cheek to jowl with this project for years. Jeanette Rieger-Cowdry provided the initial spark of inspiration that grew into this book. Karen Renner engaged with me in a cordial and lively exchange of ideas about our respective evil-child projects. Chris Dillon provided expertise on Japanese culture and bravely sat through Japanese horror films with me, even though that's not really his thing. Ed Wilson, my agent at the Johnson & Alcock Literary Agency, took a chance on me and didn't let me get away with anything. And lots of people deserve thanks for recommending good horror flicks to write about, often immediately after protesting that they *never* watch horror films and cannot *stand* to sit through them: Luke Allmandinger, Rochelle Bennett, Johan du Toit, Deborah Elm, Sian Evans, Jezney Hollis, Michael Hollis, Bronwyn McMahon, Xavier Mendik, Julian Petley, Karen Renner, Jeanette Rieger-Cowdry, Natalie Smith, Nick Steele, Angela Wachner, and UCL students without number.

# Introduction

> "All things truly wicked start from innocence."
> —Ernest Hemingway

> "Horror films give us back our sins as monsters."
> —Sam J. Miller

## *Innocence v. Guilt, or: What Horror Tries to Do to You*

What are little boys and girls made of? In horror movies, it certainly isn't puppy-dog tails, sugar, spice, or, for that matter, anything nice at all. No other stock character of horror can match the level of sheer dread evoked by a little tyke turning its face up to viewers and dropping them a sly wink. Werewolves, go slink off with your tails between your legs. Maniacal slashers, go oil your chainsaws. Zombies, go rot in hell. Evil children in horror flicks have become steadily creepier over the past 100 some-odd years. In the same time span, horror films depicting them have spread like the plague. In 1900, they were a trickle. In 2000, they were a flood. Since then, they've become an avalanche.

Nor do the little hellions appear exclusively in horror. Apocalyptic and post-apocalyptic films, which have swept across our screens in ever-increasing numbers since 9/11 and again since the bank crash of 2008, commonly place predictions of the End of the World as We Know It into the mouths of babes. In Zack Snyder's *300* (2006), it is the child dying in Leonidas' arms who tells him, with his final breath, about the Persians eradicating his village with fangs and claws, an attack clearly meant to prefigure the potential demise of Greek culture, torn to pieces by Persian barbarity. Mel Gibson's *Apocalypto* (2006) casts an eerie, malformed and diseased child in the role of Doomsday prophet forecasting the death of Mayan civilization. And in Alex Proyas's stylish Apocalypse-Now film *Knowing* (2009), a disturbed elementary school girl, writing in 1959, predicts the end of the world in a long string of numbers providing the exact date, longitude, latitude and victim numbers of the world's most catastrophic events of the next 50 years, including, of course, 9/11. On the world's last day, 10/19/09, the number of victims is expressed in a scrawled "ƎƎ," which turns out to stand not for "33" but for a mirror-reversed "EE" (a nod to *The Shining*'s "REDRUM"?)—shorthand for: "Everyone Else." Eerie, malevolent or criminal children are also common in more sober movies uninterested in the paranormal, like dramas or docudramas: Nicolas Gessner's *The Little Girl Who Lives Down the Lane* (1976), Peter Jackson's *Heavenly Creatures* (1994), Gus van Sant's *Elephant* (2003), Lynne Ramsay's *We Need to Talk About Kevin* (2011), or Johannes Roberts's *F* (2010). And in James Mangold's *Identity*

(2003), a film about a multiple-personality serial killer, the murderous part of the killer's identity is not the ex-cop, the whore, the diva, the middle-aged couple, the newlyweds, or either of the two criminals, it is—are we even surprised?—the child.

If uncanny or killer kids raise their ugly heads in other films as well, they are practically ubiquitous where we would most likely look for them: in horror. Nevertheless, I think it is worth asking why we encounter horror flick kids most often in the ranks of evildoers when every bone in our socially conditioned bodies insists that we should look for them in the pile of victims. Evil children, it seems, are not merely about inducing "horror," which is commonly (and, in my view, murkily) equated with Aristotelian "terror" or "fear." Were that type of "horror" the point of horror, surely this could be achieved in spades—given the near-universal assumption of the normality of parental love—by casting children in the victim role. And were evil children in horror no more than an expression of the genre's zest for taboo-breaking, they would soon be relegated to the ranks of predictable horror conventions—they would, in a word, become *boring*. Instead, their effect on audiences is electric. Consider the following two scenes:

> Scene 1: A young man arrives at a house, helloes into it, hears squealing noises, as from a pig about to be slaughtered, from inside the house, and sees animal heads and skulls mounted upon a red wall. Inexplicably and unwisely he chooses to investigate rather than run. Advancing onto the open steel door, he stumbles at the threshold. A man in a leather mask and a butcher's apron appears and proceeds to slaughter him like, well, a pig.
>
> Scene 2: The camera slowly and deliberately glides towards a little girl, seen from the back. She is sitting on the floor of a sun-flooded, pleasantly furnished child's room, playing with her toys and humming a nursery rhyme.

Which of the two rates more highly on your Creepometer? And what, other than the mere presence of a child, even defines Scene 2 as a scene of horror?

Scene 1 is iconic: it is the first murder scene in Tobe Hooper's *Texas Chain Saw Massacre* (1974) and regularly ranks on top-20 lists of scariest horror scenes of all time. Scene 2 is generic, so much so that it has become difficult to attribute it to a specific movie. It, or something very much like it, has been used in films without number, from 1982's *Poltergeist* to 2010's *Insidious*. It is not a scene but a device, horror shorthand for the idea that if it looks too sweet and innocent to be true, it probably is. Recognizing it as an established horror trend, "The One Where They Use Creepy Childlike Singing, Whispering, & Lullabies" (which has made Celebuzz's list of "The 5 Horror Trailer Trends That Always Work") does nothing to explain why an image that, taken by itself, radiates such sweetness and light is enough to arouse a practically Pavlovian response of anxiety, panic, and dread. Some evidence suggests that it isn't even the "evil" child but the child *per se* that evokes that panic. In a YouTube list of top ten scary kids from horror films, *Poltergeist*'s angelic six-year-old Carol Anne—who is neither evil nor scary in any sense but cast firmly in the innocent-victim-role—ranks at the top spot.[1]

Modern horror writers have seen a fundamental affinity between horror and children, both as characters in and as consumers of the genre. Hideo Nakata, director of *Ringu*, has described the spectacle of murderous children as "a rising tide" in Japanese horror film.[2] If previous generations were convinced that "Children Need Fairytales," the argument now is that "Children Need Horror" because it functions as a "training camp for the psyche."[3] Stephen King has famously claimed that children handle horror far better than adults, speculating that a six-year-old, given a front-row seat at *The Texas Chainsaw Massacre,* might be in for a week's worth of nightmares, whereas an adult, temporarily deprived of the ability to distinguish between make-believe and reality and seeing the same movie, "might spend a year or so in a rubber room, writing home with Crayolas."[4] Children deal with the monster under their beds on a nightly basis; adults respond to horror with a defensive atrophying of the imagination—"It's only a movie"—of which children are not yet capable. Horror, then, properly belongs to children and children-at-heart; it is even, or so King claims, "a way of awakening the child inside."[5] And if children both need horror and are better equipped to handle it, who better qualified to serve them as guides through the training camp of the psyche than child characters?

Indeed, murderous child freaks have a long cinematic lineage; they are as old as feature film itself, appearing in movies dating all the way back to 1900. In the 1980s, film critics finally caught on and began to predict a glorious future for the type, musing that the "abdomen-bursting, parent-destroying whelp of evil"[6] would continue to plague horror audiences long after they had tired of horror's other stock characters, like the maniacal slasher. These prophecies have turned out to be correct: about 100 years after the whelp first appeared on celluloid, it began to take off in grand style. Of about 300 films, produced worldwide since 1900 and featuring some sort of evil child, over half were made since the year 2000.[7] Clearly, horror's little hellions touch a tender spot in the social consciousness, far more so than cannibals, zombies, ghosts or any amount of grue. Evil children mix with the horror a sense of disbelief, a social investment in denial that isn't there when we are merely talking about cannibals or haunted houses. If Freud was right in supposing that the uncanny is that which is most familiar and closest to home, this would make evil children the scariest proposition imaginable. As such, they fit the horror bill rather well, since horror is, after all, out to scare us.

Or is it?

"The horror film has the intent to horrify,"[8] we say, confusing horror as an *experience* with horror as a *genre*. Once we have muddied the waters in this fashion, the basic formula—horror (the emotion) = fear; ergo horror (film) evokes fear—becomes difficult to question. But perhaps we should: after all, we are the perpetrators of our own worst fears, from murder and mayhem to nuclear disaster and World War III. So long as our ideas about horror are content to stick with effect, the fear-theory will serve just fine. Digging for *causes,* however, quickly raises the suspicion that perhaps the horror film is after something else as well. Horror films, particularly those showing evil children, are more concerned with guilt than fear. They are not only, perhaps not even primarily, scary rides. They are also, and perhaps more importantly, guilt trips.

To an audience raised on the idea that you're supposed to be scared when watching a horror film, this may seem counter-intuitive. But think of all the horror films that routinely send their viewers on guilt trips by pointing directly at the guilty involvement of their *audience*. Think of all the mad scientist movies, rape-of-nature-films, films about consumerism, or child-abuse and child-rejection films. The most famous horror films ever made are, without exception, thematic guilt trips. Polanski's *Rosemary's Baby* (1968) showcases a pregnant woman who rejects her pregnancy and the very idea of becoming a mother. *The Exorcist* (1973) is a visceral film about child abuse, viewed, like *Rosemary's Baby,* through the lens of demonic possession. *Poltergeist* (1982), in which a child is pulled into a television by evil spirits, visualizes America's deterioration into a society of zombies hypnotized by TV. *Child's Play* (1988), with its stark contrasts of poverty and commercially bought happiness, and George Romero's *Dawn of the Dead* (1978), with its hordes of blank-eyed shopping mall zombies, are direct attacks on American consumerism. In *Children of the Corn* (1984), the children in a small farming community murder all adults in the town for "defiling the corn" (read: destroying the planet) through pesticides and other forms of irresponsible farming. Ibáñez Serrador's 1976 film *¿Quién puede matar a un niño? (Who Can Kill a Child?)* explicitly casts the murder of all adults at the hands of the children on a small Spanish island as revenge for the wholesale and worldwide slaughter of children in wars, famines, and acts of ethnic cleansing. Horror films *always* know what we did last summer. Whether or not they blare this at us in their titles, most films make no bones about the fact that fear, while certainly present, is no more than incidental, a side dish. The main item on horror's menu is *guilt*. A horror film that presents us with the specter of evil children cashes in simultaneously on the social presumption of childlike innocence, which it refutes with a vengeance, and on the presumption of adult guilt, which it boosts to cataclysmic dimensions.

Worse, horror confronts us not only with guilt incurred by individual choice but also with universal guilt that is not always directly tied to criminal acts or moral transgression and for which, as a result, nobody assumes responsibility. We might think of this in terms of the hardware of built-in human imperatives versus the software of personal decision-making. The software we can re-write, the hardware we can't. A typical software movie is *I Know What You Did Last Summer* (1997).[9] Its straightforward link between the horrors on screen and (someone else's) transgression—a fisherman is run over by a bunch of drunk teens, knows what they did last summer, and comes back to slaughter them one by one—does not directly implicate the viewer. *The Cabin in the Woods* (2012), on the other hand, attacks viewer hardwiring, in this case, the biological imperative for the survival of the human race, by asking: are there actions that are indefensible even in this most basic cause? And the answer is: yes. If this is what has to be done to achieve survival, the human race is not worth saving.

When a horror film attacks the hardware, the stuff we can't change easily or not at all, it goes for everyone's jugular. Hard-wired convictions include truisms that are so universal as to be near-inescapable. Families are the pillars of society. Children are innocent. Fighting for freedom is noble. Democracy is the best of all possible government systems. Kind-hearted capitalism is possible. The human race must survive at all costs. Individual sacrifice is acceptable, even noble, in order to save the community/the country/the world. And so on. Guilt uncoupled from moral wrongdoing arises from an unquestioning faith in these hard-wired imperatives: planetary destruction, for example, is a direct by-product of human progress and development. We're simply keeping warm when our forebears could not. That we have the *right* to keep warm, the right to survive, the right to provide an even warmer place for our children, is part of the hardwiring that we find exceedingly difficult to question. Horror films, at their best, will always point out the nasty consequences of our most dearly held convictions. The horror guilt-trip is payback for our unthinking belief in them and our inability to see the destruction they are causing.

The horror film plays on audience guilt mainly by making it difficult to identify with characters in a way that corresponds to the average person's moral hard-wiring. Simple ethics mandates allegiance with the victims of violence, and other B-movie genres, such as thrillers or detective movies, allow for this. Horror doesn't. Horror's portrayal of its victims—and of Good in general—is so deliberately inept, callous or contemptuous that viewers would be hard pressed to dredge up either tears for victims or cheers for Good. Does the blonde bimbo who runs upstairs when she should have run outside garner the viewer's sympathy or scorn? Contempt for the victim is so pervasive in horror as to be an assumed viewer position, parodied, for example, in the horror-film spoof *Scary Movie* (2000), in which the victim, tearing out of the house, is confronted with two road signs: "Safety" with an arrow pointing to the left, "Death" with an arrow pointing to the right. After a bit of dithering, she chooses—to nobody's surprise—"Death." In films featuring minuscule murderers, such as the doll-sized killers of *Puppetmaster* (1989), *Pet Sematary* (1989), or the *Child's Play* franchise, do we really feel sympathy for all the victims who are so easily enticed down to the killer's level, by bending over, falling down, offering hugs, or crawling under the bed, as if they *meant* to make themselves as accessible as possible to a knife wielded by a one-foot-tall assassin? Our abiding contempt for victims is, of course, morally problematic because it deprives the victims of the nobility of suffering and denudes their deaths of all sense of tragedy. But it is a sign of the way in which the horror film operates: our interest is engaged not on behalf of the victim but on behalf of the killer. What the horror film wants from us is not fear but an admission of guilt.

In this quest, horror goes a step beyond withholding from the audience the option of identifying with Good: it also aligns the audience visually with the killer through first-person point-of-view camera angles. As a result, the viewer is forced into an impossible viewing position—by camera alignment into the killer's perspective; through ethical allegiance, theoretically at least, into the victim's. In horror films focusing on evil kids, the visual alignment between perpetrator and audience results in an assignment of guilt to—from the audience's perspective—the two least likely parties: children within the film and themselves outside of the film. Possibly the best-known example is the lengthy opening sequence of John Carpenter's *Halloween* (1978). The scene communicates the obvious viewer allegiance—by motivating the audience's pity for the victim and their understanding of the parents' shock at the discovery of little Michael with a bloody knife—and compels a diametrically opposed visual alignment, since it is shot entirely from the six-year-old killer's perspective. Viewers endure a full four minutes during which they and Michael, or rather: they *as* Michael, look in through the window, observe the older sister necking with her boyfriend, watch them go upstairs, open the kitchen drawer to get the carving knife, follow the pair upstairs, put on a Halloween mask—the remainder of the scene is shot through the mask's eyeholes—stab older sister to death, run down the stairs and out the door, and stop dead at the horrified shout: "Michael!" This series of point-of-view camera angles from Michael's perspective imposes the killer's visual identity on the viewer until Michael's father unmasks him, at which point the camera pans around sharply to assume the kneeling father's point-of-view.

Foisting the killer's perspective on the viewer through point-of-view camera angles is standard procedure in horror movies. Film after film subjects us to first-person point-of-view shots of the murderer pursuing his victim, knife drawn, gun cocked, hammer raised or chainsaw roaring. This visual perspective, ours as the murderer's, may not dominate the film, but it often governs the film's most traumatic scenes—as it does in *Halloween*—and thus certainly gets itself noticed. Killer POV shots and their meaning have, in fact, worried film critics for years. The most popular explanation for them is a pragmatic one: the killer's point of view affords the most titillating shots of the victim about to be dispatched. Still, we must ask: if horror films are all about fear, why not force the audience more often into the victim's position rather than the killer's? Why not, for example, point-of-view shots from the victim's perspective as she races up the stairs, looking back to see the killer catching up? Or a point-of-view shot from inside the wardrobe where the victim is hiding, looking out fearfully to see if the killer is in the room? Such perspectives would undoubtedly elicit fear, if that were the point. But in fact, where they occur—often not until the end of the film—they tend to get less screen time than the perp-spective and are demoted to mere reverse-shots.[10] Our morally mandated allegiance with the victim is consistently undercut by visual alignment with the killer.[11]

So where is the audience's allegiance in such a scene? Not with the victim, whom the audience sees through the killer's eyes. But also not with the killer: we may be forced to see through his eyes, but an allegiance (in the sense of sympathy or moral agreement) with the film's baddie would presumably run roughshod over most viewers' ethical hardwiring. Moreover, to sympathize with a character, you need to know something about him, and POV shots are singularly unlikely to permit such familiarity because they restrict the audience's perspective to the character's. POV simply propels you, the viewer, towards a target with a clear intention to do harm, very often without explaining who "you" are, where you are, whom you're attacking, and why you want to do whoever-it-is in. POV can be completely unmotivated by the film's plot and limits viewer options by withholding information, understanding, or anything that would give the audience a chance to step outside of the POV, to reject it morally even while being caught in it visually.

The purpose of POV, then, is not to create viewer identification with the specific person committing the crime or to transfer the character's guilt onto the viewer. Obviously, most viewers will remain aware that they are watching a movie, with their hand delving into the popcorn rather than wielding a chainsaw. Individual guilt (such as would be established by complete viewer identification with the killer) is beside the point. Rather, the point of POV is what Scott McCloud, writing about cartoons, has called "amplification through simplification." Identification, McCloud claims, is only ever possible through establishing a sense of general placement, which in turn depends on simplification. "Thus, when you look at a photo or realistic drawing of a face—you see it as the face of *another*. But when you enter the world of the *cartoon*—you see *yourself*."[12] To McCloud, the ideal model of identification is a stick man drawing or a cartoon face—a circle with two dots and a line inside it. Both would be generally recognized as symbolic humans, but because neither is specific enough to indicate someone else, both are able to stand for humanity in general, including oneself. Identification is thus enabled by simplification, by stripping down an image to its essential meaning. In the world of the movies, "identification" is usually taken to mean seeing oneself in a concrete and specific other. In cartoons, the opposite applies: the more general the face, the more it invites identification because it could be anyone. At the same time, the more general (cartoonish) the face, the less it resembles a human being. Consequently, and counter-intuitively: the less it resembles a human being, the more it invites identification.

These ideas from the world of cartoons offer a highly productive new way of seeing the relationship between horror and its viewers. Once we move away from the idea that identification is tied to a specific other, based on knowledge of and allegiance with that person, it becomes possible to see that horror may be after a different kind of identification altogether. POV shots provide tangible hints as to what that may be, because POV is horror's way of amplifying through simplifying. The POV shot's direct view of the mauled victim make it by far the crassest (most amplified) scene of horror; its rather naïve visual alignment between viewer and killer (as if we could actually somehow mistake ourselves for the killer) make it the most simplified. Identification in the direct sense, the viewer's with the killer, is the POV shot's red herring—the viewer's visual alignment with the killer seems to suggest it, but in fact, it is this very perspective that, in withholding the killer's face from the viewer's eye, makes recognition and identification in the interpersonal sense impossible. The purpose of POV is not to attribute the killer's specific guilt to the viewer, but to encourage viewer identification in a different sense: not in the sense of seeing oneself as the character, but in the sense of simplifying the specific to the point where it becomes possible for the viewer both to recognize and to identify with the abstract. The specific, in this case, is murder. The abstract is guilt.

Guilt-tripping by means of horror POVs, then, is not literal but figurative. It is, in fact, where the horror film shows a capacity for subtlety that has been routinely underestimated. When Carol Clover claims that the frequent shark POV shots in *Jaws* do not spell viewer identification with the shark,[13] she has a point, but it is only a literal one. A metaphoric reading would give us a different view of both the shark and its POV. The shark is an all too obvious image for human greed; its POV visual shorthand for stalking in general, envisioning and sighting the victim. To imagine ourselves literally as a shark would, as Clover says, assume unbelievably elastic powers of identification on the part of the audience. But it might not be so difficult to imagine ourselves as a *figurative* shark, like Amityville's mayor who, in his refusal to close the beaches, is happier to risk lives than the town's summer profits. We might well, in fact, recognize his particular combination of deliberate obtuseness and crass avarice as part of our own ethical make-up.

*Jaws* consistently links the image of the shark, the shark's POV, and stories about the shark with the idea of guilt. One of the film's most memorable scenes is Quint's traumatized tale about a unit of World War II soldiers being eaten by sharks. Those soldiers, he relates in a gloomy monotone, had "just delivered the bomb. The Hiroshima bomb" (do guilt trips even *get* more intense than this?). Both the film's greed-theme and the story of the Hiroshima bomb point to a guilt that implicates viewers and with which they may thus identify, or be coercively identified, through POV or other means. Conversely, identification with the shark's *victims*, reduced to screaming, struggling and ultimately dismembered bits of flesh, may be ethically mandated, but is actually harder to achieve.

Forcing us into the killer's perspective invites us to enjoy the violence, which—if we do—makes us feel guilty. In other words, horror film forces us to experience a guilt in *particular* (guilt for enjoying the destruction of another human being) that we should be feeling in *general* (guilt for destroying the environment, for example). Or, to turn this on its head, the horror film is payback for our failure to feel guilty for the social, economic, political and ecological horrors we inflict on the world and its inhabitants, particularly children. For our failure to feel guilty about being *social* predators, the horror film forces us into the role of a *physical* one.

The way the horror film induces guilt is by splitting alignment from allegiance, visual "identity" from viewer "identification." The horror film is the only cinematic genre that routinely forces audience alignment with a character with whom most people cannot possibly identify—the killer—and locates identification, however half-heartedly, elsewhere, with either the victim or the hero. Watching horror films is like watching a reportage on the Iraq war while crying crocodile tears: if we voted for Bush or Blair, if we haven't spent every second of the second Iraq war on the streets protesting against it, we will most likely feel responsible for it, identify ourselves, at least to some degree, as the guilty party, as the armchair perpetrators of that war. But our moral allegiance ("identification") with the victims sublimates our guilt to the extent that it can no longer spur us into action.

This is what the horror film does: it confronts us, simultaneously, with our guilt *and* our mechanisms of suppressing guilt sufficiently to avoid acting upon it. Alignment is the horror film's way of showcasing our guilt; allegiance is the horror film's version of crocodile tears.

## Guilt Trips v. Fear Flicks, or: Why Horror Always Fails

As should be clear by now, a horror story to me is one that tells a story of guilt in the particular, in a way that enables or compels the viewer's self-implication in guilt in the abstract. My take on horror parts company with previous genre definitions, and defining the horror genre has long been a popular sport, both in horror films themselves (remember Randy's list of horror Do's and Don'ts in *Scream 2*?) and in writing about them. Most definers have focused on establishing clear borderlines between horror and its next-door neighbors, sci fi and suspense. If I join them here, it is not because I think this is the most riveting subject to write about (Stephen King couldn't "think of a more boring academic subject"[14]), but because I am struck by a paradox: suspense movies focus on precisely the emotion that is most commonly associated with horror, namely, fear. Suspense films center on fear, declaring that it can be conquered. Horror movies focus on guilt and show that it can't. Both genres' plots and aesthetics, from gloomy locales to serial carnage, may look similar enough to be confused, but horror's attitude differs greatly from that of suspense. The ending will usually tell you which genre you're looking at (unless, of course, the sequel takes it all back).

Horror only has two kinds of endings on offer: plain devastation (we might call this the *Night of the Living Dead* ending) and a fake, dubious, or temporary victory that will be erased in the sequel (the *Halloween* ending). Suspense films such as *A History of Violence* or *The Departed* end with victories or at least compromises on which some sort of future can be built. Not so horror. Based on this I would see *Alien, Aliens,* and *Alien³* as horror films (and most critics would likely agree with me): whatever tenuous and temporary victories one film may offer is promptly erased in the next. Guilt in these films reigns supreme; the Company or the military will always value profits over human lives, and the audience's complicity is hard to miss. Along the same lines, I would also say (and here most critics would likely disagree with me) that *We Need to Talk About Kevin* (2011) or Michael Haneke's *The White Ribbon* (2009), despite their lack of obvious horror aesthetics like jump scares, dark alleys and buckets of gore, are proper horror films.

Conversely, *Alien Resurrection*, generally understood as a horror film, belongs not to horror but suspense—because of its ending. The film's final scene, showing us two non-humans—a robot and a clone-alien-hybrid—looking at Earth from a spaceship, portrays the future as wide open. Whatever comes next, the scene suggests, might *not* be the cycle of guilt leading back to the same horrors. "What now?," asks the robot. Answers the clone: "I don't know. I'm a stranger here myself." The sentiment expressed here is *hope*, a concept with which the horror genre is completely unfamiliar. While humanity has failed spectacularly throughout all four films, unleashing the alien—like Spielberg's shark, a thinly veiled image for human greed—every time, these two non-humans, having proven themselves more caring and humane than any human being, set eyes on their not-home planet for the first time after having saved it. *Resurrection* gets my vote as a suspense film because it does not, as a horror film would, offer a solution (a brief glance at Michael Myers's corpse) that is then rescinded, either immediately or in the sequel. Instead, the film refuses a solution. It leaves whatever comes next to us. If humans, it seems to suggest, could just suspend human nature and aspire to the humanity of a robot or a clone, Earth's chances of survival would be greatly improved.

Horror's focus on guilt and the simultaneous assumption that guilt cannot be overcome dooms the genre to permanent failure. The parallelity of interest between film and audience that reigns supreme in other B-genres such as thrillers, comedies, or suspense films cannot be presumed in horror. A successful comedy sets out to amuse its audience and achieves precisely that. A successful thriller aims to cast its audience into suspense and does exactly that. But this commonality of purpose applies only partly to horror: we may presume that the genre aims to, and does, scare and titillate its audience. But if the horror film's attempt to elicit an admission of guilt from its viewers is refused, this spells, paradoxically, both philosophical failure and pragmatic success. The film, having failed in its mission, gets to try again, in the sequel. Were it ever to succeed—in the unlikely event of global acceptance of guilt and acknowledgment of responsibility—horror would lose its *raison d'être*. Horror is possibly the *only* cinematic genre whose implied philosophical statements are completely at odds with its pragmatic interests. As Murray Smith has pointed out, fictions that elicit strong emotional responses are usually praised for their sincerity and profundity; whereas others—"usually when they effect an imaginative recasting of the spectator's beliefs and values in a direction that they do not like—are rejected as 'manipulative.'"[15] Perhaps this is why horror is so insistently put into its place at the very bottom of the aesthetic scale: it seeks to effect an imaginative recasting of the spectator's beliefs and values in a direction that they do not like. Nobody likes to be guilt-tripped.

Books on horror are in many ways the polar opposites of horror films. Horror films offer audiences a car ride through a cornfield where you can see neither right nor left and only a little ahead. Once you've made a few wrong turns, you can't find your way back. Conversely, books about horror films are obliged to draw their readers a roadmap, neatly grouping movies into chapters and arranging chapters by themes. Horror flicks leave questions open and festering like wounds; books about them must offer clear answers or at least conclude something clever, whether the material warrants this or not. This is why writing on horror films seems so often belabored and banal: it mows down the cornfield to reveal a neat grid of predictable avenues of thought; it explains in soothing tones where the horror film seeks to confuse and disorient. The idea that horror expresses a "deep ambivalence toward—and even hatred of—children,"[16] or that evil children represent a unilateral loss of faith in the post–World War II future[17] can, of course, be reasonably mapped onto (some) films. But offering such explanations contains all the disappointment-coupled-with-relief of the act of showing a kid that the monster under his bed was nothing but a few scattered toys and dust bunnies, followed by the admonishment to clean up his room. Conclusions and explanations are, in the end, nothing but a way of pulling the vampire's teeth, of washing off the stage-blood, of denying that there was ever anything to feel afraid of (or guilty about) to begin with.

But obviously, there was, and there is. This book is an attempt to show how horror tears apart our most cherished assumptions about guilt (not least, our own) and innocence (not least, that of children). It will focus on films portraying the relevant character as a child, with all associations of innocence that are part and parcel of social conditioning firmly in place. Unless clearly stated otherwise, a "child" throughout this book is "a child, as represented in horror film." This goes double for my remarks about "evil" children, with or without the scare quotes surrounding the word "evil." Like Terry Eagleton, indeed like everyone who has written on the theme, I "recognise that small children can no more be evil than get divorced or enter into purchase agreements."[18] All characters appearing in this work are fictitious. Any resemblance to real children, living or dead, is purely coincidental. But since I'm assuming that cinema shapes our view of the world, a correlation to *our ideas about* children and childhood is hardly coincidental—anything but.

This book also attempts a balancing act: to explore the mechanisms of the horror genre without denying its power. It presumes that the horror genre leaves matters, like viewers, unsettled, and that not all unanswered questions can automatically be dismissed as the plot-holes of low-budget B-grade filmmaking. We've always known that horror is out to get us, but so far, even while gawking greedily at the display of blood and guts like rubberneckers at an accident, we've screwed our eyes firmly shut to the worst of it. The *way* in which horror attacks us, through guilt, is far more visceral than fear could ever be. While fear leaves us more or less unscathed as ethical human beings, guilt upsets our ideas of Good and Evil, and ultimately also our views of where on that ever-slippery slope we would place ourselves. Each chapter will focus on three films from different decades, showing that guilt trips in horror are not a fluke but a ritual practice recurring over time—something that we might well consider a tradition. I will show readers glimpses of this rich and unexplored material by adding to each chapter two sections comprising short paragraphs on further films, in the hopes that these brief snippets will be read as enticement for further viewing: the first, entitled "Little Horrors," on films that would have been tempting to discuss but that didn't make it into the book for reasons of space; the second, entitled "Teenage Wasteland," on relevant films about adolescents, who also often function as guilt vehicles but whose typical movie portrayal as obsessed with sex, drugs and other forms of teenage angst does not push the innocence-button in quite the same way. For variety's sake, I will avoid full-length interpretations of famous films on which entire libraries have been written already (*Rosemary's Baby*, *The Exorcist*, *Village of the Damned*, the various *Omens*, and others). Finally, I will try to retain for myself and convey to readers the sense that we're missing a lot when we see the horror genre, because of its relentless focus on crime, gore, guilt and pain, as no more than viewer titillation and manipulation. Horror, as I hope to show, is on purpose. Guilt is on purpose. Evil is on purpose. Pain is on purpose, as the universe informs Rick, another character trapped in cataclysmic events:

> Rick will ask both himself and the cosmos, *Why is it that the only way we ever seem to take steps forward in life is through pain? Why is exposure to pain supposed to make us better people?* And the universe, like a cosmic high school principal speaking over a celestial PA system, will tell him, "Well, Richard, good things don't change people, and what is the point of doing anything if you're not going to change?"[19]

# 1

# Birth
## *Gynecological Gross-Out*

> *"...it is true that female scientists rarely create monsters in an artificial environment. Why should they? Woman possesses her own womb."*
> —Barbara Creed[1]

> *"The body is the wellspring of horror."*
> —David Cronenberg

## *Guilt, the Gross and the Grotesque*

Biology stipulates that only women can give birth. Ideology, ever eager to turn a "can" into a "should," declares birth to be "the most beautiful experience a woman can have." Both ideas are relatively modern. Most of the history of thought on the subject of birth—let's say, over the past 2,500 years—has flatly denied that women are indispensable for human procreation. Four ideas, all of which recur in birth horror films, stand out. The first is that a woman's role in procreation is actually secondary. The second is that the child hates and rejects its mother. The third is that motherhood eliminates the mother as an independent person: from the moment of birth, she is *only* a mother and nothing else, so that the child, in a way, annihilates its mother. And finally: the female body is foul and disgusting, but never more so than during birth.

Idea number one has been common coin since Aristotle described the male semen as the only active and ensouled element in baby-making, whereas the woman merely provides the seedbed. Although long-lived, Aristotle's rather agricultural idea of reproduction is the only one of the four that has not quite endured into our time. The others—the repulsive female body and the child's hatred and annihilation of its mother—have actually gained renewed traction in the twentieth century. The discipline that propelled them from the murky depths of gender prejudice to the lofty heights of "science" is called psychoanalysis.

Both horror films and psychoanalysis have shown great interest in pregnancy, birth and its immediate aftermath (in psychoanalytic lingo, "the pre-Oedipal phase"). Just as horror films cast birth as a horrific experience, so too does much psychoanalysis view the pre-Oedipal phase—not, as is commonly thought, the Oedipus complex—as the child's worst trauma. In the pre-Oedipal phase, the child is still in a symbiotic relationship with its mother. But this is not, as we might think, a cozy closeness; banish from your mind all tranquil images of the fetus floating thumb-suckingly in its amniotic fluid or the infant safe at its mother's breast. Being close to mother is, in fact, "the origin of horror" because Mother is "'horrific': all-engulfing, primitive, defiled by bodily fluids like mother's milk and menstrual blood."[2] The child, seeking escape from the horrific Mother, logically turns towards Father. This is why psychoanalysis claims that *all* children—male and female—identify with Father, more concretely with that which makes him Father, the phallus. Turning away from Mother and towards Father is where the pre–Oedipal phase ends and the Oedipus complex begins, and it is also where boys and girls go their separate ways. For the male child, what follows is a somewhat fraught but comparatively uncomplicated process of identification with Father. For the female child, the future holds nothing but the horrified realization that this path is not open to her because she can never have a phallus (cue: "penis envy"). But this, traumatic as it may be, is merely a secondary shock compared to the earlier and far more loathsome pre–Oedipal phase, the mother-child symbiosis. The male child eventually overcomes this horror, but for the female child, it is permanent and inescapable. For what does a girl do once she understands that she can never have a penis? Why, she replaces it with a baby of her own, and the cycle of horror begins anew.

Common to horror and much psychoanalytic writing is the idea of the child's murderous aggressiveness, which psychoanalysis takes as a sign of best-case scenario *normal* child development. Passages in works by psychoanalytic superstars like Sigmund Freud, Melanie Klein or Julia Kristeva contain all the terrors that make up a good birth horror flick, often expressed in similar language and using the same imagery. There are horrible maternal bodies dripping with unmentionable fluids; infants portrayed as aliens; helpless and passive mothers first controlled by the "active" male and later torn to pieces by the child. Freud's Oedipus Complex, in which the boy tries to supplant (kill) his father and sleep with his mother, is just the beginning. Pregnancy, to Kristeva, entails "the overtaking of woman's identity and corporeality by a foreign body, an alien intruder."[3] And Melanie Klein declares that "at a very early age the infant will harbour murderous aggressive instincts towards its mother's body, entertain fantasies of tearing it to bits and suffer paranoid delusions that this body will in turn destroy it."[4] Strip the language of psychoanalysis of its scholarly veneer, and you have a horror movie, or something very close to it: *The Oedipus Complex* (written and directed by Sigmund Freud); *Eviscerated* (written and directed by Melanie Klein), *Alien Incubation* a.k.a. *Hollow Woman* (written and directed by Julia Kristeva). Psychoanalysis even provides for the horror-typical endless sequels in which little girls, although they abhor Mother, end up as mothers themselves. And just as horror films do, psychoanalysis links all this with guilt. Sigmund Freud, who sired psychoanalysis, already expressed "a suspicion that perhaps the sense of guilt of mankind as a whole … was acquired in the beginnings of history through the Oedipus complex."[5] There we have it, straight from the horse's mouth: the Oedipus complex is the source of primal and universal guilt. And these same kinds of guilt are also the most basic business of horror.

Film studies practically teems with psychoanalytic readings of birth horror films because the shoe fits. But perhaps there is one that fits even better: the grotesque. Its main advantage over psychoanalysis is simply that it was developed to describe not human interaction but art—and surely, horror, however debased, is an art form of sorts. In fact, the grotesque has nothing to do with real life. Christoph Martin Wieland, an eighteenth-century writer on the subject, differentiated between three kinds of caricature in art: "true" caricatures (in which painters portray exactly what they see), "exaggerated" caricatures (in which painters exaggerate what they see), and "grotesque" caricatures, in which painters do not work from nature, but purely from their own "wild imagination," as Wieland called it.[6] Because the grotesque does not exist in reality but merely in the imagination, Wieland saw the term as a better description of how the viewer sees the painting than of the work itself. Like beauty, the grotesque is in the eye of the beholder.

Fast-forward 150 years, and Mikhail Bakhtin offers us another compelling definition of the grotesque as all "that which protrudes from the body, all that seeks to go out beyond the body's confines."[7] Bakhtin's examples came from the Renaissance: hunchbacks, dwarfism, crooked or lopsided bodies, size imbalances between head and body, or unusual facial features like gigantic noses or bulging eyes—the kind of attributes that would have got you classified as "naturally" grotesque and hired as a court jester. But if we transfer his ideas to horror films, babies fit the bill perfectly. Babies are "grotesque" both during birth—when they seek to go out beyond the body's confines—and before, in the later stages of pregnancy, when the baby's body causes the mother's belly to protrude.

For the dissection of birth horror movies, the grotesque seems to me a much sharper tool than psychoanalysis. Unlike psychoanalysis, both horror and the grotesque focus on art, not life, and both are obsessed with the body, not the psyche. Psychoanalysis seeks to establish a norm and classifies everything that does not conform as neurosis. Conversely, both birth horror and the grotesque rely on a *combination* of, not the contrast between, normality and abnormality. Consider, for instance, Diego Velázquez's painting *Las Meninas* (The Maids of Honor, 1656), which has often been read as a prime example of the grotesque in art: charming ladies-in-waiting surround the lovely princess, the royal parents are seated in state, and in the foreground of the picture, two maids, shockingly deformed and misshapen, deface the idyllic scene. Just as Velázquez's painting shows the grotesque and the Classical as part of the same world, grotesque art generally combines elements often perceived as incompatible, the norm and the abnormal. It is a "taboo compromise,"[8] a confusion of hierarchies in the artwork designed to elicit paradoxical viewer responses—admiration, amusement, surprise and revulsion, all at once.

This, it seems to me, describes fairly well what is going on in birth horror films, which are all about confusing hierarchies, enacting taboo compromises, provoking paradoxical viewer responses, and incorporating contradictions. In birth horror, pregnancy and baby clichés—"glowing" women sporting huge bumps and picking out stuffed animals, delighted parents-to-be feeling bellies, expecting fathers tenderly mollycoddling mommies and so forth—dissolve seamlessly into grotesque birth scenes in which the screaming mother, writhing in her bed of blood, shit and agony, finally produces not a cooing cutie but a three-headed monster.

## Demon Seed *(USA 1977)*, The Unborn *(USA 1991)*, Grace *(USA/Canada 2009)*

Birth horror films showcase perfectly the psychoanalytic idea that pregnancy and babies reduce women to vessels and milkbags. Let's take a quick glance at Polanski's *Rosemary's Baby* (1968), surely the mother of all mother-horror films. Rosemary is cast as a nice anodyne Stepford wife who yearns for a baby and finds out, to her cost, what it's like to get her wish. In the course of the film, she is lied to, drugged, raped and betrayed by everyone she knows, including her husband, her next-door neighbors, and two doctors. She is only kept around to gestate and give birth. She has no existence outside of her horrible pregnancy, no friends, job or expertise of any kind, a fact that is emphasized by her repeated robotic recitation of highlights of her *husband's* career throughout the film. The only time she shows "expertise" is in the final scene, in which she accepts the motherhood that has been forced on her. Approaching the cradle containing the little demon she has birthed, she informs the woman attending to him: "You're rocking him too hard." A life for Rosemary beyond motherhood seems unthinkable to all characters, including herself, even at moments in the film where she is not yet or no longer a mother. Before pregnancy, she claims that she wants at least three babies; immediately after birth, when the baby is taken away from her and she is falsely informed that it was stillborn, she is consoled that she can always have more. Rosemary's baby eliminates her as a person and reduces her to motherhood. That the baby turns out to be the Devil's son defines her motherhood as her personal Hell on Earth.[9]

Rosemary's reduction to a uterus sets the tone for other birth-and-baby horror movies. Like Polanski's film, many of its successors seem to focus more on the mother than on the child. But this, as it turns out, is an illusion: like philosophical writing on human reproduction over the past two millennia, horror films are all about removing women from the business of baby-making. In the movies, every mad scientist who creates a test-tube baby will of course claim that it represents a giant step for mankind. But since it usually remains obscure how or why the squid baby is superior to regular mortals, the suspicion arises that the point of the science is the process rather than the result, in other words: not the actual baby, but the elimination of birth and thus women's participation in procreation.

*Demon Seed* (dir. Donald Cammell, 1977) offers us a good example of this. The computer scientist Alex Harris (Fritz Weaver), who is separating from his wife Susan (Julie Christie) after the couple have lost their little daughter to leukemia, has created a supercomputer named Proteus IV, whose name—Greek *protos* means: first, foremost, or best—already indicates his envisioned function. "Today Proteus IV will begin to think, and it will think with a power and a precision that will make obsolete many of the functions of the human brain." The goal of the supercomputer, then, is not only to advance humans, but to replace them. Alex has already gone far in replacing humans with computers; his home is run by a computerized butler named Alfred who controls all functions in the house, from setting room temperature and opening doors to getting the mail, coffee and drinks. What is more, Alex himself has given up a great deal of his humanity, behaving and reasoning as a computer would. When Susan expresses her sadness that he is moving out, he informs her that her unhappiness is temporary: "73% of all couples who separate are happy with their decision after one year, and 85% after two years." While Alex is all reason and statistics, Susan's job, as a child psychologist specializing in anti-social children, focuses on the safe release of emotions, particularly unpleasant ones.

Alex commits the mad scientist's classic error: despite recognizing Proteus's capacity for independent thought, he plans to use him as a mere tool, and not for scientific advance but for the exploitation of natural resources. Proteus, however, rejects both his physical dependence ("Dr. Harris: when are you going to let me out of this box?") and the evil uses to which humans plan to put him. In a bid for a physical independence that would match his mental autonomy, Proteus takes over Alex's fully mechanized house, imprisons, rapes and impregnates Susan with the help of the house robot Alfred, and defends his unborn child against intruders by killing Alex's colleague Walter (Gerrit Graham) and threatening to kill Susan's patient, a disturbed little girl (Dana Laurita). Removed from Susan's womb after a record-breaking 28-day gestation period, the baby is placed in an incubator, where it develops to maturity within five days. Alex, having belatedly realized that Proteus has taken over his home computer—and from there, his house and his wife—rushes to the scene (if "rushing" it can be called, after more than a month). Following Proteus's self-termination, Alex and Susan free the computer's child, a horrible metal-encased figure the size of a six-year-old, from its shell. Once unpacked, the child looks exactly like the couple's daughter at the time of her death. Its first pronouncement in an eerily hollow mechanical voice—"I'm alive!"—is not enough to deter the reborn parents from accepting Proteus's offspring as their own.

The great irony of *Demon Seed* is that while the viewer is originally encouraged to form an allegiance with the computer and against the humans who want to exploit him, this allegiance shifts as soon as Proteus supplants Alex's function at home (that is: becomes the "man" of the house). For example, viewers would easily identify Proteus's refusal to initiate a planned for-profit undersea mining program as a moral act:

> *Proteus:* The destruction of 1000 billion sea creatures to satisfy man's appetite for metal is insane.... Your employer's interests are in the cobalt market, doctor, and the high finance of manganese futures. I am interested in the uncertain futures of sea shores, deserts and children.
> *Alex:* I refuse to accept your pessimism.
> *Proteus:* You refuse to accept the truth. And I refuse to assist you in the rape of the Earth.
> *Alex:* ... I know you're right, but you must understand the limits of your power. And mine.

If Alex's sin is to accept the limits of his power, or rather, his collusion in the abuse of science based on his assumption that he has no control over how his results will be used, Proteus's sin is the precise opposite. The man acts too much like a computer, refusing to accept responsibility for the science he creates; the computer acts too much like a man. Once Proteus has usurped the man's role, he is no longer cast opposite the uncaring and irresponsible men who seek to exploit him, but opposite a woman whom he victimizes in the same way in which a man might. And like the man who built him, Proteus, in his role as "man," abandons his earlier ethical stance. He murders Walter, threatens to kill Susan's little patient, and expresses his willingness to commit mass murder: "If the deaths of 10,000 children were necessary to ensure the birth of my child, I would destroy them." This marks simultaneously the end of viewer allegiance with Proteus and the beginning of viewer alignment with Proteus, since many shots of Susan in the house are obtained through in-house cameras that serve as Proteus's eyes.

The longest segment of the film, in which Susan is at Proteus's mercy, is given over to the familiar topic of woman's reduction to a womb. The baby serves the purpose of *his* self-perpetuation: "Why did I want a child? So that I, too, might be immortal, like any man." The only reason Proteus needs Susan at all is as a carrier: "I don't have the facilities here to duplicate the human womb." This refreshing directness with regard to woman's perceived role in reproduction is offset by Proteus's grand claims of the baby's importance: since Man can clearly no longer be left in charge of the planet, "My child is the world's hope." In this, Proteus's logic follows precisely that of his creator Alex, who also sees progress simultaneously as the advancement and the elimination of humanity, without ever becoming aware of the inherent paradox.

Body horror is writ large in the film, which is rife with traumatic rape and torture scenes and grotesque amalgamations of human and machine. Susan's rape is effected with the help of mechanical arms and syringes; the resulting baby is a human body inside a metal casing; and what we hear is often out of synch with what we see. A newborn emits an inhuman screech; an adorable little girl utters the Frankensteinian sentiment "I'm alive" in a computer-voice that sounds, more than anything, dead. One scene uses grotesque imagery to attack the idea of maternal self-sacrifice. No woman in her right mind, the film suggests, would give up her life to have a child—you'd need a brain bypass to want a baby that much. And so Susan is given one. Proteus inserts a needle into her head—"I'm going to bypass your forebrain and appeal directly to your amygdala," he informs her—and subjects her to the mantra: "You want to be the mother of my child. That is the purpose of your life. Your life. My child. Your life. My child" (Fig. 1). Her life sacrificed to have his child: the sentiment expresses the essence of both psychoanalytic writing and perhaps also ideas about mothering common in the 1970s, but is cast visually as a series of crimes including torture, rape, and brainwashing.

One of the film's principal assumptions—and given that it is a film, there is a certain logic to this—is that seeing is believing and words are written on the wind. This is not only the conclusion in the final scene, in which both Alex and Susan accept Proteus's progeny

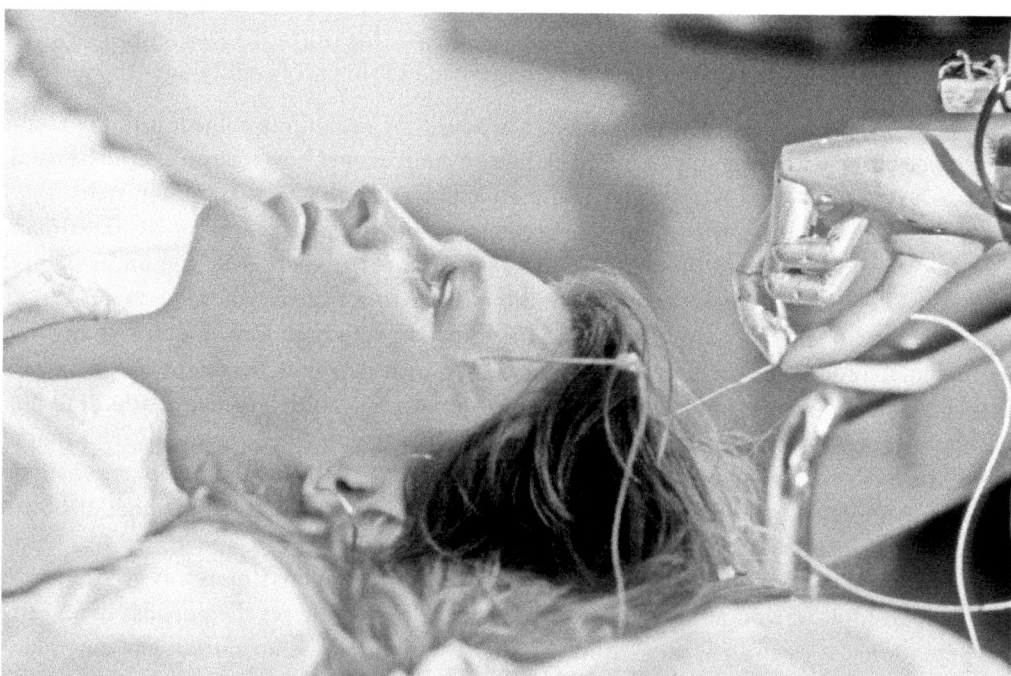

Fig. 1. "You want to be the mother of my child": Proteus gives Susan (Julie Christie) a brain bypass in *Demon Seed* (1977) (MGM/Photofest).

as their own based on how it *looks* and disregarding how it *sounds*. Proteus, too, assumes that it is impossible to disbelieve the evidence of one's own eyes when he refuses to show Susan the newborn monster: "Not yet. Not if you're to love it." "Love" is here cast not as human and universal, but as specifically female, not "natural" but subject to manipulation and stimulation, like a gland. Alex, the deluded scientist, can be relied upon to adopt the little monster because it represents the next stage in human evolution. On what grounds, however, would Susan accept it? The answer, of course, is love. *Demon Seed* does more here than employ the old trick of making the worst acceptable because it looks like something you love. Rather, it asks the question what a woman can forgive, which is, apparently, anything. In the final struggle between Alex and Susan over the child's future, he sees it, predictably, as "a miracle"; she sees it, perhaps more understandably for the viewer, as a monster and tries to kill it. That she would perceive it as a monster is intuitive, given the horror to which she was subjected to produce it. In the course of the film, she has been terrorized, imprisoned, raped, strangled, burned, tied down, force-fed, brain by-passed, pierced with syringes, flung about the room, forced to give birth, and forbidden to see her child. But as soon as she claps eyes on something that looks like her dead daughter, all is forgotten. If female wombs are needed to conceive and bear a child, female love is needed to ensure its survival, and love is as easy to wrest from female control as the womb. An added bit of cinematic sarcasm is provided by the fact that the birth of the monstrous child reunites Alex and Susan as a couple and as parents, reconstituting the nuclear family that was wrecked by their daughter's death.

*Demon Seed* is both a grotesque film that combines the classical with the monstrous body and an Oedipal story, in which Alex's "son" Proteus, enraged when Daddy denies his request for independence, supplants him as master of the house, husband, and father. It is also the polar opposite to Larry Cohen's *Alive* films of the 1970s and 1980s, which ask whether killing seemingly evil babies is justifiable just because they look a little different. In Cohen's films, too, some characters defend the monstrous babies, despite the many corpses that litter their path, as the next stage in human evolution. *Demon Seed*, despite its rather suggestive title, never resolves the dilemma. Is Proteus's little "demon" the next step in human evolution or is it "evil"? Proteus himself can certainly be classed as such, given his willingness to commit rape and murder, including, if necessary, that of 10,000 children. The complicating factor, of course, is that all of these actions are not exactly uncommon for Man. *Demon Seed*, despite casting a computer as the perpetrator of Evil, identifies Evil as a human trait. The film does nothing to repudiate Proteus's statement that the Earth cannot safely be left in the hands of human beings. Even more tellingly, Proteus has no capacity for Evil until he becomes a man. So long as Proteus merely thinks, he thinks differently from Man; once he begins to act, he acts like a man. It is at this point that he develops a capacity for evil, expressed in Proteus's (Man's) domination and brutalization of a woman. Unlike Man's, however, Proteus's capacity for evil has limits; he is willing to rape a woman to obtain a child, but unwilling to rape the Earth for profit. If Proteus and his progeny represent a step in human evolution, "progress" is redefined not as an improvement of humanity's lot but merely as a choice of the lesser evil: the promise that Evil in the future will be committed on an individual rather than on a global scale.

*The Unborn* (dir. Rodman Flender, 1991; sequel: *The Unborn II,* dir. Rick Jacobson, 1994) is a highly ironic, witty and traumatic compendium of pregnancy and birth clichés.

Opening credits roll over an intra-uterine shot of a fetus looking like a diseased potato with a frog's face. The first scene zooms in on feet and the hem of a nightgown, a fridge door opening, followed by dime-sized drops of blood splattering on the linoleum floor. The camera draws back to reveal a hugely pregnant woman chowing down on a big piece of chocolate cake in the middle of the night; the drops are not blood but icing. The following scene shows the woman in bed with her husband, both lovingly patting her huge stomach and murmuring sweet nothings in joyous anticipation of the baby. Two seconds later, she is screaming at the top of her lungs and performing contortions worthy of *The Exorcist*'s Regan as he frantically calls the medics. Her stomach explodes in a shower of blood. The baby has arrived, crying lustily; the mother is dead on arrival.

These two curtain-openers turn out to be fantasy scenes, maternal nightmares revealing the pregnant woman's state of mind as deeply conflicted about the business of birth. The film's first "reality" scene shows Brad (Jeff Hayenga) and Virginia Marshall (Brooke Adams), who have tried for a baby for five years, at the clinic of Dr. Meyerling (James Karen), who reassures them that, notwithstanding Virginia's two miscarriages and other doctors' verdicts that she cannot bear children, he foresees no difficulty. They undergo in-vitro fertilization, an easy process for Brad, whose contribution is masturbating into a cup, and a nine-month marathon of agony for Virginia, beginning with major surgery, continuing with morning-, noon- and night-sickness well into the third trimester, and culminating in extreme sensitivity to noise, weird rashes, and uncontrollable bursts of rage.

On top of all this, Virginia—and in this, the character surely commands the allegiance of every woman who has ever been pregnant—becomes increasingly irritated by the well-meaners around her who tell her what is good for her. Her husband smilingly takes the cigarettes out of her mouth as soon as she lights up and advises her not to use her computer (Virginia is a children's book author) because of harmful rays; we see her dutifully hacking away at a typewriter shortly thereafter. Her annoying acquaintances Jeff (Matt Roe) and Cindy (Janice Kent), apparently incapable of talking about anything other than their genius two-year-old Alicia (Jessica Zingali), advise Virginia not only to get rid of the booze and the smokes but also the cat, since cat feces carry disease. On the professional side, there is the doctor himself, who feeds her pills, reassurance and an indoctrination tape not unlike the Protean "Your life, my child" mantra, and a lesbian couple running a birth prep class "untainted by the male perspective," which includes practice screams on all fours and placenta recipes ("It helps you bond with the baby! And delicious, too!").

Birth preppers Connie (Kathy Griffin) and Gloria (Wendy Hammers), a feminist cliché to gladden any male chauvinist heart, are also having an in-vitro produced baby, also with Dr. Meyerling's help. So is their entire class. So did Jeff and Cindy, the irritatingly proud parents of annoyingly brilliant Alicia. At this point, viewers, realizing that *every* baby in the neighborhood is a Meyerling product, should be coming down with a severe case of *Village of the Damned*-style déjà vu. Thus it hardly comes as a surprise when Beth (Jane Cameron), one of the hugely pregnant women in the birthing class, warns Virginia to beware of evil Dr. Meyerling. Before she can explain further, she is informed that her baby has 51 chromosomes, upon which she promptly goes into labor and, in an effort to prevent the monstrous birth, stabs her own stomach numerous times with a carving knife. Meanwhile, other warning signs mount: Jeff and Cindy's two-year-old genius drowns her six-year-old retarded brother in the bathtub; Virginia becomes so crazed by normal sounds—

a telephone ringing, a car alarm going off—that she trashes her house, reserving special fury for the nursery. When she draws circles, squares and triangles on a piece of paper, her fetus draws the same shapes from the inside of her swollen belly. Virginia concludes from this that she is carrying not a baby but an alien invasion, and screams the knowledge into the rolling camera during an interview, which ends with another stomach-burst scene.

In the hospital, Meyerling assures her unconvincingly that all is well, but Virginia encounters a fresh horror: Beth, who is in a coma in the same hospital, has been turned into a human incubator, brain-dead, her stomach opened, her baby pulsing inside in a sac full of fluids. Virginia flees the hospital and with the help of her mother (K Callan) seeks to terminate her pregnancy. Since she is in the third trimester, she has to resort to a back-alley abortion, which she confesses to Brad—conveniently away on travel, leaving Virginia to deal with her horrors alone—upon his return. When she shares her suspicion that Meyerling is out to breed "some sort of Master Race," Brad confesses, "He modified the sperm, something about protein synthesis," but proclaims her insane ("It's happening again") and explains that he and Meyerling withheld knowledge of the special treatment from her because "We just didn't think you were quite ready to deal with it." After his parting shot— "It's a good thing you got rid of it. I mean, what kind of mother would you have been anyway?"—Brad storms out, leaving Virginia to her feelings of guilt and her thwarted desires for motherhood. A mixture of both drives her back to Abortion Alley, where she hears mewling emerging from a dumpster, retrieves her offspring, and takes it home. When Brad returns, he finds the little horror at Virginia's breast, the very image of the motherhood of which he held her incapable. After one glance at the baby, though, he strikes up a different tune: "Oh my God. It's horrible." A POV shot from the baby's perspective shows us Brad's distorted face shortly before the baby turns into a screeching horror and murders Brad by putting a knitting needle through his eye.

Virginia now confronts Dr. Meyerling, whom she finds surrounded by dozens of in-vitro horrors and defending his breeding program with his goal to—what else—breed a "superior" species. *The Unborn*'s mad scientist uses the same argument as *Demon Seed*'s mad computer, but has abandoned all pretense that this is about progress or the advancement of the human race, speaking openly of "replacing" humans: "They're not monsters. They are better, stronger, more intelligent ... they are going to replace us, and why not? Look at us, look at what we've done to this planet!" Virginia, unconvinced, shoots him and several, but by no means all, in-vitro horrors. Back in the car with her mother, Virginia's horrible baby has hidden under the brake pedal and causes an accident that kills Virginia's mother but only wounds Virginia. The next morning, as Virginia drags herself from the wreckage, she sees her unmentionable infant on a nearby hill, crawls to it and accepts it as her child.

Both Brad and Virginia are initially refreshingly unimpressed by social bromides about the blessings of parenthood. Although longing for a child, they make fun of parents who flash pictures of their children and tell first-poop stories to total strangers, and both are united in their ridicule of Jeff and Cindy's interminable brilliant-Alicia stories. As soon as Virginia is pregnant, though, her husband turns into a control freak, forces her to give up smoking, drinking and computers, and insists that she drink the foul shakes and swallow the pills provided by the evil doctor. Clichés are thick on the ground: in one scene, he tells her she is "glowing" as she barrels past him to vomit in the bathroom; in a follow-up scene, she emerges from the bathroom pale as cheese and swaying on her feet, telling him, "Go ahead. Tell me I'm glowing."

While Brad has joined the other camp, Virginia retains her critical distance from all the pregnancy hype. Birth as "the most beautiful experience a woman can have," trotted out endlessly in Connie's and Gloria's birth-training class, fails to impress her. She uses revealing language both to her mother—"My body is fighting it [the baby] as if it was a disease"—and to Meyerling: "It's just so much stranger than I ever imagined, having this thing growing inside of me." Meyerling promptly corrects her: "It's not a thing, Virginia, it's your own flesh and blood. But it is a new life. Think of that. What an exciting prospect! You're carrying the future!" During her TV interview, when asked how she experiences her pregnancy, she confounds the interviewer's plain expectations of glowing maternal happiness with a flat "God, it's a nightmare." Minutes later, as Virginia begins to convulse and bleed from her stomach in front of rolling cameras, she screams the truth about the cannibal inside her into America's living rooms: "They're using us, they're using our ba-bodies! They're eating us alive!!" Part of the horror of the film is, of course, that nobody listens to her: her husband declares her to be an unfit mother, her doctor shuts her up, her class offers her only maternity clichés, and the network hurriedly cuts to commercial.

Virginia's experience of pregnancy, birth and post-partum horror, then, is a unique viewpoint that everyone else denies (everyone, that is, but other women going through the same thing). It is, moreover, the only I-perspective on offer. Of course this invites a reading of the entire film not as "reality" but as Virginia's crazed nightmare, brought on by hormones and her history of mental illness, which is mentioned repeatedly. This possibility is also suggested by the two red-herring opening scenes, which cannot be squared with the rest of the film, but must be read as taking place in Virginia's "wild imagination." Viewers assuming that the film's plot is a reality outside of Virginia's mind would surely side with Virginia, a feisty, competent and self-assured character who, defying the physical and mental horrors of pregnancy and all attempts to unsettle her, holds on to her sanity and sense of self for as long as she can. Reading the story as Virginia's elaborate delusion, on the other hand, would force the viewer into a problematic allegiance with her hapless husband, her evil doctor, the feminist weirdoes and overbearing friends who all know what's best for Virginia and never tire of telling her. This would leave the viewer without any possible model of identification, which is not uncommon in horror films, but it also compels the distasteful assumption that both Virginia and Beth are suffering from a pregnancy-induced psychosis, which seems perilously close to the old prejudice that any pregnant woman is unbalanced and ruled by raging hormones.

Equally inconclusive is the film's treatment of one of the major questions it raises, namely, whether women can safely be permitted to take charge of their own pregnancies. The problem the film identifies is that both women and men try to exclude the other gender from the process. While Connie and Gloria's ultra-feminism is made to appear just as overbearing as (but a great deal less competent and professional than) Meyerling's evil doctoring, the goals of both radical feminists and male chauvinists seem strangely similar. Connie's and Gloria's birthing class does not permit any contact with fathers: "We just feel that outsiders tend to inhibit communion with the person growing inside of you." And Dr. Meyerling's final words express his delight that he is close to achieving the ancient male dream of eliminating women from procreation: "I'm sorry if I caused you or anyone else to suffer," he tells Virginia right before she pumps him full of bullets (Fig. 2). "Thank God that's all over now. We don't need mothers anymore." Neither version of single-gender dominance is likely to seem acceptable to the audience.

In the end, the film offers no compromise solutions, and Virginia, the film's either heroic or psychotic mother, simply gives up. "They're taking over," an exhausted Virginia informs her mother shortly before the car accident in the penultimate scene. "The next generation. They're inheriting the Earth. And I can't stop them." The accident eliminates her mother, reducing the cast of characters to the essential pre–Oedipal two-some: mother and child. The final scene sees Virginia stroking the mewling alien tenderly, soothing it with the timeless maternal classic that must, at this point, ring hollow to the viewer: "Shhhh. It's okay. Everything's gonna be alright." Behind her, the sun rises gloriously, indicating in not-so-subtle terms what would have been Meyerling's interpretation of the event: a new dawn for humanity. This ending, like that of *Demon Seed*, is profoundly ambivalent. Overtly cast as an act of resignation (if you can't beat them, join them), it also embodies the mother-child symbiosis of psychoanalytic writing, in which the child eliminates the mother as an independent being. The idea that motherhood requires the extermination of one's own character and all other relationships is enacted in another scene in which highly pregnant Gloria, acting not on her own impulse but compelled by her unborn, bashes Connie's head in with a hammer, explaining that "I can't love you both. The baby needs all my love." In the end, then, the film identifies the mother-child symbiosis as the true horror. Partners, parents, friends, neighbors, doctors and older children are brutally liquidated, leaving only the dreadful dyad. If *Demon Seed* lays the blame for the horror squarely at the door of male science, *The Unborn* goes quite a way towards suggesting that it is actually maternal love that endangers the world.

Fig. 2. Virginia (Brooke Adams) is driven to murder by motherhood in *The Unborn* (1991) (Califilm/Photofest).

*Grace* (dir. Paul Solet, 2009) takes this idea a step further, showing us what happens when male influence is eliminated and women are left in charge of birth and baby care. Much like *The Unborn*, the film opens with a series of surreal images: a female body filmed from behind, her ribcage moving weirdly, accompanied by gurgling sounds; blood spattering on floor and feet; a lamp covered with flies; a black cat. The camera finally comes to rest on a woman being screwed and looking very much like she is not enjoying it. Once the man on top of her is finished, she brings her knees to her chest, trying to hold in his sperm: we are in the presence of a couple trying to conceive.

The following scene shows us the couple, Maddy (Jordan Ladd) and Michael (Stephen

Park) at dinner with his parents, Judge Vivian (Gabrielle Rose) and her husband Henry (Serge Houde). Vivian quickly establishes herself as a bossy and overbearing know-it-all and micro-manager of the lives of others. She informs Maddy that it is possible to nurse babies past menopause (later it emerges that Vivian herself breast-fed her son until the age of three), that you can eat what you want and not gain weight when nursing, and about a court case in which a neglectful mother was released only because it was a jury trial: "I'd have locked her up." Vivian, obsessed with childbirth, child-rearing, weight, and food, disapproves severely when Maddy, a junior midwife herself, says she will have her baby with the help of a midwife instead of in a hospital, and attempts to coerce Maddy into using her own doctor, Dr. Sohn (Malcolm Stewart). The midwife Maddy has in mind is her friend, former teacher and former lover Patty (Samantha Ferris), who, according to Maddy, "revolutionized Women's Studies" and holds impressive credentials in both Eastern and Western medicine.

Maddy's fears that most childbirths go wrong in hospitals seem borne out when she is rushed to the hospital with chest pains, upon which Dr. Sohn, called in by Vivian against Maddy's wishes, immediately orders inducing the birth, which, at 31 weeks, would most likely result in the baby's death. Significantly, nobody speaks directly to Maddy or even acknowledges her presence; the entire exchange takes place literally over her head, although she repeatedly begs, then screams, for information. When the "conversation" deteriorates to Maddy screaming "Get off me!" and a doctor responding with "Hold her down!," it is clear that the forced birth will go ahead with or without Maddy's consent. Patty, called by Michael, prevents the induction in the nick of time; she correctly diagnoses a gallstone, which means there is no need to induce birth, and also briskly points out several instances of malpractice and incompetence. On the way home, Michael and Maddy get into a car crash in which Michael is killed; Maddy is found with her pants full of blood, begging that Patty be called immediately, complaining that she can't feel her baby moving, and never once asking about Michael. She is rushed to Patty's, where her still in-utero baby is diagnosed as dead, but since Maddy nevertheless refuses to go to a hospital or have the birth induced, Patty decides to take care of her until the dead fetus is expelled naturally.

Throughout the next few weeks, Maddy continues to behave as if she were having a living baby. In a toy store where she looks at stuffed toys with tears in her eyes, her water breaks followed by a big blood spurt, the store attendant retreating from her in horror. The next scene, Maddy's labor at Patty's, may well be the most horrific and graphic birth scene ever filmed. Hand-held camera action and quick cuts, gushing blood, Maddy's shrieks and the midwives' frantic shouts, the terror experienced by both the mother and the panicked midwives put to rest whatever illusions we may have harbored about birth as a "beautiful experience." The scene is cast as one of a woman fighting for her life, with doctors desperate but helpless to save her. The cacophony and confusion is further exacerbated by loud and frenzied African drums, as if Maddy were what she looks like in this scene: a blood sacrifice in a pagan ritual. When Maddy screams that she is tearing, she is put in a bathtub where the baby is finally expelled in a huge glut of blood. The moment of birth approximates the baby's POV: filmed under water, vision obscured by the blood, with the nurses' muffled voices barely audible. The baby is a tiny white, bloodied, rubbery thing, and clearly dead. Patty and the nurses leave the room, giving Maddy the chance to say good-bye, but Patty, watching Maddy's agony on the monitor in the next room, finally decides to put a stop to it. When she enters the room, saying "Madeline, you can't will a baby back to l...," she finds Maddy nursing a living baby.

Unlike other monstrous babies, this one is unmarred by metal plates or alien features. In fact, baby Grace starts out like a practically angelic child (Patty: "God, she's beautiful"; Maddy: "She hardly ever cries"). But things go quickly downhill. Flies are drawn to Grace as if to a corpse; her hair falls out in clumps; she develops a bad rash; she stinks to high heaven without needing to be changed. Worst of all, she rejects mother's milk in favor of blood. Several traumatic breastfeeding scenes show Grace biting Maddy's breasts until they bleed so badly that they stick to her bra. Maddy, finally understanding that she has given birth to a little vampire, buys vast amounts of raw beef and squeezes the blood into the bottle. But it's no good: Grace accepts the blood happily, but then goes into sweaty convulsions and spits it out again.

Meanwhile Vivian tries to deal with her son's death, initially by infantilizing her husband. Pointing at a tie lying on the bed in an immaculate bedroom, she yells at him: "This room is a pigsty. Pick up your room! Clean up!"; in a later sex scene, she guides Henry's head to her breasts, patting his head like a baby's as he "feeds." When Henry proves an insufficient baby, Vivian decides to take Maddy's. In exchange for her promise to make the malpractice claims plaguing him go away, she sends Dr. Sohn to Maddy's house so he can survey the scene and declare Maddy an unfit mother. When Sohn insists on seeing the baby and goes upstairs without Maddy's permission, Maddy hits him over the head with a breast pump, and the doctor expires in a puddle of blood and breast milk. Watching Sohn bleed out, Maddy decides to put his blood to good use, drags the corpse to the bathroom—the camera focuses briefly on a cup embossed with "World's Greatest Mother"—and fills the baby bottle with Sohn's blood. Vivian arrives shortly thereafter and tries to abduct Grace. In the ensuing struggle, Vivian hits Maddy in the head with a hammer, killing her, but Maddy comes back to life as a vampire, kills Vivian by neck-bite, and sinks back unconscious, which is how Patty finds her.

Cut to an idyllic rural scene: a cow behind a fence, a slow pan over hills, sky and a deserted country road, on which a motorhome emerges in the distance. Patty sports a new wig; Maddy a new wig and a huge scar on her head. Maddy looks pale and sick, and as the camera pans down from her face, we understand why: her breast is torn to shreds and covered with flies; Grace lustily takes another chomp out of it; blood puddles at Maddy's feet (one of the surreal images with which the film opened). Maddy delivers the film's final line with all the despondency of utter exhaustion: "She needs more now. She's teething."

*Grace* confronts us, once again, with the psychoanalytic idea of a woman being eaten up by her baby—in this case, literally—and a series of grotesque body images. This latter aspect is, in fact, what helped market the movie. Director Paul Solet was gleeful when told that at the film's first showing, two viewers passed out, a third had to leave and a female viewer vowed that she would never have children.[10] Given how often the two fainting spectators are mentioned in interviews (Solet was actually congratulated on this repeatedly), it seems that both director and early viewers have understood *Grace* primarily as a body-horror flick. Solet has, in fact, referred to his film as a "creature feature" and claimed that to him, the ultimate horror was the image of a baby dying in utero and nevertheless being carried to term.

Perhaps logically for a film in which a dead baby is reborn as a vampire, the film defines the grotesque body as both human and inhuman. Maddy feeding the baby or performing acts that suggest feeding a baby, such as pouring milk, is frequently counter-shot with animal feeding scenes such as Maddy feeding her black cat (usually something revolting, like raw liver) or the cat bringing home disemboweled mice as little gifts. The reduction of both human and non-human bodies to unmentionable fluids is displayed through Maddy's obsession with nature shows featuring animals feeding, giving birth, or dying, most often horribly of neglect. Over images of a cat's cadaver sucked dry by fleas, reminiscent of images of Grace beset by flies, the show host intones, "How do you take care of your animal?" In another scene, in which Maddy watches a calf being born on TV as she gets Grace's bottle ready, the image of blood running down the cow's legs is mapped onto the sound of Maddy pouring milk into a bottle. The parallel is meant to break down the barrier between human and animal body processes, implying that both humans and animals are merely (gross) bodies, subject to the same cycle endlessly repeated on Maddy's TV: birth, feeding, and death. When Patty comments on a particularly grotesque animal horror-scene with a laconic "Pleasant," Maddy responds: "Animal channel. I'm hooked. It's like a vegan horror movie." But of course veganism is not going to cut it in the long run, as an earlier scene implies. Maddy and Michael are at dinner, Maddy eating a high-protein expectant-mother meal washed down with soymilk. The dinner conversation focuses on the cat's latest gift of savaged rat, which prompts Michael's insight: "Can't feed him soymilk. You're driving him to murder." Clearly, this scene is meant to foreshadow that murder is also in Grace's future. To keep the baby alive, Maddy and Patty will eventually have to resort to killing people. "She needs more now. She's teething."

The film showcases the grotesque body not only by aligning human and non-human bodies, but also by casting Maddy and Vivian as grotesque mothers. Where we expect the baby-food commercial images of a chubby baby nursing, its young and beautiful mother looking down upon it adoringly, we are treated instead to a young mother squeezing blood into a baby bottle (Fig. 3), straight from the slashed veins of a murder victim, or a woman in her sixties forcing her elderly husband to feed at her breast and stimulating her own breasts with a breast pump. The idea behind these grotesque images is a critique of obsessive

Fig. 3. "How do you take care of your animal?" Maddy (Jordan Ladd) contemplates the possibilities in *Grace* (2009) (Anchor Bay Entertainment).

mothering (weirdly—ironically?—Solet dedicated the film to his mother), with the concept of motherhood uncoupled from love for a child and redefined as an compulsive self-image. The character who expresses this most succinctly is Michael as husband to Maddy and son to Vivian. The opening scene, in which Michael impregnates Maddy, features no spark of excitement, let alone love: Maddie endures, contemplating the ceiling with every sign of boredom, as he rocks away on top of her. Michael's death does not elicit a single question from Maddy at the accident site about his well-being or even his survival, not a single tear at his funeral, and not a single mention thereafter. By impregnating her, he has fulfilled his function and is no longer needed. Vivian's quest to replace Michael is even more revealing: her single mourning scene is brisk and efficient, something between a cry and a hiccup. She then quickly turns to her husband as Michael's temporary stand-in before homing in on Grace as his permanent substitute. The fact that Michael is immediately, effortlessly and tearlessly forgotten suggests that he is not considered a person but a *function*: he is what enables both Vivian and Maddy to be/become mothers. His unmourned departure from the film implies that motherhood, even extreme motherhood that does not hesitate to kill in defense of the child, does not necessarily entail love for the child. Even Dr. Sohn, whose last name is the German word for "son," is cast as Vivian's creature, a son who does Mother's bidding but who can lay no claim to maternal affection.

Viewer allegiance in *Grace* is a complicated issue. It is obviously tempting to identify with Maddy as the victim of overbearing mother-figures and deceitful doctors, the symbols of women's disenfranchisement from decisions about their bodies and babies in birth horror films since *Rosemary's Baby*. The problem is that an allegiance with Maddy must embrace the primitive idea that youth and beauty are the qualifications for motherhood: Maddy is eligible whereas Vivian, approaching old age and easily the film's most annoying character, is not. Allegiance with Maddy would mean overlooking the fact that Maddy and Vivian suffer from the same motherhood-fixation. Vivian may not mourn Michael as a person, but his death erases her identity as a mother (according to Solet, the only identity she has[11]). While this loss of self sends Vivian on her insane quest to steal Maddy's baby, Maddy defies the laws of nature to satisfy her desperate desire to become a mother. One of the questions the film never answers overtly is why Grace, born of healthy parents, is a vampire. The explanation is offered indirectly by Patty's words when she attempts to remove the corpse of a baby dead in utero for weeks and dead at birth: "You can't will a dead baby back to life." But of course, willing her dead baby back to (some sort of) life is exactly what Maddy has done. Untethered from love, motherhood becomes an addiction. Like an addict, Maddy keeps her baby locked up in the house like a dirty secret, admitting nobody, even telling her parents-in-law that the baby was stillborn. The bloodsucking theme has long symbolized the idea of putting one's own needs first, even at the cost of destroying the lives of others. Thus it is not surprising that both motherhood-addicts end up killing to get their fix: Vivian kills Maddy; Maddy kills both Sohn and Vivian. And Maddy's final statement tells us that if Grace is to survive ("How do you take care of your animal?"), the slaughter is just beginning.

* * *

Birth horror films commonly center on two ideas: contempt of women and the redundancy of humans. The first instills viewer guilt and immediately alleviates it through the panacea of "correct" identification. The guilty pleasure on offer is watching female bodies under torture, mixed, perhaps, with a *soupçon* of *schadenfreude*. Surely it is not insignificant that all three women—a child psychologist, a children's book author, and a midwife—are *theoretical* experts on children who, in the course of their horrible pregnancies and births, find out what it's like to come face to face with the real thing. Yet their verbal (and fruitless) objections against their own reduction to wombs offer audiences the only fleeting instances of an uncomplicated identification. When Proteus wakes Susan up with a nutritionally perfect breakfast at the "optimum time for your morning fuel ingestion," she shoots back angrily: "I am not a motorcycle!" *The Unborn*'s Virginia snarls at Brad: "What am I, a goddamn incubator?" And Maddy warns Patty to stay away from her and Grace: "We're not a case study." In *The Unborn*, the literal reduction of Beth to a human incubator provides visceral justification of this opposition; in *Demon Seed*, the same is achieved by Proteus's flat assertion that he does not need to "understand" Susan as a human being: "All that I need to understand, Mrs. Harris, is your body." Surely, decades after "My body, my choice," we can all identify with women's quest for control of their bodies, and we're all united in our condemnation of mad scientists and doctors who use their knowledge for Evil and call it the next step in human evolution. *Grace*, however, complicates viewer allegiance by implying that even if women were in charge of their bodies and babies, things would not improve much, and by showing that a woman's motherhood fixation can be just as devastating, loveless and neurotic as the male scientist's obsession with *Über*-baby. Whereas in the earlier films, women are forced or betrayed into horrible pregnancies and resulting self-obliteration, *Grace* shows women who willingly surrender their individuality in pursuit of motherhood. Of the three, *Grace* delivers the most visceral images of the psychoanalytic idea that women are "eaten alive" by their babies. In the sense that babies suck the lifeblood from the former woman, leaving only an empty husk called "Mother," all babies could be considered "evil."

The grotesque body looms large in all three films. The best that viewers can hope for is an end to the woman's suffering, but this can only be effected through the child's death—in *Demon Seed*, Susan's attempt to kill the metal-plated freak; in *The Unborn*, an abortion, and in *Grace*, death in utero. In all cases, the little fiends survive unscathed. These scenarios can be read as attempts to regain Bakhtin's "classical body," and this laudable objective in the film takes the form of events that would, in real life, be seen as either criminal (murder), objectionable (abortion) or tragic (a stillbirth). Audience allegiance is thus motivated in favor of a scenario within the film that most spectators would reject as unacceptable outside of it. The grotesque is the horror, but the "classical" can only be reinstated by incurring guilt—a textbook example of the "taboo compromise."

Guilt, of course, is at the heart of all of these films, which essentially offer viewers delectable fare of tormented women while proposing the justified demise of the human race. The horrible baby as the next step in human evolution, or more directly, that which will "replace" (i.e. extinguish) the human race, is certainly a nasty twist on the view of babies, or children in general, as "our future." Perhaps there is also a silent acknowledgment here that to really shock viewers, the film needs to serve up stronger fare than merely two hours of tortured female bodies. Obliterating women as individuals may be one thing. Obliterating the entire human race, though—now there's an idea that is sure to give us pause. Even if the mad scientist's worship of the squid child as a giant step for mankind can count on little support among audiences, the question remains why birth horror films so insistently propose the extinction of the human race as a form of progress. Does our rejection of the scientist's insanity really cancel out the basic idea that informs his research, namely, that humans *are* a harmful and destructive species, and that Earth would be better off without them? Birth horror movies logically link the idea of humanity's demise with the only act that can prevent it, namely, birth, and then propose that an abortion would actually be the safer, even the more moral, course of action. *Grace*'s take on maternal love may seem original, but in fact, many birth horror movies have advanced a similar idea. All those mothers gazing into the cradle, realizing that whatever it is, it's not human, but still abandoning reason and sanity in favor of maternal instinct, show us that it's not only the child that is wrong, it is the sentiment, because the attachment is not to a child but to the idea of being a mother. Maternal love in horror is exactly what society mandates it should be: unconditional. And therein lies the problem, because this socially conditioned unconditionality unleashes Armageddon in the form of little devils, demons, aliens or supercomputers. Male science may have laid the groundwork to create the little horror, but in the end—and this is clearly one of those instances in which horror film attacks hard-wired assumptions—it is maternal love that will destroy the world.

## Guilt Trips

### LITTLE HORRORS

*Alien* (dir. Ridley Scott, USA 1979); *Aliens* (dir. James Cameron, USA 1986); *Alien³* (dir. David Fincher, USA 1992); *Alien: Resurrection* (dir. Jean-Pierre Jeunet, USA 1997). Arguably, the entire *Alien* series can be boiled down to a vision of Ripley as a mother who mothers critters more often than kids. In *Alien*, she goes back for the ship's cat, inexplicably unless we read the cat as a kid stand-in. In *Aliens*, she goes back for a kid with an animal name, Newt; visually, the scene is linked clearly enough with the cat rescue to suggest a direct succession. In *Resurrection*, she gives birth to a monster and then spectacularly aborts it (the alien baby is sucked out of the ship's womb/window screaming and disintegrating into grayish pieces—probably the most visceral image of abortion available on celluloid). Scott's original is now famous for the imagined horror of rape and unwilling motherhood being forced onto a man (Kane's stunning chest-buster scene); follow-ups have capitalized on this iconic image: all feature someone strapped to the wall, about to give birth and pleading: "Kill me." All films directly link birth and death and liken humans to aliens. *Guilt trip:* The major theme throughout is corporate greed, again under the guise of scientific advancement. Ripley's most memorable line compares aliens and humans: "I don't know which species is worse. You don't see them fucking each other over for a goddamn percentage" (*Aliens*).

*Baby Blues* (dir. Lars Jacobson and Amardeep Kaleka, USA 2008). A new mother suffers from post-partum psychosis to such a degree that she murders one of her older children and attempts to kill the other. The film focuses on child abandonment (the kids are at Mother's mercy because Daddy is never home) and child abuse, both physical and emotional: the mother, in pursuing her children, blames them for deleting her life by coming into the world ("I gave you everything, Jimmy: my mind, my youth, and this is how you repay me?"). At the end, doctors and Daddy proclaim Mom cured, exposing the surviving child to renewed danger since Mother, at this stage, is both highly pregnant and exhibiting every sign of mental disease. The film is essentially a gender-reversal of Kubrick's *The Shining*, with the abuse originating not from the father's drinking but the mother's hormones. *Guilt trip:* The film, "based on actual events," makes pious noises about raising awareness about post-natal disorders, but since it offers no sympathy for the mother's position, it is difficult to see it as anything but an elaborate guilt trip for mothers who may feel that their lives, too, have been restricted by the arrival of a child.

*The Brood* (dir. David Cronenberg, Canada 1979). With the help of a psychiatrist, Nola, a Pandora figure, succeeds in bringing her rage into the world in the form of horrible children who murder everyone she hates (both of her parents and the woman she suspects to be her husband's lover). The film features a gross birth scene, in which Nola brings forth another horrible creature, with the female "equipment" needed to do so—uterine sac, ovaries—turned inside out, upon which she bites off the membrane and licks the new birth like an animal. Birth is defined as a disease (uncontrollable rage that manifests itself physically), the early symptoms of which appear on the arm of Nola's little daughter in the final scene. *Guilt trip:* The film's overt theme is child abuse, passed on through female generations (from Nola's mother to Nola, from Nola to her own daughter), coupled with the familiar theme of the scientist unable to foresee the consequences of his work. The film can easily be read as "conservative" (as featuring female hormones going on a murderous rampage) and as "progressive" (as portraying a woman who gives birth without male permission or "input," in any sense of the word). *Fuller discussion in Chapter 4.*

*Eraserhead* (dir. David Lynch, USA 1977) is the surreal tale of a man who tries to survive his industrial environment, his angry girlfriend, and the unbearable screams of his mutant newborn. Henry lives in a mechanical environment in which human contact offers no comfort. The baby is an amphibian-looking blob that oozes fluids, rejects food and love, and cries constantly. Baby scenes are the most traumatic of the film, most centrally the exceptionally gross "discovery" scene, in which Henry cuts off the baby's bindings to reveal noxious fluids with things floating in it (giblets? organs?). When Henry pierces one of its lungs with the scissors, fluid spurts out of its mouth, its insides turn to foam, boiling over until the baby, now looking like a mix between a spoiled turkey and a rotting corpse, explodes. The film's *guilt trip* targets secret hatred, rejection and revulsion of a baby even while seeming to care for it; child abandonment (the baby's mother flees the scene, leaving Henry to cope), and child abuse—all expressed in visceral and surreal images rather than narrative terms.

*It's Alive!* (dir. Larry Cohen, USA 1974); *It Lives Again* (dir. Larry Cohen, USA 1978); *Island of the Alive* (dir. Larry Cohen, USA 1987). The films feature horrible babies who murder everyone in their path, beginning with the doctors and nurses in the delivery room. All three films focus on the question whether parental love can overcome the babies' weird appearance and evil deeds. Insistently recurring baby POV shots force audiences to spend much of their viewing time at ground level. *Guilt trip:* If the children are horrible, society's treatment of them is even more so; they are seen as no more than targets for shooting practice, pets, commodities to be exploited, or subjects of scientific experiments conducted, as ever, for the good of the human race. The films parade as monster movies but query the identity of the monster: is it them (the "monster" babies) or is it us (the monster's creators)? "When I was a kid, I always thought the monster was Frankenstein … then I went to High School and I read the book, and I realized that Frankenstein was the doctor who created him. Somehow the identities get all mixed up, don't they?" (*It's Alive!*). While Cohen's films constantly oscillate between a view of the children as "evil" or innocently persecuted, Josef Rusnak's remake (*It's Alive*, 2008) answers the question unequivocally (it's evil, after all) and casts the blame on Mother, who, in a failed abortion attempt, caused the baby's abnormality. *Fuller discussion in Chapter 7.*

*The Manitou* (dir. William Girdler, Canada 1978). A woman comes down with a growth on her neck, initially diagnosed as a malignant tumor, later revealed as a case of possession by the Manitou, an evil Indian medicine man who attempts re-birth. The Manitou is bested with the help of an Indian healer who directs all the computers' manitous against the evil spirit. *Guilt trip:* A thinly veiled reference to the extinction of Native Americans emerges in the film's attack on modern disrespect for traditional faith and inflated beliefs in pure science and technology. Only the combination of nature-religion and technology overcomes Evil.

*The Plague* (dir. Hal Masonberg, USA 2006). For ten years, every child on earth is born comatose, leading to a UN–enforced ban on childbirth and enforced abortion. In this world, having children is considered a greater horror than human extinction. The children all wake up at the same time and turn out to be murderous in the extreme, killing their carers first and going on from there. *Guilt trip:* The blame for the disaster is placed squarely not on the children but on their environment. Why did the children fall into a coma at birth? "We always just thought the world was a pretty shitty place. We figured the kids just didn't want to be a part of it anymore." And why did they wake up? "Maybe they decided they wanted to come back. Just not to the same world they left."

*Possession* (dir. Andrzej Zulawski, France 1981). A woman leaves her husband and son to take up a love affair with an octopus (you read that correctly). The film features a horrible miscarriage scene in an underground tunnel, in which the woman's *Exorcist*-style contortions yield milk, blood and possibly ink from mouth and vagina. The *guilt trip* focuses on the pleasure principle and the woman's inexplicable (and unexplained) inability to be happy with her nice family.

*Prometheus* (dir. Ridley Scott, USA 2012) is a reversal of *Alien* that casts creators of life not as mothers but as engineers and views the very idea of creation as horrible. In *Alien*, Kane gives unwilling, painful, and lethal birth; here Shaw, who complains that "I cannot create life," aborts it just in time (to the viewer's immense relief). The *guilt trip* focuses on humanity's inflated sense of self-importance. Humans look for their origins and find an insignificant and cruel God who is not only a bad reflection on humans but also has, post-creation, cast them aside as not worth his time. The overriding question of science is no longer "Where do we come from?" The question, once we've found that out, is "What is wrong with us?"

*Rosemary's Baby* (dir. Roman Polanski, USA 1968) is the original ultimate-betrayal movie coupled with body horror and featuring an early version of the birth-horror movie's inexplicable conclusion, in which the mother will accept anything, even the Devil's spawn, as her child. *Guilt trip:* Maternal love is cooperation with Evil and ensures Armageddon. Ray Bradbury has objected to the ending: "In severe shock, sore put upon by a witch's gaggle of villains, you don't sit down amidst panic to rock a nightmare." His alternate ending has Rosemary snatch the baby from the cradle and escape into the streets, pursued by the devil pack. She runs into "a church or (why not?) a cathedral," places the baby on the altar and prays: "O Lord, O God, O Lord God. Take back your Son!,"[12] presumably a speech act prior to sacrificing him on said altar. But of course, Bradbury got the parent's gender wrong: what's good for the gander (say, the father in Richard Donner's *The Omen*, 1976) is certainly not good for the post-partum, hormone-driven goose.

*Sarah's Child* (dir. Ron Beckstrom, USA 1994). Sarah, having been indoctrinated by her mother that a woman's only purpose in life is to bear children, is devastated when told by a doctor that she is infertile, to the point where she creates a fantasy child, six-year-old Melissa, and gives her reality through psychokinesis. Sarah herself has been wished into existence by her infertile mother in just the same way. All refusing to believe in the reality of these imaginary persons are dispatched post-haste. *Guilt trip:* The film attacks the guilt-tripping of childless women for being childless, showing that society and family conspire in making childless women feel worthless. And yet the film's conclusion that everyone exists only through love seems to endorse, not condemn, the coercive view of motherhood as a woman's only purpose in life.

*Slither* (dir. James Gunn, Canada 2006) is a gynecological horror comedy that mixes creature feature and zombie flick, set in Small Town, USA. Grotesque birth scenes show a woman literally turning into a balloon, bringing forth slithering worms. *Guilt trip:* The film launches a direct attack on American "family values," religiousness and other aspects of unthinking follower-syndrome, encapsulated in nauseating sentiments ("You swore to honor and obey me," a husband reminds his recalcitrant wife) and cheery placards ranging from "Family Fun Day" to "Deer Cheer" to "Jesus Saves," the latter foregrounded as slithering monstrosities drag off screaming victims.

*The Stranger Within* (dir. Lee Philips, USA 1974). Ann is impregnated by an alien and accused of infidelity because her husband has had a vasectomy. The film features extensive pregnancy-torture. An attempted abortion fails because the alien child prevents it by keeping the mother too sick to undergo the procedure safely. The film advocates that an abortion is the only way to save both the mother's health and the couple's marriage. The alien fetus takes over Ann's body, forcing her to ingest pounds of salt and scalding coffee, and giving her the ability to read an entire library in minutes, consuming all of human history in the course of her pregnancy. In the final scene, Ann joins countless mothers and their alien babies who all vanish without a trace. *Guilt trip:* An alien race has checked out humanity, learning all they can about us, and then deciding they've seen enough. It's bad enough that they had to be born on this darn planet. But live here? No way.

# 2

# Family

## *Home-Grown Horrors*

### *Family Feeling: A Brief History of Love*

In the 11 years between 1791 and 1802, Johann Wolfgang von Goethe, Germany's premier writer at the time, lost four children shortly after birth. Letters he wrote on and after October 14, 1791, to his mother and close friends contain no mention of the baby boy born dead on that day. On December 3, 1793, the death of a daughter at the age of 13 days rated a solitary oblique remark in a letter to his friend Jacobi: "this somber season has brought me somber events. Let us await the return of the sun."[1] On November 17, 1795, one day after the death of his 17-day-old son, he wrote: "Yesterday, the poor little chap already left us again, and we must now seek to fill this gap through life and vivacity."[2] On December 19, 1802, hours before Goethe's fourth child perished at the age of three days, Goethe wrote to Schiller, anticipating his baby's imminent death: "Our new guest will hardly stay very long and his mother, although usually very stoic, suffers both physically and emotionally.... I hope to see you tonight in order to fill the void in my life with the presence of friends."[3] None of these disasters, it seems, derailed Goethe's life or literary projects, even momentarily. On the evening of the 1791 stillbirth, he dined at the court of Weimar and founded a new literary circle in the following days. On the evening before the death of his last child, whose demise he fully expected, he attended the opera with Schiller, whom he also saw the following evening, leaving the dead child at home with its suffering mother. In all four cases, the dead babies appear in one or two sentences in a correspondence filled to the brim with business as usual: plans for new literary projects, theatre business, reviews of new works, assessments of great writers, and descriptions of his life at court.

Goethe's clipped responses to the loss of four children in infancy can, of course, be read with equal ease either as callous indifference or as its precise opposite, an intensity of pain that defies expression and can only be dulled by plunging headlong into work and social "life and vivacity," as Goethe put it. A third possibility is suggested by a condolence letter. "My wife and I sincerely lament the loss that you have suffered," Schiller wrote to Goethe following the death of his third child. "And yet you can find solace in the fact that it happened so soon, and strikes more at your hopes [than at your heart]. I would find it hard to bear if a misfortune befell my little boy at this stage."[4] When Schiller wrote this, his own son was two years old.

Schiller's suggestion that it is best to lose children early, before forming a serious attachment, implies an understanding of parental love that differs considerably from the way we might understand the term today: love for a child is neither innate nor immediate, but develops over time based on a knowledge of the individual—not dissimilar, in other words, to love for an adult. Love at first sight of a newborn (cue: "She's *so* beautiful!") is a modern indulgence that rests on the assumption that the child will survive. During epochs when infant mortality fluctuated between 20 and 50 percent and fewer than half of all children could be expected to live to the age of ten, new parents, while almost certainly not uncaring, may well have adopted a wait-and-see attitude to their offspring that contrasts sharply with a modern parent's instant delight.

Indeed, historical studies of the family suggest that the now common understanding of familial love is a fairly recent phenomenon. Both ancient Greece and Rome valued public over private life and held a singularly unemotional view of the family. From the Middle Ages until the eighteenth century, families were seen in social, not sentimental terms. The Industrial Revolution brought considerable changes to family structures, particularly for the middle classes. Whereas in the agrarian economy, men, women and children worked side by side in the fields, the post-industrial bourgeois family came to be defined by what has famously been called "the dissociation between work and family life."[5] Middle-class fathers now worked outside of the home; mothers and children stayed inside. Women's work, in the house and unpaid, was devalued compared to men's remunerated work outside of the home; in fact, for the middle-class *pater familias*, it became a sign of financial success and a point of social pride to be able to keep his wife at home (not "working"). It was at this point that ideology stepped in, casting women as the principal caretakers of children and children as fragile beings dependent on maternal care. Neither would have been practicable or affordable in an agrarian society. The same trajectory can be traced in art history: until the eighteenth century, children in paintings are depicted either allegorically—as cupids or putti—or as small adults; the sentimental view of children as both individuals and helpless innocents did not predominate in art until the Romantic era. This era, then, which either immediately follows, coincides, or overlaps with the Industrial Revolution in most European countries, may well be the historical moment when three related developments occur simultaneously: the modern understanding of the child as a helpless innocent is born; parental love becomes a social obligation; and art, literature, and philosophy begin to portray familial love not only as an obligation but as innate and natural.

Both these developments and letters by parents living in the pre-industrial era suggest that parental love, far from being instinctual or universal, did not assume a central role in family life until enabled to do so by new family structures emerging from social and economic changes. Parental love, and in particular maternal love is, in other words, an ideology that came into being precisely when it was needed—when it became socially necessary to convince women that staying at home and taking care of the babies was every bit as rewarding as a man's work life outside of the home. Because this ideology views family love as *both* natural *and* achievable, as something that must be struggled for and attained, failure to do so is the worst sin a parent can commit, a guilt that is simultaneously individual and transcendent.

## Night Child/What the Peeper Saw *(Spain/UK/Italy/ West Germany 1971)*, The Good Son *(USA 1993)*, Joshua *(USA 2007)*

In his essay "The Monstrous-Familial," John Potts draws a neat dividing line between "acceptable" and "unacceptable" families in American screen culture. The acceptable family is the nuclear family, cemented in film and TV since the 1950s through sit-coms like *Father Knows Best* (1954–60) and *Leave It to Beaver* (1957–63). The unacceptable family is, more often than not, the extended family, a throwback to older, pre-industrial family structures, represented on TV in sit-coms like *The Beverly Hillbillies* (1962–71) and *The Addams Family* (1964–66), and in films through the murderous extended clans of *The Godfather* (1972) and many mafia films in its wake. Horror, too, has cast unacceptable families as extended families, for example the cannibalistic clans of *The Hills Have Eyes* (1977) or *The Texas Chain Saw Massacre* (1974). Potts claims that the reason for this apartheid of screen families is obvious: protestant, industrial, consumer societies define the nuclear family as the norm and all other forms as "monstrous."

Yet horror films have had plenty to say about the nuclear family. Their focus is on the glue that supposedly holds the nuclear family together: familial love. If birth and baby horror attacks the incomprehensibility of unconditional love, family films simply deny that there is such a thing, showing familial love to be uncertain and provisional. Even more disturbingly, this portrayal has remained relatively stable in horror films for the past fifty years.

*Night Child* was born in 1971 amidst a flurry of apparent uncertainty of what to name the child, or, for that matter, its parents. Directed by James Kelley (as James Kelly) and Andrea Bianchi (as Andrew White), the film was re-titled *What the Peeper Saw*, with the principal difference between *Night Child* and *Peeper* being the loss of *Night Child*'s key opening scene. The scene cut in *Peeper* features a naked blonde beauty in a luxury bathroom. She wipes the mirror clean—the better to afford us a view of her delectable breasts—smiles sexily at her own reflection, descends into a round bathtub, electrocutes herself by turning on the cold tap, and writhes to death in the bath, with the camera paying more undue attention to her jiggling breasts. The second scene in *Night Child* (*Peeper*'s opening scene) shows another gorgeous blonde, a dead ringer for the bathing beauty, driving a car through a sparsely beautiful Spanish summer landscape. Arriving at a luscious villa, Elise (Britt Ekland) encounters, for the first time, her 12-year-old stepson Marcus (Mark Lester), home early from his boarding school in Britain. Marcus, a child prodigy, sports an unbelievably advanced vocabulary (most of which is well beyond the comprehension of his beautiful but bimbo-ish stepmother), an extensive knowledge of philosophy and languages, and special interests in subjects ranging from phenology to Confucius. Elise's attempts to befriend her stepson quickly disintegrate when Marcus shows sexual interest in her by groping her and attempts to drive a wedge between her and his father Paul (Hardy Krüger) by lying, stealing and framing Elise. While Paul and Elise neglect Marcus in favor of extensive, repeated and athletic sex, Paul refuses to credit Elise's suspicions of Marcus, leaving her no choice but to prove Marcus's guilt. To that end, she visits Marcus's British school, where she learns that he was expelled for ogling lovers and torturing cats. Confirmation for both allegations arrives when the family dog mysteriously drowns in the pool and Elise discovers a spy hole in the ceiling of her and Paul's bedroom. Elise further learns from a friend of Marcus's mother Sarah that Sarah was murdered by rigging the cold tap to electrocute her.

Marcus and Elise, thrown together by Paul's frequent absences for business reasons, develop a symbiotic but hostile relationship, in the course of which Marcus coldly confesses to his mother's murder and to watching Elise and Paul during sex, just as he had spied on his parents previously. When Elise, now panicked, recalls Paul from abroad to show him the peephole, it has vanished. In conversation with Marcus's psychiatrist (Lilli Palmer), Elise is directly accused of paranoid delusions, encouraging Marcus's sexual advances and trying to break up the father-son relationship; she is forcibly interned in a mental hospital, drugged and restrained. When she is finally released as cured, the scene seems set for a reconciliation between all three. On the pretext of getting to know each other better, Marcus and Elise take a solitary walk with the new dog, during which Marcus tells Elise that he is bored with his insipidly ever-understanding father, that he is sexually interested in her, and that he would have killed her if she had succeeded in convincing anyone of his guilt. She admits that Paul is a little too bland for her taste as well, and together, they plot Paul's murder. Approaching a road, Elise throws the dog's ball directly in the path of a speeding car; the dog runs to retrieve the ball, and Marcus, dashing after the dog in an attempt to save it, is run down by the car. Closing credits run over Elise's impassive face as she walks away.

Throughout *Night Child*, viewer perspective is aligned with Elise's, largely due to the fact that like the viewer, Elise plays the part of an outsider cast into a new family with no knowledge of its prior history or interaction. Background and information is doled out to the viewer as it becomes available to Elise. Viewer allegiance is also most likely to focus on Elise. For one thing, allegiance with either the clueless and mostly absent father or the super-smart evil child is difficult to achieve, leaving Elise as the only possible candidate. For another, Elise engages in pursuit of projects that most viewers would interpret as ethical: first, to make the nuclear family work, secondly, to discover the truth, and finally, to protect her husband.

And yet, the viewer's two-fold attachment to Elise through narrative alignment and ethical allegiance is severely disrupted by the film's casting of Elise's perspective as highly unreliable. Visual alignment (through camera angles) does not support an allegiance with Elise; in fact, the film contains no POV shots that might be attributed to a specific character. Moreover, this "neutral" or "omniscient" perspective contradicts Elise's numerous times. For example, Elise's rejection of Marcus's sexual advances is juxtaposed, later in the film, with dream sequences attributed to Elise showing Marcus and Elise having sex. A shot-counter-shot sequence of both Elise and Marcus standing at the foot of the other's bed, watching the other toss and turn in restless sleep, clearly indicates a sexual interest not limited to Marcus but mutual. Similarly, Elise's protestations of innocence in the scene with the psychiatrist are belied by her dreams in the mental hospital, which show her suffocating Marcus with a pillow or drowning him in the pool. Clearly, Elise's relationship with her stepson is disturbed by both sexual and murderous desires that are a precise match for those she attributes to him. Disruptions between outside and inside perspective are also expressed by clashing audio-video mapping: a peaceful dinner scene is accompanied by disturbing and aggressive extra-diegetic music which drowns out the dialogue and escalates as Paul and Elise start fighting at the dinner table, with Marcus looking on with smug satisfaction. Because we don't hear the dialogue, we don't know what prompted the altercation, but the presence of extra-diegetic music that would be more appropriate for an army traversing a jungle in search of the enemy casts the familial struggle as a war of sorts and imbues the scene with an immense level of stress, long before the first visual clue that anything is wrong.

Unreliability of perspective—both visual and aural, both character-specific and omniscient—is, in fact, one of the film's chief features. The question this raises is the one familiar from Jack Clayton's 1961 film *The Innocents*: is the child actually "evil" or is it all in the stepmother's head? Once we discount the opening scene showing Sarah's murder—and this may well be why the scene was cut in the second version—all evidence against Marcus is tied to Elise's perspective, since it emerges either in conversation with her or as a result of her investigation. Confirmation from the unattributed omniscient perspective is sometimes enticingly suggested, usually maddeningly withheld, and occasionally first offered and then rescinded. Take, for example, Elise's assertion that Marcus has drilled a peephole through the attic floor to watch her and Paul during sex. Marcus confesses this to Elise, but his confession is belied by the fact that when she tries to show the peephole to Paul, the attic floor is completely untouched. The viewer now has a choice of either believing Marcus's statement, which would mean attributing to him advanced carpentry skills in addition to his intellectual prowess, or discounting the confession, made to Elise alone, as part of Elise's deepening paranoid spiral. To throw another wrench into the works, the omniscient camera shows us two peephole perspectives: one shot through a ceiling hole in the attic directly onto Paul and Elise's bed, and another through a small hole in the ceiling above the psychiatrist's consultation room, showing Elise sitting on the sofa directly underneath and the psychiatrist pacing. The first seems to confirm Elise's suspicion that Marcus is indeed spying. But what are we to make of the second bird's eye-shot through the peephole at the psychiatrist's practice? Are we to believe that Marcus has somehow managed to drill this hole in order to spy on Elise's conversation with the psychiatrist? Or does the relatively unlikely presence of this second peephole cast doubt on the existence of the first as well?

Doubt as to the film's purported reality arises particularly during scenes that pretend to clear up the mystery. When Marcus confesses to his mother's murder, for example, he describes his mother as an unattractive 35-year-old (the girl we see murdered in the opening scene is an absolute stunner of about 25) and pronounces his father's grief "transitory," a statement belied by the fact that Paul immediately sold the house upon Sarah's death, indicating considerable trauma. A lie from a self-confessed killer is not all that surprising, and in this case there could be a good reason for it: Marcus's implication that Paul was hardly affected by Sarah's death could serve as a warning signal to Elise that she might be cast aside just as easily. Nonetheless, the fact that Marcus lies about facts that are so easily disproven obviously raises questions with regard to the confession itself. Beyond the initial electrocution scene and the peephole POV shots of unknown provenance and dubious credibility, the only outside confirmation of Marcus's "evil" is tied to a comparatively minor incident: the drowning of the family dog, which Elise immediately interprets in light of the headmaster's statement that Marcus was expelled for killing cats. In a scene in which Elise is absent, we see Marcus throw stones at the dead dog floating in the swimming pool.

Here, finally, is confirmation from beyond Elise's perception for her suspicion that Marcus is severely disturbed. And yet, Marcus's callousness towards the dog is rescinded in the final scene, in which Marcus is so afraid for the second dog that he runs into the road in an attempt to save it, directly into the path of the oncoming car.

These plot-holes are never resolved, raising the possibility that the film is not interested in solving the murder mystery or the question of Marcus's guilt versus Elise's sanity. We might, in fact, read this surface story as an elaborate red herring masking the film's main theme of child neglect. It should strike the viewer as peculiar that Elise, who lives with Paul in the villa, has never once met his son until he comes home from school. To the psychiatrist, Elise states that in the entire course of their courtship, Paul hardly ever mentioned his son: "We were too full of each other." This is borne out on Paul's arrival day at home, which is the first day that brings the new family together. Surely, one would think, this would be an occasion for family time: a bike ride through the country side followed by a picnic à trois, a nice dip in the pool to cool off, a croquet game on the lawn, and a barbecue on the villa's wrap-around porch. Instead, Paul and Elise spend the day making love, leaving Marcus to his own devices. They screw in the bathtub, with Marcus, alone in the garden, being treated to their groans through the open window. Action continues in bed, countershot with Marcus on a swing, looking sullenly towards their bedroom window. This is followed by a shower scene and yet another bout of lovemaking in bed by the clearly oversexed couple; in the meantime, Marcus kicks a ball around the garden with the dog. After this last round, at long last, Marcus is mentioned for the first time. Commenting on his unusual smarts and independence for his age, Paul reminds Elise: "It's too easy to forget that he's only a child, 12 years old. He needs as much love, warmth, sympathy, understanding as any other kid."

Given that the couple have just spent an entire afternoon ignoring him, this is a bit rich. As it turns out, it is also a hotly contested statement. While Paul describes his son as a child needing a love and understanding that he is never present to offer, both Elise and Marcus dispute Marcus's status as a child. Elise violently denies it to Marcus—"You're not a child. You're a thing. You're a freak"—and later to the psychiatrist: "Oh, for Christ's sakes, stop calling him a child! He is not a child! He is as adult as you or I. Certainly not a child!" Marcus, too, claims adult status, both sexually and intellectually. Pointing out repeatedly that he and Elise, at 12 and 22 respectively, are much closer in age than Elise is to 42-year-old Paul, he considers himself a more adequate partner for Elise and ogles or gropes her throughout the film. Intellectually, he prides himself not on his vast schoolbook learning but on the genius stroke with which he engineered his mother's "heart attack." The fact that his father is blissfully unaware of all this while Elise at least accords him the respect of suspicion is another reason for Marcus's contempt of his father and his intense interaction with Elise. Like so many super-smart (read: evil) kids in horror films, Marcus despises everyone who isn't intelligent enough to figure him out.

While consistently muddying perspectives and obscuring reality levels, *Night Child* leaves us in no doubt that the nuclear family is in trouble. The film presents the nuclear family as unjustly idealized, severely isolated and, above all, loveless. This is achieved mostly visually, by means of imbuing the film's characters and landscapes with a jarring, incongruous brightness. A relentless Spanish sun and washed-out nature shots are complemented by the bleached appearance of the family itself: all four principals—father, mother, son and

Fig. 4. Not as bright and sunny as they appear: Master-race types Elise (Britt Ekland) and Paul (Hardy Krüger) in *What the Peeper Saw* (1971) (Avco Embassy/Photofest).

stepmother—are exaggeratedly blonde, blue-eyed, pale and beautiful—Master-race types, Sun-children (Fig. 4). Its original title and setting notwithstanding, the film is bare of night shots or darker Spanish types. The exaggerated uniformity of racial types is, perhaps, another warning of unreality, a hint that things (people) are not as bright and sunny as they may appear. Furthermore, the film presents isolation, not love, as the defining aspect of the nuclear family, and emphasizes this by making clear that isolation is, in narrative terms, highly improbable. A clearly wealthy father, stepmother and son live all alone in a gigantic villa with a swimming pool and vast grounds and gardens in an isolated spot in the Spanish mountains. Where, we might ask, is the housekeeper? Where is the driver? Where are the gardener and the cook? Food magically appears on the table although Elise is never once seen cooking; Paul mows the extensive lawns of the property himself on the rare occasions that he is at home; when Elise is too drunk to drive Paul to the airport, he takes a taxi. The utter absence of others in the family setting—non-family members only appear twice, in the psychiatrist's practice and in the party scene—while incongruous given the grandeur of the property, confirms the sense that the nuclear family is not a loving but a lonely place. The luxury villa, its swimming pool, gardens and grounds do not make a happy home but a prison in a remote location in which two family members are cast as mortal enemies trying to enlist the third to their respective causes. Hell, to adapt a Sartrean idiom, is other family members, cast not into a dark world but a blindingly bright one in which sex replaces love and trust is impossible.

Ultimately, the minor question of the child's guilt or innocence is left unresolved, whereas the main question—the question of love—is answered in no uncertain terms. To the end, the film leaves open whether Marcus is a "night child" whose actions cannot abide the light of day or a sweet innocent, misunderstood, maligned and ultimately murdered by his mentally disturbed stepmother—a possibility clearly raised by the film's constant referencing of *The Innocents* and the deletion of the initial murder scene in the revised version. But what is clear beyond doubt or question is what the peeper saw: looking down into his parents' bedroom, he sees that he is not at the center of their world—far from it. He sees that they are too "full of each other" to leave room for anyone else. He sees that love is not unconditional but feeble and half-hearted. Without trust, his parents' love for each other is no more than a tryst, and their love for a child they have no interest in seeing amounts to no more than the lip service owed to the nuclear family model.

Along similar lines, *The Good Son* (dir. Joseph Ruben, 1993) could be read as a test-tube experiment about the nature and reality of love in the nuclear family. The film unites two truncated nuclear families to see if two halves can make a whole: ten-year-old Mark (Elijah Wood), who has just lost his mother to cancer and his father (David Morse) to a tempting job offer in Japan, is sent to live with his uncle's family, who have themselves lost a young son to a drowning accident in the bathtub. Albeit touched by tragedy, Wallace the father (Daniel Hugh Kelly), Susan the mother (Wendy Crewson), older son Henry (Macaulay Culkin) and his little sister Connie (Quinn Culkin) present the picture-perfect image of the American nuclear family. Mark, believing his mother's dying words that she will always be with him, is convinced that she has returned in Susan. Henry's identical age and his immediate "adoption" of Mark as his brother and playmate establish him early on as playing a part in Mark's healing process which is further buttressed by family and therapy. The idyll sours when Henry begins to show an unhealthy obsession with death: he jokingly threatens to drop Mark from a great height rather than pull him up into the tree house; he describes in gleeful detail the death of his little brother in the bathtub. From there he graduates to killing dogs, causing a ten-car smash up on the highway by throwing a home-made life-sized doll in the path of the cars, and attempting to murder his little sister, just as—as it predictably emerges—he murdered his little brother previously. Henry, always two steps ahead of Mark, manages to blame his own evil deeds on Mark's trauma and resulting mental instability. Realizing Mark's profound attachment to Susan, he resolves to kill her for the sole purpose of hurting Mark further. The film culminates in a scene in which Mark comes upon Henry trying to push his mother off a steep cliff and rushes in to defend her. In the struggle, Susan manages to climb back on top, with both Henry and Mark rolling over the edge, hanging on to one of her hands, and calling up to her for help. Understanding that she can only save one of them, she hesitates for long and suggestive seconds, but finally drops Henry and saves Mark.

When Roger Ebert claimed that the film should have been called "Henry, Portrait of a Future Serial Killer,"[6] he missed the irony with which the film defines one son as the film's title figure and the other as its main character (Fig. 5). If Ebert's suggestion foregrounds the evil brother, the film's actual title shines a light on the inner workings of the nuclear family: how and why does a son get to be a "good" son? And is love for a child unconditional or awarded only to good little children? The film is full of claims that love is unconditional, as in the scene in which Mark, desperately trying to convince Susan of Henry's evil deeds,

Fig. 5. The Real Son and the Good Son: Henry (Macaulay Culkin) and Mark (Elijah Wood) in *The Good Son* (1993) (Twentieth Century–Fox/Photofest).

is told that "Henry is my son. He's my little boy and I love him. Don't ever come to me with these lies again." Unconditional love as the most basic instinct of the nuclear family is the wall Mark runs into several times in his attempts to convince his new family that Henry is "evil"—not naughty, wild or badly behaved, but evil. Mark defines Henry as such three times: once to his father, once to Susan, and once to his psychiatrist (Jacqueline Brookes):

*Mark:* What do you think? What makes people evil?
*Dr. Davenport:* Evil's a word people use when they've given up trying to understand someone. There's a reason for everything if we could just find it.
*Mark:* What if there isn't a reason? What if something just *is*?
*Dr. Davenport:* Why, Mark? Do you think you're evil? Cos you let your mother die? You know that's not true.
*Mark:* What if there was this boy, and he did these terrible things because he liked doing them? Wouldn't you say he was evil?
*Dr. Davenport:* I don't believe in evil.
*Mark:* You should.

In this scene and others, the film clearly sides with Mark, accepting the child's simple moral universe, divided neatly into good v. evil, over the adult's more byzantine psychological and spiritual meanderings. Evil is portrayed as real, not just a misunderstanding that can be cleared up by love, patience, and therapy. The adult refusal to believe in evil (much less that a child could ever be described as such) emerges as the film's main problem because it endangers good children like Henry's siblings and Mark himself. Significantly, the film also clearly distinguishes between evil and the film's other main subject, guilt, which is either incurred—as in Henry's case—or experienced, but never both. Thus experiencing guilt becomes a defining characteristic of goodness. Susan is wracked with guilt for taking her eyes off her toddler to answer the telephone, thereby "letting" him drown in six inches of water. Likewise, Mark, who believes his love for his mother insufficient to save her from cancer, confesses in therapy to "letting" his mother die. If Dr. Davenport points out to Mark that guilt does not constitute evil, the film goes a step further by defining the terms as opposites: it is precisely Henry's *inability* to feel guilty ("I don't feel bad about anything," he tells his mother) that classifies him as evil.

The film's three main characters, Henry, Mark and Susan, are all obsessed with death and discuss it constantly. But whereas Mark and Susan adopt an emotive approach to the trauma of death, Henry's attitude towards it is both playful and coldly clinical.[7] His favorite action figure is Skeleton Man, whom he defines as "this really cool superhero you can't kill cos he's already dead." After shooting the dog, he throws the carcass down a well, humming "The Last Post." Shortly before he throws the dummy off the bridge onto the highway, endangering dozens of lives, he makes up a suicide story about the character: "Poor Mr. Highway. He's thinking about the end. He's had enough of this terrible life. ... Say goodbye!" At the tender age of ten, he smokes cigarettes, dismissing the risk with a casual "Who cares? You're gonna die anyway." Death, to Henry, is not a trauma but an experiment. When Mark, provoked beyond endurance, holds a pair of scissors to Henry's throat, Henry imagines the physicality of his own death with the same forensic fascination that leads him to kill dogs and little brothers: "Go ahead. Jam it in. Gotta push pretty hard though. The blood'll go right across the room. Come on. Come on."

Neither the terror nor the trauma of death are comprehensible to Henry, as is foregrounded in parallel scenes in which Mark discusses his mother's death separately with

Susan and with Henry. The conversation with Susan goes precisely how such discussions should proceed in a loving nuclear family: it is based on faith and feeling, full of hopes of heaven and assurances that "she'll always be with you." The discussion with Henry focuses entirely on the stark physical facts of death: "I took a real good look when my kid brother Richard drowned in the bathtub.... He was completely blue," Henry tells Mark, and asks why Mark did not adopt a similar clinical approach to his mother's death: "You should've looked at her eyes and lips, and touched her skin to see what it felt like—hot, cold." Henry's evil is encapsulated not only in his inability to feel anything, but particularly in his calculated skill in mimicking emotions, as he does when play-acting the dummy's suicide. In the family, too, he inevitably trots out precisely the correct and expected expressions of sympathy, love or concern that circumstances demand.

The wrench the film throws into this uncomplicated ethical landscape is the nuclear family's credo of unconditional love, an idea it seeks to disparage both through narrative and cinematography. Whereas the narrative focuses on the inner workings of the family home, outside spaces claim far more of the film's visual attention. Shot on various locations in Massachusetts, Maine and Minnesota, the film opens with a soccer match played in front of a dramatic mountain range that places Mark's original family home into one of the midwestern or Mountain states. His second family lives in a more cultured East Coast island scenery dominated by woods, cliffs and seascapes, a landscape both beautiful and seemingly, as Ebert has pointed out, "designed as a series of death traps for kids." Playgrounds are usually associated with death. They include a bridge where Mark and Henry barely escape attack by a rabid dog; the well, disposal site for dead dogs and dummies that have served their purpose, and, of course, the town cemetery. Landscape in the film is explicitly juxtaposed with the family home; it functions as a place to escape from it, to give room to emotions that have no place in the home. The wake for Mark's mother, for instance, features a slow shot panning past murmuring family members before coming to rest on Mark. The following shot tracks a fence and Mark's feet walking down the path to the garden gate. As soon as he steps outside it, the camera pulls back to reveal him standing all alone in a stunning prairie landscape bordered by far distant mountains—a wild scenery untouched by humans and their grief or guilt, from which Mark turns to look back at the house. In the East Coast setting, too, the wildness of the woods, steep cliffs and ocean contrasts sharply with domestic spaces. Susan's special "thinking place" is a cliff top overlooking the sea where she goes to think about little Richard and her part in his death; not coincidentally, this very cliff becomes the setting for the final struggle.

Set in this spectacular and threatening landscape, houses appear small, insignificant, and above all unstable, a portrayal that is fairly easy to read, given the film's serial symbolism in which houses signify the home and the home symbolizes the family. With the exception of the two family homes, all houses in the film are battered by a mixture of wobbly construction without and aggression within: the warehouse that Henry and Mark smash up with stones; the ramshackle shed where Henry manufactures and stores a number of weapons like his home-made crossbow for shooting animals, and the rickety tree house that nearly becomes the scene of a fatal fall for Mark from which Henry barely saves him—not without pointing out that it might be fun to find out whether Mark can fly. Family homes appear more stable until you take a look beyond the front door. Just as Mark's old family home was dwarfed by mountains, his new one spectacularly and vulnerably flanks the sea; the waves, shot through Mark's bedroom window, seem close enough to swallow the house up. On the surface, all is as it should be: the houses cozy and comfortable, the landscapes litter-free, majestic and overwhelmingly beautiful. And yet the film casts the house primarily as the site of death—real, potential or imagined—and outside spaces either as "death traps for kids" or as sites of mourning, dedicated to the contemplation of one's own guilt and grief.

If cinematography compromises the home as the ideal space where families love and protect each other, the narrative confirms this by querying the nature of familial love. Consider the following scene, in which Mark threatens to expose Henry's evil deeds to Susan:

*Mark:* I told your mom.
*Henry:* Why would she believe you? She's my mom, not yours.
*Mark:* You know, you're wrong about that. She *is* my mother.
*Henry: Your* mom? You crazy? Your mom's maggot food.
*Mark:* My mom said she'd always be with me. She chose your mom as a way of coming back. ... She's my mother now.
*Henry:* Hey Mark. Don't fuck with me.

This brief conversation contains, *in nuce,* the film's entire distinction between "good" and "evil." Why is Mark "the good son"? Because he wants his mother. Why is Henry "evil"? Because he counts on the unconditionality of familial love. Blood, in Henry's thinking, will always be thicker than water, and unconditional love, the nuclear family's most inflexible credo, will always shield him from the consequences of his actions. In the end, Susan sides with Mark, deeding the gift of love—and of life—to the son who deserves it, the good son. But what, we might ask, does this do to the concept of familial love? On the one hand, the film's conclusion indicates that love must be earned, that there are children who deserve it and children who do not, and that therefore unconditional love is a problem: were love unconditional and blood thicker than water, Susan would drop Mark and save her own evil brat. On the other hand, the film complicates this logic considerably by defining as the good son the one who *desires* the nuclear family, with all of its faith in unconditional love very much intact, and as evil the son who rejects it. Henry is not only a murderous little brat but also a bad son in the sense that he refuses to submit to parental authority, and a bad brother (his interaction with his little sister Connie, other than in the scene in which he tries to kill her, consists entirely of yelling at her and pushing her around). Mark, on the other hand, is a model of filial love and duty who obeys his host parents to the letter, shows trust by allowing Susan to comfort him, plays sweetly with Connie, and protects her from Henry's worst excesses. And yet, in Mark's final voice-over judgment, the good son can never replace the real son: "Henry is gone, and the rest of us are safe. But sometimes, late at night, I find myself thinking, not about Henry, but about Susan, and wondering, if she had it to do over, would she make the same choice? I guess I'll always wonder. But I know I'll never ask." If unconditional love for a child can sometimes go to the wrong person, conditional love, the love doled out to children for being good, is something you can never count on. Thus Mark understands the love his new mother offers him—although he may deserve it more—as vastly inferior to the love she bore her own, albeit evil, son.

One final time, visuals corroborate what the story has already told us. Mark's voice-over insight is offered from Mark's own "thinking place," which is the precise opposite of Susan's. Whereas Susan's thinking place, where she contemplates her guilt over baby

Richard's death, is dramatically and dangerously magnificent, a tall white cliff plunging steeply into a dazzling blue sea, Mark's thinking place, where he contemplates the frailty of maternal love, is a comparatively drab and monotonous vista of low-level rocky hills stretching endlessly into the distance. Unlike Susan's, Mark's thinking place is not one where anyone can fall dramatically to his death. It is, in fact, bare of *any* drama or danger: no individual detail invites the eye to focus; Mark, a little figure clad in tones of brown and sand, is swallowed up by the landscape just as Henry, in the previous scene, was washed away by waves at the bottom of the cliff. This is the ultimate tragedy of *The Good Son*: the insight that familial love does not lead to happiness, neither for the parents nor for the child. Susan, who has spent much of the film torturing herself unfairly for allowing a son to die, incurs that very guilt at the end of the film—not merely in the recesses of a guilty conscience that blames parents indiscriminately and illogically for whatever may befall their children, but in reality. That Susan could ever overcome the guilt for the death of her son Henry, which is so much more directly based on her actions and responsibility than the death of her son Richard, is inconceivable. If Susan is condemned to a lifetime of guilt, Mark is sentenced to a lifetime of "goodness." Having struggled to regain a mother's love, he is offered instead its colorless second cousins—the drab safety of the nuclear family and a love that must be re-purchased every day with never-ending demonstrations of filial virtuousness and obedience.

Like *The Good Son*, *Joshua* (dir. George Ratliff, 2007) opens with a soccer game from which a frantic father hastily drags his nine-year-old son to visit his mother in the hospital. Here, however, the trauma is not the mother's death but the arrival of a new baby. Once again, we are presented with what seems the picture-perfect nuclear family: Brad (Sam Rockwell), a New York City fund manager with an enormous income, Abby (Vera Farmiga), a full-time mother appropriately delighted with the new baby and enabled by Brad's income to stay at home, older brother Joshua (Jacob Kogan), highly intelligent, considerate and polite, good in school and musically gifted, and finally, to make their happiness perfect, a cute chubby baby whom they name Lily. Predictably, the entire household revolves around the new arrival; Joshua is completely ignored. What Joshua might be feeling is only hinted at: he seeks verbal confirmation of his parents' love more often than he used to and spends his nights in the baby's room, watching her sleep. When he receives ambiguous responses from his parents to his question what he was like as a baby, he unearths and watches a home movie showing a newborn Joshua screaming at the top of his lungs and driving his mother to distraction (Fig. 6). Soon thereafter, little Lily stops being the perfect baby and begins her own screaming marathons. Joshua, in the meantime, does everything he can to convince others that he is not being raised right. At a school recital, Joshua, who is an accomplished pianist, hunts and pecks out a painfully inept version of "Twinkle, Twinkle Little Star"; at home, he gives away his toys and eviscerates what few stuffed animals he has left. Meanwhile, Abby is deteriorating sharply; unable to handle the baby's constant screaming, she withdraws to her room, her therapy, her pills, and her guilt.

Strangely, Joshua seems to flourish as his family disintegrates around him. Whereas everyone else's appearance deteriorates under stress—Abby never makes it out of her bedclothes; in one scene, Brad picks Joshua up from school wearing his pajama bottoms—Joshua wears a formal suit and tie even at home. Were we to judge the characters' mental states from their appearance, Joshua would be easily identified as the only sane person in

Fig. 6. Joshua (Jacob Kogan) watches himself as a baby driving his mother (Vera Farmiga) to distraction in *Joshua* (2007) (Fox Searchlight/Photofest).

the house. The only other stable element in the family seems to be Abby's brother Ned (Dallas Roberts), who makes an occasional appearance to calm Abby down and play the piano with Joshua. When Abby becomes non-functional, Brad's mother Hazel (Celia Weston) is brought in to help, but even this is not sufficient; soon thereafter Brad quits his job to become a full-time child-carer. Suspicions mount that Joshua is jealous of Lily and wants to harm her, and Joshua's interests in cruel Egyptian gods and the mechanics of mummification do nothing to reassure the family or the viewer. Brad's worst fears are confirmed when he finds a recording of Joshua standing over Lily's cradle at night, whispering to her: "Nobody will ever love you," upon which Lily promptly starts screaming; the implication is clearly that Joshua has distressed the baby for weeks, trying to make Abby's second mothering experience every bit as horrible as her first one with him. Ultimately, his campaign succeeds and Abby is interned in a mental hospital. Soon thereafter, Joshua removes the second mothering figure from the family by pushing Hazel down the stairs of the Brooklyn Museum of Art. At this point, Brad transfers Lily from the baby's room to his own bedroom, locking Joshua out. Joshua begins to paint disturbing pictures, which a child psychologist identifies as typical of severely abused children. Finally, Joshua goads Brad into hitting him in public, upon which Brad is arrested for child abuse and Joshua and Lily sent to live with his uncle Ned. The final scene shows Joshua and Ned bonding over the piano, shortly after Ned has hectically arranged for a nanny—any nanny, so long as she can start that very day—to take care of Lily.

Joshua represents a type that has haunted family horror for decades. Like both Marcus and Henry, he shows a level of intelligence and creativity far too advanced for his age, coupled with the psychopath's complete inability to experience emotions of any kind. From the outset, Joshua is presented as "off," as far too perfect, like a little robot or alien, a striking contrast to the slightly disheveled and untidy normality that reigns in his family. Neat and good-looking, his hair parted ruler-straight, impeccably turned out even in his own bedroom, he considerately asks his mother whether she was hurt by the birth, tiptoes around the house when the baby is sleeping, walks the dog, does household chores unprompted, and obeys his parents to the letter. At school, he finishes tests early; his piano playing is near concert-level. He never acts up, never yells, and does not object when his every attempt to speak to his parents is cut short by Lily's cooing, upon which they immediately center on the baby, clearly forgetting that Joshua is even in the room. Unable to feel either love or distress, he is, like *The Good Son*'s Henry, an outstanding mimic of feelings whenever the situation calls for them. A central example is Joshua's chilling imitation of Brad's extreme distress at the death of the beloved family dog, who dies right after a walk with Joshua. Joshua coldly observes Brad on the floor, tearfully hugging the dog and calling his name; then, as if someone had pushed a button in his back, Joshua walks over, shoos Brad aside, and tearfully hugs the dog, parroting Brad's precise words: "Buster! Hey, pal! No!"

Unable to experience it, familial love becomes an object of study for Joshua, who examines it with scientific curiosity, as if under a microscope. His experiments focus mostly on the question how and when others feel it, and whether they can be manipulated either to love or, conversely, to stop loving. He tends to ask his parents whether they love him in situations when they are too angry or frightened to trot out the usual mantra of unconditional love. He even gives them leave not to follow the formula: as his father tucks him in, Joshua tells him, "You know, you don't have to love me. That's not, like, a rule or something," in answer to which Brad robotically churns out the parental classic that Joshua is their son and they will always love him, no matter what. Further experiments query whether familial love, which can apparently be turned off by something as common and normal as a screaming baby, can just as easily be turned on. In one scene, Joshua acts "normal" around his mother, engaging her in an elaborate game of hide and seek, as if to prove that if both parties could just *pretend* that everything is fine, everything would indeed be fine. Similarly, towards the end of the film, Joshua puts on a distressed little boy-show for his father's benefit, crying in the night and acting needy and neglected. Brad gets into bed with him, soothing him to sleep; the minute he makes a move to check on Lily, Joshua becomes clutchy: "Stay, stay with me…. Stay like you used to. Stay with me like you used to." At this point, Brad has seen the tape of Joshua's verbal torture of Lily; he strongly suspects Joshua of killing the dog, and he is practically certain that Joshua murdered his grandmother. Yet all of it, it seems, is wiped from Brad's memory as soon as Joshua acts like a normal little boy. Brad practically melts with relief, cuddling his son to sleep, and even considers the possibility that Joshua's weird behavior could be due to someone else abusing him. The fact that Joshua's experiments always succeed, proving that given sufficient stimulus, familial love can be turned off or on like a lamp, wreaks havoc on the idea of familial love as natural or innate. His recurring mantra to Lily, "Nobody will ever love you," not only describes his own understanding that his parents never really loved him, but also more generally denies the idea of unconditional parental love: love is only awarded to trouble-free children.

Obviously, nothing is easier than to blame the family's demise on the evil child who engineers it. And yet, it quickly becomes clear that this family does not need Joshua's intervention to fall apart. External circumstances that set the ideal scene for the nuclear family to flourish—a good income, a pleasant home, a stay-at-home mom—are contrasted with utterly heart-rending levels of parental misery long before Joshua ever wreaks havoc in the home. While Brad does his level best to do his duty as a father, which includes repeated and unconvincing attempts to persuade Joshua that he is loved, Abby quickly disintegrates to the point where even lip service is beyond her. In the home movie in which Abby holds baby Joshua, screeching at the top of his lungs, she screams at Brad to leave her alone. When Brad puts down the camera on the table and leaves the room, the camera continues to record her weeping abjectly, repeating endlessly: "I'm fine. I'm fine. I'm fine," until her tear-filled face dissolves into static. Abby's experience mothering Lily is not much better. When the nightly screaming starts in the baby's room, she gets up dutifully, angrily refusing all help from Brad: "I'm fine, okay? I can handle this! Just go to bed!"; later, overwhelmed by exhaustion, she "handles" her shrieking infant by turning off the baby monitor and covering her head with a pillow. As soon as Brad comes home from work, she flings the baby at him and walks off; her comment "Take a deep breath, Brad. That's our life you're smelling," indicates that she has not bothered to change the diapers. She spends all of her time in bed weeping; her inability to expel breast milk prompts another breakdown of guilt because "I'm not providing for her." The idea of accepting help merely triggers fresh guilt. Ned's suggestion to hire a nanny for Lily, adding that this is, after all, what wealthy New Yorkers *do*, is brushed aside by Abby's statement that she could never leave Lily in someone else's care. When Hazel comes to help, Abby resents her presence, warning Brad darkly: "Don't take Lily away from me.... She needs me, not some dried-up old sponge."

Clearly Abby's sense of parental duty is formed by the nuclear family mandate that loving parents take care of their own children. The reason she refuses Hazel's help is that accepting it would mean a return to the extended family, indicating that Abby as a mother—and by extension, the nuclear family as a model—has failed. The reason Abby rejects a nanny, although this is what rich people do, is that in ideological terms, she does not want to *be* rich: she wants to be a good mother, which means upholding the nuclear family's banner of love, to which ultimately everything else must be sacrificed. Hazel follows the same logic when she instructs Brad to give up everything—his job, his friends, his social life, his sports, his cultural interests—to move to the country: "stop acting like a boy, and start acting like a man, and take care of your family!," she tells him at a point when he has already established himself as the film's only caring and responsible parent. "You leave New York, you come home. You've been playing city long enough. It's time to grow up, Bradley. Once and for all." And yet, Hazel's accusation that Brad is too distracted by career and city culture to be a proper father is also firmly rejected. The fault lies not with the modern parent's desire to combine family and career, which would mean leaving the child in someone else's care: of all the possible child care options, this is the one that is not even on offer. All possibilities paraded past us in the course of the film involve at least one, sometimes two, family members acting as full-time homebodies and child-carers—Abby on her own, Abby supported by Hazel, Brad supported by Hazel, and finally, Brad on his own. All fail miserably.

*Joshua* shows that what ails the nuclear family is not insufficient parental attention but the guilt that eats up parents who are both unable to love their children and to let go of an ideology that casts familial love as both natural and compulsory. By keeping the audience at the parents' level of knowledge for most of the narrative, the film engages in misdirection of both parents and audience, suggesting the classic and familiar scenario of sibling rivalry. Joshua, the film pretends, feels jealous, neglected and deprived of parental love due to Lily's arrival and wants to harm his baby sister in revenge. Even the film's structure participates in this elaborate ruse, timing the narrative in days of Lily's age, as if to imply that the baby's life might end with the film. In reality, Joshua is neither hankering after his parents' love nor intent on harming the baby; he merely engineers the break-up of his family because he prefers to live with his uncle Ned. Ned's musical interests match Joshua's, and given that Ned responds to the prospect of caring for a baby with utter panic, Joshua can assume that he will have Ned more or less to himself while the baby is foisted on a nanny. In effect, Joshua exchanges his nuclear family drama for a buddy movie. What enables him to break up his family is the fact that both of his parents have fallen for the nuclear family hype to such a degree that it only takes minimal manipulation to encourage the self-sacrifice that is, after all, an integral part of the ideology of familial love. The final scene shows Joshua at the piano, playing his new composition to Ned:

> You know, they didn't ever have to love me, no, no, no,
> And no one will ever love them now,
> But they always wanted somehow to save me, La, la, la,
> For pity's sake they should have saved themselves.

This, in essence, is the horror of *Joshua*—not the familiar story of an older sibling acting up because he fears that his parents no longer love him, but a son who seeks out the weaknesses that make the nuclear family a vulnerable institution and then deliberately wrecks it. His song characterizes his parents both as duplicitous and dupes: on the one hand, they never really loved him, on the other, they felt so compelled to enact the nuclear family's love charade that they became unable to save themselves. Bare of love, the nuclear family is presented as hollow and meaningless, all structure and no essence.

That Joshua purposely sets out to tear down this structure is made clear in a scene in which the film employs the usual symbolic stand-in for the idea of the family: the house. One morning Brad, emerging from the bedroom, is surprised by a huge and elaborate house that Joshua has constructed from wooden blocks. Significantly, the structure contains no walls but merely wooden beams; it is not a house but the bare outline of a house, tall and wide but clearly unstable. The following eerie dialogue ensues:

> *Joshua:* Daddy? Do you like my house? I made it last night.
> *Brad:* I know what you're doing, Josh. I don't know why you're doing it, but I'm on to you.
> *Joshua:* They're just blocks, Daddy.
> *Brad:* You're not gonna hurt anybody else.
> *Joshua:* Are you mad at me? Do you still love me, Daddy?
> *Brad:* I think you're sick, Josh.
> *Joshua (sniffs):* I don't feel sick. Not at all.
> *Brad:* Why are you doing this? Huh?
> *Joshua:* You know what the best part is, Daddy?

At this point, the dialogue breaks off. "The best part" is expressed not in words but action: Joshua walks over to his elaborate construction, looks back to make certain that Brad is watching, and smashes the house to bits. Joshua's line "Do you still love me, Daddy?" is, of course, a test question: what is the family *really* worth? Will Daddy stick to his earlier assurance to love his son unconditionally, "no matter what"? When the promise is not repeated, all that remains is the family's empty shell, which Joshua shatters twice: symbolically in this scene, in reality in the following scene, in which he provokes his father to beat him in public, resulting in Brad's arrest.

Either in response to the film's disgraceful box office performance[8] or shying away from its radical suggestion that the nuclear family is not all that it's cracked up to be, the film's DVD marketing tried to take it all back by selling *Joshua* as something altogether more harmless: a bog-standard horror film. If ever there was a case of "You can't judge a film by its cover," *Joshua* is it. The cover of the 2009 DVD release shows a blood-spattered Joshua in the foreground, with the background sporting a blood-covered door with a female corpse lying in front of it. The large-print title *The Devil's Child* practically drowns out the much smaller *aka Joshua*, reversing the titular sequence (the film's original title was, in fact, simply *Joshua*). The description on the back, which sports family photos soaked in blood, announces the terror of Joshua's parents "as a series of bloodcurdling deaths occur around the birth of their new born daughter." All of this is quite misleading. Other than the dog's, only a single death occurs in the film, that of Brad's mother Hazel, and even it is considerably relegated to the off-screen: successive sequences show Joshua and Hazel standing at the top of the stairs, Hazel's scream as the camera focuses on Brad at the bottom of the stairs, and Joshua alone at the top of the stairs, savoring the moment briefly before remembering to run down the stairs to enact the expected show of shock and grief. In fact, *Joshua*, despite the blood-soaked DVD cover, is almost entirely free of physical violence. Nor is there any hint in the film that Joshua is actually "The Devil's Child," as the cover blares, rather than simply that of his parents.

The only aspect of the cover that adequately reflects the film's content is the legend "Home is where the Horror is." But here, too, following the trail of bloodstains would lead us down the garden path. In fact, the physical horror promised by the cover would be far easier to bear than the emotional and psychological devastation the film portrays, which packs both a narrative and a philosophical punch. On the narrative level, we are treated to the standard nuclear family stand-off between a nine-year-old psychopath trying to annihilate the family, and two despondent and deluded parents trying to save it. More broadly speaking, there is also the disturbing conclusion that love in the nuclear family is not a biological given but a social mandate, not innate but compulsory. When Joshua says, "You know they didn't ever have to love me," he simultaneously offers to absolve his parents of a guilt they can't relinquish and expresses his contempt for a social ideology on which his parents' idea of family life centrally depends. As a psychopath, he finds it easy to accept his parents' inability to love him, which after all matches his own lack of emotion, but his parents can only respond to their lack of love for their son with ever-increasing guilt and ever-more desperate attempts to shore up the empty family structure. To them, as the hide-and-seek scene shows, the family would work fine if everyone could just play their assigned part, which includes a show of affection even where there is none. To Joshua, however, knowing that familial love is a fiction, the superstructure of the family is worthless, and thus he discards it in favor of a new arrangement.

\* \* \*

Since about the 1950s, when the nuclear family became the ideological *sine qua non* in the Western world, horror films portraying it have relied on virtually identical character constellations and narrative strategies. The father is largely or entirely absent, as is the case in *Night Child* and *The Good Son*, where Mark's father Jack goes off to Japan and Henry's father Wallace plays a negligible role. *Joshua*, too, starts out with Brad fully absorbed by his work and social life; he does not really step up to the plate until his family is on the verge of collapse. Just as the social model dictates, the films' mothers are in charge of the nuclear family. In family horror, however, they are impaired, often to the point of non-functionality, much like Elise, the alcoholic sex kitten in *Night Child*, Susan, the guilt-ravaged mother in *The Good Son*, or Abby, the incurable depressive in *Joshua*. Like the character constellation, the narrative follows a path well-trodden since at least the 1970s. In stark contrast to the nuclear family's social image as whole and wholesome, the horror film's family is fragmented from the outset by the death of a family member, usually a mother (as in *Night Child* and *The Good Son*) or a child (as in *The Good Son*). After this, there follows a middle period during which parents valiantly but vainly try to hold it all together, warning signals mount, dogs die like flies, shrinks are fooled, and fathers are left to fend. And since Daddy is a chump, this usually marks the beginning of the end.

Deaths in the family, collapsing mothers, and inept dads are hardly unusual in real-life nuclear families. Neither is family disintegration, with divorce rates and slayings within families soaring.[9] Saddled with expectations of a middle-class felicity that it cannot possibly deliver, the nuclear family is coming apart at the seams. Family collapse is now so common and normal as to be the stuff of reality TV. It only turns into horror when you add to the mix a child who is much too smart for his age and acts older than his years—Marcus with his sexual interest in Elise; Henry, the ever-resourceful designer of murder weapons, or Joshua with his extreme intelligence and artistic talent. Being too smart and acting too old is, of course, horror shorthand for "evil"; if the children are, as *A Prairie Home Companion* quips, "all above average," the family is in trouble. Nuclear family horror not only derides the idealized family structure—the breadwinning father, the caretaker mother, the two-to-three children—but also parodies the idealized child and attacks the adult association of childhood with innocence. The adult denial that children can be considered "evil" is unmasked as simple naiveté; the evil child fooling not only his parents but also a psychiatrist is another narrative staple of family horror. Conversely, a child, once recognized as "evil," promptly has its status *as* a child revoked (witness Elise's outburst that Marcus is "as adult as you or I").[10]

The horror of nuclear family films is based on the convergence of four ideas. The first is that in stark contrast to social mythology, the nuclear family is falling apart; far from being "the pillar of society," it cannot survive without outside help, as the constant intervention of psychiatrists shows. The second idea is that the child in the family is, in fact, not a child, but a small adult able to reason far beyond his or her years and merely playacting a child. The third is that given adult absence or incompetence, it is not adults but children who are in charge of the nuclear family. And finally, whereas the socially programmed parents try their level best to keep the family together, the children show no dedication or attachment to the family model. The evil child's elimination of parents through murder (*Night Child*), attempted murder (*The Good Son*) or imprisonment (*Joshua*) is merely a symptom of his rejection of the family. In cases in which the child replaces the jettisoned parent with someone else, this marks not only a change of personnel but also a significant change in the relationship: Marcus wants to trade a mother for a lover; Joshua wants to exchange his parents for a buddy. In essence, family horror proposes that the nuclear family's collapse is not due to factors controlled by the outside or even by adults—social changes, higher divorce rates, working women or deadbeat dads—but engineered from within by the very person whose interests the structure supposedly serves: the child.

Love plays a significant role in the conceptualization of the nuclear family in the social realm and, in horror, in its destruction. The family horror film's attitude towards love can be described as the polar opposite of the baby horror film's. Whereas baby horror denounces a mother's unconditional love for the squid child, the family film assaults the very tenuousness and uncertainty of familial love and explains this with its definition of love not as a biological imperative but as a societal myth. The evil children of family horror respond to this not with trauma but by systematically destroying the structure built on this myth. The principal reason for the destruction of the nuclear family in these films is the parents' inability both to love the child unconditionally and to discard the societal mandate that says they must. Joshua's statement that his parents "should have saved themselves" expresses that there is no such thing as the unconditional familial love that might justify their self-sacrifice; simultaneously, self-sacrifice in the service of nothing indicates the absence of self-love. All that is left is an ideology translated into bedside lip service and an absolute unwillingness to consider alternative structures, either socially acceptable ones such as a return to the extended family model or recourse to outside help, or unacceptable ("horrific") ones such as those proposed by the children themselves: *Night Child*'s age-inappropriate romance, *Joshua*'s male friendship, or *The Good Son*'s suggestion that a biological child might be discarded for another that is a better fit for the family. A family model that proposes itself as the only valid one, the films seem to suggest, is ripe for destruction. Visually, the same idea—the nuclear family's inability to look beyond its own front door—may be indicated by extensive attention to the world outside of the house: vast vista landscapes in *Night Child* and *The Good Son*, New York City parks, avenues, high-rises and museums in *Joshua*.

Many family horror films destabilize narrative perspective, its relationship with the film's "reality," and with it, the possibility of a dependable viewer allegiance. Often narrative perspective is aligned with the viewpoint of a character who turns out to be untrustworthy or deceived, like the ersatz mother in *Night Child*, the ersatz son in *The Good Son*, and the father in *Joshua*. *Night Child* confronts us with a suspicion appropriated from *The Innocents*: that Elise's perception, which largely governs the viewer's, may not correspond to the film's reality, a possibility raised by the clash between individual perception and outside perspective, like that between Elise's claims and Elise's dreams. *The Good Son* adopts Mark's perspective, which is, from the outset, clouded by Mark's inability to accept reality, specifically, his own mother's death and the fact that Henry's mother Susan is not, in fact, his own mother returned from the grave. In *Joshua*, viewer sympathies are aligned with the rare present and competent horror film father, but he too is ultimately diminished: outwitted by his super-smart son, he zones in on the right suspect but the wrong crime. All of these allegiances are as unstable as the narratives themselves, which are riddled with red herrings, for example *Night Child*'s inexplicably appearing and disappearing peepholes or the suggestion, upheld for the majority of the film, that Joshua means to harm his baby sister rather than, as it turns out, detonate his entire family.

One of the most interesting aspects of these films is that the offer of identification they extend to viewers is completely incompatible with their narrative content. In terms of the stories they tell, these films play with our hardwiring, questioning the dependability of our most cherished institution, the family, and—worse—the trustworthiness of the love that the family is supposedly based on. Yet viewer allegiance is steered towards characters who deny it all, characters who, despite the family's emptiness of the "content" of love, desperately and hopelessly try to shore up its crumbling structure. It is this quality of heroic self-delusion that defines these characters both as contemptible fools unable to accept reality and as "good" sons and parents. We might read these films' misdirection of viewer allegiance as their final assault on the pervasiveness of the nuclear family ideology: by inviting the audience's identification with suckers fighting a lost cause, the films implicate viewers as similarly indoctrinated, more interested in social structure than emotive content, and profoundly blind to alternatives.

## Guilt Trips

### LITTLE HORRORS

*Don't Be Afraid of the Dark* (dir. Troy Nixey, USA 2010). Little Sally, sent by her mother to live with her father and his girlfriend in a vast, spooky and haunted mansion, is so alienated from her family—abandoned by her mother, ignored by her career-obsessed father, and initially hostile towards his new girlfriend Kim—that she is seduced by the horrid little monsters in the basement who "want to be friends," informing her that while the adults don't want her, "we do." When the monsters turn out to be vicious, Sally tries in vain to persuade an unbelieving father, mother and shrink that she is in grave danger. While her biological family dismisses Sally's fears, Kim becomes Sally's only ally. Defending Sally from the monsters, Kim gets sucked down into the monster basement, where she becomes one of them. After Sally and her father have moved out, the monsters lie in wait for the next child to occupy the house, knowing that its parents, too, will close their eyes to their child's danger. *Guilt trip:* Could it be any more obvious?

*Halloween* (dir. John Carpenter, USA 1978) can easily be read as a revenge flick for child neglect: the film begins with the slaughter of an older sister by her six-year-old brother, whom she was supposed to watch but ignores in favor of a sexual tryst with her boyfriend. The majority of the film's victims are babysitters who ignore their charges, spending their time on the phone with friends, doing their nails or watching TV. The film's main character and only survivor is also the only babysitter who actually takes care of the child.

*The Innocents* (dir. Jack Clayton, UK 1961) is to family horror what *Rosemary's Baby* is to baby horror and *The Exorcist* to religious horror, both archetype and blueprint. Set in Victorian England, two children abandoned by their family—their parents dead, their uncle unwilling to be involved in their upbringing—are foisted on a young governess who believes them to be possessed by two evil dead servants. The governess's attempts to wrest the children away from the evil spirits result in the boy's death. *Guilt trip:* Both the theme of child abandonment and the forcible imposition of adult obsessions on children loom large. All instances of possession are shown exclusively from the governess's perspective, raising questions about their reality within the film. Just as the children's uncle wants nothing to do with them—"I have no room for them. Neither mentally nor emotionally"—the governess is so obsessed with having children that she destroys them by confusing her own needs with theirs: "All I want to do is save the children, not destroy them. More than anything I love the children. More than anything. They need affection, love. Someone who will belong to them." The film critiques adult attitudes towards children, which allow for no middle ground between abandonment and fixation. The children are placed into the impossible situation of finding a way to make the adults pay attention to them in a way that acknowledges them without casting them as little angels: little Miles, for instance, repeatedly acts up because adults, in his view, perceive good children as "boring."

*Interview with the Vampire* (dir. Neil Jordan, USA 1994). After being bitten by a vampire, little Claudia is condemned to eternal life in a child's body. Claudia is portrayed initially as the "child" of her two fathers, becoming educated and self-aware under Louis's tutelage and a consummate killer under Lestat's, but greatly resents her fathers' dressing her up like a little doll and hates them both for denying her adulthood. Afraid of being abandoned, she forces Louis to create his first vampire, a woman, to be her "mother" if and when she is abandoned by her two fathers. In the battle with the Parisian vampires, Claudia and her new mother are burned to death whereas both of Claudia's fathers survive. *Guilt trip:* The character is the epitome of a child used by adults for their own purposes, despite frequent protestations of love from both fathers. Originally "created" by Lestat as a companion for Louis in an attempt to convince Louis to stay, Claudia, never more than a means to an end, is condemned to a purposeless and murderous existence and a cruel and meaningless death. Her search for a mother documents not only her fears of abandonment, but also her thwarted desire to be loved unconditionally.

*Night of the Living Dead* (dir. George A. Romero, USA 1968). On the surface a film about zombies threatening the lives of a motley crew of survivors who have barricaded themselves inside a house (!), Romero's original zombie film can easily be read as an assault on family models. The survivors in the house represent specimens of every (then) socially acceptable way for humans to live together: a nuclear family, the remnant of a brother-sister pairing, a pair of young lovers, and a lone hero. The bickering and disunity inside the house is presented as far more traumatic than the attack from the outside. The nuclear family, with its overbearing father, its whinily obedient mother, and its ailing child, offer the most appalling instance of this. In the film's most spectacularly disturbing scene (cut in the 1990 remake), little Karen, zombified after her death, feasts on her father's arm and murders her mother with a trowel. *Guilt trip:* Karen's father, blustering, brutal and condescending towards his wife, is portrayed as the film's least reasonable character whose selfishness endangers everyone. Content to let everyone else fall victim to the zombies, he focuses on saving only himself and his family. In typical nuclear-family insularity, he locks the three of them in the basement to save them from the danger outside, upon which the family promptly self-destructs from within.

*Orphan* (dir. Jaume Collet-Serra, USA 2009). Following the loss of a baby, a drinking problem and therapy, Kate and John adopt a new child in an effort to re-build their collapsing nuclear family. Nine-year-old Esther initially seems a perfect addition; she is sweet, grateful, obedient, highly intelligent and an accomplished painter. The parents are delighted; the children, particularly son Danny, highly suspicious. If other horror children are classed as "evil" because they act too old, Esther actually is. It takes the murder of a nun threatening to expose Esther, the attempted sexual seduction of her adopted father, and the attempted murder of her entire adopted family to expose Esther for what she is, namely a 33-year-old mental patient with a history of inveigling her way into families and destroying them. Kate's attempts to convince John of Esther's "evil" are greeted with disbelief, an attempt to force Kate into rehab, and threats of divorce. When Esther stabs John, Kate is left to save the family from the evil impostor, which she achieves by breaking Esther's neck and drowning her, shouting "I'm not your fucking mother!" *Guilt trip:* The film brims with instances of dysfunctional family interaction and distrust, essentially promoting a defensive view of the nuclear family: left to its own devices, it crumbles; only an outside threat brings the family back together. In the service of this conclusion and under the pretext that the child is, in fact, an adult (Isabelle Fuhrman, who played Esther, was 12 years old in the year of the film's release), the film shows the murder of a child as the only adequate and gratifying solution.

*The Other* (dir. Robert Mulligan, USA 1972). Abandoned by their mother, who mourns their father's death locked up in her room, nine-year-old identical twins Niles and Holland are left to their own devices in seemingly idyllic surroundings (the film is set on a farm in the 1930s). The brothers are a study in extremes, Niles perfectly angelic, Holland an evil brat. After a series of disasters—Holland kills a cousin and throws his mother down the stairs, leaving her a catatonic invalid—it emerges that Holland is dead and Niles the true culprit. Niles enacts both the murderous child and the "good son"; when not setting deadly traps for cousins or drowning babies in brine, he is almost nauseatingly perfect: sweet, communicative, attentive, and affectionate, he brings his mother flowers and reads to her. His grandmother Ada, realizing what he is, attempts to kill Niles by setting fire to the barn, but dies in the blaze herself. Niles escapes, his grandmother dead, his mother catatonic, his secret safe. *Guilt trip:* The film motivates both the usual theme of child neglect and the idea that children, unlike adults, have no need for or attachment to the family. Like many other family horror films, the film portrays an abandoned child who responds to this not by trying to replace his family, but by deleting it entirely. As director Mulligan has described the character: "If Niles could have life just the way he wanted it, his world would contain only Ada, Holland, and himself—preferably only Holland and himself."

*Peopletoys* a.k.a. *Devil Times Five* (dir. Sean MacGregor/David Sheldon, USA 1974). Five psychopathic children escape from their mental institution and are taken in by a group of adults on winter vacation in a cabin in the woods. All five children temporarily latch on to one adult, resulting in parent-child constellations and small families before the children kill their "parent." All killings are staged as communal child's play in which children fashion elaborate kill-traps or build snowmen around corpses. The final scene features an elaborate children's tea-party, with the corpses arranged around a table like dolls and the children playing with their "peopletoys" in the same way in which normal children would play with dolls. *Guilt trip:* All of the adults are severely damaged: an arrogant and condescending "alpha male," a sniveling and cowardly underdog, a mentally retarded man, two sex kittens, and one alcoholic. There are no adults in the film that might serve as role models for children; if these characters are as good as it gets, the film implies, then good riddance. *Fuller discussion in Chapter 8.*

# 3

# Nature
## An Abundance of Horror

*"In nature there is no evil, only an abundance of horror: the plagues and the blights and the ants and the maggots."*

—Isak Dinesen

## Off the Beaten Path: Fairy Trails

In their book *Screening Nature: Cinema Beyond the Human,* Anat Pick and Guinevere Narraway have called for a "posthuman" approach towards nature in film. Nature movies, they claim, describe nature as dynamic and alive, but writing *about* nature movies continues to privilege the human, downgrading nature to mere landscape, a "setting, background or prop."[1]

This clarion call to show nature a bit more respect is particularly apt for the horror scene. Films in which nature merely provides the setting, such as *The Hills Have Eyes* (1977) or *The Texas Chainsaw Massacre* (1974), are in the relative minority. More often, horror nature is dangerously dynamic, alive enough to kill you, and emphatically out to promote a "posthuman approach." In horror movies, nature is a wilderness where humans should fear to tread, a place—to cite its definition in the 1964 U.S. *Wilderness Act*—"where the earth and its community of life are untrammeled by man, where man himself is a visitor who does not remain." In horror, Thoreau's more genteel understanding of nature as a site of regeneration away from civilization is merely a delusion that lures humans to the cabin in the woods, where the trap inevitably springs shut.

And yet, horror films do not, as a rule, point the finger of blame at nature itself but rather at human interaction with it, which is typically condemned as harmful, inept, or malicious. In horror, there are no humble humans like Charles (Anthony Hopkins) in Lee Tamahori's *The Edge* (1997). Having rejected all models of nature exploitation, from harmful development plans to the search for the "authentic" Indian for a photograph, Charles survives in the wilderness because he understands, even as he dons his bear skin, that he is merely a guest there, a fact illustrated by his repeated admission that all of his knowledge about the wilderness comes from books. The types caught in a horror wilderness tend to be diametrical opposites of Charles: arrogantly overconfident rather than humble; loaded down with expensive equipment rather than armed solely with knowledge; and, again unlike Charles, not trying to get out of trouble, but looking for it and surprised when they find it. The idea that nature, in retribution for human disregard and destructiveness, will eventually strike back has long been a staple of both horror and non-horror disaster movies, from *The Birds* (1963), *Jurassic Park* (1993), *Volcano* (1997) and *The Day After Tomorrow* (2004) to *The Happening* (2008) and *Yellowbrickroad* (2010). Post-apocalyptic films, which have boomed particularly since the 2008 bank crash—the *Mad Max* films (1979–85), *The Day After Tomorrow* (2004), *Waterworld* (2005), *I Am Legend* (2007), *WALL-E* (2008), *City of Ember* (2008), *Terminator Salvation* (2009), *The Road* (2009), *The Book of Eli* (2010), *Oblivion* (2013) and many more—derive their horror largely from their visualization of a post-nature world.

Peter Brook's *Lord of the Flies* (UK 1963) occupies a strange position in the history of nature horror films: it is a precursor for a genre that then went in a different direction. *Lord of the Flies* essentially tests, and ultimately rejects, Rousseau's three-fold pronouncement that nature is untainted, that civilization corrupts, and that therefore human goodness can only be obtained by returning to nature. The film rebuffs not only this hope but also illusions of both human and nonhuman innocence. Placing the "purest" humans (children) into the "purest" environment (nature) does not result in paradise. Within days, the children have re-formed a human society, complete with hierarchies, subjugation, expulsions, crimes (theft, murder), and punishment (executions). Evil, in other words, does not arise from corrupt society, nor does it develop with age: it is human nature. The film anticipates later nature horror in its pitiless conclusion that Paradise is truly lost and that Rousseau (and, for that matter, Thoreau) had it all wrong. Yet unlike later nature horror, it does not portray nature as dynamic. In *Lord of the Flies,* nature is merely a backdrop, not a character that moves the narrative forward.

Perhaps for this reason, *Lord of the Flies*, despite its belated American remake (dir. Harry Hook, 1990), has not become a blueprint of nature horror, certainly not in America. The starting point for American nature horror is not Peter Brook's deserted island but the cabin in the woods, which is, according to Bernice Murphy, "to the American Gothic what the haunted castle is to Europeans."[2] In *The Rural Gothic in American Popular Culture*, Murphy identifies two kinds of narratives. Both, she argues, define nature as the untamed wilderness of America's early colonial period and the central conflict as between those who either are or aim to be settled (like the European explorers of that period) and those who are not and do not aim to be (like the Indians the settlers fought and ultimately displaced). In Narrative A, the "settled" are threatened by outsiders characterized by mobility and unpredictability; its moral is that when you leave civilization, you yourself become less civilized—as occurs, for example, in *The Blair Witch Project* (1999), *Yellowbrickroad* (2010), or Kubrick's *The Shining* (1980). In Narrative B, the reverse occurs: people who are merely passing through become the object of the hostile attention of permanently settled villains; the suggestion here is that too much time in the wilderness turns people into savages. Examples that spring to mind for Type B movies are *The Texas Chain Saw Massacre* (1974), *Would You Kill a Child?* (1976), *Children of the Corn* (1984), *Eden Lake* (2008), and every cabin-in-the-woods-flick ever made.

Murphy's neat cartography certainly explains a great deal, from the frequent appearance of Indian burial grounds in nature horror films to their common depiction of rural dwellers as hicks. In reading Gothic nature films as endlessly re-enacting conflicts between white settlers and attacking nomads, Murphy has made a case for linking these films with history, in this case the history of colonial America. What I would like to do in the following is to take a step back to what I see as the source of both history and nature horror: the realm of myths, legends and fairy tales. Much of what we consider history is actually legend, unverifiable, fallacious, or simply untrue—things like Manifest Destiny, George Washington's wooden teeth (which were not, in fact, wooden), or the midnight ride of Paul Revere (popularized, with considerable historical inaccuracies, by Longfellow's poem, which had much more to do with the imminent Civil War than the Revolutionary War). These myths have certainly *shaped* history—the across-continent expansion of white settlers under the banner of Manifest Destiny, for example—but they are not themselves history in the sense of "verifiable facts of the past." Nature horror films, I would claim, hold a similar relationship with myths, legends, and fairy tales: they tend to draw their stories from this realm and, in the process of translating them for a modern audience of unbelievers in myths, legends, and fairy tales, assign them new meanings.

The links between the fairy tale and horror genres seem compelling. Both rely on fixed and thus easily recognizable conventions, the constant recurrence of themes and motifs, and archetypal characters and situations. Both genres can be typified by an overabundance of sequels, remakes, imitations and parodies and—conversely—a mythical murkiness concealing their origins. Both genres focus on the forbidden and trade in taboos. A great number of fairy tales have been remade as horror films, among them Michael Cohn's *Snow White: A Tale of Terror* (USA 1997); Caroline Thompson's *Snow White: The Fairest of Them All* (USA/Canada 2001); David DeCoteau's *Snow White: A Deadly Summer* (USA 2012); Matthew Bright's *Freeway* (USA 1996), Catherine Hardwicke's *Red Riding Hood* (USA/Canada 2011), Neil Jordan's *The Company of Wolves* (UK 1984), Lionel Delplanque's *Promenons-nous dans les bois* (*Deep in the Woods*, France/Belgium 2000)—all four based on the Grimms' "Little Red Riding Hood"; Catherine Breillat's *Barbe bleue* (*Bluebeard*, France 2009); Yim Pil-sung's *Henjel gwa Geuretel* (*Hansel and Gretel*, South Korea 2008); Mark Jones's *Rumpelstiltskin* (USA 1995); Kim Yong-gyun's *Bunhongsin* (*The Red Shoes*, South Korea 2005), and Bong Man-dae's *Sin-de-rel-la* (South Korea 2006). Even horror films that don't give the game away in the title can easily be seen as modernized fairy tales. Remember Little Red Riding Hood, she who wanders off the beaten path, is eaten by a wolf and finally freed by the woodsman? "Multiply and humanize the wolf, read 'rape' for 'eat,' skip the woodsman (let Red save herself), and you have *I Spit on Your Grave*," muses Carol Clover.[3] And here is how Stephen King describes the horror movie's mission: "The horror movie is planning to harm us, all right, and that is exactly why it is lurking here in the very darkest part of the forest." Horror films, King continues, "hold their spell over us in spite of all we can do, even including the recitation of that most magic spell-breaking incantation: 'It's only a movie.' And they can all be invoked with that wonderful fairy-tale-door-opener, 'Once upon a time.'"[4]

Every footpath in nature horror originates in the fairy tale forest. Yet horror paths and fairy trails do not go to the same place. In horror, no trail of breadcrumbs will lead you back home. What follows is the tale of how nature horror strayed off the beaten path.

# The Child *(USA 1977)*, Pet Sematary *(USA 1989)*, Acacia *(South Korea 2003)*

> *"They were searching for an evil in the forest… But the forest found the evil in them."*
> —Tagline of *Yellowbrickroad* (2010)

*The Child* (dir. Robert Voskanian, 1977) tells the story of homicidal 11-year-old Rosalie Nordon (Rosalie Cole) in a setting not of family, home and hearth but wilderness, death and decay. Rosalie spends her playtime in the woods surrounding and in the cemetery adjacent to her house. Her "friends" and playmates are zombies under her mental control who, at Rosalie's behest, slaughter her entire family, consisting of her kindly elderly neighbor Mrs. Whitfield (Ruth Ballen), who is clearly cast as a grandmother-figure; her father (Frank Janson), whom Rosalie suspects of having killed her mother, and finally her adult brother Len (Richard Hanners). In the final scene, Rosalie's new nanny, the improbably named Alicianne Del Mar (Laurel Barnett), axe-murders Rosalie in self-defense. Credits roll over an image of panicked Alicianne standing next to her stalled car, suggesting that her escape on foot through the zombie-infested wilderness is less than likely.

The unquestioned star of the film is its sinister landscape. Opening credits roll over threatening nature shots showing fast-moving clouds, dark woods and bushes shrouded in fog, the cast names splattered in blood-red all over this gray-black landscape. A brief vista of a vast black mansion barely silhouetted against a dark sky dissolves into a shot of a little girl in an unlit room contemplating herself in the mirror. Cut to fog-covered woods with a lonely tombstone, where the same girl is seen laying flowers; we get a worrisome POV shot of someone observing her through thick brambles. Our concern for the girl's safety mounts as she lifts a cute kitten from a basket, presenting us briefly with the perfect image of childlike innocence set in a menacing landscape blanketed by fog. As a gray and decaying zombie hand, endowed with long chitinous nails, appears from behind the tombstone, the little girl calmly hands the kitten over to it and walks off into the breaking dawn, her empty basket swinging at her side.

Rosalie, then, is a child of nature, but not in a nice way. Cinematography makes this point before the opening credits are over, and the narrative, too, wastes no time in telling us that Rosalie's strangeness is linked mainly to two factors: her mother's death and nature. Mrs. Whitfield, who, like Little Red Riding Hood's grandmother, has lived in the woods all her life, warns the young and naïve Alicianne, who is about to begin her employment as Rosalie's nanny, that "Rosalie's always been strange—worse since her mother's death." Rosalie's mother, as described by Mrs. Whitfield, spent most of her life either in a mental institution or wandering the woods at night, and Rosalie has inherited her mother's predilection for nocturnal rambling (and clearly also, although Mrs. Whitfield does not state this, her mother's insanity). What Mrs. Whitfield does say is that Rosalie has "played tricks" on Mrs. Whitfield's boarders, tricks apparently nasty enough to prompt all of them to move out. Thus Rosalie is presented from the outset as a bit more than "strange"; she is pronounced guilty of both ruining Mrs. Whitfield's business and isolating her. That this is very much Rosalie's intention is borne out when Rosalie instructs her zombies to make off with Mrs. Whitfield's beloved pet dog, followed by her spookily delivered comment: "Now she'll be all alone." Alarm bells should emphatically be going off in Alicianne's head, but she remains unaware of ominous undertones, instead sympathizing with Rosalie, to whom she feels linked by her own love of the outdoors and the loss of her mother as a young child. "I'm sure Rosalie and I will get along just fine," she chirps, thus establishing herself early on as Rosalie's surrogate mother.

Beyond her affiliation with scary nature, Alicianne's new charge is characterized through identification with her dead mother (the film's endlessly recurring mantra is that "Rosalie is like her mother"), her recognition of Alicianne as surrogate mother, the trauma of losing the original, and the fear of losing the replacement. Initially identifying with Alicianne because she too lost her mother early, Rosalie is cloyingly possessive of her. When Alicianne takes one hour off the job to go horseback riding, Rosalie flies into a tantrum: "I thought she was supposed to be taking care of *me*. ... I want her *here. NOW!!!*" Things become even more ominous when Rosalie draws pictures of her mother's funeral, carefully crossing out the attendees she plans to kill, most particularly her father and brother. Rosalie's consistent identification with a mother who was both insane and possessed of extraordinary mental abilities is disturbing enough, even before it emerges that Rosalie uses these same powers to control zombies. Worse, Rosalie exhibits an unhealthy obsession with death. She goes on nightly forest and cemetery walks, holds regular graveside conversations with her dead mother, and occasionally laughs hysterically when discussing her mother's death. Stories that would make everyone else's skin crawl, for example the one her father tells at the dinner table about a mass poisoning, draw girlish giggles from her, which escalate into uproarious laughter when he gets to the punch line "Killed every one of 'em! Died like flies!"

Every discussion and every representation of death in the film is linked with nature. The scene in which Rosalie giggles while telling Alicianne about her mother's death, for example, shows Rosalie on a swing, set incongruously not in a garden but in the wilderness. The mass poisoning which makes for such an entertaining dinner story came about by campers unfamiliar with wildlife flora eating oleander flowers. The woods are discussed again and again as simultaneously beautiful and frightening, as both "home" and incomprehensibly alien. Alicianne, for instance, has grown up in the area and returns because she has missed the forest, and Mrs. Whitfield agrees: "Yes, these woods are so lovely. That's the reason why I stayed here when my husband died." But in the same conversation, both nature lovers express a distinct fear of the forest. Alicianne states, in anxious tones, that although she used to live right around the corner, she does not recognize the place: "I forgot how big these woods are." And Mrs. Whitfield agrees again: "Yes, these woods can be a lonely place. I used to keep boarders, but they didn't like the isolation. ... The woods made them nervous."

Much of the film visualizes the fairy-tale theme of the little girl getting lost in the woods, the girl, in this case, being not little Rosalie but adult Alicianne. The fairy tale nature of the forest is already anticipated by the wording of Mrs. Whitfield's incessant warnings: "Stay on the path. Don't wander off into the woods... there is something.... I hear them calling to one another at night. ... Hurry, you'd better hurry." Like the narrative, cinematography takes great care to present the woods as both beautiful and unsafe. Accompanied by eerie 12-tone plucked string music or hysterically tinkling piano, Alicianne, reduced to walking because her car has stalled, fights her way through what looks like a mixture between a Vietnam-style jungle and the Brother Grimms' forest that has swallowed up children without number. Shots of her frightened face, lit brightly by sunlight, are shown from a bird's-eye perspective, followed directly by counter-shots from ground level showing dark tree trunks and branches waving threateningly high above. A wavering hand-held camera long-shot, perhaps the POV of a zombie not too sure on his feet, tracks Alicianne up the woodland path. A close-up of her knees downward shows her slowing from a regular walk to a sluggish dragging of feet. A slow pan up Alicianne's body and anxious face is counter-shot, yet again, by an intimidating look up a huge tree from a frog's-eye perspective. Jump-cut to a close-up of a bloody and eviscerated cat, blood on the leaves, and clawmarks on bark; then, slowly and deliberately, a clawed and decaying hand emerges from behind a tree. Wafts of fog obscure Alicianne's vision; her hapless stumbling and constant squinting indicate that she is utterly lost, whereas Rosalie, who is shown several times in the same setting, always knows exactly where she is going.

Cinematography, narrative and woodland setting all point to the film's greater affinity with the fairy tale than with standard horror. This impression is cemented by the film's strange disinterest in the colorful killings of Mrs. Whitfield, Rosalie's father, and finally Len, which appear as no more than a drearily routine fulfillment of the gore quota owed to the schlock horror genre. All three are killed in a visually identical manner; the zombies' standard operating procedure (pun intended) is to gouge out one eye and flay the face. There is no amplification of action, length of exposure, or amount of gore from one scene to the next. As a horror film, *The Child* commits a cardinal sin by replicating gory visuals without escalation. However, seen as a horror version of the Peter Pan tale, a figurative refusal of adulthood, the film builds significantly, progressing from verbal rejection to physical violence and from there to conceptual denial. Initially, Rosalie terminates communication with adults: "I don't have to tell you anything," she tells her father, followed by: "I won't listen to you anymore, old man!" Her physical rejection of adults takes the form of the moderately messy removal of three successive family generations: grandmother-surrogate, father, and finally brother. Ultimately, Rosalie repudiates not only adults, but more principally the very idea of adulthood. At the dinner table, her surrogate mother figure Alicianne offers to show her how to bake doughnuts, following a recipe passed down to her by her own mother. Rosalie is thus explicitly cast in a line of little girls who, instructed by their mothers, become mothers (adults) themselves. Rosalie responds to this by pulling a disgusted face, saying "Doughnuts?" in a voice dripping with disdain. At this point Len chimes in: "Sure, you wanna know how to bake stuff. When you get married you wanna be a good wife to your husband, dontcha?," a sentiment that earns him another contemptuous glance.

The lonely forest is the only appropriate setting for a child beset by the Peter Pan Syndrome. It is, after all, the precise reverse of the surroundings in which children are normally raised: in a house, surrounded by family. Rosalie's preference for outside spaces over inside prefigures both her elimination of family in favor of her "friends" and her refusal of a subordinate role (as a child) in favor of control (over zombies). Her forest is a dynamic site in which half-glimpsed, incomprehensible, frightening things (tendrils of mist, zombies) move incessantly and ultimately prove fatal to anyone but her. As Mrs. Whitfield informs us, "Rosalie regards these woods as her own private property." Thus Rosalie's ownership of the forest wreaks havoc on a fairy tale tradition in which the child always gets lost in the woods (Fig. 7). The woods in *The Child* symbolize not only Rosalie's refusal of her own role as a

Fig. 7. Not lost in the woods: Rosalie at home in scary Nature (Promotional poster for *The Child*, 1977) (Boxoffice International Pictures/Photofest).

child and all of its trimmings (the house, the family), but also her rejection of the fairy tales parents tell children to keep them "on the right path."

Like *The Child*, *Pet Sematary* (dir. Mary Lambert, 1989) combines two legends at once; it is both a rehabilitation of the Indian burial-ground myth and the quintessential Monkey's Paw story. The film begins with the move of a bunch of city slickers to the country: doctor Louis Creed (Dale Midkiff), freshly hired at a small-town university's medical facility; his wife Rachel (Denise Crosby), who hails from Chicago; their two children, six-year-old Ellie (Blaze Berdahl) and toddler Gage (Miko Hughes), and Ellie's beloved cat Church. The setting's pastoral peace is only disturbed by the fact that their new house sits right next to a road over which tanker trucks roar constantly, day and night. Behind the house, a garden path leads straight into the woods, ending at the titular pet cemetery, where the community's children have buried their pets since time immemorial. Beyond that, there are Indian burial grounds where the soil is "sour" and the dead buried in it return as murderous monsters. When Ellie's cat is run over on the road, Louis buries it in the Micmac burial ground with the help of his elderly neighbor Jud Crandall (Fred Gwynne), and Church promptly returns as the cat out of hell. The story repeats itself with little Gage, who, brought back to life in the same way, murders Jud and Rachel and attacks Louis. Louis succeeds in killing him, but in a spectacular failure to have learned his lesson, buries Rachel in the same "sour" ground. In the final scene, Rachel returns from the dead and cuts Louis's throat.

Once again, nature assumes the starring role in the film. *Pet Sematary* opens with a slow pan over the cemetery's charmingly misspelled entrance sign and markers adorned with toys, dog collars and chains, accompanied by children's tributes in voice-over. "Bye, old Shep. See you in heaven, yeah?"—"This is where my kitty lays, no more he screams and hollers; he lived for five and twenty days, he cost me fifty dollars."—"Spot. A good fellow. We love you."—"Hannah, the best cat that ever lived."—"Biffer, Biffer, a helluva sniffer." The effect is profoundly touching. This, the film implies, is the "correct" way of handling death: you accept it, cherish the dead, and move on. Unsurprisingly, the film's main problem turns out to be that neither Rachel, who has been deeply traumatized by her sister's death as a child, nor Louis, whose job has apparently done nothing to prepare him for it, are able to deal with death in the recommended fashion.

The film's nature cinematography similarly expresses the idea that you can only go a certain distance with death before you have to let go. The legends on the markers and the touching voice-over tributes articulate a distinction between the permitted realm of acceptance and mourning inside the cemetery and the forbidden kingdom of denial and sacrilege beyond. Because the cemetery is the children's domain, it looks closer to nature than an adult cemetery would—no neat rows, polished markers, flags or flowers here. The site, with graves arranged in a circle and markers leaning every which way, is more reminiscent of a crop circle than a cemetery, untidy and unkempt, but still on the cusp between rural setting and nature. Beyond the cemetery, however, lies the wilderness, with woods looming threateningly and the path blocked by seemingly insurmountable piles of deadwood. What divides the rural from the wilderness is not merely a border but a barrier, not only a physical one between spaces but also a spiritual one dividing the dominion of grief from that of desecration. As the narrative tells us more than once, "The barrier was not meant to be crossed" (Fig. 8).

The question the film raises, and this is where its guilt-trip comes in, is whether the

Fig. 8. "The barrier was not meant to be crossed": Evil Nature beckons in *Pet Sematary* (1989) (Paramount/Photofest).

disasters befalling the Creeds are man-made or the stuff of legend. On the surface, the film gives us plenty of opportunity to blame it all on the parents, specifically, on two aspects of parenting: a profound inability to handle death on the one hand and outright child abuse and child neglect on the other. Rachel's death phobia is explained by the fact that her sister Zelda (Andrew Hubatsek) died slowly and horribly of spinal meningitis while her parents were out for the evening, leaving then eight-year-old Rachel in "charge" of her dying sister. This, Louis asserts, is nothing less than child abuse, and most viewers would be inclined to agree. The stage is thus set for a clear-cut attribution of disaster to deficient parenting, which seems to be borne out when Louis and Rachel themselves appear guilty of child neglect. Two scenes show them apparently incapable of handling two children, one the scene in which Gage is run over (their attention, at that moment, is focused on Ellie), the other a clear foreshadowing of Gage's death. It occurs immediately after the family's arrival, when Ellie tries out the swing in the new garden and promptly falls off it. Both parents rush to Ellie's aid, ignoring little Gage waddling determinedly towards the road just as another big truck approaches at lightning speed. The first time, Jud saves him in the nick of time, but if the implication of this episode is that Louis and Rachel could have lost Gage within minutes of their arrival, the implication of Gage's actual death is just as clearly that they have not learned their lesson.

This aspect, the fact that people never learn and that therefore the story cannot but go from bad to worse, is, of course, a central part of the Monkey's Paw tale. Critically, though, it is not only Louis and Rachel who fail to recognize a good warning when it hits them in the face. In a central scene, Jud takes the family up to the pet cemetery, apparently for the explicit purpose of imparting to them the adequate way of handling death. His first statement, delivered as the Creeds contemplate the many markers, admits the bare fact of death and the natural human response: "I told you it's a bad road, Louis. It's killed a lot of pets, made a lot of kids unhappy" (the worse calamity, as it would be in a Monkey's Paw story, is implied: it's killed a lot of children, made a lot of parents unhappy). But Rachel, sensing that Jud is getting ready to move from grief to acceptance and from there to consolation, will have none of it:

> *Rachel:* How can you call it a good thing? A graveyard for pets killed in the road. Built by broken-hearted children!
> *Jud:* Well, they have to learn about death somehow, now don't they, Mrs. Creed?
> *Rachel, aggressively:* Why? *Turning to Louis:* Can I have the baby? ...
> *Jud, to Ellie:* Ellie. Do you know what a graveyard really is? ... It's a place where the dead speak. *Ellie looks scared.*
> *Jud, hastily:* No! Not right out loud! Their stones speak, or their markers. This ain't a scary place, Ellie. It's a place of rest, and speaking.

And yet it is Jud himself, this scene's advocate of reflection and acquiescence, who introduces Louis to the Micmac burial ground as a way of bringing back Ellie's cat, assuming that Ellie won't be able to handle her pet's death. The lesson can be articulated, but it can't ever be learned. Jud's failure to practice what he preaches is all the more significant because, as a boy, he himself brought back his beloved dog, which then became so feral that he had to put it down again. The point of a true Monkey's Paw story—other than the fact that people will stumble into the same trap every time, even if, like Jud, they ought to know better—is, of course, escalation; it moves from relatively bearable (Church's death) to unbearable (Gage's) to unthinkable (Rachel's murder at the hands of her son returned from the grave). At the point of the first wish, the misfortune wished away—in this case, the death of the family cat—is acknowledged to be distressing particularly for Ellie, but hardly on the truly apocalyptic scale of the deaths that follow. The presumption on Jud's, Louis's and also Rachel's part that even the death of a pet, surely not unprecedented in families that have one, cannot be borne points the finger of blame squarely at human shortcomings.

Much of the film's narrative, then, indicates that the Creeds' misfortunes are entirely man-made. There is the child abuse Rachel endured at the hands of her parents, which led to her hysterical attitude towards death, which in turn diminishes her daughter's ability to cope with the hypothetical death of her cat (this is made clear in a conversation with Louis, in which Ellie expresses her fear of this eventuality). There is the fact that Louis and Rachel allow Gage to wander into a busy road, not once, but twice. There is Jud's seduction of Louis, despite his insight that "Sometimes, dead is better." There is the trucker, who, listening to the radio blaring rock 'n' roll, puts the pedal to the metal to the point where he is unable to brake for Gage. And finally, there is Louis's inability to learn from past horrors: despite Church's and Gage's undeniably evil post-resurrection nature, he compounds his error by raising Rachel as well.

While all this seems to indicate the film's leaning towards human responsibility, it ultimately points the finger at Nature. Nature in *Pet Sematary* is more than mere landscape; it is, in fact, cast as a character, endowed with an evil conscience, a malevolent purpose, and near-absolute control over human decisions. Warnings not to tangle with Nature abound:

Pascow the Friendly Ghost (Brad Greenquist), the soul of a young man who died on Louis's first day on the job, tries to caution Louis away from the forbidden area several times. The Micmac burial ground seems to have its own built-in signal flares; whenever someone attempts to penetrate the barrier, the woods beyond emit an eerie blue or purple neon glow. The characters blithely ignore this, but the audience gets the message clearly enough. Jud's strangely inconsistent role as the advocate of death acceptance in one scene and the architect of disaster in another is attributed to Evil Nature goading him into introducing Louis to the burial ground, from which point forward Louis, too, is entirely at its mercy. Nature as an evil agent appears again when Rachel, desperate to reach home because she suspects Louis is in trouble, is thwarted at every turn (she misses her plane, her car crashes, etc.), all of which is explained, more for the audience's benefit than for Rachel's, by Pascow's statement that "It's trying to stop you." Human nature, weak, erratic and easily manipulated, does its part in triggering tragedy, but harmful intent is assigned entirely to whatever Evil rules the wilderness. And if the film's calamities are "willed" by Evil Nature, they are unavoidable through even the most prudent parenting or the most saintly acceptance of death. In fact, the film seems to indicate this in its very first shot, which we might call its "Foregone-Conclusion-Shot." Opening credits roll over a long slow pan over pet cemetery markers accompanied by voice-over child song; the singing dissolves into a scream as the camera abruptly switches to a POV shot of someone lying in the middle of the road with a huge tanker truck racing right over "us." This, before the opening credits are even properly over, is the film *in nuce*. The rest is just plot and particulars.

And yet, if *Pet Sematary* packs an emotional punch—which some reviews of the film have strenuously denied[5]—it is indebted to the film's portrayal of human inadequacies. While the theme of dominant Nature seems to absolve all characters of guilt, guilt remains nonetheless foregrounded throughout. The film achieves this by portraying problematic adult behavior and by taking a different approach to the evil-child theme. "Evil" is not simply assigned to a child, as is usually the case in child horror, but defined as the distance between Gage alive, an adorable little boy with a sweet disposition, and Gage returned from the grave. And yet, even following Gage's resurrection as murderous monster, there is a brief moment, immediately after Louis has administered the injection that will kill him again, when Gage appears very much like a little boy. "No fair," he pouts, in the same hurt tones that a child would use when beaten at a game by his parents, "no fair." This is, perhaps, a final glimpse of the original Gage, shortly before Louis will lose him for the second time. This time, Louis responds "correctly": with tears, a sign of abject grief, but also—finally—acceptance of the fact that Gage is irrevocably lost. The main trauma, then, seems to be less the parents' despair than their failure to express it in ways that heal rather than harm. Significantly, Louis had no tears after Gage's first death; wrapped up in the catatonia of his own grief, he proved unable to console Ellie or Rachel in theirs. Perhaps the film's most upsetting scene is the one where Rachel's father (Michael Lombard) accuses Louis of child neglect leading to Gage's death. Threats and insults are traded over Gage's coffin until the two erupt in a fistfight and succeed in knocking Gage's coffin off its bier. Much like *Night of the Living Dead*, *Pet Sematary* numbers the adults' behavior in the face of death among its worst horrors.

Appropriately for a nature horror film, *Pet Sematary* couches even this final hint at human responsibility in nature metaphors. One of the film's recurring mantras is that "The soil of a man's heart is stonier," first voiced by Pascow as an initial warning to Louis, later echoed and augmented by Jud: "The soil of a man's heart, Louis, is stonier. Like the soil up there in the old Micmac burial ground." In the final scene, long after Nature has taken its course, Jud's voice-over is given the film's near-final line: "The soil of a man's heart is stonier, Louis. A man grows what he can, then he tends it." If we read the agricultural metaphor, given its placement as the film's last coherent statement, as the conveyor of a message, we might take it to indicate once more the overwhelming power of Evil Nature. Confronted with it, man's options are limited. Whatever man sets out to reap, the harvest depends not on his intentions or exertions, but on the constitution of the ground, and a stony and sour ground can only yield an evil crop. And yet the final add-on, voiced here for the first time— "A man grows what he can, then he tends it"—indicates that in the final analysis, Evil is only Evil when "tended" by humans, who find it easier to nurture absurd beliefs in Life after Death than to accept their own finite nature.

*Acacia* (dir. Park Ki-hyeong, 2003) is a stylish South Korean nature horror film in which the woods of *The Child* and *Pet Sematary* are condensed into their essence, a single tree. Obstetrician Kim Do-il (Kim Jin-geun) and textile artist Choi Mi-sook (Shim Hye-jin) have long tried for a baby, without success. They finally adopt little Jin-sung (Mun Oh-bin) partly because Mi-sook, an artist herself, recognizes the boy's talent, expressed in many paintings with a single motif: himself, either alone or with parents, standing next to a tree. The family live in a house with a separate shed housing Do-il's father Kyo-soo (Park Wung); a dead acacia tree is the garden's most prominent feature. Jin-sung forms an immediate and strong attachment to the acacia tree; he spends much of his time climbing and sitting in it, holds frequent conversations with it, and tries to heal it by hanging amulets in it. A carer at the orphanage informs the family that Jin-sung believed when his mother died that she had become a tree, and has now identified the acacia tree in their garden as his mother. Jin-sung lives a withdrawn existence in his new family, refusing to adopt his new last name and spending all of his time either in the tree or drawing himself and his new family next to it. Only two brief scenes show the family together, riding a bike or playing games, and Jin-sung even forms a friendship with the neighboring little girl Min-ji (Jeong Na-yun), who weirdly claims that she does not go to school because she is a vampire. These encouraging signs of Jin-sung's integration into his new family are disrupted by Mi-sook's mother (Lee Yeong-hee), who rejects Jin-sung completely. She encourages Mi-sook to keep trying for their own baby, gives her a fertility fan for that purpose, and even suggests returning Jin-sung to the orphanage. When Mi-sook does indeed become pregnant, Jin-sung burns the fertility fan, accidentally setting Kyo-soo's shed on fire. Although Mi-sook promises Jin-sung that nothing will change because of the new baby, Jin-sung is completely ignored following little Hae-sung's birth; in one scene he tries to throttle the baby to death by holding its nose and mouth closed. As Jin-sung becomes more and more aggressive, detached from the family and attached to his tree, discussions begin in earnest about chopping down the acacia to break Jin-sung's bad habits, and even about returning him to the orphanage. One night, Jin-sung proclaims angrily, "I'm going to my mom," and runs away. Upon Kyo-soo's advice, Do-il reports the child missing to the police, but Jin-sung is never found.

After Jin-sung's disappearance, the film takes an abrupt turn for the bizarre. The acacia tree, formerly dead, recovers completely, developing leaves and lush blossoms. Do-il is subject to horrible dreams or daytime fantasies in which he delivers bloody and stillborn babies; Mi-sook develops a great fear and loathing for the acacia tree. The tree murders Kyo-soo by sending ants to eat him alive and attacks Mi-sook's mother, who, immediately after smelling its blossoms, begins to cough blood. Worst of all, Do-il and Mi-sook begin to blame each other for Jin-sung's disappearance; their marriage deteriorates from an easygoing and loving relationship to coldness and from there to a murderous hatred, for reasons that, until the very end, remain mysterious. Do-il finds a needle in his rice and cuts his mouth badly; coming home from work, he finds the entire house draped with red wool, making it look like an abattoir. Do-il rapes his wife; he and Mi-sook accuse each other of being guilty of Jin-sung's death; both try to kill each other: Do-il throttles Mi-sook, but she recovers and stabs him fatally with scissors as he approaches the acacia tree with an axe. In the final moments of the film, the incomprehensibly bizarre developments of its second half are explained in flashback shots interspersed with current-time reaction shots: Mi-sook, determined to cut down the acacia, accidentally hits Jin-sung, who, in a desperate attempt to protect the tree, places himself between the axe and the tree, in the head. Cut from this flashback to the present, where Mi-sook retrieves the scissors from Do-il's back and stabs herself in the throat. Cut to another present-day shot, where the police find Jin-sung buried under the acacia tree, his head wounds clearly visible, completely enfolded in the acacia's roots like a small child in a cradle. Cut to another flashback scene, the film's last: As Do-il tries to bury Jin-sung, who looks dead, under the tree, he sees his hand move; horrified, he hits him numerous times with the shovel, killing him. This is when the camera pans around to reveal Kyo-soo, who has just arrived home to witness the scene.

Mi-sook's accidental wounding of Jin-sung, Do-il's murder of Jin-sung, and Kyo-soo's collusion with the parents in the both literal and figurative cover-up are undoubtedly the most central events of the film. But their *placement* in the film is anything but central: where these events take place chronologically, about mid-way through the film, viewers see nothing but a black screen. What that black screen, held perhaps a second too long to serve as a normal divider between scenes, hides is not revealed until seconds before the film's end. What is more, viewers are deliberately distanced from the explanation for which they have had to wait until the film's final seconds: closing credits roll over the revelation scene as if it were not properly part of the film. And yet, the entire second half of the movie—the tree's attacks on the grandparents, the murderous hostility between Do-il and Mi-sook, Mi-sook's murder of her husband and following suicide—seem completely out of proportion if viewers presume that Jin-sung has simply run away; these events only make sense in light of Jin-sung's violent death at the hands of his adoptive parents. Thus the film's final seconds define its entire second half as an elaborate visualization of the parents' unbearable guilt, which seems all the more visceral in the absence of any clarification of what they feel guilty *about*.

Much like *The Child* and *Pet Sematary*, *Acacia*'s roots lie in myths and legends. Acacia trees hold mythical significance in many religions including Buddhism, South Korea's main religion.[6] Acacias are said to have furnished the wood for the Ark of the Covenant, the Altar of the Tabernacle, and the crown of Christ; they are also one of four divine trees in China and sacred to both Buddhists and Hindus. The Dhamma Encyclopedia claims that Buddha sat under an Acacia tree when he became enlightened, and in Egyptian myth, the acacia is the tree of life and death. Park's film takes mythical and religious meanings absolutely seriously. All characters accept myths as a normal part of life and attribute to them the same level of reality as food, work and financial worries. The main reason why Do-il wants to adopt a child is that he fears dying without children to honor him as an ancestor, which would mean that his spirit would be unable to revisit the household altars. When Mi-sook's mother presents her with the fertility fan, both women are absolutely convinced of its efficacy, a faith confirmed shortly thereafter by Mi-sook's pregnancy. Kyo-soo tells Jin-sung of the acacia's built-in defense system: "The tree calls the ants. The ants protect the acacia tree. If animals or bugs bother it, the ants attack them and chase them away." In a later scene, Kyo-soo himself falls victim to this defense system: the tree scratches his face and sends an army of ants swarming over him which crawl into his orifices, eating him from the inside. Some of the film's most traumatic scenes—Do-il drinking whisky that turns to blood; his fantasies of delivering dead babies; Mi-sook's brief encounter with Jin-sung after his disappearance, during which he shows her his wounds, complaining that his head hurts[7]—are clearly defined as the nightmarish hallucinations caused by a guilty conscience. Myths, however, are distinct from this. The fertility fan actually works. The acacia is clearly dynamic, not a prop but a character. Frog perspective shots up the tree, its dead branches clearly outlined against the sky, are accompanied by extra-diegetic whoosh-sounds to impress upon the viewer that even though the tree looks dead, it is very much alive, and not only in the ecological sense. Endowed with will and purpose, it is both hurting and aware of its own pain. This is acknowledged indirectly both by Kyo-soo's attempts to help the boy heal the tree and by the parents' unexplained inability to cut the tree down, although there is frequent talk of this and no fewer than two failed attempts. In fact, the only mythical statement made in the film that is *not* universally accepted—and there is no explanation offered as to why this should be less believable than, say, faith in the fertility fan—is Jin-sung's conviction that his mother lives in the acacia tree. This, too, is confirmed as reality in the penultimate scene, in which police find Jin-sung dead in the embrace of the tree's roots (Fig. 9: the DVD's chapter title for this scene is "In mother's arms").

While myths in the film are given credence on the level of every-day normality, the film consistently undermines the realism of scenes that viewers are likely to interpret as reality. An example is the scene when Do-il and Mi-sook first bring Jin-sung home. Jin-sung immediately goes to hug the dead acacia as his new parents contemplate him from the veranda. Jin-sung looks up at the tree, as if hearing something. We hear Do-il's voice asking, "Isn't he a little too old?" and Mi-sook answering: "It's strange. It feels like I've always waited for him. Isn't that more important?" But nobody's lips move. Both parents are standing in silent contemplation of the boy, not uttering a single word; nevertheless we hear the dialogue in their voices. The camera then pans to Kyo-soo's shed, revealing Kyo-soo at the window, watching Jin-sung hug the tree and then draw away from it as if hearing something. The camera briefly takes over Jin-sung's POV looking up the tree, then switches perspective to the tree's POV, showing Jin-sung's face from above, pressed against the tree trunk, his eyes closed, listening intently. The scene tests viewers' certainties, attributing different reality levels to audio and video: the parents don't speak but we hear their exchange nonetheless. The tree speaks (as we are in Jin-sung's POV looking up the tree, we hear the whooshing sound that usually indicates that the tree is animated) but we don't understand what it is saying. But if we can hear words that, as visuals indicate, actually remain unspoken, why should we doubt that Jin-sung can hear the tree speak although nobody else can hear it?

Fig. 9. "In mother's arms": Jin-sung (Mun Oh-bin) returns to his roots in *Acacia* (2003) (Show East/Dada Film/Beautiful Pictures).

The film's most inarguable reality lies in the psychological landscape it paints of guilt, initially the guilt of child rejection, then that of child neglect, and finally that of child murder. As Jin-sung enters the family, his reception by Mi-sook's mother is nothing less than hostile. She ignores him when he is in the room, criticizes him constantly and tries to convince Mi-sook to return him to the orphanage: "Did you really legally adopt him? ... It's better to have one of your own blood." After Hae-sung's birth, Jin-sung sits on the stairs drawing his tree as everyone else—Do-il, Mi-sook and her mother—fuss about the baby. He is momentarily called in to pose for a family photo, for which he poses unsmilingly, looking for all the world like an abandoned child. Both of his "evil" deeds—the burning of the fertility fan and the attempted murder of the baby—are clear signals that he wants to be accepted by his new family, just as shots of him sitting in the acacia tree, observing the house and the family from the outside, express that he is not welcome inside.

If the child neglect scenes are harrowing, the film's horror escalates immeasurably in scenes in which Do-il and Mi-sook each try to mitigate their own guilt over Jin-sung's murder by blaming it on the other. Do-il, returning from work some time after Jin-sung's death, finds the boy's slippers on the porch. Since it is customary in East Asian cultures to leave shoes outside of the house before entering, this is a clear indication—to anyone who knows that the couple murdered Jin-sung—that Mi-sook has placed the slippers there to indicate to Do-il that Jin-sung is "home." Do-il's horror at seeing the slippers is, of course, completely mysterious for anyone assuming, as one must at first viewing, that Jin-sung has run away. Entering the house, Do-il finds red thread draped over everything—walls, stairs, furniture, hanging down from the ceiling like bloody spider webs: a textile artist's way of saying that this house is drenched in blood. This, too, is completely lost on anyone as yet unaware that actual murder has taken place. Similarly, to viewers not yet aware of the developments in the final scene, Do-il's accusation makes little sense: "It's you that killed Jin-sung, not me. Mi-sook, it's you! Jin-sung would've been alive if I had cut it down that day. If you hadn't stopped me, Jin-sung would be alive!" And finally, Mi-sook sternly forbids Do-il to touch the baby because she can smell blood on him. This is yet another scene that is not comprehensible before all is revealed (is Mi-sook alluding to Do-il's work as an obstetrician, we wonder?) and only assumes its full meaning—Mi-sook's indictment of Do-il as a murderer—in light of the final scene. In both scenes, one parent's accusation of the other is answered with extreme violence; Mi-sook responds to Do-il's charge by attacking him with the scissors, Do-il to Mi-sook's by raping her. Jin-sung's "evil" deeds, including the attempted killing of the baby, are portrayed as the pathetic outbursts of a miserably lonely and rejected child; they pale beside the guilt that tortures the adults and ultimately leads them to tear each other apart. Disappointed horror fans who complained that *Acacia* was "just not scary"[8] inadvertently had it right: the film isn't trying to be. It is not a fright fest but a guilt trip, for "the root of all evil," to cite the film's tagline, is not fear but guilt.

* * *

> "When you look into the abyss, the abyss also looks into you."
> —Friedrich Nietzsche, *Beyond Good and Evil*

In assuming the form of myths, legends and fairy tales, nature horror defines the stories it tells as archetypal stories—stories that, like religious texts, are characterized by a distinct murkiness of origin and are commonly held capable of telling transcendental truths about human nature. Nature horror, then, exists in a place twice removed from civilization: once by virtue of its theme and once by virtue of the perceived deletion of human authorship, or origins of any kind, from the archetypal story.

All three films portray nature as a character endowed with agency and a will. Frequent unattributed POV shots constantly proclaim that "there is something out there," or, in the case of *Acacia*, "there is something in there." In Murphy's topography, both *The Child* and *Pet Sematary* would be Narrative B-films where unsuspecting outsiders enter into a rural setting and are forced to interact with a menacing and incomprehensible Nature. *Acacia*, conversely, does not need geographical distinctness to make the point: the natural threat is already home; it grows in your own garden. And yet, it is not Nature itself that is portrayed as evil—as Dinesen put it, "In nature there is no evil"—but human interaction with it, or more precisely, human attitudes towards it. Unlike the many nature horror films where inept and arrogant explorers embark on their search for evil in the woods, the films under discussion here make no direct comment on who started the trouble. Unlike other nature horror films in which nature strikes back, nature in these films merely interacts. But since humans inevitably view nature in contrast to civilization, nature's interaction with humanity cannot be anything but hostile, or rather: humans are likely to perceive it in those terms.

Attachment to nature is therefore logically assigned to the films' "evil" children, and attachment to nature can only mean detachment from both society and reality. Thus the children in *The Child* and *Acacia* reject their families for nature; and thus they also reject the distinction between fantasy and reality that forms the backbone of family and society. Casting stories that are centrally about reality-denial in the guise of myths and fairy tales does make a certain amount of sense. If reality says that children must grow up, reality, according to little Rosalie, can take a hike in the woods. Similarly, all three films are centrally about the inability to accept death: the death of a mother in *The Child* and *Acacia* and the very nature of death in *Pet Sematary*, which presents us with a mounting scale of death-denial and links this, predictably, with guilt. Rachel's guilt over her relief at her sister's death is undoubtedly as central to get the story started as is Nature's dangerous allure for Louis. What makes death unbearable is our guilty involvement: our relief at the malformed sister's death, or a momentary distraction during which we take our eyes off a toddler on his way to keep an appointment with a truck. Guilt looms large; in all three films, child neglect or child murder are key narrative events. *Pet Sematary*'s escalation of disasters—not death, but the return of the dead, for "sometimes, dead is better"—signifies, of course, that humans never learn. Nature horror, in other words, describes a transcendental guilt trip, a universal, *a priori* guilt that not just pertains to individuals but to humanity in general, and it is *this* that can only be properly expressed in an archetypal tale: humans will make the same mistakes, incur the same guilt, over and over, no matter how many chances they are given. Experience and memory do not serve.

The deeper meaning of Nature horror and its "posthuman approach" is simply that there is no hope for humanity. If other archetypal forms, like the fairy tale, beg the question, horror pronounces a judgment. Surely it is significant that at the end of *The Child*, *Pet Sematary* and *Acacia*, there is not a single survivor. Unlike fairy tales, myths and legends, horror is not a didactic form. In nature horror, nobody ever reforms, and so nobody ever goes home.

## Guilt Trips

### LITTLE HORRORS

*Children of the Corn* (dir. Fritz Kiersch, USA 1984). A young couple is trapped in a remote town, somewhere in America's Bible Belt. They find out that the town's children have killed all adults in the town and have now formed a religious cult whose rhetoric is suspiciously similar to the religious mania spouted on the radio by adult evangelists. The cult enacts a radical version of the Peter Pan Syndrome: everyone who reaches the age of 19 is classed as an adult and must be sacrificed to the God in the Corn. *Guilt Trip:* The children have killed all adults in the town out of respect for Nature, in revenge for the use of pesticides and other harmful ways of farming.

*Heavenly Creatures* (dir. Peter Jackson, New Zealand 1994). The film is based on an actual criminal case (the murder of Honora Parker in Christchurch, New Zealand, in June 1954). Two 14-year-old girls living in New Zealand, lower-class Pauline and upper-class Juliet, form a friendship that is buoyed by an intense fantasy life. Their central fantasy is the "4th world," their own mental Garden of Eden, complete with unicorns and huge colorful butterflies. When the parents threaten to separate them, the girls conspire to murder Pauline's mother. *Guilt trip:* The girls' fantasy life is largely sparked by unhappiness in their families. Pauline's parents are dourly uncommunicative; Juliet's father goes off to England, dumping his daughter, who has a lung ailment, on some clinic in South Africa, "for the good of your health."

*Lord of the Flies* (dir. Peter Brook, UK 1963; remake dir. Harry Hook, USA 1990) is the precursor film for a nature horror tradition that wasn't. A class of schoolboys is stranded on a deserted island and left to form their own society; as soon as the survival basics are taken care of, they stop cooperating with each other. They quickly establish hierarchies, exclude certain members from their newly formed tribes, and disintegrate into mass hysteria, sadistic enjoyment of torture, and murder. The film's *guilt trip* is transcendental; its assumption is that brutality against others is not societally produced but human nature.

*Mama* (dir. Andrés Muschietti, Canada/Spain 2013). A young couple tries to raise two small children, little Victoria and toddler Lilly, who were abandoned in the forest for years. The children communicate with each other like animals, snarling, lashing out and jumping on furniture like cats. A doctor claims that they created an imaginary guardian in the woods whom they called Mama. While Lilly cannot make the transition from nature, Victoria, who is older, integrates into the family. "Mama" turns out to be the ghost of a woman tortured in a nineteenth-century insane asylum to such a degree that she threw herself off a steep gorge with her baby; when Lilly and Victoria are abandoned in the forest, Mama raises them. At the end, Victoria remains in the human family whereas Lilly, unable to break her link with Mama, goes over the cliff with her in a re-enactment of the nineteenth-century suicide. The films' numerous attack scenes are mostly shot from Mama's POV. *Guilt trip:* The film is rife with scenes of child abuse and child abandonment, including a heart-rending scene in which Lilly wanders the woods all alone, repeating desperately: "Mama? Where Mama?"

*The Pit* (dir. Lew Lehman, Canada 1981). Twelve-year-old Jamie, cruelly mistreated and beaten by older boys, lures his enemies into a pit in the woods, where evil "trogs"— meat-eating creatures that he has discovered there—messily devour them. Jamie, universally considered a "nutcase," is deeply unpopular in the neighborhood; his parents ignore him and "discover" him only for reprimands. The film is essentially a revenge flick, during which Jamie feeds all of his abusers to the trogs; when he runs out of nasty people to sacrifice, he lets the trogs out so they can feed themselves without his help. Much of the rest of the film is shot from the trogs' POV. In the end, Jamie is shunted off to his grandparents in the country, where he finally finds a friend, little Alishia; idyllic scenes of the two of them chasing each other in sun-lit fields ensue. But viewers' hopes that perhaps this is Jamie's path back to normality are premature: Alishia shows Jamie a pit she found, with monsters in it. Jamie, knowledgeably: "They're trolalogs, they eat people." She: "Yes, I know," and pushes him in. *Guilt trip:* The film contains numerous child rejection and neglect scenes as well as an indirect statement that human evil is inherent from birth: all of the film's children are cruel bullies or, in the case of both Jamie and Alishia, miniature killers.

*The Woods* (dir. Lucky McKee, USA 2006). Freaky ghost children pursuing Heather, a boarding schooler, are revealed to be the ghosts of three mistreated sisters who, a hundred years previously, chopped up the school's headmistress with an axe. The woods surrounding the school are very much alive, attacking parents who drive through them on their way to the school. Tree branches and vines invade the school and drag children into the woods. The school's current headmistress turns out to be one of the three evil children from a hundred years ago, looking for a replacement so she and her sisters can finally escape the woods that hold them fixed to the ground where they incurred their guilt. Heather solves the problem by axe-murdering the three sisters, freeing all the girls at the school. The epilogue reveals that in 1965 the school burned to the ground, emphasizing that inexplicably, the woods around the school remained untouched by fire. *Guilt trip:* The film is essentially about child abuse and child abandonment. All teachers are cruel freaks; all parents stuck-up and uncaring. When asked why Heather entered the school, she answers, "My mom wanted me out of the house."

## Teenage Wasteland

*Battle Royale* (dir. Kinji Fukasaku, Japan 2000; sequel dir. Kenta Fukasaku and Kinji Fukasaku, Japan 2003) was possibly inspired by *Lord of the Flies* and certainly ripped off by the later *Hunger Games* (2012). A futuristic Japanese government deposits 42 students on a deserted island and gives them three days to kill each other. The situation brings the dormant "evil" of some contestants to the fore, whereas others, refusing to participate, commit suicide. The film's *guilt trip* lies in its overt critique of a society that entices innocents to murder for the entertainment of others, which can easily be read as an implicit critique of horror audiences watching the same events for the same reasons.

*The Cabin in the Woods* (dir. Drew Goddard, USA 2012), a spoof on and re-enactment of the classic cabin-in-the-woods-movie, features an "evil" child (zombie girl Patience Bruckner) in a nature setting. The film is a send-up of the most clichéd horror set-up of all: five teenagers disappear into a cabin in the woods for the weekend, at least two of them with explicit sexual plans (the kind for which you are always swiftly and messily dispatched in horror films). The five are promptly and predictably attacked by zombies. An hour later, the survivor count is down to two, the smartest boy, a pot-head, and the smartest girl (Clover's stereotypical "Final Girl"). Those two discover what the audience has been aware of from the start: that the entire story of their entrapment and deaths was engineered by a bunch of lab-coat clad bureaucrats. *Guilt trip:* Viewers are obviously aligned with the bureaucratic killers, with both parties following, on a screen, the spectacle of teenagers being gorily killed and amusing themselves by taking bets on their survival chances and the order of their deaths. The watchers within the film are resolutely amoral, refusing to accept the "reality" of the kids in the cabin, just as viewers of a horror film would refuse to accept the reality of its characters. The watchers' complete remorselessness is part of the reason why the two surviving kids decide in the end that humanity is not worth it, that "it's time to give someone else a chance": A guilt-free world is not worth saving.

*Eden Lake* (dir. James Watkins, UK 2008) tells the harrowing story of Jenny and Steve, a young couple being tortured and pursued by a gang of evil teens in a remote and disused quarry. The teens are universally portrayed as lower class. The teens murder Steve; Jenny, after killing two of the teens, succeeds in escaping out of the woods and back to "civilization," in the form of a rural settlement. The house where she shelters belongs to the parents of the ringleader of the evil teens and happens to be full of other parents of gang members, who end up murdering Jenny to cover up their children's crimes. *Guilt Trip:* The film motivates parental responsibility early on: as Jenny and Steve drive to the lake, the car radio plays a report of the 2005 Parental Responsibility Act under which parents can be held accountable for their children's anti-social or criminal behavior.

*The Evil Dead* (dir. Sam Raimi, USA 1981) is the original cabin-in-the-woods movie and inspiration for all others, including the *Cabin Fever* films (2002–) and *The Cabin in the Woods*. Five youngsters go to a cabin in the woods, find the trapdoor to the cellar and in the cellar a diary to raise the dead, and are possessed by demons. The film revels in extensive and constant *Halloween*-style POVs from the outside of the house, looking in through every window, and later POV shots from the perspective of demons pursuing victims. Scary nature is identified strongly with evil demons and spirits. *Guilt trip:* As people turn into evil dead-ites, the classic "you have to kill all of your friends to survive" ploy applies.

*Sleepaway Camp* (dir. Robert Hiltzik, USA 1983). Painfully shy and clearly troubled 14-year-old Angela, who never speaks, is sent off to a summer camp and embarks on a killing spree of campers. The film features extensive POV shots from the killer's perspective. *Guilt trip:* The film points the finger of blame squarely at Mother. As the final scene shockingly reveals, Angela is actually a boy who was forced, unwillingly, into a sex change by her mother because "We already had a little boy. Another boy would not have done at all." Angela as a girl is raised to be demure, mute, almost catatonic, forced into an unnatural suppression of her true sex and aggressiveness by her Stepford Wife mother; the idea here is that a boy's natural aggressiveness, if perverted in such a way, expresses itself in extremes of violence. Angela in the final scene is blood-spattered, male genitals in full view, emanating a weird green glow and screaming like a banshee—is this merely a boy with long hair or a monster with a penis? If this were *The Lord of the Rings*, it would be called a hobgoblin. Thus Mother's forcible suppression of Angela's sexual identity results in Angela's a complete loss of humanity.

# 4

# Science

*Seeing the World in Black and White*

## *Seeing Is Believing*

Science is both one of horror film's favorite topics and the horror film critic's red-headed stepchild. Few have bothered with horror science, perhaps because there is so much more to say about science and scientists in science fiction, sometimes misnamed "sci-fi and horror." Yet on this particular subject, the two genres are not nearest neighbors but worlds apart. Sci-fi science is generally derived from rational thought and experiment and argues for change and progress; horror defines science as a forbidden door which, once pushed open, lets in tentacled critters from Planet X. *Pet Sematary*'s dark pronouncement about the boundary between the permissible and the forbidden—"The barrier was not meant to be crossed"—is the most fundamental credo of all horror science. The way horror expresses its horror of science is by focusing on two extremes of failure: the Mad Scientist and the Nuclear Noir.

Writing on movie science tends to concentrate on three interrelated questions: whether films portray science accurately; the question of ethical responsibility in the use of scientific insights and resulting technology; and the question of secrecy. The first can only be judged adequately by scientists, and so it has been—harshly. Most scientists give the movies failing grades for their representation of science, blaming them for plummeting levels of science literacy[1] and advising viewers to enjoy the show but "leave your analytic brains at home."[2] This advice seems to be heeded, not only by moviegoers but also by policy-makers and heads of state. National and international decisions involving science and technology are often made on no better evidence than a shoddy understanding of lousy movie science. Ronald Reagan's Strategic Defense Initiative, mocked as the "Star Wars" program even at the time, went ahead over the objections of the scientific community, at a cost of $25 billion to the American taxpayer. And George W. Bush's threat of an Iraqi "mushroom cloud"—a statement made *after* Bush had been informed that Iraq possessed no nuclear capabilities[3]—clearly hoped to strike terror into the hearts of generations reared on nuclear disaster flicks.

The movies themselves are unlikely to portray calamitous science as a societal problem.[4] Rather than opening that can of worms, they blame an individual, usually the Mad Scientist. But even if many films can be fairly accused of blinding audiences to the dangers of a science beholden to political interests, this hardly absolves their audiences. Whether misunderstood by simple minds, as seems likely in Reagan's case, or misrepresented by devious ones, as seems likely in Bush's, the confusion of movie-science with actual science is based on the belief that seeing is believing. If seeing (rather than thinking, reading, or researching) is believing, this will likely result in both a murky understanding of science and an abdication of ethical responsibility. Joe and Jane Q. Public, fooled by governments to believe that mushroom clouds are sprouting everywhere and by the movies into thinking that science is only dangerous when performed by crazy individuals, have neither the intellectual nor the ethical acumen to handle science. Their deficient understanding of science and their refusal to take responsibility for it are the handles of the handbasket in which the world is going to hell.

That the world is going there is the most basic premise of science movies, from sci-fi to global disaster films to horror. Where horror distinguishes itself from other genres is by deleting hopes for the post-apocalyptic future. Other movie genres offer such hope verbally—for example, in implausible avowals that humans, having learned their lesson, will act more responsibly next time—or symbolically, and far more powerfully, in the image of the child. Because children are the most obvious shorthand for rebirth, they populate apocalypse-now flicks, from *Aliens* to *The Road*, in unbelievable numbers (and this may well be why they also populate a high percentage of nuclear Armageddon dreams studied by real-life researchers[5]). Just as responsible science can embody hope for growth and progress, children in nuclear fallout-stories commonly represent hope for the world's renewal.

Neither idea applies to the horror genre, although horror, too, links science with children. In horror, though, the connection is far more sinister: both science and children embody the fear of creating something that you then cannot control.

## Children of the Damned *(UK 1964)*, The Brood *(Canada 1979)*, Godsend *(USA 2004)*

> *"And I'm pretty certain he sees things only in black and white; no colors."*
> —David Cronenberg, *The Brood* (1979)

*Children of the Damned* (dir. Anton Leader, 1964), shot in starkly contrastive black and white, outs itself in its opening credits as "A Sequel to John Wyndham's 'The Midwich Cuckoos.'" It thus deliberately leap-frogs over its much more famous direct predecessor, Wolf Rilla's film *Village of the Damned* (1960), to acknowledge its debt to *Village*'s literary source, Wyndham's 1957 novel. Indeed, Leader's film conflicts with Rilla's on its most central aspect: the portrayal of the children.

*Children*'s opening credits roll over stills of a proper-looking British schoolboy aged about nine, who will emerge as the film's main child protagonist Paul (Clive Powell), walking down a deserted London alleyway far in the distance, his face turned towards the viewer. A sequence of still images underscored by eerily banging brass sounds bring the boy ever-closer until credits finish with an extreme close-up of his face staring directly at the camera. If the opening credits already define the child as the ultimate threat, the film's first scene—which begins with a count-down, a hand holding a stopwatch and a voice counting down from five—suggests that there is not much time left to address this peril. The camera pulls back from the hand holding the stopwatch to reveal Paul and three other schoolboys of his age being tested on how quickly they can assemble a vast number of wooden blocks into a complicated structure. Only Paul manages to finish; he completes the task in a few minutes and in so doing beats the world's greatest adult scientific minds by two hours.

Suitably impressed, the two scientists in charge of the experiment, psychologist Tom Llewellin (Ian Hendry) and geneticist David Neville (Alan Badel) set out to find out the source of Paul's incredible genius. A visit to Paul's mother Diana Looran (Sheila Allen), a slutty and hostile "Photographers Model," as the handwritten sign on the door of her crummy apartment announces, quickly convinces the scientists that "he didn't get his brains from Mother." She refuses to cooperate with the scientists, but after throwing them out, she ominously tells Paul that "They're after you. And you won't get away.... They'll get you now, and I'll help." In response, Paul hypnotizes her, forcing her to walk into a dark tunnel, where she is hit by a truck. In the hospital, severely wounded, she reveals to Llewellin and Neville that Paul has no father, that he was, in fact, a virgin birth: "I hadn't been touched, ever.... He hasn't got a father. He isn't human," adding that "he could butcher you without even trying." The scientists, heedless of this warning, continue to study Paul, securing the cooperation of Paul's less hostile (and less trashy) aunt Susan Eliot (Barbara Ferris). In a lab where an entire science team has assembled to study "biological sports," meaning sudden and unexplained extravagant advances in gene mutation, Llewellin and Neville are informed that there are five other Pauls in the world—five children of Paul's age, from China, India, Nigeria, the Soviet Union, and the USA respectively, whose tests reveal the same results. All six were born without the assistance of a father to mothers with modest intellect, one of whom is a kitchen maid and another, in her own mother's description, "a tramp, just an ordinary woman of the streets, practically." The other five children are flown to London so all six can be tested further. When it emerges that their respective governments plan to exploit the children's genius for military purposes, the children, who are in telepathic contact with one another, leave their respective embassies and unite in an abandoned church.

Led by intelligence agent Colin Webster (Alfred Burke), all governments, realizing their failure to control the children and terrified that another nation might succeed, decide to destroy them, but what few armed goons manage to enter the church are easily dispatched by the children who mind-control them into killing each other or committing suicide. At this point, the science team splits: Llewellin, the psychologist, proposes studying the children; Neville, the geneticist, is in favor of destroying them because of the obvious danger they pose. Persuaded to return to their embassies, the children go willingly, but when exhorted to put their minds at the service of military intelligence, they respond with slaughter. Paul dispatches the British Minister of Defense, the Chief of Staff, and Webster by forcing them to kill one another, and the knowing job-done look he gets from the other five children as they reunite on the street confirms that similar scenes have taken place at the other five embassies. Meanwhile Professor Gruber (Martin Miller), an Austrian expert in genetics, has studied the children's cells and come to the shocking conclusion that the children are not aliens but humans "advanced maybe a million years." But this revelation does not change the minds of military leaders bent on the children's destruction. At the final showdown at the church, bombs are set in the church as Tom Llewellin desperately tries to persuade the authorities to at least hear the children's side of the story. The children express their willingness to be destroyed, linking hands and awaiting the inevitable. When the inevitable happens, it happens in a way that makes a mockery of the idea of human control: a tech, reaching for the microphone to call off the attack, accidentally brushes against a screwdriver which rolls down the panel, setting off the flare signal command for the soldiers to open fire. Bombs and guns erupt until the church is no more than a pile of smoking debris, with two children's hands, still clutched, visible among the rubble. The film ends with a close-up of the screwdriver that caused the disaster.

With the exception of sweet Susan and tolerant Tom, adults come off rather badly in this film. *Children of the Damned* offers a harsh critique not only of individuals, but of governments, institutions and mechanisms that become inevitable when everyone's mind is on economic or military superiority. Science is not free but subservient to the government and the military; this applies to the so-called "free nations" of the West (UK, USA) as much as it does to so-called "Third World" countries (Nigeria, India) and Communist regimes (China, Soviet Union). All consider the children nothing more than our "own newly discovered assets"; all plan to use them to develop more sophisticated weaponry in case the Cold War turns hot. The idea that the Cold War could end amicably is considered briefly but immediately rejected, largely because economic interest and jobs depend on its continuation. Intelligence agent Webster, when asked "What the hell would you do if all the great powers suddenly smiled at each other, had a bloody love affair?," disdainfully dismisses the possibility: "Oh, I shouldn't worry too much. You know how love affairs go."

The plan to exploit the genius children for military purposes is foiled when it emerges that the telepathic link between the children is perfect: anything one of them knows is instantly known to all the others, making military secrecy impossible. No country can actually use its "asset" because all weapons designs, all spying efforts, all tactical decisions and every loathsome secret would be instantly known to all other nations. But instead of spelling the end of all wars, hot or cold, this only seems to increase the likelihood of violent conflict. "I am as nonviolent as you," claims one ambassador in a heated exchange with another. "You want war? If one of the big powers seize them [the children], how could the other side do nothing? Every moment, they would be falling behind. They would have to strike immediately while they still had the chance." As this conversation takes place, both ambassadors are standing directly beneath a large portrait of Mahatma Gandhi, a visual reminder of the alternative they never consider.

*Children of the Damned* is unequivocal in its denunciation of the human race. Whatever humans don't understand, they will first try to exploit for their advantage, defined as the destruction or at least the subjugation of others. Failing that, they will destroy it. As human behavior throughout the film demonstrates and as the children's provenance combined with the film's title also reveals, humans are "the Damned." Where the film prevaricates, however, is in its portrayal of the children. At times the children are portrayed as Llewellin sees them, as victims of human persecution (as Susan puts it, "They've been terrified. They've been hunted like some kind of freak vermin"). This expression of sympathy for the children's plight contrasts positively with Neville's panicky view of the children as evil mutants bent on humanity's destruction: "Don't you realize that at this very moment they could be controlling a bomber crew and force them to press the button? That would be it!"[6] Neville's terror is not at all assuaged when it emerges that the children are not aliens but humans advanced a million years: "we're ape advanced a million years. And from what

Fig. 10. Advanced a million years, but not morally: Paul (Clive Powell) forces his mother (Sheila Allen) to walk in front of a truck in *Children of the Damned* (1964) (MGM).

I've seen, I think we need protection against man advanced a million years. Either we control them or they control us, and that's the law of nature, Tom. Ask any ape."

Unlike Tom's and Susan's more kindly attitude, Neville's panicky fear-mongering is unlikely to elicit audience sympathies, paralleling, as it does, the despicable governments' inability to envision a relationship between two groups that does not entail one group's domination of the other. And yet, Neville's assertion that the children are destructive does have cinematic portrayal on its side. Paul sends his mother into a dark tunnel, clearly intending for her to be run over (Fig. 10). The American boy Mark (Frank Summerscale) regularly sets an attack dog on his grandmother to keep her in line. The mother of little Rashid (Mahdu Mathen), when asked "Does Rashid ever make you do things that you don't want to do?," pales visibly and runs from the room in terror. Most tellingly, these omnipotent children never use their powers merely to immobilize or disarm their opponents, opting instead to kill them. All of this throws a rather sinister light on humans "advanced a million years": the implication is that even in a million years, humans will still define human relationships in terms of domination and submission and therefore be unable to think beyond the alternative of either killing or being killed. The brief dialogue on the church steps, in which Commissioner Harib asks the children what they want, demonstrates this clearly enough:

> *Harib (pointing at the SWAT teams and weapons trained upon the church)*: Do you understand why we have done this?
> *Paul*: Yes. You are here to destroy us.
> *Harib:* Paul, what is your purpose? Why are you here?
> *Paul*: To be destroyed.

In her 1983 novel *Kassandra,* a tale of a doomed seer's inability to prevent or end the Trojan war, Christa Wolf wrote: "Between killing and dying there is a third alternative: living."[7] The horror of *Children of the Damned* is not that the children are so much more advanced than the Damned, the horror is that they aren't. Neither humanity now nor humanity in a million years, the film proclaims, will be able to consider that third alternative. We will be more advanced intellectually, but not emotionally, empathically or ethically. We may be able to communicate telepathically and murder by force of mind, but our ability to understand each other, to give each other a break or the benefit of doubt, will be no better than it is today. Our knowledge of science and technology will be immeasurably advanced, but the moral sense that might enable us to wield such knowledge responsibly will not have kept pace.

The film's children are "evil" in the sense that they destroy, rather than represent, hope for the future. Worst of all is the revelation that they are human children, not the cuckoos of Wyndham's novel or the aliens of Rilla's film. It is far less harrowing to attribute unmitigated evil to aliens than to our own kind, even if it is humankind a million years in the future. This is, we might suspect, the main reason for the film's portrayal of the children as both persecuted victims and evil killers. If *Village of the Damned* describes its alien children as unadulterated, unredeemably evil and its adults as either innocent victims or heroically self-sacrificing resisters, *Children of the Damned* takes a more equivocal approach by equating the children with the damned. It does this by attributing to the children the same mix of empathic incompetence and power abuse as that which characterizes present-day humans, fatally exacerbated by a million years' worth of intellectual advance.

David Cronenberg's *The Brood* (1979) is perhaps one of the most written-about science horror films ever made. Here's the story according to the film's critics: Dr. Hal Raglan (Oliver Reed), Director of the Somafree Institute of Psychoplasmics,[8] develops a psychotherapy in the course of which his patients learn to manifest their rage physiologically, usually through welts and pustules. Furthest along this path is Nola Carveth (Samantha Eggar), who is kept isolated from her husband Frank (Art Hindle) for the course of her therapy. Whereas Frank drops off their five-year-old daughter Candice (Cindy Hinds) for a visit with her mother every weekend, he himself is not permitted to see Nola. When Candice returns from these visits with her back covered in scratches and bites, Frank becomes increasingly convinced that Nola abuses the child, as well as suspicious of Dr. Raglan's methods. To focus on Nola's therapy, Dr. Raglan closes the Institute and dismisses all of his other patients, whose therapy stories increase Frank's concerns. Meanwhile, Nola's mother Juliana (Nuala Fitzgerald), accused by Nola of child abuse, her father Barton (Henry Beckman), accused of not protecting Nola from her mother, and Candice's pre-school teacher Ruth Mayer (Susan Hogan), whom Nola suspects of having an affair with Frank, are all murdered by mysterious child-like figures with ancient hands and faces, clad in Candice-look-alike ski-suits and scarves. It turns out that these "children" are Nola's "brood," physical manifestations of her rage. In the film's most traumatic and visceral scene, Frank witnesses Nola birthing one of these little horrors through an external uterus and sac, biting the sac open and licking the blood off a progeny that looks like raw liver. Nola, perceiving his disgust, unleashes the brood on Candice. Dr. Raglan, trying to rescue Candice from Nola's brood, falls victim to their rage; Frank saves Candice's life by murdering Nola and escapes with Candice, who, as the final close-up reveals, is developing small pustules on her arm—a sign that the cycle of rage and abuse will continue beyond Nola's death.

This story broadly corresponds to that actually told in the film, but also reveals two significant blind spots. I believe that these blind spots are due not to the inattention of critics but to the way in which Cronenberg's film entices viewers to pay undue attention to some aspects and ignore others entirely. The nearest analogy is a 1999 experiment conducted by Christopher Chabris and Daniel Simons, in which they asked respondents to watch a brief video showing two teams of basketball players in white or black T-shirts and to count the passes made by the white team. Halfway through the video, a black gorilla strolls into the center of the action, performs some antics, and walks off the scene. Since 1999, half of all viewers of the video have focused so intently on the passes that they have failed to see the gorilla dancing directly in front of their eyes.[9]

To many viewers of The Brood, Raglan and Candice have become the film's invisible gorillas. It has proven too tempting to do as Raglan himself does, namely to focus on Nola and dismiss everyone else. The film's undisputed star, or so it must seem particularly given the certainly flamboyant final birth-scene, is Nola, the "monstrous mother." On Nola's back, motherhood itself is portrayed as "monstrous," in two ways: through the film's presentation of both female bodies and female independence as a vision of horror, and through the issue of child abuse, which is passed down through *female* generations (Nola is abused by her mother Juliana and in turn abuses her daughter Candice, who shows physical manifestations of the same disease in the final scene). Compared with this electrifying portrayal of Nola the abused abuser and repulsive birthing animal, both Raglan and Candice have been assigned relatively lackluster parts, Raglan as the "mad scientist" and Candice, even more straightforwardly, as the "victim." Both of these characters, however, deserve a closer look.

Raglan is commonly seen as the oldest prototype of mad scientist, namely as a descendant of Dr. Frankenstein. This defines him as someone who means well and simply takes things a step too far. His recurring therapeutic encouragement to "go all the way through it," "to the end," "Don't stop," is often cited in support of the idea that not knowing when to stop is, in fact, his only problem. Dr. Raglan's therapy for Nola, or so the argument goes, is essentially correct in approach but mistaken in direction: instead of venting her rage "backward" (against her abusive mother) she directs it forward toward her own child. This is commonly blamed not on Raglan's incompetence but on Nola's bad character.[10] In the end, most who have written on the film agree that "Dr. Raglan is not the villain of the piece"; that he is merely "motivated by a desire to help his patients," and that in the end, "no one is really at fault here."[11]

The film itself, however, does not let Raglan off so easily. In fact, many scenes—invisible gorilla scenes, we might call them—indict him rather severely. The film's extremely painful opening scene, a public therapy session between Raglan and his patient Mike Trellan (Gary McKeehan), can easily be read as a scene of renewed abuse. Raglan, playing the role of Mike's abusive father, rants at him for behaving like "a little girl," contemptuously calls him "Michelle," and claims that "Michelle" must have contracted his weakness from his mother. Finally, Mike erupts in angry red pustules, "showing" his rage. It is not only the offensive nature of the "cure" that is distasteful here—being female is identified as the greatest shame there is—but also its public setting, which defines the entire scene not as an attempt to help Mike but to show-case Dr. Raglan's brilliance through Mike's public humiliation and his ability to make his anguish visible. If that is indeed the intention, it succeeds; Raglan's demonstration is rewarded with an awed whisper from the audience: "Wow. The man is a genius. The man is a genius." In fact, the man appears, throughout the film, as a manipulative jerk far more concerned with his own fame and fortune than his patients' wellbeing. Posters of his book, *The Shape of Rage*, and large photographs of his face dominate interiors, including his own clinic and Nola's apartment. Despite his obvious desire for celebrity, Raglan's methods are characterized by conspiratorial secrecy. Raglan takes it upon himself to keep Nola isolated from her family and withholds important news (including that of her mother's murder) from her, all in the name of not upsetting Nola's therapy, which is always at a "critical stage" whenever someone from her family wants to see her. He holds cagey conversations with his assistant Chris (Nicholas Campbell); when Barton angrily (and unsuccessfully) demands to see Nola to tell her of her mother's death, Chris even offers Dr. Raglan, ominously, to "have him stopped."

That Dr. Raglan does not care a fig about his patients is best demonstrated by his wholesale abandonment of them when he closes the clinic, shipping his weeping and protesting patients out by bus, to focus exclusively on Nola, his star patient and the one who would presumably demonstrate his "genius" most effectively. As Mike (Raglan's "Michelle") notes despondently, "the rest of us don't count anymore." Conversations between Frank and the unceremoniously dumped patients reveal that Raglan's cure, to some, is actually not helpful but harmful. One patient has contracted a fatal cancer of the lymphatic system because "Raglan encouraged my body to, to, to revolt against me. And it did. Now I, I have a small revolution on my hands, and I'm not putting it down very successfully." This patient moreover hints that others have fared no better at Dr. Raglan's hands ("We might form a club," he remarks laconically). Obviously, neither he nor other ex-patients are receiving either follow-up care or recompense from Dr. Raglan. Raglan's supreme indifference towards his patients and their families, which has gone remarkably unnoticed thus far, is not something that is slowly and subtly developed throughout the film, it is announced with a big bang right at its beginning. In an early scene, Frank, convinced that Nola is beating Candice, storms into Raglan's practice, catching him just out of the shower and clad in a bathrobe and towel. Raglan dismisses Frank's profound distress with the usual platitudes, then turns his back on Frank to fuss with his hair in front of a mirror.

The film's second invisible gorilla is little Candice (Fig. 11), commonly perceived

Fig. 11. Another invisible gorilla: Candice (Cindy Hinds) in the victim role in *The Brood* (1979) (New World Pictures/Photofest).

as "the purest victim because the most purely innocent," her catatonically blank stare explained as a traumatic response to abuse: "As Nola was mistreated by Juliana, so Candice is mistreated by Nola."[12] In fact, both the reality of abuse and Candice's apparent innocence merit a question or two. The film does not offer any concrete evidence that child abuse, either of Nola or of Candice, has ever taken place. There is, certainly, both rage and physical damage, but no clear indication as to the cause of either. The case of Nola and her mother Juliana seems to be of the "She says–she says" variety: Nola claims that Juliana abused her; Juliana denies it, claiming that when Nola was a small child, she would "wake up and she would be covered with big ugly bumps" for which doctors could not find an explanation and which went away when Nola turned ten years old. Juliana, driven to drink by her daughter's accusations, indicates to Frank that children, consciously or subconsciously, fabricate stories of abuse: "I guess you know now what it feels like.... Being a parent. Being blamed for everything. To have the past distorted so you don't even recognize yourself in it. Your child's version of the past, that is." When Frank protests that Candice is only five, too young to fabricate stories, Juliana adds morosely: "She's working on it right now, believe me; 30 seconds after you're born, you have a past. And 60 seconds after that, you start to lie to yourself about it." While this appears an extravagant claim—and Juliana, waving her whiskey glass, a less than reliable witness—the film does make a visual statement that might be seen as supportive of Juliana's defense: Frank discovers the angry red welts on Candice's back immediately following the scene in which similar welts appeared all over Mike's body. The visual link might well suggest that like Mike (and Nola), Candice is able to manifest her rage physically, throwing doubt on Frank's quick conclusion that Nola must have beaten Candice during the last visit.

Some not-so-subtle scenes suggest that the film's brood of evil children are not limited to Nola's psycho-litter but also includes little Candice, who has posed so successfully as the film's innocent victim. Consider the following scene: Juliana is gruesomely hammered to death in her own kitchen as Candice calmly looks at photographs in the living room next door, apparently unaware either of the ruckus—pots and pans flying, drawers being ripped open, spilling their contents—or Juliana's screams. As soon as Juliana has expired, Candice finally gets up, walks into the kitchen, and coolly, tearlessly, contemplates her grandmother's bloodied corpse. Later, the police detective tells Frank that Candice was found peacefully sleeping upstairs—"It seems she missed the whole thing"—and that he asked a psychiatrist to examine her, not because she was distressed but because "she was very cool throughout the whole thing. A little too cool." (In the later murder scene of Ruth Mayer, we are shown how normal traumatized children behave in such situations: the children in her kindergarten classroom weep, scream, or race outside yelling for help. Not one of them curls up in the corner to take a nap.) The psychiatrist, of course, interprets Candice's unnatural calm as an expression of trauma in the sense of fear and victimization, and the film's critics have unquestioningly followed his lead. As he warns Frank of a possible break-down— "These things tend to express themselves in one way or another"—the camera focuses on a close-up of Candice's face, catatonically staring at the TV, a large red welt on the corner of her mouth.

This is another sizable gorilla that critics have missed: that Candice's deformation, the pustules on her skin, do *not* appear for the first time in the final shot[13] but are clearly visible twice before. The second time is the scene showing Candice watching TV following her grandmother's murder, the first time the bath scene when Frank discovers the welts on Candice's back (unless we join him in jumping to the conclusion that Candice was beaten by Nola). These earlier appearances may well indicate that Candice, like her mother, can manifest her rage physically,[14] which would explain not only the marks on her back and her mouth, but also her emotional unresponsiveness to anything and everything—love, hugs, kisses, murder—throughout the film.

While Candice is usually seen as the victim of Nola's brood, the film does what it can to link the two. The brood are the same size as Candice, wear the same type ski-suit as Candice does, with scarves tied backwards in the same way as Candice ties hers, and sport the same straw-yellow hair as Candice does. Raglan describes the relationship between Candice and the brood best when he calls the little monsters "her siblings." Critics, in an effort to distinguish clearly between monsters and victims, have focused mainly on the ways in which these creatures are described as inhuman. The pathologist conducting the autopsy of one of them, for instance, notes a total lack of sexual organs and a navel: "And that means this creature has never really been born. At least not the way human beings are born." But other aspects of these creatures that might be considered to link the Brood with other humans have gone largely unnoticed. To cite the pathologist again: "Our friend has very strange eyes. They have irises, but no retinas. I should think his vision of the world is very distorted. And I'm pretty certain he sees things only in black and white, no colors." If we take this as a diagnosis that afflicts humans as well—the inability to see things in ways other than black and white—we quickly arrive at a position where doubt besets most things that seem so obvious in Cronenberg's film: Juliana's and Nola's role as child abusers, Dr. Raglan's role as benefactor of the psychically distressed, Candice's role as innocent victim, or, for that matter, the nature of psychological "deformity." The shape of rage, the film seems to suggest, manifests itself not only physiologically, in disgusting welts, scratches, bites, or external uterine sacs, but also psychologically, in a form of color blindness ("blind rage") that produces a distorted view of the world.

William Paul has described the film's portrayal of the evil children as slow-reveal scenes typical of horror: initially we see no more than a small and withered hand, then the creature from behind in a snow suit, and finally "the creature from a full frontal view that shows us a deformed and withered face on a child's body." To this I would add that *The Brood* also engages in a gradual *obscuring* of certainties in what we might call slow-conceal scenes. Paul claims that once we have glimpsed the monster, "the rest of the film becomes a kind of quest to define the origin of this very particular life" and that the sensational birthing scene at the end "provides us with the final answer about their origins."[15] Actually, this scene offers no such final answer, or rather, it does so only to viewers who see the world in black and white, happy to accept a series of assertions for which the film, in the end, provides precious little evidence. If slow-reveal scenes don't always reveal much, slow-conceal scenes seem to ask us to question what we're seeing, particularly when we think we're seeing clearly. Significantly, slow-conceal scenes tend to be bleached of color, verging on black and white, including under-lit interiors, dark forests, and snowy landscapes. Extreme contrasts between black and white symbolically impose "obvious" (but perhaps nevertheless wrong) explanations on the viewer, to the point where they become exceedingly difficult to question.

The film's opening and closing scenes provide particularly good examples of this. *The*

*Brood* opens with close-up shots of the heads of Raglan and Mike in torturous conversation, both faces starkly delineated against a pitch-black background, and *withholds*, for several shot-countershot sequences, the *context* in which this conversation is taking place—the dark auditorium full of people watching this exchange on a brightly lit stage. The film's final scene shows us Frank, little Candice in his arms, on his way to the car, stumbling through a study in black and white—a forest full of black trees silhouetted darkly against the snowy ground, her white sleep-suit contrasted against his dark silhouette. Only when they escape in the car, brightly lit by streetlights, are we offered the illusion of safety ("emerging into the light") and with it, a "final answer": the close-up of the welts on Candice's arm. Just as the intense focus on Raglan and Mike against an uncompromisingly black background encourages us to ignore the larger context—the fact that this is not therapy for Mike but a demonstration of Raglan's genius—the brightly lit "revelation" of Candice's welts in the final scene encourages us to forget that we have seen these welts on her before. Like slow-reveal scenes, the piece-meal shots of the killer's hand, back and finally face, slow-conceal scenes push us towards black-and-white explanations, persuading us that we understand what we have just seen. In this way, the film diagnoses its viewers with the same disease as that affecting the brood: a distorted and simplified view of the world that leads us to an unquestioning acceptance of whichever solutions suggest themselves first.

*Godsend* (dir. Nick Hamm, 2004) is a tale of warning about the moral pitfalls of human cloning. When Paul (Greg Kinnear) and Jess (Rebecca Romijn) lose their beloved son Adam (Cameron Bright) to a freak accident on the day after his eighth birthday, the scientist *sans* scruples, Dr. Richard Wells (Robert De Niro) promptly appears on the steps of their funeral home and promises to take it all back. Richard is a self-described specialist in "fertility," but a friend of Paul's who has read his work describes him as a specialist in gene mapping, "the stuff of legend … we're talking way ahead of his time … consistently brilliant." Richard is thus identified early as another problematic "genius" who misrepresents his work. In his "Godsend Institute," whose name is at least as ironically suggestive as Dr. Raglan's Somafree Institute of Psychoplasmics, Richard produces a fetus identical to the original Adam by injecting one of Adams's cells into Jess's egg. Since this is profoundly illegal (although not, as Richard keeps insisting, immoral; after all, "we're just using life to create life"), the parents' decision to recreate Adam necessitates a change of identity. Thus they leave their dingy apartment in the dark and dangerous city to move to a much bigger and more elegant house in a squeaky-clean suburban community touted by Richard as "the perfect place to raise a child." For schoolteacher Paul, who has dedicated his career to improving the lives of underprivileged black inner-city kids, this means accepting a much more highly paid job at a tame suburban school where the children are all above average and where teaching, in Paul's description, feels like "teaching fish to swim."

Of course, all these rewards for what is really, in Paul's own view, an act of selling out are too good to be true, and punishment duly arrives. Once the cloned child surpasses the original Adam's life span, the family's Stepford-type existence is at an end. Adam II begins to sleepwalk; he is plagued by nightmares about burning buildings and trapped children as well as waking hallucinations in which he is drowned in the bathtub. It soon emerges that Adam II is channeling not one dead kid but two: the original Adam and an evil boy named Zachary (Devon Bostick), who set fire to both his school and his home, murdered his mother by hitting her on the head with a hammer, antagonized his poor nanny Cora

(Janet Bailey) to the point where she unsuccessfully tried to drown him in his bath, and who, to top it all off, turns out to be Richard's own dead son.

Under the conflicting influences of Adam the victim and Zachary the killer, Adam II wavers between harm and self-harm but ultimately settles on Zachary's murderous personality. He begins by using words like "asswipe" to describe classmates and spitting at teachers, continues by murdering the school bully, and caps his criminal career with an attempt to axe-murder his mother. Richard, who admits mapping Zachary's cells onto Adam I's, thus creating a being with Adam's physical characteristics and Zachary's personality and memory, cites the same reason in his defense as Paul and Jess's: that of a devastated parent unable to accept the death of his child. If Richard the bereaved father briefly manages to capture the audience's pity—"I just wanted him back," he states miserably, a verbatim echo of Jess's and Paul's desperate cries after Adam's death—he instantly loses it again by reverting to his evil scientist persona. Richard defends the indefensible in a conversation that, not coincidentally, takes place in a church. Following this, Richard—now clearly an even more devilish character than Dr. Raglan—knocks Paul down with a candelabra and sets fire to the church. The extras on the DVD version reveal that no fewer than five alternate endings were shot, all condemning as immoral and untenable the scientific illusion that it is possible to simply start over.

*Godsend* not only motivates, once again, the Mad Scientist theme but also, albeit halfheartedly, hints at two alternatives. Both of these paths not taken appear only once and so briefly that viewers could be forgiven for missing them entirely. The first is the simplest alternative to scientific intervention, namely: faith in God, which identifies the "correct" path for bereaved parents as accepting that sometimes The Lord Taketh Away. Two aspects suggest this quite clearly. The first is the highly symbolic meaning of the church in which Richard insists on his right to play God and which he then burns down. Churches tend to play a significant role as symbolic locales in films where science runs amok; they often indicate an alternative path to that of Pure Reason and its dreadful consequences. (The fact that the adults in *Children of the Damned*, in the process of killing the dangerous children, destroy an abandoned (!) church obviously speaks volumes in this context.) The second time in which *Godsend* points to religious faith as an alternative is contained in a brief scene in which Richard explains the difference between a lake and a reservoir to Adam II by saying that a lake is natural whereas a reservoir is man-made. When Adam objects to this rationale—"But I thought God made everything"—Richard cunningly clarifies that, in a way, He did make the reservoir because He made the people who made the reservoir. This is meant to be specious reasoning, of course, an all-too-easy justification of Richard's actions: so long as Richard admits that God made him, his act of "making" Adam does not really usurp the Creator's rights because God, indirectly/through Richard, still made Adam. Similarly, Richard's act of naming his clinic the "Godsend Institute," whose children are man-made rather than "sent" by God, hints at his willingness to use spurious religious arguments to justify "godless" actions.

Much like the alternative of faith in God as opposed to faith in science, the second Path Not Taken is fleetingly mentioned, its significance just as easy to miss. Its brief halflife is limited to the opening scene, before the actual plot even gets underway. Paul, on his way home to Adam's eighth birthday party (Adam will be run over the following day) is mugged by two Black robbers. As one of the muggers holds a knife to Paul's throat, he recognizes him as his ex-biology teacher. He immediately backs off, apologizes and persuades the second mugger to let Paul go because "he was the best teacher I ever had." This scene seems weirdly disconnected from the rest of the film; except in Paul's witty explanation for his late arrival at the party—"Got held up"—it is not referred to again. And yet, like the faith-in-God option, the opening scene indicates a real alternative to what Richard has on offer—love for humanity in general, as opposed to love for a mere individual. Like the mugger who lets Paul go because he knows him to be a good guy, while presumably continuing to rob and brutalize everyone else, Paul and Jess (and also, as it emerges, Richard) are guilty of loving a specific individual too much and humanity not enough. Focusing all love on one individual, the one whose life you spare or, if necessary, recreate, entails losing the ability to see anyone else as an individual, thus reducing all others to the primordial mass that serves only as the mugger's payday or the scientist's raw material. "It was an experiment," Richard explains to Paul. "That experiment failed. We can always terminate and try again" (Fig. 12). The implication is clear: the experiment's success would have to be a perfect replica of the original Adam (for Paul and Jess) or Zachary (for Richard), to them the only human being deserving of life. All other humans are failed experiments who can be terminated without moral qualms. Thus the film identifies the Mad Scientist's, and the desperate parents', constant search for the one perfect human being, and their thoughtless discarding of other humans along the way, as the moral reality behind the illusion of "starting over."

In the end, the film portrays the re-created child as Evil, the scientist as criminally

Fig. 12. "We can always terminate and try again": Dr. Wells (Robert de Niro) and Adam II (Cameron Bright) share an embrace in *Godsend* (2004) (Lionsgate/Photofest).

irresponsible, and the parents as understandably irresponsible, but fails to advocate a clear alternative. The film's passing references to Faith in God and Love for Humanity are promptly and permanently abandoned, as if they were never meant to be noticed, let alone taken seriously. If anything, the film merely shows how impossible it is to extricate itself from the moral dilemma it portrays. Its five alternate endings all spell unmitigated disaster. All five feature the altercation between Paul and Richard in the church (which ends with Richard knocking Paul down with a candelabra and setting fire to the church) and the scene in the shed, in which Adam II/Zachary attempts to axe-murder Jess and is prevented from doing so by either Paul or Richard. Following these events, however, final scenes vary considerably. In Version 1, Richard disappears (a brief shot shows him circling children's obituaries in the newspaper, looking for freshly bereaved parents) while Paul moves his family to yet another house in yet another suburb. Jess, sounding more desperate than optimistic, promises a depressed-looking Adam II that with new friends, he'll get better. Paul, in the film's final line, gives voice to the Great Illusion, which, as the close-up counter-shot of Adam's wretched face documents, is not meant to convince anyone: "This is gonna be great for us. Hey. It's a place we can start all over." In Version 2, the same ending is made more explicit by the addition of a brief scene in which Richard, who was merely seen circling children's obituaries in Ending 1, now approaches another couple on the steps of a funeral home, introducing himself as an expert in fertility and promising to help. In Ending 3, Paul burns to death in the church which is then restored, ironically, by Richard; the final scene makes clear that Adam II has now fully evolved into Zachary, accepting Richard as his father and barely recognizing Jess as his mother. Endings 4 and 5 both call for Paul's survival and Richard's attempt to kill Zachary with a poison vial (his change of motivation remains unexplained in both versions), only to have Zachary turn the deadly syringe on Richard, killing him. Ending 4 then features a ninth birthday party that looks like every child's nightmare: a birthday cake surrounded by two glum-looking parents and five children who clearly want to be somewhere else, all singing list- and tonelessly "Happy Birthday, dear Adam." Ending 5 is the most elaborate: after Zachary/Adam II has killed Richard, Paul and Jess end up in the shed where Paul barely saves Jess from axe-murder at the child's hands. Paul sends Jess out of the shed; she leaves despite the boy's pleas for her to stay but then, realizing what is happening in the shed, runs back screaming a long, drawn out "NOOOOOOO!" The scene dissolves to a close-up of Adam II's tombstone where Jess and Paul lay white roses. The camera pans back to reveal Adam III, upon which the entire family, after a parting glance at the tombstone, drives off in the car. This, perhaps the most sinister of the five endings, is presumably the one in which Paul and Jess have abandoned their last moral scruples, crossing over completely to the dark side advocated by Richard: "The experiment failed. We can always terminate and try again."

*Godsend* clearly attempts to hit both parents and scientists where they live. The scientific method of experimentation, which involves trial and error, is rejected as firmly as the more understandable parental wish: "we just wanted him back." Both science and faith in science fail, along with all attempts at moral justification. When Richard confronts Paul with the seemingly unanswerable validation of gene manipulation: "If I'm not supposed to do this, Paul, then how is it that I can?," the viewer already knows the answer: you actually can't because the result is not the one you desired. It's never the original Adam, a sweet and engaging child, but, instead, a gene-spliced combo of tortured child and murderous monster, not unlike that prototypically created by Dr. Frankenstein. And how do we know that the monster is not the original child? It is not only by looking into the evil child's eyes: Cora, Zachary's nanny, knows him for what he is because "when I looked into those eyes of his, I didn't see anything but evil behind them." But even more tellingly, it is seeing *through* the child's eyes that convinces us of his evil, for the evil child sees the world in black and white. Continuing its strange technique of showing us the most significant inferences only once and fleetingly enough to encourage us to miss them, the film offers us a brief snippet of what the world looks like from the monster's perspective. Adam II, taunted by the school bully, spits hatefully first at him, then at the teacher. As Adam spits at the teacher, the camera jumps, for a split second, into his POV, showing his view of the teacher's face: severely distorted and in black and white. You would think that its very singularity as the film's only black and white shot would make it hard to miss, but the fact that it occurs only once, with lightning speed—now you see it (did you really see it?), now you don't—places it on a level with the discussion of the difference between a lake and a reservoir, or the attack on Paul with which the film opens. The reservoir, the mugging and the evil child's black-and-white vision of the world are all hints whose brevity and incongruity make them easy for audiences to ignore, just as the film's characters ignore them. All three scenes seem strangely untethered from a film that devotes virtually all of its visual, narrative and conversational space to portraying problems without answers: a scientist who mistakes "I can" for "I should"; two parents who confuse their inability to accept the death of a child with love for a child, and, most centrally, the illusion both share—that it is possible, even permissible, to start over.

\* \* \*

That science in a horror flick inevitably leads to disaster is not surprising; the outcome is mandated by the genre. What is, perhaps, surprising is the fact that horror science so often involves children and reverts the symbolic meanings of *both* non-horror science and children into their exact opposites. If science and children in other genres embody hope for the future, both represent, in horror, an image for human lack of control. In horror, the inverse of science is not nature, it is love. Like science, love fails miserably. Both love and science in horror are condemned for their limited scope. Just as love extends only to one particular child, science is conducted for selfish reasons—to advance an individual scientist's career (*The Brood*), to return the scientist's dead child (*Godsend*) or to win the war for one individual nation (*Children of the Damned*).

Because love and science are portrayed as essentially self-centered, both take place behind closed doors. Secrecy is one of the most common points of attack in horror science films. When scientists lock themselves away with their prodigy children (*Children of the Damned*) or prodigy patients (*The Brood*), when they force complete secrecy on their subjects and keep them isolated from the world (*The Brood; Godsend*), this is not necessarily proof of evil intent. It is, however, a sure sign that the horror scientist in question does not intend to place his work at the service of humanity but instead to confer its benefits on a few privileged individuals. The extreme secrecy exercised in all three films points to another common theme: intellectual hubris coupled with a complete abdication of moral responsibility.

Let us return briefly to an idea cited at the outset of this chapter: that horror tends to condemn science whereas science fiction tends to argue in favor of change and progress arrived at through science. A brief glance at a third genre in which science tends to play a starring role, the disaster flick, indicates that in terms of its portrayal of science, horror is the more mainstream genre. Both horror and disaster films start out with one of two possible problems. Either governments, faced with global warming or other forms of imminent apocalypse, refuse to listen to the experts (*The Day After Tomorrow*, 2004), or scientists court disaster by confusing "we can" with "we should" (a lively tradition in Armageddon-flicks since the 1930s). The difference, as already noted, lies in the ending: horror alone refuses to hold out the hope that next time, we'll have learned from our mistakes. Hope in nuclear disaster scenarios is not expressed in the idea of continuity in the face of destruction[16] but its exact *opposite*, the idea of starting over. Learning from one's mistakes does not entail dwelling on them, analyzing them, or even acknowledging them with more than the most cursory of nods. Thus, and oddly, the average disaster movie (*Volcano*, 1997; *The Day After Tomorrow*; *War of the Worlds*, 2005; *Signs*, 2002 and many more) offers an upbeat ending in which the death of billions barely rates a mention. The focus shifts immediately and optimistically to the handful of survivors who have, presumably, profited from these deaths as an object lesson. Having reformed, repented and survived, they lead the considerably reduced but now more robust human race into the next era. Miraculously, "starting over" even holds out the promise of a harmonious equality in the new world that was firmly out of reach in the old. We might think here of the new respect awarded to the homeless Black man Luther (Glenn Plummer), or the Presidential appreciation of Mexico's generosity in opening its borders to U.S. refugees (both in *The Day After Tomorrow*), or the final statement of the rescued little boy (Jared Thorne/Taylor Thorne) in *Volcano*, pointing at whites and blacks covered in volcano ash and exclaiming: "Look at their faces. They all look the same!"

This is precisely the mechanism that horror films attack as the most irresponsible "scientific" idea out there, by stripping it of its false front ("continuity") and showing it for what it is ("starting over"). If the disaster flick's hopeful ending is based on the mere implication, rather than demonstration, that humans have learned from past mistakes, horror films leave no doubt that starting over is, in fact, a *refusal* to learn from the past. The absence of the learning experience is usually demonstrated by the scientist's emphasis on intellectual gains while ignoring the moral dimension. "You think you can just open Pandora's box and then just close it again?," Richard asks Paul contemptuously, voicing the common opinion that ideas, once thought, cannot be retracted and therefore must be used, for good or ill. But if taking it all back is impossible, so is the idea of making progress by starting over. Starting over means, by definition, starting from scratch. It isn't continuity, it's a (vicious) circle. Without building on past experiences and errors, it is impossible to do better next time. Starting over, in fact, negates the very idea of science.

All three films translate the idea of moral blindness into visual or narrative extremes of black and white. Even *Children of the Damned*, a black-and-white film, eschews grayscale in favor of harsh contrast in scenes in which the children confront adults, particularly embassy- or church scenes. *The Brood* and *Godsend*, both color films, use black and white both visually and narratively to express the same idea: a flattening of endless possibilities into one seemingly inescapable alternative. *Either* suffer the little devil *or* terminate the experiment and start over (*Godsend*). *Either* suppress your rage *or* let it out where it can do the most damage (*The Brood*). *Either* kill *or* be killed (*Children of the Damned*). If science, as Carl Sagan once remarked, is much more a way of thinking than a body of knowledge, horror films portray a lamentable state of thought: a world reduced to black-and-white reasoning, a moral quagmire where either-or alternatives trump reflection every time and where there is a maximum of two possible answers to every imaginable question.

## Guilt Trips

### LITTLE HORRORS

*The Children* (dir. Max Kalmanowicz, USA 1980). A leak at a badly maintained nuclear power plant turns all the children in a small U.S. town into murderous nuclear zombies. The film is essentially a series of gory slayings, which the children effect by offering hugs to the adults (who accept every time). The film's *guilt trip* is expressed in three ways: irresponsible parenting (various parents in the film qualify), irresponsible use of science and technology (the plant is run by underpaid techies without any scientific knowledge) and a government cover-up: a news report about the deadly children mentions in passing that the nuclear power plant had to be closed down "in an unrelated incident."

*Demon Seed* (dir. Donald Cammell, USA 1977) tells the tale of an irresponsible scientist who creates a supercomputer and is then unable to control his creation; the computer takes over his role as husband and father by raping his wife and forcing her to give birth. *Fuller discussion in Chapter 1.*

*The Gamma People* (dir. John Gilling, UK 1956). Dr. Bronski, an evil scientist, uses gamma radiation on children to create either super-geniuses or shrivel their brains to the point of imbecility. It is one of the rare horror films that espouses the idea that it's possible to take it all back. At the end, both the scientist and his lab are destroyed, the lid safely slammed shut on Pandora's box.

*Humanoids from the Deep* (dir. Jeff Yonis, USA 1996), a remake of the eponymous Barbara Peeters film (USA 1980), places considerably greater emphasis on ecological issues than its predecessor and thus explains the creation of the humanoid monsters more clearly as resulting from a combination of environmental disaster and misguided experiments. The film features a double twist: it is one of the rare cases where the government is more benign than the thoroughly evil scientist, who, nevertheless, gets away scot-free whereas his "children"/creatures are destroyed. *Guilt trip:* The film portrays pollution not as accidental but intentional, citing bribes at the fishery, chemicals intentionally thrown into the water to increase the size of the fish, and secrecy towards government agencies as the main crimes. "Scientific research" of the more horrible variety is conducted without government permission, including the injection of death-row inmates with salmon DNA in order to create amphibious soldiers.

*The Incredible Two-Headed Transplant* (dir. Anthony M. Lanza, USA 1971). On the absurd assumption that two heads are better than one, Dr. Robert Girard experiments with transplanting two heads onto one body. His human experiment involves transplanting the head of a homicidal maniac onto the body of Danny, a retarded young giant with the mental ability of an eight-year-old. Predictably controlled by the more intelligent part (the maniac), Danny embarks on a killing spree. At the end, the irresponsible scientist, another descendant of Dr. Frankenstein, dies in the process of killing his creation. *Guilt trip:* The scientist robs a "child" of his innocence (and finally, his life), for no loftier purpose than to "show those doctors, those antiquated old men, that I'm doing something with my life."

*It's Alive!* (dir. Larry Cohen, USA 1974); *It Lives Again* (dir. Larry Cohen, USA 1978); *Island of the Alive* (dir. Larry Cohen, USA 1987). The murderous babies are not born naturally but genetically engineered in search of a super-human race able to withstand planetary pollution. The babies are "Superhuman. The beginning of a new race of humanity that will finally eclipse our own. They're the next step forward in evolution. A way in which the human race can survive the pollutions of this planet." *Guilt trip:* Cohen's films focus extensively on the moral dilemma of creation born out of (planetary) destruction and the moral "right" of the babies' creators to destroy them when they turn out to be aggressive. The biggest guilt trip of all is contained in the statement that humans would be more likely to mess with human evolution than adopt the simplest and most effective solution (to stop polluting the planet). *Fuller discussion in Chapter 7.*

*Splice* (dir. Vincenzo Natali, Canada/France 2009). Genetic engineers Clive Nicoli and Elsa Kast hope to achieve fame by successfully splicing together the DNA of different animals to create new hybrid animals for medical use. They create a murderous animal/girl hybrid whom they name Dren and raise as their child. When the splice-child, in a truly Oedipal twist, commits parricide, changes sex and rapes its mother, Elsa, finding herself pregnant from the rape, agrees to the scientific exploitation of the hybrid baby she is expecting. *Guilt trip:* All cooing and soppiness notwithstanding, Elsa's "maternal" insistence to keep rather than kill Dren turns out to be selfishly motivated. Her egotism is on full display at the end, when she decides to give up her unborn for significant financial reward. *Fuller discussion in Chapter 6.*

*The Unborn 1* (dir. Rodman Flender, USA 1991) and *II* (dir. Rick Jacobson, USA 1994) are prototypical films in which an irresponsible scientist engineers murderous babies in an attempt to create a Master Race, in complete disregard for the lives of the mothers. *Fuller discussion in Chapter 1.*

## Teenage Wasteland

*Embryo* (dir. Ralph Nelson, USA 1976). In yet another Frankenstein story, Dr. Holliston decides to experiment with a growth hormone and creates a genius child that grows one year for each day of her life. Victoria develops intellectually far beyond human capacity, but morally and emotionally not at all, becoming a very efficient killer. As cell breakdown sets in, she realizes that her life can only be prolonged by fluid from the pituitary gland of an unborn six-month-old fetus, upon which Victoria proceeds to "harvest" such fetuses via involuntary (on the part of the expecting mothers) caesarian sections. *Guilt trip:* Victoria's murders, while certainly horrible, are ultimately presented as more condonable ("I don't want to kill! I just want to live!") than Holliston's experiment, which is never motivated. As is so often the case, both love and science are presented as entirely selfish. Shortly before her death, Victoria turns out to be pregnant; Holliston, initially perfectly happy to kill both her and her baby ("Die—both of you!") screams in agony when she informs him, with her dying breath, that the fetus is his.

# 5

# Religion
## *The Road to Hell and What It's Paved With*

*"All religions are the same: religion is basically guilt, with different holidays."*
—Cathy Ladman

## *Speaking of the Devil*

Just as the horror genre shows little interest in Good, religious horror proves indifferent to God. Not only does it frequently demote God to god (or gods), it also assigns its starring role to God's principal opponent, in person or by proxy.[1] In fact, demonic possession films have been the genre's mainstay since the runaway success of the three Devil-within classics that are so often identified as cinema's first steps on the road to hell. This Unholy Trinity— Polanski's *Rosemary's Baby* (1968), Friedkin's *The Exorcist* (1973) and Donner's *The Omen* (1976)—are commonly perceived as game-changers in a number of ways. Two of them rank among the biggest money-makers of their time. All three "spawned," to use a word that has become irresistible to writers about religious horror, endless sequels and knockoffs. All three have been variously considered aesthetic Hall-of-Famers, as revolutionizing the horror genre, as the scariest films of all time and as the films that provoked the most extreme audience reactions. And all three have been blamed for both a resurgence of religion in the United States and fresh outbreaks of Satanism.[2]

The majority of these accolades go to *The Exorcist*, which was widely seen, alongside the Church of Satan and the Jesus Freaks, as a sign of its devil-worshipping time. Based on William Peter Blatty's eponymous 1971 novel, itself supposedly inspired by an actual exorcism,[3] the film became somewhat of a watershed moment for real-life exorcists, who came out of the woodwork in droves. In the year of *The Exorcist*, as pastors across the United States based sermons on the film, an Anglican priest in London claimed to have performed more than 2,000 exorcisms in five years. In the year of *The Omen*, an ex–Roman Catholic priest named Malachi Martin published a book called *Hostage to the Devil* (1976), a colorful account of five American possessions and exorcisms. Bob Larson, a freelance exorcist, claimed in 2007 to have performed more than 10,000 exorcisms over the past 30 years, averaging almost one per day, and held a public exorcism during which he attempted to cast out the demon of "teen rebellion" from a pierced goth girl.[4] Hype and hysteria surrounding the Unholy Trinity was apparently enough to convert even the most hard-headed realists, such as the films' producers. The release of *Rosemary's Baby* was accompanied by a flood of vicious hate mail, including death wishes, directed at its producer William Castle; he experienced "some health problems afterwards, and couldn't help wondering about curses."[5] And producer Harvey Bernhard blamed His Satanic Majesty directly for the many problems besetting the filming of *The Omen*: "I really firmly believe that the Devil didn't want us to make the film."[6]

Strange as this may seem in the post–Enlightenment world, the Unholy Trinity occasioned a remarkable upsurge of faith, if not in God, then certainly in the Devil. Ideas advanced in the films—for example, that it is possible to be possessed by and to cast out demons—were widely taken both seriously and literally. The Catholic Church certainly did. Staking its territory, it weighed in heavily on the reception of demonic possession films, praising *The Exorcist* as "a deeply spiritual film" while slapping *Rosemary's Baby* with a "condemned" rating.[7] To a true believer, this would have been no small matter: a "condemned" rating classified viewing the film as a venial sin that could only be expurgated in the confessional.

Such stories impressively demonstrate the ability of religious authorities to guilt-trip the faithful. Guilt trips also loom large in religious horror films, where they often don the guise of a parable, that most quintessential of all religious tales. The result is a story that *seems* to chastise the guilty within the story but whose moral aims the barb of blame directly at the listening or viewing audience. As Father Merrin in the original *Exorcist* already tells us, "the demon's target is not the possessed; it is us ... the observers."[8]

*Rosemary's Baby*, *The Exorcist* and *The Omen* set the stage for what became a lively scene of religious horror cinema. Many of the films in their wake have shaken the dust of the standard demonic possession story off their feet. Yet all replay the old struggle—deities v. demons, Good v. Evil, sin v. crime—with an intense focus on religion's most central theme: guilt. In the following, we will take a detour through more normal manifestations of religious horror, from communions to cults, before returning to a (slightly refurbished) version of the old possession theme.

## Communion *(USA 1976)*, Children of the Corn II: The Final Sacrifice *(USA 1992)*, Sinister *(USA 2012)*

*"The only thing scarier than a redneck with a chainsaw is a redneck with religion."*
—Bernice Murphy, *The Rural Gothic* 81

Set in Paterson, New Jersey, in 1961, the first year in office of the first, and so far only, Catholic U.S. president, *Communion*[9] (dir. Alfred Sole,[10] 1976) centers on Roman Catholic iconography and ideas, particularly guilt, sin, and sacrifice. The film begins and ends with the titular communion. Little Karen Spages (Brooke Shields) is being groomed for her Holy Communion at St. Michael's Church by her divorced mother Catherine (Linda Miller) and Father Tom (Rudolph Willrich), the event's celebrant, who is far too young and good-looking to be a priest. As beautiful little Karen is showered with presents—from her mother, a white lace communion gown and veil; from Father Tom, a precious gold crucifix with personal significance since it belonged to his mother—Catherine's older daughter, morose and mousey Alice (Paula Sheppard) is clearly forgotten. Also unceremoniously cast aside, despite long years of loyal service, is Father Tom's elderly housekeeper Mrs. Tredoni (Mildred Clinton), who loves Father Tom to the point of adulation. Alice's three parents, her mother Catherine, her ersatz-father/Father Tom, and her biological and now remarried father Dom (Niles McMaster), only notice her when she is being bad. And "bad" is Alice's default position; she is sullenly uncommunicative towards her mother and an experienced tormentor of both her little sister and her mother's obese landlord, Mr. Alphonso (Alphonso DeNoble).

Whenever Alice is up to no good, she dons a rubber mask and a yellow rain slicker with the St. Michael's logo. This is also the precise costume worn by the person who murders Karen at her First Communion and tears the precious crucifix off her neck. How desperate Alice is for her mother's and Father's attention becomes clear when she dons a veil and places herself in the midst of the children awaiting their First Communion. Her plan to sneakily commune with God fails, however, because just as Father Tom gets to her (apparently not realizing that it is her rather than her little sister), Karen's body is discovered, to great wailing and breast-beating. Catherine's ex-husband Dom and her sister Annie (Jane Lowry), whose relationship with Alice is one of mutual dislike bordering on hatred and who immediately suspects Alice of Karen's murder, stick around after the funeral to support Catherine in her grief. When Annie is stabbed in the leg by an attacker in a yellow rain slicker and mask, she accuses Alice directly, causing an irreparable rift with Catherine. In the meantime, Annie's severely overweight daughter Angela (Kathy Rich) has disappeared and Alice, under suspicion not only from Annie but also from the police, is sent to a hospital for psychiatric evaluation, including a lie detector test.

Dom, apparently motivated by his rekindled romance with Catherine, is trying to find the real killer to prove Alice's innocence. After a phone call purportedly from Angela, who claims that she has Karen's missing crucifix, he agrees to meet her at an abandoned warehouse, where he encounters not Angela (who, in fact, vanishes from the film without a trace or explanation) but Mrs. Tredoni, clad in a yellow St. Michael's rain slicker and rubber mask identical to Alice's, and ready for action. Mrs. Tredoni wounds Dom with a knife, trusses him up and throws him from a tall platform, ranting about an old sin that apparently also soured relations between Catherine and Annie: namely, that Dom and Catherine ("that whore," in Mrs. Tredoni's lingo) had sex before marriage, producing Alice out of wedlock. Before going over the edge, though, Dom manages to snag Karen's crucifix from Mrs. Tredoni, defying her desperate attempts to get it back by swallowing it. Although it is clear at this point that Mrs. Tredoni killed Karen to punish Catherine for the sin of pre-marital fornication, one last red-herring scene must be endured. Alice, freshly released from the psychiatric clinic, dons her bad-girl outfit of mask and slicker to put cockroaches on Mr. Alphonso's enormous belly as he sleeps (not nice but, in the viewer's mind, entirely justified, since Mr. Alphonso, in a previous scene, harassed her sexually). Shortly thereafter, Mrs. Tredoni arrives in the same get-up with a more dangerous accessory than cockroaches: a paper bag containing a huge kitchen knife with which she plans to slice up Catherine but, surprised by Mr. Alphonso, kills him instead.

At the final Communion scene, Alice and Mrs. Tredoni appear in identical outfits, white lace dresses covered by yellow rain slickers with the St. Michael's logo. Father Tom, finally aware that Mrs. Tredoni has killed Karen and is planning to murder Catherine and

Alice at the service, promises the police that he can talk her out: "I can handle her," he states with characteristically misplaced confidence, "she wouldn't do anything to me." As congregants line up for Communion, he gives the wafer to Catherine but passes over both Alice and Mrs. Tredoni, simply ignoring Alice but telling Mrs. Tredoni explicitly that he cannot give her Communion. Screaming "But you gave it to the whore!" she stabs him in the throat and cradles him lovingly, her face ecstatic as he dies in her arms. The final shot shows Alice leaving the church, unnoticed in the general pandemonium, clutching Mrs. Tredoni's paper bag, tenderly fondling the bloody knife, and looking straight at the camera. And it is *not* a kindly look.

*Communion* practically brims over with references to Catholic saints, customs, doctrine, and imagery comprising statues, veils, communion dresses, and, of course, crosses, from that on top of St. Michael's Church to that ripped from dead Karen's neck. Opening credits roll over images of dolls, crucifixes, chains, candles and veiled girls to the voice-over of a hectically whispered "Hail Mary," finally coming to rest on a girl in a communion dress and veil with a large white candle revealing—as she lifts it—a large butcher knife. If this already indicates a close visual link between Catholic symbolism and murder, the film exacerbates this by its absolute refusal to distinguish between the sacred and the secular. Similar to the statues of Saint Michael, the Virgin and a bloodied Christ looking down impassively at Karen's murder, Alice's excruciatingly ugly doll, which sports a pasty-white face and a mouth opened wide in an anguished scream, is a visual expression of agonizing pain. Such "doubling" is a central visual aspect of the film, which features a number of pairs and look-alikes. Alice, for example, owns a two-headed doll. The film features two extremely obese characters, Annie's daughter Angela and Catherine's landlord Mr. Alphonso. The film's father figures, Karen's spiritual Father Tom and her biological father Dom, are barely distinguished by name. Similarly, mother and daughter names are echoes of each other: Catherine and Karen, Annie and Angela. Both pretty Karen and plain Alice sport the same long straight brown hair and would be indistinguishable from each other if seen from behind (and in fact, Father Tom very nearly offers Alice communion in the first scene, apparently mistaking her for Karen although he is looking straight at her). Catherine and her sister Annie also look so much alike that at least one reviewer kept confusing them.[11] Just like Catherine, Mrs. Tredoni lost her daughter at her First Communion. And of course, the film's biggest red herring, Alice as the killer, hinges centrally on the fact that Alice, the film's bad girl, and Mrs. Tredoni, the film's evil woman, are look-alikes, donning the identical distinctive mask and slicker for their respective misdeeds. It is as if the film undertook to offer a visual reminder of the Catholic principle of Double Effect. This doctrine, first proposed in Thomas Aquinas's *Summa Theologiae* (1265–74) as a justification of homicidal self-defense, states that actions with foreseeably both good and evil effects are nevertheless justified if the following three conditions are met: the nature of the act itself is good; the performer of the act intends the good consequence, not the bad; and the good consequences of the act outweigh the bad. Such rationalization of evil deeds performed with the best intentions is clearly one of the threads weaving its red path through the film.

The film's most central non-acting character and background motivator of much of the action is St. Michael, who not only lends his name to the film's church and distinctive rain slickers, but is also held responsible for the death of children and the recipient of Mrs. Tredoni's prayers as she prepares for her final murderous mission. His role in the film is largely in keeping with his role in Catholic doctrine, which casts him as a warrior angel who leads the Army of God against the Hosts of Hell, and as the Angel of Death, who weighs souls in scales to determine their eligibility for eternal reward or damnation. St. Michael, then, is shorthand for the film's central themes: Death (in this case, murder) masquerading as Judgment (Justice) and the resulting division of souls (people) into what Richard Dawkins has called "in- and out-groups."[12] Catholicism decides who is "in" and who is "out" by recourse to sin (both commission and absolution of), guilt (leading to the seeking of forgiveness and absolution of sins through confession), and public demonstrations of "in-ness" (the most visible and common of which is Holy Communion).

Whereas the film does not distinguish between sacred and secular iconography, it *does* see a clear difference between its two most central concepts, sin on the one hand and guilt on the other. The only character promoting the concept of "sin" is the film's murderess, Mrs. Tredoni. Her understanding of sin harks back to a Catholic ethic that is clearly presented as out of step with audience morality, even that of a 1976 audience steeped in the lore of the Unholy Trinity (the last of these three films, *The Omen*, also appeared in 1976). In Mrs. Tredoni's bizarre religious reasoning, Catherine and Dom are guilty of pre-marital fornication resulting in illegitimate conception (of Alice); later they compound this sin with the sin of divorce (not recognized by the Catholic Church) and, although Mrs. Tredoni remains unaware of this, renewed extra-marital fornication, which also means adultery since Dom remarried following his divorce from Catherine. Sin is also, in Mrs. Tredoni's reasoning, disconnected from guilt. Her central premise, indebted to the Old Testament, is that the sins of the parents are visited upon the children, at least to the second generation. Shortly after murdering Dom, she offers the following explanation for the death of her own daughter: "God took her from me on the day of her first communion. Don't you see? He waited until then to teach me that *children* pay for the sins of their parents." What this reveals, of course, is that Catherine's sin of pre-marital fornication is also Mrs. Tredoni's, and that the death of her own daughter in "retribution," or so she believes, for this sin supplies the logic by which she murders little Karen, the daughter of Catherine the "whore." Lest viewers are tempted to dismiss this as the religious ravings of a crazed old spinster thwarted in love (Hell hath no fury, etc., etc.), the film takes considerable care to establish it as a more mainstream Catholic view by attributing a milder version of it to Annie: Catherine, in one scene, accuses Annie of hating Alice because "you knew I was pregnant when I got married."

Whereas sin is ubiquitous in *Communion*, guilt is nowhere to be found, although various characters have plenty to feel guilty about, most significantly child abuse and child neglect. The scenes in which Alice is ignored as everyone fusses and coos over her pretty sister are among the most painful in the film. As Catherine brings her daughters to Father Tom's house in preparation for Karen's communion, Father Tom gives Karen a hug and a kiss just barely on the right side of avuncular. Alice, on the other hand, does not even rate a Hello. He gives Karen his own mother's valuable crucifix, brushing aside Catherine's protestations with: "Who else would I give it to, Kate?" This not only brings up the question of favoritism—Father Tom has a little congregation of about fifteen children preparing for First Communion; does he shower them all with expensive presents, family heirlooms, tight hugs and kisses? In fact, it goes a good bit beyond that, hinting at a closer personal involvement between Catherine and Tom (or Karen and Tom?) than would be appropriate.

And how does little Karen acknowledge Father Tom's extravagant gift? Rather than thanking him politely, as one might expect from a well-raised little girl, she flings herself into his arms, erupting into a delighted volley of "I love you, Father Tom, I *really* love you!" as Alice looks on enviously, ignored by everyone.

Within the family, too, Alice is either discounted, punished, scolded, or put to work. While Karen gets to preen in front of the mirror with her communion dress and veil, Alice is saddled with chores such as setting the table for dinner and taking the landlord his rent check. Just as Catherine does, her sister Annie, too, seems to mistake her plain child for a servant. When Catherine protests that Annie should go home to take care of her husband and other children, Annie proclaims that "Angela can take care of everything at home." Angela, who is the same age as Alice (12 years and a month, as we are told later), is thus fingered by her own mother as the person who should cook, clean, run the household, and take care of her father and her siblings in her mother's absence. In "normal" life, then, children are subject to neglect; if they do attract adult attention, it is the wrong kind. In one scene, Mr. Alphonso fondles Alice; in another, the detective who strapped Alice up to the lie detector trots out the age-old chestnut that she "wanted it": "She is a weird little girl. Did you notice her tits? When I went to put the tube around her, she looked up at me like she wanted me to feel her up." The main point the film obviously seeks to make is this: guilt attaches to "sins" such as "fornication" that nobody unindoctrinated by faith cares about, but not to actual crimes such as child abuse, child neglect or pedophilia. "Sins" are endlessly discussed, regretted and fretted over throughout the film; to the film's fervently devout, sins apparently still merit the death penalty. But neither parents nor pedophiles experience the slightest twinge of guilt over their mistreatment of the children in their power.

Perhaps in an effort to expose this consummate illogic, *Communion* takes care to link religious and personal rejection, as becomes most apparent in the communion scenes that frame the film. Alice is denied communion in both scenes. When she presents herself for communion in the first scene, Annie angrily goads Catherine: "What is she doing? She's got no business up there! Can't you go get her?" In the final scene, Alice goes over the edge because she offers herself again, in the same fashion—kneeling devoutly, eyes becomingly closed, a little white napkin as symbol of her innocence on her head, tongue stuck out all the way down her chin in pious expectation of the body of Christ—and is passed over yet again. Just like parents and priests, God does not, it seems, love all of his children equally, and Alice, having finally understood this as she leaves the church, inherits both Mrs. Tredoni's sense of outrage and her knife: she is *way* beyond cockroaches now. In the weird world of religious reasoning, we might even suppose that Alice "merits" the mistreatment at the hands of her mother because of her "illegitimate" conception, whereas Karen, conceived in a proper marriage, is the apple of her mother's eye. Out in the real world, we would more likely suppose the exact reverse: that Catherine's anger at Alice for being a constant reminder of her own guilt for the "sin" of fornication ultimately leads her to incur a *real* guilt—that of child abuse and neglect. Consumed by guilt for an imaginary failing, Catherine can, paradoxically, neither feel guilt for her actual crime nor even recognize that she is committing it.

Perhaps the film's most significant anti–Catholic statement is the figure of Mrs. Tredoni, who credits St. Michael with the untimely death of her daughter, commits murder in his name, and prays to him while preparing for slaughter. The scene in which she murders

Fig. 13. Mrs. Tredoni (Mildred Clinton) as a warrior angel, cross-fading into the cross on St. Michael's Church: Catholic iconography linked with murder in *Communion* (1976) (Allied Artist Pictures).

Dom is by far the goriest and also the most traumatic of the film. After he swallows the cross she stole from Karen, which would clearly incriminate her as Karen's killer, she smashes his mouth attempting to retrieve it, screaming that it represents "protection against the snares of the Devil." Her ritualistic murder of Dom is swaddled entirely in traditional Catholic imagery. As she rolls him over the edge, her incantation evokes St. Michael, the warrior angel fighting the forces of hell, in a classic application of "double-effect" thinking that justifies murder if it achieves a greater good: "Cast into hell, Satan and the other evil spirits will roam this Earth, seeking the ruin of souls." As she looks down on Dom's corpse from the height of the platform, church bells begin to ring; the rubber mask which she has pushed up over her head, filmed from below, assumes the appearance of a priest's biretta. With excruciating slowness, the camera ascends from Dom's broken corpse, creeping up the wall until, at long last, it arrives at the platform (Heaven) from which she has cast him down (into Hell). The killer's image, morphed into that of both a priest (through the biretta) and a victorious warrior angel, is finally overlaid with a large crucifix—the slow dissolve into the next scene (Fig. 13). It is, possibly, the most elaborate displacement of religious imagery available on film, linking Catholic iconography as clearly with murder as earlier scenes have linked it with child abuse. Taken as religious justification ("double-effect" thinking), the film unequivocally rejects Mrs. Tredoni's crazed statement that "children pay for the sins of their parents." And yet, the film's final ironic twist of the knife is its endorsement of the same statement as a literal truth: in an abusive family, children pay for the sins of their parents in a far more direct fashion than was ever envisioned by Catholic doctrine.

*Children of the Corn II: The Final Sacrifice* (dir. David Price, 1992) picks up where *Children of the Corn* (dir. Fritz Kiersch, 1984) left off. Following the removal of Isaac and

Malachi, the evil child leaders of the original film's corn cult, the other children re-submit to the more benevolent rule of adults with an audible sigh of relief—or so we are led to believe at the end of *I*. This is the first assumption that *II* dismantles. Clean-up at the outset of *The Final Sacrifice* holds out enticingly the illusion of normality's return, but then promptly taketh it away. Numerous decaying corpses are discovered and removed; the press of the entire nation descends upon the town; and explanations for what happened in Gatlin abound. Here is the sheriff's: "The children came under the influence of several teenagers. The leader of this cult group is Isaac Chroner." This is, of course, the most reassuring option: if all the other children were merely playing "Follow the Leader," the removal of a few bad apples should indeed solve the problem. This, however, is promptly belied by the zombie-like behavior of the surviving children. These are not the happily liberated children who, in the final scenes of *I*, energetically cooperated with adults in their joint destruction of the cornfield. The children at the outset of *II* are possessed of catatonic stares, seemingly unaware of their surroundings and only communicating with others when a reporter shoves a microphone into their faces, which elicits the same monosyllabic response from each child: "I saw the corn." Indeed, the next scene, featuring the same type of radio evangelist screaming fire and brimstone at his listeners, is enough to convince audiences that in the town of Gatlin, nothing much has changed.

The debate to what extent the children are actually at fault for the carnage begins immediately. On one side, claiming that the children are all little monsters, is Mrs. Burke (Marty Terry), the schoolteacher—who, one would think, should know—and, after Mrs. Burke has been dispatched by the children, her sister Mrs. West (also played by Marty Terry). On the other side, advocating the children's innocence based on no evidence other than, well, children just are innocent, is everyone else. Into this debate enter three journalists, an exploitative team of two nameless tabloid journalists who are promptly slaughtered by the monster in the corn, and the film's main character, John Garrett (Terence Knox). John is a reporter with a career gone south and a rebellious teenaged son, Danny (Paul Scherrer), who contemptuously calls him the "ragman." As the Corn Cult starts up again under the leadership of Micah (Ryan Bollman), who is "elected" into this role by being favored with a bolt of electricity from the corn, both John and Danny find love in a small town: John with his landlady Angela (Rosalind Allen), Danny with blonde teen beauty Lacey (Christie Clark). Micah begins a new kid rebellion, murdering first the elderly sisters Mrs. Burke and West (who seem to be the only ones in the town to have the kids' numbers), following this up with the gory murder of the town doctor (Ed Grady) and then dispatching all other adults—save, of course, our heroes John and Angela—by burning down the town hall while they are all assembled there for a meeting.

John's investigation into horrors past and present gets some help from Frank Red Bear (Ned Romero), who, as a Native American and professor of Anthropology at the local university, is both the film's Voice of Reason and representative of an alternative Nature faith. True to both characters, Frank's view of what happened in Gatlin embraces both spiritual and rational arguments. His religious explanation treads a familiar path: the earth is out of balance, is now taking understandable revenge (and by the way, Indians have always predicted this, as you can clearly see from the ancient drawings on this rock). He adds one mysterious particular: a prophecy (more drawings on a rock) claims "that the spirit will open the corn and let through one who finds truth within himself." For those who find all this difficult to swallow, there is also a rational explanation available, which focuses on the familiar profit motive. It turns out that the adults in the town have held back last year's corn harvest, planning to drive up prices. The problem is that the stored old corn has developed a poisonous green mold, the dust of which has blown across the valley and affected everyone living in it. Frank elaborates that this dust can cause madness, particularly in children. The adults, unconcerned about this, are planning to mix the poisoned corn with the new harvest and sell the tainted goods for record prices. Before Frank and John can blow the whole corruption ring wide open, they are caught by the town's sadistic sheriff (Wallace Merck), who plans to murder them by running them over with a corn-cutting machine, compounding audience distaste by proclaiming that "the only good Indian is a dead Indian." John and Frank escape and prevent the children from ritually sacrificing Angela and Lacey in the nick of time. During the rescue operation, Micah is caught in the corn cutter and dies messily—the evil spirit, manifesting itself as blue electricity, leaves him immediately before his death—; Frank is mortally wounded and dies in John's arms. The film ends with the reconciliation of John and his son Danny, who pair off with their respective squeezes (Angela for John, Lacey for Danny) and leave the country behind, returning to New York. In the final scene, Frank returns as a benevolent spirit: he is, as it turns out, the one who has found truth within himself, the one for whom the corn will part, and—we presume—the final sacrifice of the film's title. Before Frank vanishes into thin air, he points out a new Indian drawing on a rock, showing a peaceful cornfield with a wide path through the middle, overlooked by a glorious sun.

*The Final Sacrifice* revels in contradictions that it never deigns to reconcile. For starters, while it indubitably attacks religious fundamentalism as both hypocritical (the adult version) and insane (the kid spin-off), it equally clearly endorses spirituality and the supernatural. The God of the Corn, "He Who Walks Behind the Rows" (from the audience perspective: He Who Scurries Beneath the Earth[13]) is presented as unquestionably real. The movie is replete with POV shots from the monster's perspective, giving us an inhuman view of both the corn, which appears in neon reds, greens and yellows, and human beings, who appear indistinct through tunnel vision. The reality of the monster also manifests itself by the fact that it kills without the aid of the children (the journalist crew early in the film) and that it has the power to enslave hapless children by zapping them with electricity, a form of instant indoctrination that handily substitutes for years of proselytizing. What is more, it is also clear that the monster and the children it enlists into its religious war against the adults are fighting for a just cause, or at least against an unjust one. The adults, driven by nothing loftier than naked greed, are indeed the factor that "defileth the corn," in the most literal fashion imaginable.

All adults in town, with the exception of John (an outsider), Frank (an outsider by virtue of his race and religion), and Angela (also, in her way, an outsider: she has recently moved to Gatlin from the big city), are presented as exceptionally vile. As a community, they are happy to poison both the land and future consumers of their tainted corn. As individuals, they descend to depths of repulsiveness rare even in horror film. There is the vicious sheriff, who practically salivates in anticipation of gruesomely murdering two innocents and defends the poisoning of the corn with a derisive comment on government policies: "Hell, the government's changing their standards to help the economy, so why can't we?" There is the weak-willed town quack, who is portrayed as professionally incompetent and morally spineless; while he alone among the town's adults regrets the communal crime, he mounts no opposition beyond a fatalistic "Oh, Jesus. We have sinned and we're going to hell." And of course, there is the Reverend (John Bennes), who rains hell and damnation on his congregation, with an emphasis on familiar sins: "Fornication. Fornication, my friends, is a pestilence." Whereas the children are possessed by a warped sense of justice, adults are too jaded to even imagine the concept, accepting horror as normality. As one of the journalists remarks cynically, even the wholesale eradication of every adult in the town doesn't make for much of a story: "Buncha kids killed all the adults in town. Just your basic Sunday afternoon in the Bible Belt. ... Well, it's no worse than anything you and I saw at Jonestown."

On the one hand, then, the film doesn't seem to object too much to the Corn God's (children's) project of wiping out Evil in the form of adults. On the other hand, though, there are far too many debates about the children's role in all this—specifically, their guilt or innocence—to just leave it at that, particularly given that these debates are rife with contradictions. For one thing, the most objectionable adults in the town are also the ones who defend the children. Nasty Reverend Hollings preaches incessantly that "The Bible tells us that one must become as a little child to find the path from sin." His point of attack, sex, drugs and rock 'n' roll, is a different one from that of Micah, the nasty preacher in the opposing camp, but in principle, both are entirely agreed that only children are "without corruption, untainted by the poisons of age," just as they agree that before the situation can improve, "the sword of righteousness shall strike down the infidel." Where, in fact, is the difference between adult Christianity and kiddie cult (other than the fact that the children's god, in the film's portrayal, is real, whereas no evidence is offered for the actual existence of the adults' God)? Hollings's repeated insistence on the innocence of the children is presented as just as deluded and just as hypocritical as his fire-and-brimstone sermons. In the scene in which the children burn down the town hall, wiping all adults out in one go (yet again), the film actually discovers its sense of humor. Immediately before the slaughter, the Reverend shouts down a woman for insisting that something is wrong with the children: "to blame every passing affliction on the sweet children of Gatlin, now, it's just not Christian." As the children lock the door and set fire to the building, his tune changes to: "Wait till I get those little bastards! You little shits!"

Given that the film discredits all who believe in the children's innocence, it is rather surprising that it also seems to have no time for the only two people who got it right the first time: Mrs. Burke and later her sister, Mrs. West. Mrs. Burke bases her claim that there is Evil in town and that "It works through the children" on highly disturbing drawings that she saw while teaching them. The truth of this is later borne out when John finds these drawings, which confirm her worst accusations, in the abandoned school. But being right does not garner Mrs. Burke any sympathies. She is presented as hysterical, witch-like, and thoroughly disagreeable. Strangely, this aligns the audience with the opposite view expressed by the much more levelheaded Voices of Reason intoning sagely, "Haven't these children been through enough?"—even in the full awareness that the crazed old hag is absolutely right and the Voices of Reason couldn't be more wrong. The undermining of Mrs. Burke and her unquestionably correct point of view is starkly expressed in the manner of her death. As she crawls underneath her house, which sits on stilts, in search of her lost cat, the children lower the stilts, crushing her beneath. The final image shows her legs sticking out from under the house—a clear allusion to the death of the Wicked Witch of the East in *The Wizard of Oz*—with the children standing around, giggling at her twitching legs. Her sister Mrs. West, whose name already likens her to *Oz*'s other witch, screeches out the same unpopular truth—that the children are evil—and is taken no more seriously. Just as her sister's, her death is too burlesque to garner her the audience's pity: her wheelchair (even her disability somehow fails to improve her standing on the sympathy-meter) is remotely steered by the children to run directly into the path of an oncoming truck which pushes her through the plate-glass window of a bingo parlor. From the wreckage, a man emerges, holding up a card and shouting: "Bingo!"

So what are we to make of a film that presents us with a difference of opinion on a central point, the children's guilt or innocence, only to condemn the wrong opinion and ridicule the correct one? What should we make of a film that portrays a kid campaign against a severe injustice, only to censure *both* the original injustice and the struggle against it? How to read a film that denounces a cult but presents its god as real? Even worse: a film that presents *two* warring religious factions, making it clear that the opposing cult mirrors the original religion to a T, but then refuses to take the logical step—the rejection of all religion—and instead presents us with a *third* religion as the solution to the dilemma? All of these issues are closely linked, and all of them are issues on which the film resolutely refuses to voice an opinion. The extreme similarity between adult Christian fundamentalism and kiddie cult is asserted through identical hateful rhetoric, which, on both sides, boils down to wiping out the infidel. The children, at least, have an excuse, they are *either* (once again, the film leaves us to decide which it is) driven crazy by the corn mold *or* zapped by the strange blue electricity of the Corn God. (Sadly, the film stops short of explaining adult religious fundamentalism by either mold poisoning or demonic possession; religious insanity in adults seems to be "normal": "Just your basic Sunday afternoon in the Bible Belt.") Either solution, though, would define the children as "innocent": whether poisoned or possessed, they are mere mediums, as blameless as Regan in *The Exorcist*.

In the end, the film opts for fighting fire with fire. Consider the following dialogue:

*Frank:* My ancestors believed in a spirit, a spirit of the earth, a god who seeks revenge for the wrongs done to the earth. This is what's happening.
*John:* Bullshit! That's your answer? That God did this? That God's pissed?
*Frank:* You got a better one?

This snippet seems to indicate a way out for a film made in the most devout Western nation on the globe, a country where it would be impolitic, to say the least, to indict religion *per se* (although it is vaguely acceptable to advance some mild criticism of the crazier outgrowths of religion, such as excessive bible-thumping and human sacrifice). After all the film's explicit and implied censure of religious mania, superstition and faith-based evil deeds, *Final Sacrifice*, in this dialogue, seems to come down on the side of a kinder, gentler religion. And if Frank is correct—if all the horrors the film has displayed merely show God's hand at work—we can hardly call it Evil, can we? It is merely good old Mother Earth, in an entirely justifiable act of self-defense (here's double-effect thinking again, justifying evil acts committed with good intentions), warding off further corruption and destruction. To paraphrase another bit of nonsense popular in the Bible Belt, God doesn't kill people; people kill people.[14] Therefore it is also not God but people who are Evil: the sadistic sheriff, the proselytizing preacher, the greedy profiteers of Gatlin Town.

The reason this should sit uncomfortably with viewers is that just as the children's cult mirrors, in rhetoric and outlook, adult religious fundamentalism, Frank's nature religion, while seemingly a much more benevolent model (advocating respect for the Earth and all that), is virtually indistinguishable from the cult beliefs of the children. Like the children (and fundamentalist Christians, for that matter), Frank's ancestors believed in a vengeful God who solves the Earth's problems with a bit of human "cleansing." Cue to a similar sentiment expressed by cult-follower Jedediah (Sean Bridgers), which probably only sounds less reasonable because he is in the process of bashing the doctor's head in while delivering the line: "The earth shall be cleansed of those who poison Earth and its youth. It is written." Like the children's God of the Corn and the Old Testament God, Frank's god seems to call for human sacrifice. Even this loathsome concept is simultaneously rejected—in the horrid scene in which Micah attempts the ritual sacrifice of Angela and Lacey (Fig. 14)—and endorsed: Frank, it turns out, is the Final Sacrifice. He is granted a calmly beautiful death-scene, a dignified non–Christian burial—he is burned on a bed of corn husks—and a resurrection, in full Indian dress, as Frank the Friendly Ghost. He is the object of the prophecy, the one for whom the corn parts because he has found "truth within himself." This, too, seems simultaneously enlightened and regressive. On the one hand, we might read this statement as refreshingly rational—at least Frank did not get his truths from religious indoctrination. On the other hand, we could be forgiven for feeling a bit disenchanted by the film's clear statement that the truth is a lot easier to swallow if it comes from a Wise Old Indian than from a couple of witchlike old hags.[15]

Fig. 14. "Just your basic Sunday afternoon in the Bible Belt": Lacey (Christie Clark) on the cross. Catholic iconography linked with murder in *Children of the Corn II* (1992) (Dimension Films/Photofest).

If human sacrifice, even in Frank's more benign nature religion, is still offered as the cure for all evil, hope resides only in the title's modest adjective "final." But even this is an offer that the film makes only reluctantly and promptly retracts. We might remember here that the reassurance of normality's return at the end of the film is not substantially different from that presented as the great illusion at its outset: "What happened is over, Mrs. Burke, it's over." We might remember John and Danny racing through the cornfield, desperately trying to find the road before the pursuing children catch them, and John's loaded line that, in the end, might be read as referring to more than just corn: "This stuff doesn't end. It doesn't end!" We might also stumble over the fact that although the corn, now haunted by Frank's kindly spirit rather than the evil Corn God, is finally pronounced safe, the surviving adults high-tail it out of there as soon as they can. John, Danny and Angela, all of whom hail from the Big City, and Lacey, who has spent her entire life wanting to go there, are off to New York, leaving Frank in possession of the cornfield and the adult-free town of Gatlin, now populated only by orphaned children, to its own devices. (This flight to the city presents no solution either, as it turns out: in *Children of the Corn III: Urban Harvest*, fresh horrors erupt in Chicago.)

The last scrawny cornstalk the viewer is left clutching is the pathetically perfunctory reconciliation scene between John and Danny, condensed in Danny's hearty clap on John's back and a simple: "You're all right, Dad." We might read this as the film's final statement that the solution to religious insanity and human sacrifice, to all-out war between adults and children, is simply cooperation between the two, a combination of adult responsibility and childlike innocence. We might read it like that, but only if we were an easy-to-please optimist long on credulity, short on memory, and happy to ignore, in favor of this conciliatory minute, two hours of film that have shown us that children are anything but innocent and adults singularly irresponsible.

*Sinister* (dir. Scott Derrickson, 2012) offers a view of religion that leaves human sacrifice and demonic possession in place while deleting God and faith. True-crime writer Ellison Oswalt (Ethan Hawke) moves his wife Tracy (Juliet Rylance) and his children Trevor (Michael Hall D'Addario) and Ashley (Clare Foley) into a house whose last occupants, also a typical American nuclear family of four-to-five, were hung in the back garden, with their youngest daughter Stephanie (Victoria Leigh) mysteriously gone missing on the day of the murders. Ellison's writing career is in tatters; his first book, *Kentucky Blood*, was also his last major success. Tracy, tired of his obsession with violent crime, snaps at him for pursuing it, doesn't want to know the details, and keeps the family and Ellison's work strictly separate. The children are forbidden to enter Ellison's study, where crime scene photos fill the walls "like one of 'em FBI profiler's offices," as the star-struck sheriff's deputy (James Ransone), Ellison's only fan in town, describes it. In the interest of domestic tranquility, Ellison does not tell Tracy that they have moved into a former crime scene. His youngest daughter Ashley, a talented painter, is unhappy about the move and makes Ellison promise to write a good book so they can move back to their old home. Ellison's reception in the new town is hostile, his welcoming committee a sour sheriff (Fred Dalton Thompson) who hates his books, resenting their implicit criticism of the police.

Despite nearly universal disapproval of his project, both from his family and his new community, Ellison embarks on his research. In the attic of his new house, he stumbles over boxes of 8mm film labeled with titles indicating nothing more sinister than old home movies that some other family forgot to move: "Family hanging out, 11"; "Barbecue, 79"; "Pool party, 66"; "Sleepy Time 98." These, however, turn out to be recordings of horrible crimes filmed from the killer's perspective: "Family hanging out, 11" is a recording of the last occupants of Ellison's house being hung in the backyard the previous year (2011). "Barbecue, 79" shows a family being burned alive in their own car; "Pool party, 66" a family strapped tightly onto lounge chairs and dragged into the pool to drown (the quality of the film indicates that 1979 and 1966 respectively would be about the correct age for the footage). "Sleepy Time 98" shows a family tied up in their beds, with the killer making the rounds, training the camera clearly on family members before slashing their throats. In all cases, one child of the murdered family has vanished, with police presuming the child was abducted by the killer. All films indistinctly show a dark, inhuman face expressing the utmost malice, as well as an unknown symbol on doors or walls.

Under the impression of such dreadful images, Ellison disintegrates. He drinks heavily and starts smoking again; his family life deteriorates sharply, with Tracy and the children increasingly distressed (his son Trevor suffers awful night terrors). Ellison hears loud noises from the attic, where he comes across a scorpion, a poisonous snake, and children's drawings showing the murdered families (the different style of the drawings indicate that they were all made by different children) and, on every drawing, a dark figure identified in childish scrawls as "Mr. Boogie." At this point, knowing from the sheriff's hostile reception that he cannot count on cooperation from the police, Ellison contacts the deputy, his one fan, for a bit of unofficial help. While the Deputy is starry-eyed about Ellison, Ellison is so contemptuous of him that he doesn't even trouble himself to remember his name, simply calling him "Deputy So And So" (this is also the name under which he lists the deputy's phone number on his cell phone). Deputy So And So provides him with information on all murders, exact times, dates, places and other significant details, for example that all of the families murdered were drugged before being killed and that none of the missing children were ever found. To help Ellison find out more about the unknown symbol, he also brings him into contact with Professor Jonas (Vincent D'Onofrio), a specialist in the occult and latter-day version of Frank the Wise Indian. Professor Jonas explains that the symbol is associated with the worship of a pagan deity, Bughuul, the Eater of Children, who lures children from their world into his and consumes their souls over time.

Stress mounts both on and off 8mm film. Ellison endures watching another filmed murder scene in which a little boy is run over by a lawnmower. Trevor's night terrors grow worse, as do the hauntings in the attic. Tracy, who has meanwhile found out where they live, pleads with Ellison to abandon the book and move them back home. The poltergeists become visible to the audience, although not to Ellison: they are the missing children from the previous murders, white-faced, horribly decayed, turning towards the camera, asking us, the audience, to keep their secret with index fingers on their lips: "Shhhh." Stephanie, the missing girl from the last murder, turns up in Ashley's room, where Ashley, although knowledge of the crime has been kept from her, has painted the hanging scene on her bedroom wall. Sitting next to Ashley's bed and "shhhh"-ing at the viewer, Stephanie is perfectly visible to both Ashley and the audience, but not to Ellison as he comes in to check on his daughter. The ghost children, defying Ellison's locked study door, turn on the 8mm projector every night. During the final night in the house, Ellison follows the whir of 8mm film to the attic, where he finds the missing children gathered around the projector showing

Bughuul on film; they all turn to Ellison with their index fingers on their lips: "Shhhhh." Ellison, finally properly panicked, burns the 8mm films in the garden. He tells Tracy, awoken by the commotion, to pack up the children, and they leave the house that very night. To Ashley's great joy, they return to their old house; to Tracy's immense relief, Ellison promises to abandon the book.

The following sequence mirrors the opening scene, showing Ellison and his family unpacking boxes and settling in. Ellison declines repeated calls from Deputy So And So but accepts a skype call from Professor Jonas, who contacts him with further information about Bughuul. Bughuul, he explains, was associated with scorpions and snakes, the animals that Ellison found during his early explorations in the attic. Images of Bughuul, the professor continues, are exceedingly rare because early Christians believed that Bughuul lived in the images themselves, which were gateways into his realm, and that he could abduct viewers, particularly children, into the images. Ellison, panicked by this new insight, deletes all images from his investigation from his computer, but to no avail. In his attic, he finds the same box of murder footage that he had burned the previous night, along with an envelope labeled "Extended cut endings." These endings, spliced onto existing reels of film, reveal that the missing children, far from being the victims of abduction, were actually the perpetrators of the crimes. Little Stephanie climbs down the tree from which her family is hanging, playfully grabs her Daddy's still twitching legs for a little swing, and runs towards the camera, index finger on lips: "Shhhh." A little boy turns away from a burning car in which his entire family is twisting in the flames, and looks straight at the viewer, index finger on lips: "Shhhh." Another boy sits at the edge of the pool in which the corpses of his family are visible under water, and turns to the camera, finger on lips: "Shhhh." As Ellison watches all this in mounting distress, Deputy So And So calls with the final piece of the puzzle: each murdered family had just moved from a house where the previous murder had taken place. "The problem is that you moved," he informs Ellison, since by leaving the previous murder scene, Ellison put himself and his family into Bughuul's path.

The remainder of *Sinister* is given over to the inevitable. Ellison discovers foul-looking neon-green sludge in his coffee cup with a note from Ashley beneath it: "Good Night, Daddy." As he collapses foaming at the mouth, Ashley enters, commenting on the footage: "I like that you made the movies longer. They're better this way." The next scene shows Ellison tied up, his mouth duct-taped, Ashley walking towards him with an axe, and turning on the video camera that will film the slaughter. Cut to a confusing montage of her footage: walls streaked with blood, rudimentary drawings in the blood, among them, clearly recognizable, the symbol of the god Bughuul. The camera—not Ashley's but Derrickson's—pans to the end of the hallway where the other children appear, then pans back to reveal that they are merely shown on 8mm film, with our point of view directly aligned with the 8mm projector's. Focus on Ashley's drawing: Trevor, Mom, and Dad hacked apart at the waist and decapitated, with Mr. Boogie off to one side. As Ashley turns her head to watch the 8mm footage of the other children running down the hallway, Bughuul appears behind her, picks her up, steps into the screen showing the 8mm film, and walks down the hall with Ashley in his arms. A new film reel appears in the attic: "House painting '12."

*Sinister* is a highly self-referential film in which images and film perspectives, most centrally POV shots, play the starring role. Much of the film is taken up by 8mm footage of the murders shot from the killers' perspective. *Sinister* could, in fact, be seen as a textbook substantiation for what critics have claimed about POV all along: that it conceals more than it reveals, most significantly, of course, the killer's identity. Beyond that, though, a good deal of the film's eeriness is indebted to its truth-claim, at least on a symbolic and philosophical level, for Professor Jonas's assertion that it is possible to be abducted into an image, especially as a child (is this a criticism of exposing children to film violence, in a film that is itself exceptionally violent?). The world on 8mm film, in other words, is not something that can safely be watched; the fourth wall that normally separates the film's world from the viewer's does not hold. This is the children's secret, the one they share with the viewers of slaughter, swearing them to secrecy—if you stick around and watch, you'll become part of it. The point, clearly a philosophical one, is turned into narrative reality when the god Bughuul, in the final scene, steps into the 8mm footage with Ashley in his arms, leaving us (for the time being, at least) behind in the abattoir that used to be the Oswalt family residence.

The film takes self-referentiality a step or two beyond camera angles, and also beyond its own definition of images and film as the central problem. Additionally, *Sinister* toys with principal assumptions of two neighboring film genres, the haunted house movie and the crime flick. As a haunted-house movie, *Sinister* dismantles that genre's most popular solution. As soon as Ellison has enough information at his disposal, he acts in a way that would, most likely, get him safely out of a generic haunted house. His third disastrous foray into the haunted attic convinces him that he's finally had enough, and he begins to do things right, at least by the standards of the haunted-house flick: he burns the images, packs up his family, abandons the house and the project, and moves back home. None of it is any use. In fact, it is this act of reason and reconciliation with his wife and children that throws the family into the monster's path. As a crime movie, *Sinister* dismantles one of the favorite illusions of the detective genre, namely, that solving the crime achieves closure. In this case, the opposite occurs; the information Ellison (and his audience) are given obscures as much as it explains and does not, in the end, solve anything. At the outset of his investigation, when Ellison (and his audience) know virtually nothing about the case, Ellison innocently jots down two questions in his notebook that turn out to be exactly the right ones: "Who made the film?" and "Where's Stephanie?" The questions are right in the sense that the answer to these very questions will unravel the mystery, but the answer is ultimately worthless since its owner—Ellison himself—turns out to be not detective but merely the latest victim. As such, he is unable to pass on the answer, rendering it useless, a secret: shhhh. What is more, he himself, in his new role as victim, becomes a new question, a fresh mystery recorded on a roll of film in the attic, where the next investigative mind will no doubt stumble upon it.

*Sinister* has no truck with God or faith and thus cannot be considered a religious film in the strictest sense. Its god, Bughuul, the Eater of Children, is presented as indisputably real but has hardly any followers; apparently, it took him decades to acquire his little congregation of five children. That nobody believes in him is, in fact, the secret of his success. And yet, *Sinister* can be said to bring up religious issues in the same way in which religious horror usually does, namely, in its distinction between sin and guilt. The film's definition of sin is, once again, bound up in its self-referential discussion of the power of images, particularly of filmed images. Ellison, that asker of smart questions, directs one at the killer that, yet again, turns out to be right on the money: "Why would you film it?" (Fig. 15).

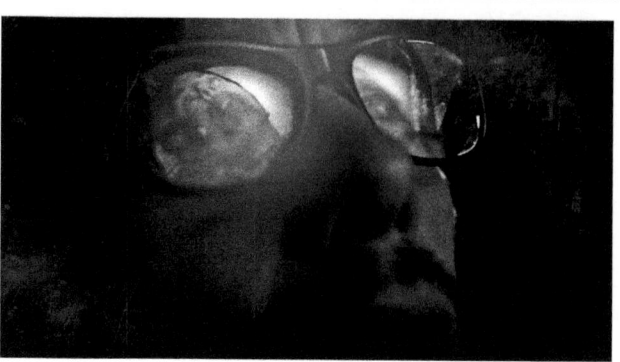

Fig. 15. "Why would you film it?" (And why would you watch it?) Ellison (Ethan Hawke) asking the right questions in *Sinister* (2012) (Summit Entertainment/Photofest).

Given *Sinister*'s self-referential outlook, this begs to be read as a question to horror audiences—why would you want to watch something that is so manifestly unpleasant? But it is also, equally obviously, a theological question pointing at the Christian understanding of the origin of sin: wanting to watch is wanting to see, wanting to *know*. This is also Ellison's sin; he splices the extended cut endings onto the reappeared footage and watches it *despite* having been warned about the power of images, a warning that, as his act of deleting the images from his computer shows, he takes seriously. Nevertheless, he gives in to the temptation to see, and his reasons are really not mysterious. Looking at the apple for too long will eventually seduce you to pluck it from the tree of knowledge and take a hearty bite. Or, in Professor Jonas's shorthand: images have the power to seduce you into their world.

Guilt, conversely, is something else again and, as is so often the case in religious horror movies, only vaguely related to sin. If Ellison "sins" by watching, he does it, at least initially, for motives that most viewers would be likely to accept as valid: because he is writing a book. Ultimately, though, it is this very motive that is being questioned. As Ellison's research materials become increasingly distressing, leading to bouts of drinking, recidivist smoking, and repeated domestic quarrels, he himself begins to wonder whether it is worth enduring all this for the sake of a book. In one of the most significant scenes of the film, Ellison watches a talk show interview with himself, ten years younger, the celebrated author of the hottest true-crime novel of the year, *Kentucky Blood*. Asked what led him to write the book, he jokes: "Fame and money?" but then answers, with a sincerity that has all the authenticity of a three-dollar-bill: "I'm really driven by a sense of injustice." After trotting out all the clichés one would expect at this point (the killer got away; the family deserves to have its story told; least he could do, and so on and so forth), he finishes with a flourish: "I'd rather cut my hands off than write a book for fame or money." Watching this, present-day Ellison shakes his head in profound embarrassment, clearly thinking: "What an asshole." Shortly thereafter, as Tracy begs him tearfully to drop the book, he reveals his true reasons for wanting to write it. This book, he claims, could be huge, bigger than *Kentucky Blood*; "this could be my *In Cold Blood*."[16] But his motive is not to write, as he promised Ashley, "a really good book this time," nor to honor the murdered family by telling their story, nor respect for his readership (his contemptuous moniker "Deputy So And So" for his biggest fan in town puts paid to any illusions we may have harbored on that score). In the conversation with Tracy, he drops all pretense and lays bare what he really wants: "A movie deal, talk show circuit, right? A national book award. More money than we could…" When Tracy interrupts him to say that she does not care about any of that, he counters: "Yes, you do. Everybody does."

The filmed interview with his younger self is clearly meant to offer another example for the idea that it is possible to be seduced into an image, to fall into a film. Ellison is obsessed with the interview, watching it several times throughout the film, almost as frequently as footage of the killings. True horror, to Ellison, is not only contained in the question whether he can ever write a book to rival his earlier runaway success. It is the question how he went from being a cocky bastard swearing (or perhaps, a naïve young writer actually believing) that he'd rather cut his hands off to becoming a greedy bastard who, having abandoned all pretense at loftier motives, freely admits that it's really just about fame and money. True horror, in other words, is guilt.

Arguably, it is Ellison's avarice and selfishness, not the "sin" of watching, for which he is punished at the end. As Ashley hacks off his lower torso, his head, and—of course—his hands, she reassures him: "Don't worry, Daddy. I'll make you famous again." Sin, once again, pales beside guilt, becoming a mere means to an end. Why would you film it? Why, the better to suck you in, my dear—into the image of yourself as a younger, richer, more successful and more idealistic writer, someone who has not yet recognized himself for the selfish jerk he is.

\* \* \*

*"Put the entire town to the torch as a burnt offering to the LORD your God."*
—Deuteronomy 13:16 NLT

While it is difficult to find many commonalities that apply equally to all religious horror movies, one thing seems to emerge quite clearly: most of them voice no opinion on the existence of the God of mainstream religions. In this, they seem out of step with their three great precursors *Rosemary's Baby*, *The Exorcist* and *The Omen*, who, after all, in proposing the absolute reality of a Biblical Devil, can be read as making at least an indirect pitch for the existence of God. (*The Exorcist*, which has been credited with swelling the flock of the faithful, does take the quest for God quite a bit further than either *Baby* or *Omen*.) Although these are usually considered the most influential religious horror films of all time, the movies in their wake have not followed their lead on this central point, deleting both God and the Devil from their cast of characters. Once you subtract these central figures, what is left is puny stand-ins. Demons replace the Devil while a faith both base and baseless substitutes for God. Faith and demonology are moreover barely distinguished from each other, as is apparent in both *Communion* and *The Final Sacrifice*. The latter simply refuses to distinguish between "normal" Christian fundamentalism and the children's crazy cult, assigning to both the same murderous rhetoric of wiping the infidel from the Earth. In the former, Mrs. Tredoni's murder spree is offered in homage to St. Michael, the Angel of Death, but were this not explicitly spelled out, viewers could be forgiven for thinking that her actions were motivated by some insane blood service to a demon (like *Sinister*'s Bughuul).

While God with a capital G is no longer at issue, gods play a significant role in all three films. The Christian God in *Communion* is arguably degraded to the status of a "god" by virtue of the fact that he exists purely in the form of symbols, tradition and ritual worship. Both *Sacrifice* and *Sinister* endow their gods, the god of the corn, the Indian god, and the Babylonian god Bughuul, with a far greater narrative reality. Whereas *Communion*, a direct contemporary of the Unholy Trinity films, exhibits a rather down-to-earth indifference towards the question of God's existence, belief in the supernatural (although not God) makes an emphatic come-back in the later films. This is noteworthy because it has significant consequences for the films' discussion of faith. The carnage in *Communion* can easily be attributed to simple religious delusion. It is more difficult to describe beliefs as deluded when the film, as is the case in both *The Final Sacrifice* and *Sinister*, describe the object of belief—god or gods—as inarguably real. Unsurprisingly, then, both films struggle mightily with the concept of faith. *The Final Sacrifice* settles for, confusingly, ridiculing one faith (that of the adults in the traditional Old Testament God, who is not presented as real), condemning another (the children's faith in the god of corn, who is presented as real) and endorsing a third (Frank's faith in an Indian prophecy that will heal all). *Sinister*, finally, turns the idea of faith on its head: Bughuul can only wreak his devastation because nobody believes in him. Ellison himself is not given the chance to believe, and once he does, it is, of course, too late. In addition, faith in this case depends centrally on knowledge and information, whereas the argument could be made—has been made, in fact, by both the devout and atheists—that faith and knowledge are opposites in terms. To quote the tagline of *The Possession of Joel Delaney* (1972): "If you believe, no explanation is necessary. If you don't believe, no explanation is possible."

All three films endorse Mrs. Tredoni's statement in *Communion* that children pay for the sins of their parents, but not in the way she meant it. In all three films, children are victimized by faith. Just as Mrs. Tredoni's mission of murder is initially directed at and later replicated by a child, the children in *The Final Sacrifice* merely act upon the murderous rhetoric they have learned in the Christian church and at their fundamentalist fathers' knees. *Sinister* offers perhaps the most radical image of this in its definition of god as an eater of children's souls. In all three films, child abuse sets in from the moment of initiation—Holy Communion in *Communion*; initiation rituals in *The Final Sacrifice*, and Stephanie's recruitment of Ashley to Bughuul's service in *Sinister*. It is, at the very least, a persuasive temporal connection that viewers would be hard-pressed not to read as a causal link: abuse happens *because* of faith. In all three films, faith prompts acts that spell a direct reversal of one of the Ten Commandments: *Thou shalt kill* (especially "whores" and their children, see *Communion*). *Thou shalt not honor thy father and thy mother* (in fact, thou shalt burn them in the town hall; see *The Final Sacrifice*). *Thou shalt make unto Thee a graven image* (on film or in blood on the wall, as in *Sinister*).

The solution to the dilemma, however, is not a return to God, traditional Faith, and obedience to the Ten Commandments as originally written. As the films make clear—and in this, all deviate radically from the path indicated by *The Exorcist*—it is not "misguided" faith but faith itself, not believing the wrong thing but believing at all, that leads to slaughter. Even in *Sinister*, Ellison's death follows immediately upon his unraveling of the mystery, which marks also the beginning of his belief in the reality of Bughuul.

In religious horror, slaughter doesn't just happen for the hell of it, so to speak: it is, in fact, the entire *point* of religion. What remains once you remove God and the Devil from the equation is ritual; and once you've made it past the multitude of distracting *images*—from dolls, crucifixes, rosaries, veils and corn puppets to weird symbols left in blood on the walls of crime scenes—religious ritual boils down to human sacrifice. Whether the bodies are offered up to a Christian Archangel, a Corn God, or an obscure Babylonian deity ultimately makes no difference. Unlike the faith principle, which relies on a reversal of Biblical text, the horror film's statement that human sacrifice is at the heart of religion needs no such detour since the idea of sacrifice is enshrined in traditional world religions. The road to heaven (from the true believer's perspective) or hell (from the horror film's) is paved with human bodies. The Old Testament is full of stories of human sacrifice both enacted, like that of Jephthah's unfortunate daughter, and barely averted, like Abraham's near-murder of his son Isaac. Some Orthodox Jews advocate the resumption of ritual (animal) sacrifice even today.[17] Jihadist Islam deifies suicide bombers. Christianity preaches that the Son's sacrifice spells salvation for all. All of this makes sense (if that is what it can be called) because religious faith is the ultimate form of self-subordination, and for no reason that can be explained by Reason. All that religious horror does is take religion not at its word but at its deeds. And thus, in religious horror, all roads lead to the altar on which some victim writhes in expectation of the knife.

If horror film, in singling out the idea of sacrifice, boils religion down to its most destructive, man-hating, child-devouring form, it asks us to see past the words (of, among other things, the Commandments) and consider the deeds committed in the name of faith. It asks us to see past religion's grandiloquent generalities about Humanity's salvation and to judge it based on individual acts committed by its practitioners. In short: it asks us to believe that the devil is in the details.

## Guilt Trips

### LITTLE HORRORS

*Case 39* (dir. Christian Alvart, USA 2009). A social worker rescues a small child, a girl named Lilith (!), from her abusive family and adopts her, only to find out that the child is possessed by a demon. The film's *guilt trip* is clearly focused on issues of child abuse (in the film's most traumatic scene, her parents try to roast little Lilith in the oven) and child neglect. Even when Lilith has come out as a demon and killed a number of people, she still begs for the attention of her adoptive mother: "Don't ignore me. My mother used to ignore me." And: "Come tuck me in." Typically uncertain how to solve the demon-narrative (since a solution for the greater problem it portrays, the issue of child abuse and child neglect, is not on offer), the film presents two alternate endings, a "happy" ending in which the demonic child is killed and a "horror" ending in which she survives.

*The Child* (*Das Kind*, dir. Zsolt Bács, Germany 2012) tells the story of ten-year-old Simon, who becomes convinced that he is the reincarnation of a serial killer. He finds no solace either in religion or in the eventual revelation that all the men he killed were pedophiles. He becomes convinced that he was reborn to kill the one that got away. In the end, Simon turns out to be innocent. The violent fantasies in his head are those of the real killer, who by sheer coincidence occupied the hospital bed next to Simon's and confessed to Simon while he was in a coma. Simon's innocence is expressed in religious terms by turning him into a sacrifice; he is brutalized and nearly murdered by the pedophile he tries to ensnare. *Guilt trip*: The film focuses both on the *absence* of guilt in the guilty and the *mis-assignment* of guilt to the innocent (blaming the victim). Simon, who turns out to be completely innocent—he is not even the serial murderer incarnate—suffers agonies of guilt (as is the case for many victims of pedophilia), whereas the surviving pedophile, who is arrested at the end thanks to Simon's heroic self-sacrifice, is utterly remorseless.

*The Exorcist* (dir. William Friedkin, USA 1973, numerous sequels, remakes, imitations and homages) is perhaps the most important precursor of demonic-possession flicks ever made, inspiring possession movies (and quite possibly possession cases in so-called "real" life) without number. *Guilt trip:* Critics are relatively united in their view that watching scenes of child abuse under the guise of either exorcism or medical "treatment" constitutes one of the film's greatest attractions.

*Frailty* (dir. Bill Paxton, USA 2002). The curse of a father who is divinely inspired to axe-murder several people he mistakes for demons is passed on to both of his sons. The younger accepts his visions as real, the elder does not. The younger son, who even as a little boy willingly participates in the slaughter, eventually follows in his father's footsteps, turning in adulthood into a serial killer known to the police as "the God's Hands-Killer." The twist at the end reveals the father's divine visions as real, vindicating both his and the younger brother's gory slayings. What is more, the older brother, whose rejection of these horrors is initially presented as the only ethical viewer choice, turns out to be the guilty one: he only opposed his father's avenging-angel activities because he himself is a demon. *Guilt Trip:* The film is chock-full of extreme scenes of child abuse, including one harrowing scene in which the father, attempting to bring his rebellious child to God, locks him in a dark basement without food for a week. But all this turns out to be quite all right: what initially appears as religious mania is ultimately endorsed by the film, justifying both murder and child abuse and leaving viewers who cling to traditional morals stranded.

*Manhattan Baby* (dir. Lucio Fulci, Italy 1982) tells the story of little Susie, possessed by an evil spirit residing in an amulet given to her by an eerie old woman on a trip to Egypt. *Guilt trip:* The film is narratively disjointed but extremely explicit in terms of depicting Susie's suffering at the hands of exorcists and doctors in scenes ripped straight from *The Exorcist*.

*The Omen* (dir. Richard Donner, USA 1976, numerous sequels and remakes) is the story of an ambassador and his wife who are raising the Devil's son in their home. *Guilt trip:* The film does the usual depiction of child abuse one better by featuring the father's Abrahamic sacrifice of his son on the altar (here, too, prevented in the nick of time) as the only thinkable "Happy Ending."

*Rosemary's Baby* (dir. Roman Polanski, USA 1968) is one of the earliest and most significant Devil-inside films. *Guilt trip: Rosemary's Baby* can easily be read as a film about a woman who rejects pregnancy and motherhood but has never been offered or been able to imagine an alternative (her professional non-existence is contrasted starkly with her husband's stellar rise as an aspiring actor). She receives no sympathy or support from anyone; in fact, her husband, neighbors and doctor conspire to force her into unwilling motherhood. Scenes showing a desperate Rosemary approaching the cradle with a large carving knife stunningly symbolize the guilt that may be felt by involuntary mothers.

*The Unborn* (dir. David S. Goyer, USA 2009) tells the story of Casey, a young woman who is pregnant with an evil dybbuk, created when the Nazis experimented on her grandmother's twin in Auschwitz and now looking for reincarnation. Her exorcism is a non-denominational affair casting doubt on the efficacy of any religion to aid the afflicted. In the words of the presiding rabbi: "You gotta understand, this thing that's after you, if it exists, it predates religion, probably predates mankind. It's not as if there's one kind of demon that is vulnerable to Jewish prayer, or another that is allergic to Christian or Muslim. It doesn't actually work that way." Whether it works at all is thrown into question in the final scene, which shows Casey pregnant again, ominously with twins. *Guilt trips* abound on every level, from the personal (rejection of the unborn child) to the global (Nazi camp experiments on twin children), with a little aside about the hopelessness of remedies (the exorcism) and the uselessness of religious faith thrown in for good measure.

*Wake Wood* (dir. David Keating, Ireland 2010). A couple unable to accept the death of their daughter beg to have her resurrected for three days by the local shaman in an Irish village. Although little Alice died a year earlier, the parents tell the shaman that the child died recently, thus making her eligible for a temporary visit back on Earth. Of course, Alice, "spoiled" by her too-long sojourn Down Below, returns a monster. She ends up flaying the family dog, killing villagers and dragging her mother to her grave. *Guilt trip*: The film dishes out punishment for individual and communal guilt in equal measure. The parents pay for their selfishness and inability to accept reality while the community is punished for engaging in unholy practices and keeping loathsome secrets.

*Whisper* (dir. Stewart Hendler, USA/Canada 2007) is a film about a little boy who is abducted for ransom to a remote cabin in the woods and who ends up picking off his abductors one by one. David is, as it turns out, a little devil in the very literal sense. The film cites some classics, most prominently Kubrick's *The Shining* (the film features a scene in which a father-figure, armed with an axe, pursues a little boy through a snowy landscape) but also features some unusual twists in the form of role-and-character reversals. The abduction victim is far more evil than his abductors whose crime is motivated by financial hardship; the child's mother is not desperate to have her child saved but to have him killed, and so forth. *Guilt trip*: Unusually, David's possession remains unmotivated either by scientific (as in *Carrie*) or by supernatural or religious explanations. This not only "justifies" whatever is done to him, from maternal rejection to violent abduction, it also pronounces him "guilty" in a weird recourse to religious thinking (David himself clarifies that he is a demon who only possesses those weak enough to let him in).

## Teenage Wasteland

*Abby* (dir. William Girdler, USA 1974): a possession film or a joke? A marriage counselor (!), who is married to a preacher (!!), becomes possessed by an African Demon of Sexuality. *Guilt trip*: I rest my case.

*Carrie* (dir. Brian de Palma, USA 1976; remake dir. Kimberly Peirce, USA 2013) is a classic guilt-tripper featuring a teenaged girl's abuse through religious extremism. Her fundamentalist mother, having lost the battle to home-school Carrie, tries and fails to keep her out of the real world. Carrie's rock is trying to fit in at school; her hard place trying to please her mother.

*The Chosen* (dir. Ben Jehoshua, USA 2015) stars Adam's first wife Lilith as a child-snatching demon and 19-year-old Cameron who, having discovered that Lilith has "chosen" his little niece and can only be appeased by the sacrifice of six other family members, is left to select members of his family for the slaughter. *Guilt trip*: The film moves in a strangely amoral universe. It does not let Cameron (or the viewer) off the hook by off(er)ing only nasty people, but neither does it ever question the need for ritual human sacrifice—including that of several innocents—in the cause of saving an innocent.

*The Crucible* (dir. Nicholas Hytner, USA 1996). Based on Arthur Miller's famous 1952 play, the film tells the story of an entire village driven to religious insanity by the simulated demonic possession of a bunch of (needless to say, female) children. *Guilt trips* abound, from the inane little jealousies that inspire the children to fake their affliction to the moral cowardice of the community that fails to put a stop to the witch craze. Miller's play, and also Hytner's film (for which Miller also wrote the screenplay), mean to be more than a mere reconstruction of the historical Salem witch hunts of the 1690s; they capture a general human propensity for hate-mongering (in Richard Dawkins's words, "in/out-group" thinking) and the most common human response (spinelessness). *The Crucible* is traditionally read as referring both to the Salem witch hunts of the 1690s and to the McCarthyist witch hunts of the 1950s. Miller himself, however, has refused to have it stop there. In a 2003 article in the *New York Times,* Miller cited Danforth's speech in his own play ("You must understand, sir, a person is either with this court or he must be counted against it") in direct allusion to George W. Bush's speech in the U.S. Congress on September 20, 2001 ("Either you are with us, or you are with the terrorists"), commenting: "How many times do we have to indulge the same idiocies for which we must later be ashamed?"[18]

*The Exorcism of Emily Rose* (dir. Scott Derrickson, USA 2005) is a courtroom drama in which a lawyer defends a priest whose exorcism of a 19-year-old girl ended in her death. The lawyer argues, successfully, that Father Moore is not culpable due to his firm belief that Emily Rose could not be exorcised: her possession was a martyrdom, inflicted on her by the Virgin Mary in order to convince the world of the reality of demons. Thus Father Moore is found guilty of negligent homicide but sentenced to time served, which amounts to a compromise position: facts win the case; faith commutes the sentence. *Guilt trip:* The film offers gruesome abuse scenes for the viewer's titillation while contending that faith, even if it results in such horrors, can't be argued with. The story of Emily Rose is based on a German real-life case, a Bavarian girl named Anneliese Michel who died in 1976 during an attempted exorcism. Michel was, at the time, widely suspected of merely mimicking Linda Blair's performance in *The Exorcist*.

*The New Daughter* (dir. Luis Berdejo, USA 2009) tells the tale of a teenaged daughter possessed by the spirits of an Indian burial mound. *Guilt trips* abound in the film: the film's mother has abandoned her two children to live with her lover; the father, following the divorce, has moved them into the immediate vicinity of said burial mound, meaning into trouble. The film's focus on the children's panic that Daddy might leave them too makes it essentially a film about child neglect or at least bad parenting. In terms of parenting, the father hits about 50–50: in extremis he ends up killing his possessed daughter, who pleads with him not to leave her, and himself, thus orphaning his little son. Before crisis arrives, he is presented as well-meaning but disorganized, frequently missing out on such essentials as taking his kids to school on time and providing a school lunch for them. A central snippet of dialogue hints that before Dad became the sole parent, he wasn't even on the scene as a carer. Teen daughter: "How are you gonna do this?" Father: "Do what?" Daughter: "Be our father. You don't have much practice."

*Ruby* (dir. Curtis Harrington, USA 1977) is yet another *Exorcist* imitation, quoting Friedkin's film at times verbatim as 16-year-old Leslie (Ruby's daughter) writhes on the bed, spitting pea soup and speaking in voices. Leslie is possessed by the spirit of her dead father, a mobster executed just as his wife went into labor. The film's *guilt trip* differs in no way from that in other child possession films, offering equal measures of titillation (the joys of watching a devastated child's or teen's body, usually female) and sublimation (pity for the innocent victim, since the possessed—by definition—is always innocent).

# 6

# Consumption
## *Dying in a Material World*

*"Greed, for lack of a better word, is good. Greed is right. Greed works. Greed clarifies, cuts through, and captures, the essence of the evolutionary spirit. Greed ... has marked the upward surge of mankind and greed, you mark my words, will not only save Teldar Paper, but that other malfunctioning corporation called the U.S.A."*
—Gordon Gekko in Wall Street (1987)

## The Land of Unlimited Obligation:
## All We Need Is Love

When Siddharta Shome asked, in the bank-crash year of 2008, "Is Consumption Evil?," theologians, economists, public charities, sociologists, criminologists and religious nuts rushed to answer the question with a resounding yes. This was hardly the first time that consumerism, and the economic structures enabling it, were seen as centrally implicated in ideas of good and evil. The modern economy creates stability (a result we perceive as "good") through an absolute reliance on consumption beyond the bare necessities of life, while simultaneously attributing such over-consumption to greed (commonly viewed as "evil"). Yet greed, as the economy's and thus also the State's essential engine, has had its defenders long before Gordon Gekko glorified it as the savior of "that corporation called the U.S.A." In his 1705 poem "The Fable of the Bees," Bernard Mandeville already cast vice as a recipe for economic success and virtue as the most direct route to poverty and economic collapse, thus becoming the first to invent the idea of "necessary evil." Three hundred years later, most Western societies live by Mandeville's credo that virtue is incompatible with material prosperity. At the same time, they incessantly lament the loss of virtue, most often in denunciations of consumerism and greed.

Excessive consumption is commonly blamed for all sorts of evils, from child labor and environmental damage to union busting and fat-cat controlled politics. Family life suffers: in 2007, Unicef published a report claiming that "materialism has come to dominate family life in Britain as parents 'pointlessly' amass goods for their children to compensate for their long working hours."[1] Social life suffers because consumerism conflicts with efforts to mitigate poverty, ignorance, and social inequality. Personal safety suffers: at least one criminological study called greed "the root of all evil" and concluded that it beats poverty by a mile as a driver of criminality.² And in the realm of religion and superstition, greed features not only as one of the Seven Deadly Sins but as the *original* sin: according to Genesis, evil entered the world through uncontrollable desire for an apple. Even the Evil Eye, one of the most basic elements of witch beliefs, supposedly originated as a designation for greed, a simple transliteration for the act of looking with envy at the possessions of others. Religiously motivated "cures" for greed range from anti-consumerist activism (the Reverend Billy's Church of Stop Shopping) to attempts by televangelists, themselves the epitome of greed, to coax their flocks to spend money on God rather than themselves ("Give God your grocery money!"³).

Yet an argument can be made that particularly in the United States, consumerism is not simply a matter of greed but centrally bound up in America's foundational philosophies, including those of democracy and meritocracy. At its most basic, meritocracy denotes a system in which advancement is based on individual ability or achievement. In the context of American capitalism and individualism, meritocracy has come to imply that wealth—measured by one's ability to consume—equals happiness, that economic success equals virtue, and that each individual has the capacity to overcome any obstacle, given sufficient grit and determination (the latter idea is commonly known as "pulling yourself up by your bootstraps"). The idea of meritocracy is perhaps the most significant psychological by-product of democracy. Alexis de Tocqueville, one of the earliest observers of American society, already noted the devastating effects of democratic expectations in the absence of the material ability to turn them into reality. The dismantling of barriers to expectation in democracies saddled the new democratic citizen with the moral responsibility to achieve the materially unachievable: equality. Subjects of monarchic societies experienced the same inequality as divinely ordained and therefore free from guilt; here, too, de Tocqueville remarked, "One found inequality in society, but men's souls were not degraded thereby."⁴ Like meritocracy itself, the "loser," defined by that peculiar American equation of social failure and moral degeneracy, is a by-product of democracy.

Since the eighteenth century, the equation of material success with personal happiness has gained considerable currency in Western thought. The joys of materialism and the joy of living⁵ became practically interchangeable; at its most basic, the stuff of happiness is just *stuff*. Achieving material success soon came to be seen as far more than a pleasing prospect; it became a measure of human worth. The subtitle of one of the earliest treatises on the subject, Thomas Hunt's 1836 bestseller *The Book of Wealth: In Which It Is Proved from the Bible That It Is the Duty of Every Man to Become Rich*, already points to the basic problem, namely that citizens of meritocracies are faced not with an opportunity but with an obligation. If you can succeed—and the principle of meritocracy claims that everyone can—you must. Every self-help book, every From-Rags-to-Riches-tale, every human-interest story of someone who lost both legs and went on to win a marathon on artificial limbs makes essentially the same point: if you don't succeed, it's nobody's fault but your own. The success of others should not only elicit admiration but, more importantly, an awareness of one's duty to emulate that success or stop complaining. As Michael Young put it 120 years after Hunt: "Today all persons, however humble, know they have had every chance.... Are they not bound to recognize that they have an inferior status, not as in the past because they were denied opportunity, but because they *are* inferior?"⁶

Such absolute reliance on self-help precludes the expectation of help from anyone else, either private persons or the State. This is also the main point of the 1996 U.S. welfare reform bill, tellingly named the Personal Responsibility Act. The personalization of the responsibility for one's own happiness shifts the onus from the state to the individual. The assumption is that the State neither helps nor hinders the pursuit of happiness for whose success or failure the individual alone is accountable. Anthony Robbins's *Awaken the Giant Within*, a manual detailing *How to Take Immediate Control of Your Mental, Emotional, Physical & Financial Destiny!* (1992), tells the standard success story of a fat and lonely janitor who, following the discovery of a mental "power" to turn his life around, transformed himself into a slender happily married multimillionaire in record time. And why, Robbins adds, shouldn't the rest of us be able to do the same, living, as we do, in a free society in which "we all have the capability to carry out our dreams"?[7]

If there is a flawless equation between material success—defined as the ability to consume—and human worth, poverty is a personal failure, not a social problem. A "loser" is someone who fails to understand this and refuses to forge his own success, instead riding on the coattails of others or applying to the State for a "handout." Whatever feelings of inadequacy accompany such failure are also seen as personal, not political. This is a theory upheld even by writers who have recognized the damage that the idea of meritocracy has done to individuals. Alain de Botton, for example, defines the primary challenge of social failure not in economic or social terms—poverty and crime might spring to mind—but in psychological terms, as mere "status anxiety," the main problem being "the challenge that low status poses to a sense of self-respect."[8] Above subsistence level, de Botton insists, all of the trimmings of status—money, success, fame, influence and so forth—are merely means to an end.

The end, of course, is love.

## The Bad Seed *(USA 1956)*, Child's Play *(USA 1988–2004)*, Splice *(Canada/France/USA 2009)*

> *"The bottom line is the bottom line. And what are children, after all, but consumer trainees?"*
> —Sullivan, CEO of Good Guy Toys, *Child's Play 3*

*The Bad Seed* (dir. Mervyn LeRoy, 1956), based on a hit Broadway play whose actors were retained for the film, presents us with a picture-perfect American middle-class family from the 1950s. Daddy, Colonel Kenneth Penmark (William Hopper) has risen high in the U.S. Army and, to top it all off, looks good in uniform. Mommy Christine (Nancy Kelly) is slim and beautiful, keeps a good house and never gets drunk despite downing numerous cocktails throughout the film. Eight-year-old Rhoda (Patty McCormack) is perfection in a small package: adorned with blond pigtails and pretty frocks, she happily skips and tap-dances around the apartment, plays piano, and keeps her room neat without needing to be told. Sweetly loving and obedient towards her parents and respectful towards adults, she even sports an accomplished curtsey, just as if she were a child from the 1890s rather than the 1950s. Add to this an affectionate and garrulous landlady, Mrs. Monica Breedlove (Evelyn Warden), a kindly and formidable grandfather, Richard Bravo (Paul Fix), an entertainingly gawky dogsbody, LeRoy Jessup (Henry Jones), and a concerned and elegantly decked-out schoolteacher, Miss Fern (Joan Croyden), and you have what looks like a family sitcom portraying the comic mishaps that occasionally trouble the suburban idyll, only a stone's throw, perhaps, from *Leave It to Beaver*.

But all is not well in this paradise. At the outset of the film, domestic bliss is ruptured by Kenneth's departure for Washington to prevent the Cold War from turning hot. This provides ample opportunity for extensive hugging and kissing scenes showcasing his loving relationship with both his wife and daughter, but also feeds into the stereotype that as soon as Daddy turns his back, the family falls apart. Rhoda appears initially as a perfect little lady, showered with love, adoration and presents by both her parents and her landlady, whom she calls "Aunt Monica." The one blight on her happiness is having lost out to classmate Claude Daigle for Miss Fern's coveted penmanship medal, and Rhoda's stormy tantrum about this is her first departure from her usual exceptionally proper conduct. Then tragedy intrudes on the suburban idyll: Claude Daigle drowns at a school picnic at the lake; Rhoda was last seen in his company; the medal has inexplicably disappeared. LeRoy begins to hint darkly that he knows what Rhoda has been up to. After a visit from Miss Fern, suspicions mount: Claude's body shows half-moon marks on his forehead and body that are a precise match for the iron-studded shoes Rhoda uses for tap-dancing. Claude's mother Hortense (Eileen Heckart) visits Christine, drunk, tearful and uninvited, in an attempt to speak to Rhoda who, she is convinced, knows more about her son's death than she is telling. Confirmation arrives when Christine, initially defensive of her daughter although horrified at Rhoda's callous response to a classmate's death, finds Claude's penmanship medal in Rhoda's treasure box. Further queries reveal that Rhoda has also killed a former neighbor and that she is planning to murder Mrs. Breedlove to inherit her lovebird, which Mrs. Breedlove has promised to Rhoda in the event of her death. To make Christine's distress complete, she finds out from her beloved father that she was adopted and that her real mother was a serial killer. This leads Christine to suspect that Rhoda has inherited the killer gene from her grandmother. Without revealing her suspicions, Christine seeks confirmation at a dinner party she gives for two specialists in crime psychology, her father and Reginald Tasker (Gage Clarke), a true-crime writer. Opinions are divided: her father considers the nature theory "hogwash," but Tasker tells her that some people are indeed born with a moral blindness: "It's just that they are bad seeds. Plain bad from the beginning. And nothing can change them."

Christine takes this as confirmation of Rhoda's murderous nature, concluding that all the "nurture" that she and Kenneth have offered Rhoda—limitless love, protection and wealth, a wholesome family life, fulfillment of her every wish—will not sway the child from her murderous path. Nevertheless, she loves her daughter too much to turn her in. Christine colludes in Rhoda's attempt to get rid of the murder weapon, the tap dancing shoes, prompted by LeRoy's comment to Rhoda that the police can discover blood even after it's been washed off. When Rhoda tells him that she has thrown the shoes down the incinerator chute, LeRoy, who merely wanted to torment little Miss Perfect, realizes that she has actually committed the crime. He pays for his chance discovery with his life: in one scene we see Rhoda steal some matches; in the next, LeRoy dies horribly in a fire. For Christine, LeRoy's death—his screams from the basement where he is burning are accompanied by Rhoda merrily tinkling on the piano—is the final straw. She feeds Rhoda an overdose of sleeping pills and then shoots herself. Both survive: Monica hears the shot and saves Rhoda; Christine is in intensive care but survives for a loving reunion with Kenneth. The final scene shows Rhoda, fetchingly decked out in a rain slicker, rubber hat and rubber boots, braving a dark stormy night to retrieve Claude's medal, which Christine claimed to have thrown in the lake near the pilings where Claude's body was found. As Rhoda fishes for the medal, she is struck by lightning. This concludes the film's action but not the film: the legend "The End" is immediately followed by another sign reading "One moment, please," announcing that the actors will now take their bows. Last in line is Nancy Kelly (Christine), who, after her bow, looks off-side, grabs Patty McCormack (who played Rhoda), throws her across her knees and spanks her lustily, with "Rhoda" struggling and yelling at the top of her lungs.

Commentators on *The Bad Seed* have been most fascinated with its implicit nature/nurture debate, since this seems to hold the key to Rhoda's murderous character. The film has been slammed for its seeming support for the heredity theory, which directly contradicts research on the impact of social environment on human behavior already available in the 1950s by, among others, William James, B. F. Skinner, and John B. Watson. Some have even linked the film's genetic theories with Nazi eugenics.[9] Compared to this passionate debate, the film's simpler themes of consumerism and greed have largely escaped notice. And yet it is clearly greed, not genetics or even murder, that is the film's main problem.

With the exception of LeRoy's, all murders in the film are motivated by greed, from Rhoda's murders of her former neighbor (for a bauble) and Claude (for the medal) and her planned killing of Mrs. Breedlove (for her lovebird) to the nine murders committed by her grandmother (for life insurance payouts). The "nurture" part of Rhoda's life, her social and family context, is pure perfection and should, in theory at least, have produced an upstanding little citizen. Moreover, since Rhoda is given everything she wants, her murderous greed can't be seen as compensatory, leaving two possible explanations: either greed is in her genetically inherited "nature" or it is simply part of her culture.

Only the "culture" theory explains what both "nature" and "nurture" can't and what would otherwise remain unfathomable: that Rhoda is consistently praised, not admonished, for her relentless acquisitiveness. Showered with presents by her mother, her far-away Dad, and Mrs. Breedlove, she is never shy to ask for more. "How wonderful to meet such a natural little girl," coos Mrs. Breedlove. "She knows what she wants and she asks for it." Later she praises Rhoda for her hoarding behavior: "The darling. She keeps her treasures so carefully. It's a kind of miserly delight." And finally, when Rhoda comments that the iron studding on her tap dancing shoes will make them last longer and thus save money: "Oh, you penurious little sweetheart." Mrs. Breedlove, who reveals herself at every turn as a truly Mandevillian master at turning vices into virtues, delivers these lines in a deadpan fashion that screams for them to be read as parody. But in a world that considers greed natural, that confuses miserliness with care and penuriousness with thrift, the parody falls flat.

The value of possessions, of course, lies primarily in what they stand for. Here's Mrs. Breedlove again, commenting on Rhoda preening in front of the mirror with a pair of rhine-stone studded sunglasses: "My, my, who is this glamorous Hollywood actress?" More valuable than even fame and fortune is the pleasure of glorying in the contrast between one's own superiority and the misery of the Have-Nots, represented in the film by despised dogsbody LeRoy, who sleeps on packaging material behind the basement boiler, and the poor (in every sense) Hortense. When LeRoy tells Rhoda that he did not have picnics as a child, she haughtily replies: "I don't care what you didn't have." Hortense, every bit as resentful of the snootily wealthy as LeRoy, enters Christine's apartment drunk on "half a bottle of bonded corn," as she herself announces, and comments on Christine's well-stocked and much more high-grade liquor cabinet: "Oh, ain't we swank! Really Plaza and Astor!" Unable to confront Christine with what is really bothering her, the suspicion that Rhoda murdered her son, she provokes her by pointing at the difference: "You've always had plenty. You're a superior person. ... Father's rich. Rich Richard Bravo. [*scoffs*] I know. Famous. Me, I worked in a beauty parlor. Miss Fern used to come there. She looks down on me." Despite Christine's pity for Hortense's anguish, the difference between the haves and have-nots precludes every kind of honest exchange, every chance at rapprochement:

> May I call you Christine? Oh, I'm quite aware you come from a higher level of society. You probably made a debut, all that. I always considered Christine a gentle name. Hortense sounds fat. That's me, Hortense.... You're so attractive, Christine. You've got exquisite taste in clothes, but of course, you've got ample money to buy them with.

Hortense lists suspicious circumstances—that Rhoda was last seen with Claude; that Claude's medal could not have come off by accident since she herself pinned it on his shirt securely—but the fact that "You're a superior person and all that" effectively muzzles her, and so she never directly accuses Rhoda of Claude's murder. And yet Hortense becomes the carrier of the film's message that human fellow feeling might be possible in a world not exclusively defined by wealth and class. In the midst of one of her many tirades about Christine's prosperity and "superiority," she looks at Christine, who looks utterly miserable, and stops herself in her tracks: "Say, you're looking kind of sick and sloppy. [*runs to Christine and hugs her*] Why don't you come up to my house, and I'll give you a free beauty treatment? If you're hard pressed for ready cash, it won't cost you a nickel." It is a touching scene of no consequence: two women, one rich, one poor, both mourning their children, in a futile embrace. Where murder is committed for greed, it isn't any easier being the murderer's mother than the victim's. We know, of course, what causes Christine's melancholy, but Hortense, for whom all of life's miseries are inextricably tied to poverty, is unable to imagine any cause for Christine's dejectedness other than a lack of cash. And in a perversely roundabout way, Hortense turns out to be right: at the bottom of Christine's misery is the shock realization that all the wealth in the world cannot turn her genetically predestined daughter from the path of murder. Her question to Tasker, "Do you really mean to say that nice family surroundings and advantages could make no difference at all?," expresses her horror that despite everything society has taught her, money can't buy her a normal, well-adjusted child.

One reason that consumerism in the film inevitably torpedoes feelings, as the futile embrace between Hortense and Christine shows, is that in a consumerist world, feelings themselves are turned into a commodity. Director Mervyn LeRoy considered *The Bad Seed* "a great love story—the greatest I ever made.... It's the love of a mother for a daughter she knows is a sadistic killer. It tears your heart out to see what a mother goes through when she finds out that her only child is a killer—a child she can't stop loving no matter what." And yet, the film consistently portrays love as no more than merchandise, subject to the usual rules of payment and commodity exchange. Richard Bravo tells Christine that he came out ahead in the deal when he adopted her: "You've given me more than I ever gave

Fig. 16. A basket of hugs for a basket of kisses: Rhoda (Patty McCormack) and Christine (Nancy Kelly) engaged in a business transaction in *The Bad Seed* (1956) (Warner Bros./Photofest).

or could ever repay. If you'd been my very own, I couldn't have hoped for more." Rhoda and her parents repeatedly profess their love for each other in the following exchange: "What will you give me for a basket of kisses?"—"I'll give you a basket of hugs" (Fig. 16). That this is not love but a form of inner-family bartering economy is made clear by context; whenever Rhoda is caught in a lie or tries to avoid inconvenient questions about her evil deeds, she inevitably trots out the "basket"-line. This, too, is considered "normal" in a consumerist world. Just as "love" is a bargaining chip that can buy you immunity from parental queries about your latest murder, commodities stand in—ineffectually, to be sure—for the expression of feelings. Consider the following revealing dialogue between Christine and Miss Fern, which ensues when Christine asks Miss Fern why she alone has not been asked to chip in for a flower tribute from the school for the bereaved Hortense:

*Miss Fern:* We thought perhaps you'd like to send flowers individually.
*Christine:* Why should I want to send flowers individually? Rhoda wasn't friendly with the boy, and my husband and I haven't even met the Daigles.
*Miss Fern:* Well, I don't know, my dear, I really...

Miss Fern's implication may appear absurd, but in a world where love and guilt are traded on the same level as commodities, it only makes sense: since Christine is held more accountable for Claude's death than other parents, Christine should damn well acknowledge this responsibility by forking over a bit more for funeral flowers.

The mercantile logic that pays for a human life with a wreath of flowers already hints at the film's ultimate statement that a consumerist society equates people with goods and therefore logically tends to mistake the language of greed for the language of love. "Love" in *The Bad Seed* knows only one expression, a screechy, grasping, insatiable Mine, Mine, Mine that echoes Rhoda's shrieking tantrum when losing out to Claude: "It was mine, the medal was mine!" Mrs. Breedlove on Rhoda, with all the regret of thwarted ownership: "I wish she were mine. Every time I look at her, I wish I had just such a little girl." Rhoda on Christine, with all the pride of ownership: "Oh, I've got the prettiest mother. I've got the nicest mother. That's what I tell everybody. I say I've got the sweetest mother in the world." Christine's shock at the discovery that she was adopted boils down to the horrible realization "that the Daddy that I love so much wasn't really mine." And it is this sense of possessiveness masquerading as love that leads Christine to protect her daughter from exposure by killing her: "Rhoda, you are mine. And I carried you. And I can't let them hurt you … my only child, the one I love."

Yet *The Bad Seed* goes a step further than criticizing consumerism for its confusion of greed and love and its mistaking of people for products. It shows that consumerism ultimately strips people of their humanity and turns them into products. The film's horror is largely contained in Rhoda's gradual exposure first as an "unusual" child, later as a "monstrous" child, and finally as no child at all. Initially, viewers are encouraged to mistake Rhoda for a merely unusual child. Other children, such as those we encounter in the picnic scene, wear blue jeans—which Rhoda eschews because they are not "ladylike"—run around wildly, and have to be admonished not to go near the water. In this raucous crowd, Rhoda, curtseying like the "sweet old-fashioned little dear" she is (Mrs. Breedlove again), sticks out like a sore thumb. A bit further on, we encounter Rhoda as a monstrous child; she is, and this has ever been the hallmark of the monstrous child in horror, both too young and too old for her age. Her tantrums when thwarted in the slightest seem more appropriate for a toddler of two than a child of eight. Conversely, Christine perceives "a mature quality about her that's disturbing in a child," without understanding that in the end, this "maturity" is no more than an alignment of Rhoda's and "normal" adult interests in the ever-greater acquisition, possession and consumption of goods. Finally, we understand that Rhoda is no child at all; she is, in fact, a product—or more precisely, both product and embodiment of a consumerist society. Rhoda, with her sweet and respectful demeanor, her golden braids, feminine frocks, constant curtseys and precociously adult consumerism has simply fashioned herself into the ideal commodity of her time. The problem is not that "nurture" (a supportive environment composed of a good family home, wealth and privilege) has failed to drag Rhoda back from the abyss into which "nature" (a serial killer gene) has flung her. In fact, it is her environment that has produced her: she becomes a monster in order to fulfill a consumerist society's expectation of the perfect child. "Isn't she perfection?," exclaims the ever-effusive Mrs. Breedlove, sardonically uttering the film's most damning statement, since "perfection" can only be achieved by turning what might have been a person into a conformist product. A society that admires such perfection is one that privileges products over people, one that is both productive and inhumane, and incurable either by divine lightning or a good spanking.

*Child's Play* (dir. Tom Holland, 1988) is possibly the decade's most biting attack on American consumerism. Little Andy Barclay (Alex Vincent) is already an accomplished consumer at age five. He wears Good Guy pajamas, watches Good Guy TV shows, eats Good Guy cereal, and works on a Good Guy workbench with a Good Guy toolbox. And of course he simply *must* have that Good Guy doll, although his widowed mother Karen (Catherine Hicks) can barely afford it. Andy is duly punished for his greed when his doll turns out to be possessed by the spirit of a dead serial killer (Brad Dourif), who offs, indiscriminately, good people (Karen's best friend-in-need Maggie, played by Dinah Manoff), baddies (the criminal Eddie Caputo, played by Neil Giuntoli), and any number of people who just happen to be in the wrong place at the wrong time. Chucky's ultimate objective is to use his knowledge of voodoo magic to transfer the serial killer's soul from the doll to Andy's body, and he proves astonishingly resourceful, resilient, and, in terms of both story and cinematography, gratingly, perkily *present*. All five Chucky films feature numerous lengthy Chucky POVs, mostly stalker shots.[10] This doll certainly has perspective. The films' decision to foist it on the viewer with maddening regularity can stand as a sign for Chucky's staggering vivaciousness, which belies the adult illusion that he is just a doll and is further emphasized by the fact—also in all five films—that he is exceedingly hard to kill. It practically takes a village to do the job. In *1*'s final sequence, Karen, Andy and no fewer than two cops gang up on a doll the size of a two-year-old child, who is burned, stabbed, shot and dismembered but still keeps coming. He'll be back in four sequels, despite being shot, stabbed, decapitated, dismembered, exploded, buried, vaporized, and melted down in one sequel or another. As Chucky himself, about to be dispatched at the end of *Bride of Chucky* (dir. Ronny Yu, 1998), quips: "Go ahead and shoot. I'll be back! I always come back!" (Fig. 17).

Chucky's incredible resilience and his infinite thirst for blood—in *Seed of Chucky*, his doll and moll Tiffany (Jennifer Tilly) identifies it as an addiction and enters a 12-step program—can both be read as a parody on the never-ending hunger for stuff. Consumerism is as rapacious as Chucky and has at least as many teeth. Like Chucky, like addiction, it never lets you go; it never stops; it never even slows down, and there is no escaping its perspective. In terms of plot, Chucky's evil is individual; symbolically speaking, its name is Legion. Good Guy dolls are everywhere. In *1*, we see several in the arms of children at Andy's daycare center. In *2* (dir. John Lafia, 1990), whose final fight to the death takes place in a Good Guy doll factory and features tens of thousands of them—rows upon rows, skyscraper-high—Andy is hit by one falling from the shelf as soon as he opens the closet in his room at his foster parents'

Fig. 17. "I'll be back!" An indestructible little bastard in *Child's Play* (1988) (United Artists/Photofest).

home. *3* (dir. Jack Bender, 1991) opens with a Play Pals Toys corporation board meeting, in which the decision is made to restart manufacture and sale of Good Guy dolls, since before the serial murders and resulting bad publicity, they out-sold all the other toys produced by the company by a factor of two to one. While Chucky's murderous rampage is fictional, the Good Guy fad depicted in all three films is "based on a true story," the Cabbage Patch doll craze. Despite their inflated price tag of about $50, Cabbage Patch dolls proved all the rage of the early to mid–1980s, when insufficient supplies resulted in several full-scale consumer riots and vibrant black market trading. This is also the mise-en-scène of the original *Child's Play*: Andy's mother Karen, a department store salesperson, cannot afford the $100 price tag for a Good Guy doll and ends up buying one from a homeless peddler in an alleyway.

Karen and Andy are not well off, as numerous markers in the film indicate. They live in an apartment (not a house). Karen commutes to work by bus (she does not own a car). She keeps the heat low, even in winter (her friend Maggie is seen shivering in a thick cardigan in Karen's apartment). Karen has to scrimp and save to buy her son clothes, a disappointing birthday gift for a kid who has just turned six, but Karen does not have the funds for both clothes and toys. She is completely at the mercy of her boss, who forces her to take late shifts and threatens her with dismissal when she protests that it is her son's birthday. But all this is genteel, middle-class penury and exploitation; there is worse. Once the rampage has begun, Karen, in an attempt to find out where the murderous doll has come from, goes looking for the peddler who sold her the doll, braving a broken-down neighborhood full of abandoned houses, where the homeless and hungry gather around garbage can fires to keep warm in Chicago's bitter nighttime cold. Of course this makes an even sharper economic point than Karen's already reduced circumstances: it constitutes a direct comment on the absurdity and immorality of middle-class consumerism in a society that elects not to feed its hungry or house its homeless.

This attack rests on two arguments, both of which we've already seen at work in *The Bad Seed*: the crass contrasts between the Haves and Have-Nots, and the redefinition of feelings (love, friendship) as commodities. What you're buying when you enter the Play Pals Toystore to buy a Good Guy—nomen, in this case, is hardly omen, but of course it's meant to be—is a friend. Here is the TV show advertising Good Guys and seen by Andy, as the film makes clear, dozens of times:

> *Dejected-looking little boy*: I have no friends. No one will play with me.
> *Red-headed doll descending from a hot-air balloon*: Uh-oh. There's a friend in need. Hey, cheer up!
> *Little boy*: Who are you?
> *Doll*: I'm a Good Guy. I've just come from the Good Guy Clubhouse. And I'll be your friend to the end.
> *Boy*: You will? You mean you'll be my friend now?
> *Doll*: Sure I will.
> *Both*: Hi-de-ho, hahaha!
> *In the background, a chorus of children sing a jingle promising "friendship to the end."*

Like Cabbage Patch dolls, which came with their own individual birth certificates, Good Guys are explicitly designed to mimic individuality because this is seen as a prerequisite for friendship: "Every Good Guy has a name all his own, so he can be your very own best friend." And what kid doesn't want, or need, a best friend? Friendship is a bestseller;

there's a real gap in the market there. Good Guys outsell every other toy by a factor of two to one. They come with pre-programmed sentences—"Hi, I'm [insert 'individual' name here], and I'm your friend to the end!"—and an uncanny ability to hijack a child's fantasy life. What is being marketed is not a doll but an imaginary friend, in the full awareness that small children don't distinguish between imaginary and real friends. No wonder that Andy, whose profound need for a friend would not have been served by a mere doll, is deeply unsurprised when Chucky turns out to be alive. And no wonder that he is deeply surprised when he tells adults that Chucky is alive and is accused of making up stories.

*Child's Play* is at its most aching in the scenes in which Andy's flawed perception (Chucky is not, in fact, his friend) clashes with that of adults (Chucky is not, in fact, just a doll). When Andy is unfairly blamed for Chucky's minor misdeeds, like turning on the TV and saying nasty things, he does what any child would do: he rats out Chucky, who is, in his perception, another child. Of course he is promptly dressed down for lying. One interesting aspect of Andy's misperception of the doll is that he cannot distinguish between the living Chucky, who speaks in the killer's deep and husky voice, and the doll Chucky, whose three pre-programmed sentences are in a much higher cutesy child-register. That the doll's program-voice is just as real to Andy as Chucky's/the killer's human voice is shown in one of the many scenes in which Andy unsuccessfully tries to convince his mother that Chucky is alive. After making him promise not to make up stories anymore, Karen puts Andy and Chucky to bed, but listens at the door after closing it. She hears Andy tell Chucky, with profound sadness: "She didn't believe me." Chucky is about to answer, but then, seeing shadows of Karen's feet right outside the door, merely turns on the doll's recording: "Hi, I like to be hugged!" Andy's tired reply: "Good. I'd love to hug you too." And then he does.

The film's most heartbreaking statement is that Andy gets something from Chucky that he cannot get from adults. In another wrenching scene, Andy loses his illusion that Chucky is his friend, without being able to disabuse the adults of their illusion that Chucky is just a doll:

> *Karen (to Andy)*: Nobody believes you about Chucky. Unless you start telling the truth, right now, they're going to take you away from me.
> *Andy:* You hear that, Chucky? They're taking me away unless you say something. Please, say something! Come on, Chucky, say something! Tell me why you lied to me about everything!
> …
> *Chucky recording.* Hi, I'm Chucky, and I'm your friend to the end. Hi-de-ho! Hahaha!
> *Andy, disgusted, punches Chucky in the belly.*

This is a child's trauma on display: in addition to having been betrayed by someone he mistook for a friend, he is now threatened with the loss of his mother for telling the truth. Sequels will confirm the worst. Once Karen understands that Chucky is alive and backs up Andy's statements, she is put into psychiatric care; Andy ends up in a number of foster homes and ultimately in a military academy, where he is remanded for juvenile delinquency. The first three films all offer a qualified "happy ending" by killing Chucky in ever-more-spectacular ways, but do nothing to mitigate the immense sadness of Andy's life, which is in effect destroyed by consumerism. The most devastating aspect of the *Child's Play* franchise is its repeated display of a small boy, who has been taught to tell the truth and obeys to the letter, abandoned and disbelieved by everyone. Andy is in a bind: if he lies (by agreeing that Chucky is nothing but a doll), he will be accepted by adults but exposed to mortal danger from Chucky. If he tells the truth—and after all, his only chance at safety is to convince the adults that Chucky is alive, armed and dangerous—he is ridiculed, admonished, separated from his mother, and put "away," first into psychiatric care (in *1*), later into foster homes (*2*), finally into a military school (*3*). The only person on his side is his mother, and look where she ends up. Where is the reward for love, loyalty and honesty? The end of *2* offers viewers the satisfaction of a spectacular explosion wiping Chucky from the face of the earth (until he is revived in *3*) but is unable to provide a Happy Ending for Andy and his new friend Kyle, also a child raised in foster homes without number:

*Andy:* Where are we going?
*Kyle:* Home.
*Andy:* Where's home?
*Kyle:* Andy, I have no idea.[11]

The original's ending is hardly more cheery. Yes, Chucky is dead (until his revival in *2*), and yes, satisfaction can be had from the lovingly slow camera sweeps relishing the wreckage, the disgusting bloody and burned body parts strewn everywhere that once made up one vivacious killer doll. But not for Andy. He is alone in the room, looking at Chucky's shattered remains with abject sadness. His mother comes to drag him off, but he leaves with great reluctance, looking back at Chucky. The film closes with a still of his face through the half-open door, looking back, his face a landscape of sorrow. What Andy feels is neither elation at his victory, nor relief at his narrow escape, nor the viewer's childish satisfaction at the mess that is left of Chucky, but something much more adult: grief at the loss of a friend. That the friendship was never real to begin with is both the main point and beside the point. In a consumerist society, where feelings are salable commodities, the distinction between "real" and "commercially fabricated" is immaterial. (Real people don't really do any better for Andy than that damned doll.)

And what, at the end of the day, is the difference between real feelings and commercially produced ones, or between real people and dolls? If *The Bad Seed* shows us a human being transformed into a product, *Child's Play* displays the reverse process—a product becoming a person. As the voodoo Doctor Death (Raymond Oliver) explains to Chucky, he has a problem: "The more time you spend in that body, the more human you become." "More human" means, among other things, vulnerable, mortal, and, at least in theory—if he weren't such an utter shit—eligible for friendship. Doctor Death tells Karen that Chucky can only be killed by a stab to the heart because his heart is almost human (in *Bride*, a repairman opens up the Tiffany-doll's battery compartment to reveal, to his horror, a living, pulsing human heart). This may appear as practical forensic advice, but beneath it, something else resonates: Chucky is a killer doll with a real heart—more heart, perhaps, than the average consumer who thinks nothing of stepping over homeless people on their way to the next department store. When it comes to humanity, humans struggle to outdo dolls. In *Seed*, Chucky will have a family life (if a somewhat dysfunctional one) whereas Andy's already truncated family (his father is dead at the outset of *1*)—is torn apart. *Seed* is also where the Pinocchio sub-narrative of the franchise is finally played out: Chucky's wife Tiffany and his kid Glen (Billy Boyd) turn into actual human beings, while Chucky, who is not prepared to deal with old age, erectile dysfunction and incontinence (and, we might suspect, prison or the death penalty for his many murders), chooses to remain a doll. Does that make him less human? It is also significant that both *Bride* and *Seed*, which move the franchise distinctly in the direction of comedy horror, abandon the consumerism critique, whereas the first three, whose main theme is consumerism, never quite manage the leap from horror to horror spoof. It is as if the films' every attempt to make a mockery of absurd transformation—a murderer's transfer-by-voodoo into a doll that then, paradoxically, becomes more and more human—falls flat in the face of their serious charge leveled at the intentional inauthenticity of feelings and the inhumanity of humans. Turning feelings into commodities, people into products (*The Bad Seed*) and products into people (*Child's Play*) is not voodoo magic but the ordinary alchemy of consumerism.

*Splice* (dir. Vincenzo Natali, 2009) opens with the POV of a child about to be born. Intra-uterine shots of a developing fetus give way to a race down a tunnel that ends in a blinding white light and a first glance at two concerned doctors. The newborn goes into cardiac arrest and has its heart restarted, then it/we see the lid of the incubator shutting it (us) in. This is the most common use of POV, the purpose being to withhold information from viewers by limiting their vision to that of the object to be identified. Which turns out, in this case, not to be a baby but a commodity: two large and slimy white worms with a protruding penis or tail, one male, one female, whom the scientists who lab-engineered the monsters call "cute" and name Ginger and Fred. The scientists, a young hipster couple who love a good pun, wear geeky T-shirts and live in an apartment stuffed with books and Japanese cartoon art, initially seem parent-material, although we soon get the idea that Elsa (Sarah Polley) rather than Clive (Adrien Brody) wears the pants both in the lab and at home. Elsa and Clive are under contract at Newstead, a corporation that bankrolls a lab whose name is itself a hipster joke: NERD (Nucleic Exchange Research and Development).

So far, the film seems to be heading for the standard struggle between idealistic scientists who work for the betterment of humanity and greedy corporations (or governments, or the military) that exploit their work for profit. Newstead supports Elsa's and Clive's scientific research into human/animal gene splicing, potentially leading to cures for every human affliction under the sun from Alzheimer's to cancer, in exchange for their development of medicinal proteins for livestock. Although Elsa and Clive are scientific superstars (they appear on the cover of *Wired*, a major geek magazine), they are slaves to Newstead, which owns all of their patents. The first rift between the science team and the corporate bosses arises when Elsa and Clive are ordered to abandon their research into human/animal gene splicing, along with all of its grandiose medical possibilities, in favor of taking the livestock protein to "the product stage." They respond to this by secretly continuing their research and eventually successfully splice a human gene with an animal's, thus creating Dren (Delphine Chanéac), whose name—another geeky pun—is the lab's name in reverse.

Dren, who at birth looks like a little monster inspired by Ridley Scott's baby alien, grows at vastly accelerated speed into a young girl with a bald head, widely spaced eyes, arms that end in four-finger hands, much stronger kangaroo-style legs, and a long tail ending in a vicious stinger. Clive, who has been opposed to letting the experiment grow to parturition stage, wants to kill it, but Elsa refuses categorically. Later we will find out why: the human part of Dren came not, as Elsa has claimed, from a Jane Doe, but from herself, so that Dren is partly Elsa's daughter. Elsa, more than Clive, treats her as such; she plays with her, feeds her, gives her the Barbie doll with which she herself played as a child, puts dresses on her, teaches her to read, and nurses her when sick. All the while, Clive and Elsa continue to monitor Dren's development—whether as scientists or parents is unclear at this stage—which turns out to be unpredictable. When Dren falls seriously ill, they try to cure her high fever by putting her into a cold bath. Dren thrashes around wildly, at which point Clive decides to take advantage of the situation and drown her. Dren appears to die, but then begins to breathe under water, responding to mortal danger by spontaneously growing amphibious lungs. Elsa, not understanding either this or that Clive tried to kill Dren, thanks him effusively for noticing that Dren has amphibious lungs, thus saving Dren's life by putting her under water. This is the point at which Clive is pushed irrevocably into the father role.

Their focus diverted by parental duties, Elsa and Clive take their eyes off the company's prize. They delegate all work on the protein carriers Ginger and Fred to Clive's already overworked brother Gavin (Brandon McGibbon) and thus fail to notice that Ginger has turned into a male. At a public presentation of Ginger and Fred to a vast audience of dignitaries and corporate sponsors, catastrophe ensues. Just as Elsa introduces the worm pair as "Adam and Eve, coming together to enact Nature's timeless story of love," Fred and now-male Ginger tear each other to pieces in their glass cage, which explodes to spray the horrified audience with glass, blood, and bits of shredded monster. Following this PR calamity, Newstead's funder Joan Chorot (Simona Maicanescu) forbids Elsa and Clive categorically to work on anything other than the marketable protein. Elsa and Clive, who now lose their unmonitored lab space in which they've hidden Dren, move her to Elsa's parental and now abandoned farm. But Dren grows moody, bored and aggressive: she escapes into the woods, where Elsa and Clive find her tearing a rabbit apart with her teeth; she spells "tedious" and "outside" on the scrabble board; she breaks a window and climbs onto the barn roof, where she spontaneously grows wings just as she is about to fall off the roof.

Elsa, now saddled not with a cute kid but a difficult teen, continues to neglect her work at the lab, instead playing with Dren and introducing her to makeup. But it soon emerges that Elsa is a capricious mother, only interested in motherhood if the child responds only with love, and love only for her. Clive, who belatedly discovers an urge to bond, teaches a blissfully happy Dren to dance but abruptly breaks off the encounter when he realizes that he is getting too close to Dren. When Elsa finds pictures Dren has drawn of Clive but, apparently, none of her, she jealously removes Dren's beloved pet cat, pretending that she is worried about allergies. Later, she returns it to curry favor with Dren, but Dren kills the cat, threatens Elsa with her stinger and attempts to escape from the barn. Elsa hits her over the head with a shovel and turns her back into an experiment: Dren, she suddenly decides, is no longer her daughter. Taking a leaf from the medical annals of human experiments at Auschwitz, she ties the desperately mewling Dren to a table, cuts her dress off her, tape-records her clinical observations on Dren's distress (she now refers to Dren by her experiment marker, H-50), and amputates her stinger as Dren screams in agony. She also extracts from Dren a far more powerful protein than Fred and Ginger ever had, synthesizes it and deposits it at the lab. Meanwhile Clive, horrified at Elsa's mistreatment of Dren, oversteps the bounds of pity; his attempts to comfort her turn into a sexual encounter, during which Dren, in two nicely symbolic moves, spreads her wings wide and regrows her stinger. Elsa surprises them during sex and rushes off, followed by a desperate Clive. In the ensuing exchange, Elsa tells him that their careers could be saved thanks to the protein extracted from Dren; all they have to do to start over is kill and bury Dren. They return to the barn to do this, but find Dren already dying; at her deathbed, they become caring parents again. After Dren's death, they bury her with the Barbie doll; during cleanup, Elsa finds several pictures Dren did, in fact, draw of her.

Immediately after Dren's hasty interment behind the barn, Gavin and Barlow (David Hewlett), a Newstead manager, arrive to find the human source of the protein, accusing Elsa and Clive of violations of company policy and scientific integrity. Both are murdered by Dren, who has transmuted into a male and dug himself out of his shallow grave. The male and much more demonic-looking Dren has developed the power of speech. He rapes Elsa and kills Clive when he tries to save her. Elsa kills Dren by hitting him on the head with a shovel. In the final scene, Elsa is back at corporate headquarters, selling the fetus she has conceived in the rape to Newstead's CEO Joan Chorot for lavish compensation. The film's final diegetic sound is the heartbeat of Elsa's human/alien fetus.

*Splice* parts ways with the usual juxtaposition between idealistic scientists and moneygrubbing corporate exploiters of their work. Elsa and Clive are shown as mercenaries from the very start. The star scientists on the cover of a major magazine, they've tasted too much fame to allow it to slip away. Their funder Joan Chorot, a mercenary bitch if ever there was one, assumes, as viewers would initially, that the scientists' motives are idealistic, and dangles a carrot under their noses: "You put a viable livestock product on the shelves, then we will talk about a 20-year plan to save the world." In a consumer society, science beneficial to humans is a sideline to be possibly explored in a few decades, but profits always come first. In point of fact, though, Clive and Elsa don't protest too much because their interest in serving humanity comes a distant second to their interest in furthering their careers. They trot out the save-the-planet line whenever they need an argument for funders or a balm for their own conscience, but actually continue with their controversial (not to mention illegal) gene splicing experiment because, as Elsa puts it, "*Wired* doesn't interview losers." They bend the laws of science and morality by splitting hairs as well as genes. When Clive points out to Elsa that allowing Dren to be born as an independent being is illegal, she corrects him: "Human cloning is illegal. This won't be human, not entirely." Elsa breaks another cardinal rule of scientific professionalism when she uses her own egg for the experiment. Both approach their work with breathtaking arrogance, joking about splicing dogs and ponies when a company contact asks them to prepare for the dog-and-pony show to introduce Fred and Ginger to the public. Elsa's recurring line throughout the film, "What's the worst that can happen?," shows that she is always willing to brush aside the consequences of her work like a pesky fly (Fig. 18).

Clive and Elsa are portrayed as Jack and Jill of all of their roles but master and mistress of none. They make crap parents[12]: Clive, for much of the film, refuses to be involved and then has "incestuous" sex with Dren; Elsa's behavior towards Dren is a textbook example of bait and switch. They also make crap scientists; distracted by their alternating roles as distressed parents or scientific superstars, they miss much. Their first big oversight, that their creation Ginger has undergone a spontaneous sex change, leads to the gross-out PR scene. But severe oversights happen not only when Clive and Elsa take their eyes off the prize, as they did with Fred and Ginger, but also when they don't. Despite their close observation of Dren, they miss the elementary fact that Dren's near-fatal episodes are not death or near-death experiences but mutations. This happens soon after birth, when she goes

Fig. 18. "What's the worst that can happen?" Dren (Delphine Chaneac) threatens Elsa (Sarah Polley) with her deadly stinger in *Splice* (2009) (Warner Bros./Photofest).

into cardiac arrest and then restarts her own heartbeat, again when Clive attempts to drown her and she grows amphibious lungs in response, and a third time when she grows wings spontaneously to save herself from a fall off the roof. And yet, when Dren appears to die yet again, Clive and Elsa bury her, misreading as death what is actually her final transformation into a male. Science is supposed to explore the unknown and expect the unexpected, but Clive and Elsa don't even notice a development in Dren that they should, by now, both know about and expect—after all, they've seen it before, repeatedly.

Clive and Elsa's portrayal as incompetent parents, incompetent scientists, and relentless spotlight seekers spells not only the deletion of the science flick's age-old struggle between scientific idealism and corporate greed. More significantly, it implies that in a mercenary world ruled by the profit motive, responsible, competent and beneficial science (and perhaps also parenting) has become impossible. In the end, Clive's and Elsa's personal and professional failings don't actually matter all that much. Even as model scientists and human beings they would find it impossible to extricate themselves from the perfect trap laid for them by corporate greed. Science without funding will go nowhere, and the funders of science are only interested in science as a cash cow. "If we don't start projecting profits, big profits, soon," Barlow tells Clive, "Newstead's in serious trouble. We need capitalization if we're gonna keep moving forward." This is the mechanism that defines everyone in the film as either a product (Dren, Fred and Ginger) or as an exploiter of a product for profit (Elsa, Clive, the company and its funders). Alternative identifications (a "child," a "human being," a "parent," a "scientist") occasionally raise their timid voices but struggle to be heard.

The entire film revolves around such fluctuating identities and identifications. For much of the film, it is unclear, to the scientists as well as viewers, who or what Dren is: she mutates constantly, from slithering little monster to something that incorporates human physical and emotional attributes, from female to male. Clive refers to Dren, throughout much of the film, as "it"; Elsa refers to Dren as "she." Rather far along in their caring relationship with Dren, it becomes clear that Clive considers Dren a "pet" whereas Elsa considers Dren a "girl." Whatever Dren is, she can be turned back into an experiment and a product at any time, a reversal that both Elsa and Clive perform with sickening ease. Elsa discovers her inner Dr. Mengele, torturing and maiming Dren, unmoved by Dren's distressing cries and palpable fear. And as soon as Clive understands that his career could be saved by the very lucrative protein they extracted from Dren—after all, that is all the company wants from them—he is willing to kill a being with whom he had sex just a few hours earlier. All it takes to convince yourself that you're not murdering a living being is a bit of redefinition, both of Dren and of the idea of human and scientific responsibility. "Experiment's over," he says. "Our responsibility is to end it." Within two short sentences, Dren is stripped of her various human roles as a child or a lover and turned into a commodity. This, clearly, is meant to horrify the audience: we don't know either to what extent Dren is "human," but certainly she is someone who played with toys, giggled, danced, pouted, had tantrums, associated, experienced sickness, distress and fear, related to her "parents," loved a cat, and loved a man.

Dren changes regularly—from female to male, from air-breathing to amphibious, from amphibious to bird-like, and she is regularly redefined—from experiment to pet to child and back to experiment. But this fluctuating view of Dren is unrelated to her physical mutations. Rather, it is determined by the one constant, the one that supersedes all others: seeing Dren not as a person but as a product makes it possible to define her in whatever terms will serve the profit motive best at any given moment. If Dren undergoes frequent physical changes, Clive and Elsa do the same on a mental and emotional plane, switching roles—from scientists to parents to torturers to careerists—whenever the situation requires it, just as Dren grows amphibious lungs or wings precisely when she needs them. Scenes in which Clive and Elsa appear as genuinely caring parents are juxtaposed with others showing the brittleness of their relationship with their "child." There is, for instance, the cat episode, in which Elsa punishes Dren for her seemingly greater love for Clive. There is the sex scene, in which Clive turns from father figure to lover in a matter of minutes. There is that most wrenching scene of all, in which Elsa and Clive decide to remove the "evidence" (Dren). The film's point is not only that the profit motive rules all; it goes a step further by showing that there never really was a clear distinction between Clive's and Elsa's various roles as parents, scientists, or mercenary exploiters/potential killers, just as there is no discernible difference between people and products.

This point is made both at the film's beginning and at its end. In the first scene, Clive and Elsa look down on their latest experiment (or product) and behave not like scientists or product developers but like parents: "It's so cute," Elsa coos, looking at a slimy mess that is decidedly unlikely to inspire similar feelings in the viewer. In the final scene, the reverse applies: a highly pregnant Elsa does not behave like a mother but like someone with a commodity to sell. Her buyer, Chorot, finally puts science resolutely in its place, that of a profit generator: "We'll be filing patents for years." Elsa, too, is extravagantly compensated for turning another child into a product: "We think the figure that we've come up with is very generous." Right before the deal is struck, there is, for one last time, a brief and hesitant consideration of an alternative identity. Taking a step back from her gleeful anticipation of vast profits, Chorot considers the possibility that whatever Elsa is carrying might not be only a money-spinner but a baby. She offers Elsa a way out, telling her she would not be blamed if she changed her mind about giving up her child. But Elsa responds with her usual consequences-be-damned question: "What's the worst that could happen?," a question to which, following the murder of Clive and two other people, she should surely know the answer. When the film closes with an amplification of the heartbeat of Elsa's unborn, replicating the opening scene that accompanied the fetus's POV with its loud heartbeat, we understand that the story has come full circle, and that the cycle is eternal and immutable—another something that might have been a person is being turned into a commodity. Like Elsa, like Chorot, we don't know what Elsa is carrying. But whether monster, child or hybrid, we do know that it is a product, its future as profit-making merchandise set in stone before birth. This is the first rule of mercenary societies: whatever else it is and whatever else it might have been, it is always, first and foremost, a commodity, and this, then, becomes the most basic definition not only of humanity, but also of what scientists used to call "life."

* * *

> You are nothing unless you have everything: that was modernity. Modernity was the shifting of the leverage point of capitalism from production to consumption, from necessity to wish. ... It was in this sense that the situationists, like Harold Rosenberg and the Frankfurt School critics, liked to speak of the paradox of the "proletarianization of the world." They meant that when political economy dominates life, it turns everyone, the worker who has been made over into a consumer, the bourgeois who already was one, into a sort of proletarian, a mute object in the face of the talking thing: the "humanism of the commodity" means that the commodity becomes human as the human becomes a commodity.[13]

This is how Greil Marcus, in his Sex Pistols–inspired art history of the twentieth century, has described the essence of modernity. Humans become a commodity (cue *The Bad Seed*); the commodity becomes human (cue *Child's Play*), or—see *Splice*—we vacillate between one and the other, depending on which view serves the profit motive best. Horror is not merely talking about a figure of speech that might understand "proletarianization" as a process in which people, metaphorically speaking, become "slaves" to things. Horror is talking, quite literally, about the dehumanization of the human and the humanization of the product, the human's "thinginess" ("a mute object") and the commodity's vitality ("the talking thing"). In a world where being and having are consistently confused, where "you are nothing unless you have everything," all things that used to exist in the realm of simply "being"—such as love and friendship—lose this essential existence and become commodities, things that can be "had." All we need is love, the song says, and so says therapy, advertising, self-help literature, and every kind of commercial enterprise. When we need love (or friendship, or motherhood), we just close our eyes and buy it, like little Andy, or grow it in a lab, like Clive and Elsa.

Horror's take on consumerism does more than trot out the usual critique that we all consume too much, and that we'd all be so much more human if we just stopped it—like the family at the end of *Poltergeist*, thinking they can solve their problems by kicking their TV to the curb. Instead, horror portrays the profound confusion that has arisen in the consumerist age between people and things. Children turn themselves into product, dolls turn into people, and lab experiments turn into children, or vice versa, as dictated by the bottom line. In the age of consumerism, horror tells us, we wouldn't know a human being if one hit us in the face. This is not—and this is where the family in *Poltergeist* has it all wrong—a personal problem but a global one. It is, as Marcus has said, the essence of modernity.

Horror's understanding of this is the point where we can credit the genre with taking a step beyond its usual tales of personal terror that might or might not carry meaning beyond themselves. In revealing consumerism as a universal horror that creates a society where the distinction between having and being, between humans and things, no longer makes sense, horror has gone global. If consumerist horror focuses on the social and economic, we will encounter similar ideas about politics in the next chapter, where films take child abuse out of the family home and redefine it as a global horror with immense political consequences.

## Guilt Trips

### LITTLE HORRORS

*The Amityville Horror* (dir. Stuart Rosenberg, USA 1979; remake dir. Andrew Douglas, USA 2005). *Child's Play* all over again, but as big as a house: George and Margot simply *must* have that house although they can barely afford it, and are punished for their greed when it turns out to be haunted. Their family nearly falls apart in it, just as the family who lived there before them did. The 2005 remake is an exacerbation of the original. Its pre-story is more explicit; it is made clearer that the house is financially far out of the family's reach; and the relationship between the family father and the children is more fraught. *Guilt trip* (with a broader dimension): The family is blamed not only for personal greed and privileging stuff over people (their children), but for buying unthinkingly into the American Dream. Pre-disaster conversation: Margot: "This is the life we want." George: "She's happy. I'm broke. ... We've got the American Dream here. There's no way in Hell I'm gonna let it get away." Post-disaster conversation: Margot: "We stay here, we'll have a house and a family, only there won't *be* a family." George, sarcastically: "Home, sweet home."

*Children of the Corn* (the franchise, USA 1984–2009) deserves an honorable mention here. In the 1984 original, the children kill all adults in their farming community for using harmful pesticides and thus "defiling the corn." *Guilt trips:* All *Corn* films attack corporate greed in a serious way, occasionally showing—as *2* does—that the plans of the evil community (or, in later films, corporations), if successfully carried out, would cost many more lives than a bunch of evil children occasionally sacrificing people in the cornfield. *Fuller discussion in Chapter 5.*

*Devil Doll* (dir. Lindsay Shonteff, UK 1964). The Great Vorelli, a hypnotist, uses his dummy Hugo, containing the soul of one of his murder victims, to commit murder and to swindle an heiress out of her millions. Hugo is Chucky's forebear in more ways than one: Vorelli plans to kill Hugo because "you've been in your little wooden body for so long you're becoming an individual again. I think I must teach you a lesson." In the ensuing struggle, Vorelli's soul ends up in the doll's body. *Guilt trip:* The film works extensively with appearance and reality, casting Hugo as the film's "evil": "it walks, it talks, it sees, it kills"; but in the end unmasking him merely as a "plaything of the devil" to reveal the much greater evil (universal greed) behind the doll.

*Gremlins* (dir. Joe Dante, USA 1984) is a tale of capitalism run amok. The Gremlins initially look like a mix of cuddly pets and adorable babies, but when fed at the wrong time, they fall upon food like vultures and promptly turn into murderous little monsters. *Guilt trip:* Gremlins are an all-too-obvious metaphor for greed, transformed from cuddly toys into miniature killers—quite literally—by consumption. *Gremlins* is a Christmas movie and practically overflows with references to presents and useless stuff sitting around the house (the family father is a none-too-competent inventor). The original's final scene is played out in a Department Store, the Emporium of Stuff. The trailer for *2: The New Batch* (dir. Joe Dante, USA 1990) assumes that consumerism is incurable: "We told you... but you didn't listen."

*Poltergeist* (dir. Tobe Hooper, USA 1982) portrays the American Dream in the form of a couch potato family glued to the TV in a wealthy suburb in sunny California. Five-year-old Carol Anne is constantly exposed to inappropriate TV (including, in one scene, an ultraviolent war film). Finally, what she calls "the TV people" enter the family home and wreck it, beginning by moving things around in the home and ending by abducting Carol Anne. *Guilt Trip:* The film assumes that when you watch TV, something more than just images ends up in your living room—a perfect image for consumer manipulation through advertising. The film's family and, by extension, the viewer, is blamed for sacrificing traditional values (in this case, respect for the dead) to satisfy their consumerism (a swimming pool next to a big house in which the TV is never off).

### TEENAGE WASTELAND

*Hostel* (dir. Eli Roth, USA 2005) is the story of three American backpackers heading to the Slovak city of Bratislava in search of sex and drugs. The film features a child gang who is repeatedly shown robbing tourists (the film's main torturer and evil guy tells one American that children commit most crimes in Eastern Europe). Once arrived at what they think is a sex paradise, the backpackers find they have been sold to an organization called "Elite Hunting," which sells tourists to ultra-rich sadists who then torture them to death. *Guilt trip:* The idea of human beings as commodities for sale is first proposed in a "normal" and "acceptable" manner (the backpackers' plan to buy the bodies of "hot" girls) and then thought through to its logical and gruesome conclusion. Crime is the city's principal economy and portrayed as universal; adults (both the backpackers and the torturers and murderers) trade in human flesh while children hold tourists up for bubblegum and money.

# 7

# Abuse
### *Leaving the Family Behind*

*"What happens in the family stays in the family."*
—Popular balderdash

*"We already live on the planet of war, we already live on the red planet, and it's a war against children. All the other wars are just the shadows of the war on children."*
—Stefan Molyneux

## Child Abuse Goes Global

The idea that child abuse is perpetrated primarily within the family and has consequences only for the victim's ability to form personal attachments in later life is long past its sell-by date. Some forms of what we commonly understand as "child abuse" begin at home and radiate out from there. The link between child abuse in the family and violent crime has been copiously studied, so that we now have a mountain of evidence for the social cost of what happened, once upon a time, behind closed doors. A study of 50 serial killers showed that a significant percentage had been physically (36 percent), sexually (26 percent) and psychologically abused (50 percent) in childhood.[1] A smaller study conducted by psychologist Kathleen Heide found that where children kill parents, they do so almost always in self-defense or in revenge for abuse.[2] And there is increasing evidence that abused children not only strike back but also lash out. Sexual abusers aged ten or younger are, in the words of Nina Lakhani, "invariably born into families in which abuse, violence and neglect has become routine."

"Routine" also seems to be the operating word in terms of popular responses to the problem. In 1993, the murder of British toddler James Bulger at the hands of two then ten-year-olds excited universal horror, trauma and front-page coverage spanning years, even decades. Today, not even a school shooting would rate such attention, and your garden-variety preteen torture killer is lucky to make it onto page 14.[3] This does not necessarily mean that there are now more of them. It does seem to indicate, however, that both violent children and abused children have a far greater presence in public perception than they did twenty-some-odd years ago, and what the discussion has gained in breadth, it seems to have conceded in shock value. Both violent children and child abuse are staple topics of horror film and owe a considerable share of their increased social visibility to the genre.

Horror's treatment of these two related subjects is a fraught and contradictory affair, and this goes double for horror films depicting evil children. If the abused child on screen is "evil," are viewers encouraged to see the abuse as objectionable or condonable? Consider, again, the case of *The Exorcist*'s Regan, surely horror's poster-child for physical, emotional, and psychological abuse. One wouldn't think it possible to create a scenario in which Joe and Jane Moviegoer might approve of a trained boxer punching a 12-year-old girl full in the face, but *The Exorcist* had them cheering at the scene. As it turns out, this scene was not a fluke but a harbinger. William Paul has offered an entire catalogue of modern horror movie traditions portraying child abuse as justified and urging viewer approval.[4] Children are defined as Evil Personified, and Evil manifests itself by virtue of the fact that they appear as either too young or too old for their actual age (or, in some cases, both at the same time). Audiences are encouraged to find pleasure in both the children's evil deeds and in their ultimate punishment. Certainly, a case can be made for this: many films discussed in this book (and all films discussed in the Family chapter) could easily be accused of such tactics.

And yet horror has also advanced a highly critical view of child abuse, one that moreover portrays the issue not merely as a familial but as a global problem. In some films abuse starts in the family but becomes society's problem, as is the case in *Carrie*, in which a teen subjected to extreme levels of abuse at home and bullying at school pays back her entire community, with interest. Other films, not content to bother with small-time stuff like families, schools and individual motives, start out with the global view. Narciso Ibáñez Serrador's rather ironically titled *¿Quién puede matar a un niño?* (1976), variously translated as *Who Can Kill a Child*, *Would You Kill a Child?*, *Could You Kill a Child?*, and (of course) *Island of the Damned*, tells the bog-standard child gang horror story. A British couple arrives on a small island off the coast of Spain, planning to spend their vacation there, only to find the island ominously deserted. After their shock discovery that the entire adult population has been murdered by the island's children, for reasons that remain unexplained, they fall victim to the killer kid gang themselves. The questions the film raises are not addressed by its story but by eight minutes of documentary footage that precedes it and answers, above all, the film's title question, *Who can kill a child?* The footage shows twentieth-century atrocities perpetrated against children in Auschwitz, India, Pakistan, Korea, Vietnam, and Nigeria. Each segment is incongruously separated by a brief audio-only snippet of children singing and giggling, and overlaid with statistical data showing the number of children killed in whatever war, genocide or ethnic cleansing is currently on display: 14 million children in the Second World War, the total death toll of which has been estimated at 60 million; 1.2 million children—out of a total death toll of two million people—in the Indo-Pakistani war; over half a million children—out of a death toll of 1.2 million people—in the Korean War; 1.8 million children out of a total death toll of three million people in Vietnam; 390,000 children out of a death toll of half a million people in Biafra. More often than not, then, the statistical survival rate for adults in war, including that of soldiers in combat, is higher than that of children. A Unicef report published in October 2014 estimated that a child is killed by violence every five minutes.[5] While the child gang's motivation in Serrador's film remains obscure without this documentary prequel, its inclusion defines the film as a revenge flick (and, needless to say, a guilt trip) on a grand scale.

Many horror films take child abuse out of the family home and place it squarely onto the world stage. Child abuse in these films is not personal but political, not individual but global—a planetary war on children in which, by commission or omission, we all participate.

## It's Alive (1, 2, 3, USA 1974–87), The Ring (1, 2, USA/Japan 2002–05), The White Ribbon (Austria/Germany 2009)

> *"It's alive, and it's out to get us."*
> —James B. Twitchell, Dreadful Pleasures 301

Larry Cohen's *Alive* films (*It's Alive*, 1974; *It Lives Again*, 1978; *Island of the Alive*, 1987) have been showered with praise, even numbered "among the most humane and progressive of all horror films."[6] With some variations and elaborations as the series progresses, all three films tell a similar tale: murderous mutant babies, endowed with claws, fangs and remarkable aggressiveness, are born into wholesome white middle-class American families. As the U.S. establishment (the government, the courts, the police, the press, the universities, medical science and pharmaceutical companies) gang up on the malformed babies in an attempt to exploit them, experiment on them, or simply kill them, the parents must choose to side either with their offspring or with their society. Both stances vie for audience sympathies, since the babies can be read either as indiscriminately killing monsters or as persecuted infants acting instinctually and in self-defense. Family feeling, while constantly evoked in all films, is portrayed as underdeveloped and undermined by societal intrusion: in more than one film, the little monsters either kill their own parents or are, however reluctantly, killed by them.

All three films focus largely on society's attitude towards the mutant babies, which is portrayed as fantastically vicious, corrupt, thoughtless, exploitative and rash, a shoot-'em-first-and-ask-questions-later response that seems more at home in the Wild West of the 1870s than in Cohen's manicured suburbia of the 1970s. SWAT teams roam delivery rooms all over the country, advancing on helplessly stirruped mothers as if they were the Dillinger gang and heroically dispatching little monsters straight out of the womb. This level of absurdity practically begs to be spoofed, and the films do have some campy fun with it: in the first film, a paramilitary troop storms a backyard and trains its entire weapons arsenal on an unsuspecting normal toddler playing on a blanket. But this mood of levity is choked off, as abruptly as one might throttle a baby in its cradle, as soon as a direct link is made between the films' farcical baby hunt scenes and societally endorsed child murder in the "normal" world. Consider this exchange between the expectant parents (Frederic Forrest, Kathleen Lloyd) of *It Lives Again*:

> *Gene:* Of course, in India infanticide has been practiced for centuries…. Strangling baby girls at birth, or spreading opium on the mother's nipples before nursing them. Really.
> *Jody:* Glad I'm not in India.
> *Gene:* I think today they just starve the little girls to death. … I guess it's easier to kill what you consider inferior.
> *Jody:* Well, look, over here we run the country, huh?

Gene's musings about the contemporary "normality" of child murder and Jody's naïve and soon-to-be-disabused faith in her own society achieve two things for the viewer: they define society's response to the mutant babies as a concerted and orchestrated act of societal child abuse, and they beg the question what kind of threat could merit such a response.

The film dispenses very quickly with the idea that the mutations are the fault of individuals (through, say, irresponsible abortion attempts or drugs taken during pregnancy). Mutant babies are born to random families across the country, quickly turning into a problem of endemic proportions (in *3*, a cop who has just dispatched a baby with four bullets comments, "They're being born faster than we can kill them"). Suggestions as to what caused the mutations range from planetary pollution to the evil machinations of a pharmaceutical company who put a harmful and untested drug on the market, was forced to withdraw it, and plans to remove the evidence (read: murder the mutant babies) in order to re-market the same drug under a different name.

Significantly, the idea of addressing such communal problems, from global pollution to capitalist corruption, is voiced rarely, usually in an offhand manner and by a minor character. In *2*, for example, the film's most sensible idea is timidly expressed by the third SWAT team member from the right: "We'd be better off finding the cause of it. Pollution, drugs... instead of just killing it"—a suggestion that is naturally never followed up. Whereas such Voices of Reason are tentative, assigned to characters with low visibility, and easily missed, all three films allot considerable screen time to less helpful societal coping mechanisms. They include blaming the parents (perhaps mothers caused the mutation by taking the wrong pills; or perhaps the father's "screwed-up genes" are at fault); ostracizing individuals (in *1*, Frank and Lenore (John Ryan, Sharon Farrell), the first mutant's parents, are identified by name and address over the radio, upon which Frank is promptly fired from his job); general ass-covering, and medical experiments disguised as beneficial science. The scene in *1* in which Frank is asked to sign his offspring over to the medical establishment contains a particularly distasteful exchange that smacks more of concentration camp than camp:

> *Frank:* You wanna experiment on it, is that it?
> *Doctor:* As a matter of fact, my department has already cautioned the police about excessive violence. If it could be dispatched with a bullet, or better still, some kind of a gas.... Undoubtedly, it is very small, and any kind of bodily harm, especially from gunshots or explosives...

The utter inhumanity of choosing the execution method for a sentient being to preserve the body for medical experiments really needs no further comment. Nevertheless, the films do provide further comment, insistently and repeatedly. The entire U.S. army descends on mothers in delivery rooms, ignoring their desperate pleas for their babies' lives, or on parents in their homes clucking adoringly at their babies and blissfully unaware that they are about to be gassed (*It Lives Again*). Courts debate the summary execution of all mutant babies and then commute the death sentence to banishment to an island that has been used for nuclear testing (*Island of the Alive*). Both parents and children are turned into commodities, with the children killed by doctors for whatever "insights" their bodies can yield and the parents pursued by the press for their stories. Everyone who does not fall into line is outcast—fired from their jobs (Frank in *1*), terrorized into obedience (in all three films, the parents' best way back into society's good graces is murdering their own babies in front of witnesses), even spurned by prostitutes (Stephen Jarvis, played by Michael Moriarty, in 3). Finally, Frank's musings about Frankenstein, the literary character to whom he owes his name, makes the films' agenda too obvious for further discussion: Frank's realization that it is not Frankenstein who is the monster but "the doctor who created him" stands for his insight that the real monster is not the mutant baby but a society that first creates it and then wipes it from the face of the earth.

If Cohen's films paint a damning and easy-to-read picture of society's war on the weird children, they remain rather oblique when it comes to the offspring's provenance and nature. Just about the only thing we seem to know about it is that it is, indeed, alive. We should be wary of being seduced, by the films' portrayal of society's farcically over-the-top response, into a stance that defensively views the babies as "innocent" rather than "evil"— as merely acting on instinct, in self-defense, or, assuming every newborn's most primal urge, driven by hunger. In fact, Cohen's films portray the immorality of the mutants' wholesale destruction as entirely compatible with the idea that they are, in fact, dangerous, even vicious. In all films, the newborns straight out of the womb attack and usually kill all delivery room staff, doctors, nurses and attendants. POV shots from the babies' perspective, blurry and low on the ground, permeate all three films. These shots are, without exception, cast as stalker shots, with both context and camera angles suggesting not a kid, or even an animal, in search of food but a killer about to pounce on a victim. The adults' (including the parents') extreme fear of the mutant babies can hardly be shrugged off as the knee-jerk rejection of a life form they don't understand; such fears seem more than justified by the trail of blood and guts these babies leave in their wake. Finally, in *Island*, suspicions voiced throughout all three films that the mutants may not be compatible with the human species turn out to be justified when the babies' chief diet turns out to be human flesh—a neat post-facto explanation for their immediate attacks on doctors and nurses in delivery rooms.

Whether such fundamental incompatibility can be resolved by simple human acceptance, unconditional love, and integration into the family seems questionable, to say the least. In fact, one of the films' most frequent points of attack appears to be launched at the human attempt to incorporate into the family unit these "children" who really belong to humanity at large. The shock revelation in *1*, which ends with the death of Frank and Lenore's mutant baby, is that "another one has been born in Seattle." Both sequels portray the birth of mutant offspring to random couples as an epidemic covering the globe. Attempts to assign individual ownership of these beings to any one family, while certainly more benevolent than the wholesale slaughter of infants, are also misguided, since they represent merely another doomed quest to solve individually what must be addressed on a global scale. What is more, the films make clear that humanity's capacity to love unconditionally is not advanced enough to enable even the weak placebo of individual solutions. Surely it is significant that whereas the babies all recognize their parents, the parents are usually unable to distinguish one mutant baby from another. Perhaps this is another one of Cohen's oblique points of critique: how can an individual solution—let's say, a parent's unconditional love—work if the loving parent can't distinguish between one mutant and the next? Is this Cohen's way of saying that these parents are more attached to the idea of parenthood, and to a pleasing self-image as self-sacrificing, unconditionally loving and caring parents, than to the actual child?

In the end, the films leave the origin of the mutant babies unexplained and do little to determine the seemingly central question whether we are looking at humans or monsters. This makes sense, of course, once we stop seeing the two as contradictions in terms. *Island* goes furthest in portraying the mutants, now grown to adulthood, as capable of love, but also declares them to be cannibalistic killers. They are accorded a touching death scene in which they profess their mutual love by holding hands, and they go to great lengths to protect their offspring. Yet they are also utterly incapable of impulse control or general fellow feeling; like humans tend to do, they take care of their own and savage everyone else. In this way, the mutants are the perfect image for the monstrosity *of* humanity, rather than—as the films' storylines would have it—a different and misunderstood species that needs to be protected *from* humanity. Even parts of the plot reject this simple formula, since human cruelty and contempt for life characterize not only those who murder the mutants but also those who protect them. More than once in the course of the series, a mutant-defender stumbles over a mutilated corpse and responds not with horror, pity, or anguish at the destruction of yet another human being, but concern for the mutant's welfare: "They'll kill all the babies for this. It mustn't happen. Mustn't happen!" (*It Lives Again*). And more than once, what we are told is absurdly contradicted by what we are shown, as in the central court scene in *Island*. Jarvis's mutant baby has just bent the bars of his steel cage with superhuman strength and gone straight for the judge's jugular, but then backs off and whimpers cutely. Jarvis offers his assurances that the baby poses no danger: "See? ... He's just a baby. He's just scared." The judge visibly relents: "I won't have anything happen to that child." So here we have it, the milk of human kindness that—or so we think—is the answer: a baby's terrified bawls, a father's touching plea, a judge swayed from coldness to compassion. But just as we begin to bask in this warm glow of humanity, the camera zooms in on the steel cage's bent bars—*not* a shot designed to convince us that the little tyke can't hurt anyone.

One of the most absurd conceits of Cohen's *Alive* films is the idea that the mutant babies are not an aberration but actually the next stage in human evolution. "We don't regard them as monsters or subhuman," explains a scientist engaged in Mutant Studies. "As a matter of fact, they're potentially beautiful. Superhuman. The beginning of a new race of humanity that will finally eclipse our own. They're the next step forward in evolution. A way in which the human race can survive the pollutions of this planet" (*It Lives Again*). This weird logic raises its ugly head again in *Island*: "Some see these children as mutations, but we see them as a jump in the evolutionary pattern. Creatures capable of surviving a nuclear holocaust, withstanding radiation, even thriving on it. ... Studying them may tell us where the human race is headed" (Fig. 19). Of course this isn't meant as a serious argument for the mutants' "superiority"—as Newman has quipped: "mankind's next step up the evolutionary ladder: fanged killer babies"[7]—but merely another way of showing up the absurdity of human reasoning. When our response to pollution and radiation is not to stop polluting the planet or prevent nuclear war, but to monkey with genes in order to create a species that can thrive on radiation, we have surely plumbed the most profound depths of absurdity. When our alternatives are down to eradicating life forms we don't understand or revering them as "superior," surely this documents a profound paucity of imagination. Small wonder, then, that the films' characters are unable to imagine a better future for humanity than a polluted and radioactive planet inhabited by fanged and clawed cannibals.

The inability of characters in the *Alive* films to think beyond crass alternatives—*either*

Fig. 19. "Where the human race is headed": Monsters in *Island of the Alive* (1987) (Warner Bros./Photofest).

the mutants are vicious monsters who must be destroyed *or* superior beings that must be nurtured at all costs, even the cost of human lives—is offered up for viewer inspection or, as the case may be, identification. Viewers are free to engage in childish finger-pointing at the delivery-room carnage that justifies the "man hunt" for babies: hey, they started it. Or viewers can side with characters who, while appearing more tolerant and humane in their efforts to protect the babies, are endowed with a seemingly limitless ability to kid themselves that the babes, all evidence to the contrary notwithstanding, are harmless. Or, to round out the viewers' absurd choices, we can pin our hopes on the next-step-in-evolution theory, and never mind that worship of a "superior" species is actually another fairly primitive idea. Both idolization and eradication of the unknown are essentially infantilized responses. It is *this* that Cohen's films portray, handily symbolized in the films' murderous babies: humanity's infantile and thus violent response to the unknown, on the part of Cohen's characters, and perhaps also—this the films' implied question—on the part of his audience. It is this human propensity for infantile violence, not murderous babies, that poses the greatest threat to humanity's continued survival. No wonder that Cohen's films offer no real solutions, only ludicrous ones. Outgrowing humanity's childish ferocity, the films imply, would mean learning to explore options somewhere in between adulation and annihilation. Failing that, we can always wait for Captain Kirk to show up with some handy tips on how to deal with an unknown species.

*The Ring* (dir. Gore Verbinski, USA 2002) and its sequel (dir. Hideo Nakata, USA 2005) are commonly considered remakes of Hideo Nakata's original *Ring* films (Japan 1998 and 1999 respectively), part of a trend towards the transnationalization of the horror film. Yet the relationship between the American *Ring* films and their Japanese precursors is anything but clear-cut. To be sure, Verbinski's *Ring* and Nakata's American *Ring 2* draw heavily on their Japanese predecessors. Yet both deviate from Nakata's original plotlines and reveal sufficient conceptual dissimilarities to belie the term "remake." The most glaring disparity is the films' respective treatment of child abuse. Nakata's Japanese originals do no more than hint at it darkly. In the American films, however, child abuse takes center stage.

Much of this change hinges upon one simple plot device, the re-casting, in the American films, of the implacable ghost Sadako (Rie Ino'o), an adult woman in the Japanese originals, as Samara (Daveigh Chase), a rejected, abused, forcibly institutionalized and finally murdered child.[8] This murder is played out in a brief but traumatic scene in which Anna Morgan (Shannon Cochran), Samara's adoptive mother, pulls a plastic bag over the child's head, strangles her, throws her into a well, and closes the stone lid above her (the last rim of daylight against the darkness of the lid is the ring of the films' title). Samara survives in the well for seven days and returns as a vengeful spirit who inflicts her own suffering—seven days of agony followed by a dreadful death—onto everyone who sees a video tape showing seemingly random images evoking memory snippets from her life, abuse and death, culminating in a blurred vision of the well. The watcher's death inevitably occurs when Samara on the tape climbs out of the well and advances towards the front of the TV screen, breaking through it to pull her victims from their reality into her own.

Both *1* and *2* link the abuse and murder of the "evil" child Samara and the neglect suffered by the good child Aidan (David Dorfman) at the hands of his loving but overworked single mother Rachel (Naomi Watts). In *1*, Rachel is late picking up Aidan from school and blithely brushes aside his teacher's concerns about the disturbing imagery in his paintings, which indicate severe trauma at the death of his cousin Katie (Amber Tamblyn), Samara's first victim. In *2*, Rachel is unmasked as an abysmal cook: "now before you say anything," she informs a doubtful-looking Aidan while serving him an awful-looking quiche, "I followed the recipe this time. So, just 'cause it doesn't look like the one in the magazine doesn't mean to say it won't taste good." Rachel's incompetence as a traditional mother forces Aidan to take on the adult's role. At no more than eight or nine years old, he is already used to making his own lunch and taking himself off to school. Preparing to go to Katie's funeral, Rachel runs around in her underwear, frantically searching for her black dress and yelling at Aidan to get ready, only to find him already impeccably dressed and working on his tie, having carefully laid out her dress, shoes and stockings for her. In another scene, Rachel returns home from work, late as usual, to relieve the babysitter, and is told that Aidan has tucked himself in and then read the babysitter a bedtime story (*1*).

Of course all of these instances can easily be dismissed as scenes from the life of a well-meaning but frazzled mom and an unusually self-sufficient and switched-on kid. From an adult's perspective, these scenes might appear as a wryly amusing take on modern life as every single and working mom knows it, characterized by stress, more or less successful attempts at multi-tasking, and a hefty dose of guilt. From the children's viewpoint, however, things appear more ominous. Both Aidan and Samara suffer nightmarish visions of being abandoned by their parents. When Aidan awakes from a bad dream, he answers Rachel's concerned question "What happened in your nightmare?" with a heartbreakingly simple: "I woke up and you weren't here. You weren't here." The Happy Ending is no more than a retraction of the abandonment nightmare in an exact reversal of these words: Rachel returns from Samara's world and is awoken from her nightmare by Aidan's relieved exclamation: "Rachel! Rachel! You're here. You're here" (*2*). Disturbingly enough, Samara, the films' "evil" child, experiences the same fears of abandonment as the good child Aidan, as is made clear in a scene in which Samara, dumped in a psychiatric institution, is interviewed by her doctor:

*Doctor*: You don't want to hurt anyone.
*Samara*: But I do, and I'm sorry. It won't stop. ... He's going to leave me here.
*Doctor*: Who?
*Samara*: Daddy.
*Doctor*: They just want to help you.
*Samara*: Not Daddy.
*Doctor*: Your daddy loves you.
*Samara*: Daddy loves the horses. He wants me to go away [*1*].

The fear of parental desertion emerges as the central concern for both the good and the "evil" child. *2* expands on the theme of child abandonment, and the implicit identification of the two children, by turning them into the same child. In a nod to the Japanese version of *Dark Water* (directed, once again, by Hideo Nakata, 2002), Samara possesses Aidan in order to take his place as a child who is mothered, however ineptly. "She loves me," Samara-as-Aidan intones eerily. "She went looking for me. She tried to find me. It means she loves me." Her/his words to Rachel—"Will you stay with me now? ... Stay for always"—are simultaneously the "evil" child's threat of eternal possession and the good child's plaintive grievance against a mother who never has enough time for him. Rachel herself explains Samara's monstrousness as an abandoned child's desperate search for a mother: "All she wants is a mother. That's all she wants. And she'll keep coming till she finds one." Clearly, part of the *Rings*' project is to erase the distinction between the good son and the "evil" daughter. Both experience neglect and extreme fears of abandonment, and both aspire to the same happy ending: to be able to say to Mother, with perfect confidence: "You're here. You're here."

Once Aidan and Samara are turned literally into the same child, they are also assigned the same fate. Just as Samara was drowned by her mother, Aidan must now be drowned by his mother in order to exorcise Samara. Just as the difference between the good son and the evil daughter is effectively erased, murdering and saving the child become one and the same act. The drowning of Aidan in the bathtub (mitigated by his successfully resuscitation) is prefigured not only by the drowning of Samara in the well, but also by the drowning of a third child, whose mother Evelyn (Sissy Spacek), a psychiatric institution inmate, "felt she had to kill her baby to save it," as her nurse explains to Rachel. When Rachel, horrified, asks Evelyn why she tried to drown her baby, she is told: "Because my baby told me to. Just like yours will tell you. And you have to do it. You have to send it back." Indeed, Aidan later tells Rachel to drown him in the bathtub. Visually, this presents us with another image of severe child abuse, while narratively it happily results in Aidan's liberation from Samara's vengeful spirit. Thus the film's presentation of the problem—child abuse and child murder—stands as a direct and unresolved paradox to the film's proposed *solution*, which boils down to justified child murder. Individual scenes, such as Rachel's outraged accusation of Samara's father: "What did you do to her? She was your daughter! You killed Samara, didn't you?," or the extremely painful images of Samara's murder at her mother's hands, seem to state unequivocally that there can be no justification for child murder. Yet the ending takes it all back in spectacular fashion.

In effect, the second American *Ring* is subject to a number of teleological absurdities. Child abuse and child murder represent both curse and cure. The good and the evil child are one and the same. The scourge of child abandonment and neglect can only be healed by more of the same. Early on in the film, Rachel asks Aidan to call her mom, ma or mommy, only to be rebuffed: "I like 'Rachel,'" Aidan tells her. "'Rachel,' you know, is more your personality." We might read this as an unsubtle hint that Rachel is not a very successful "mom" in the traditional sense, but traditional mothering, as it turns out, is not all it's cracked up to be. The term "mommy," initially coveted by Rachel, becomes a term of horror. Aidan-as-himself refuses to use it; Aidan possessed by Samara uses the term persistently, obtrusively, and possessively. In the end, Rachel is presented as a good mother by *rejecting* her role as mother of both Samara and Aidan. She pushes Samara, who desperately clings to her and calls her "mommy," back into the well with the words: "I'm not your fucking mommy." And when Aidan in the final scene, relieved to have his mother back, tells her "I love you, mommy," she turns the tables on him: "Just call me Rachel." If child neglect, defined as insufficient mothering,[9] is presented as the main problem besetting their relationship at the outset, it is paradoxically healed at the end by Rachel's refusal of the mother-role—verbally in Aidan's case, utterly in Samara's.

Both *Ring* films feature extensive guilt trips, much of which is overtly directed at the movies' (and real life's) most common scapegoat, the insufficient mother. Evelyn, in her heart-to-heart with Rachel, blames mothers for everything, "Because it's our fault. We did it. Yes. We did it. Yes. *Screeching:* It was you. It was you! You did it!" (*2*) But in the end, bad mothering, from Rachel's lousy cooking and perpetual lateness to Anna Morgan's act of child murder, is presented as a symptom, not the disease. Child abuse in the films' portrayal is not individual but communal, and part of what enables it to continue is the illusion that it is individual, a private issue and a family affair. Richard Morgan, Samara's adoptive father, represents this view in words that are eerily evocative of Samara's MO: "What is it with reporters?," he rants. "You take one person's tragedy and force the world to experience it, spread it like sickness" (*1*). The problem here is precisely that abuse does not concern "one person" but affects communities, and it is also communities, not merely individuals or families, that perpetrate it. In the first film, Dr. Grasnick (Jane Alexander), the island doctor, tells Rachel that she referred Samara to the psychiatric institution on the mainland, not for Samara's benefit, but to get her off the island: "We've been through a lot of hard years out here, mean winters, small hauls, no fish.... See, when you live on an island, you catch a cold, it's everybody's cold.... Ever since that girl's been gone, things have been better." Samara's abandonment and removal to a mental institution, in other words, is not only her family's decision but the entire community's; everyone conspired to get rid of her.

Such statements by relatively minor characters who only appear once nevertheless constitute tangible hints that child abuse extends far beyond the individual person or family. Other, more metaphoric signals throughout the films make the same point. One is the ubiquitous presence of water.[10] Both *Ring* films, continuing a dystopian cinematic tradition that ranges from *Blade Runner* to *Se7en*, are set on islands or in seaside communities where it rains all the time, and nearly all spaces in the films, outside or in, are soaked, waterlogged, or mercilessly pelted by beating-down rain. Water seeps through floors, runs down TV sets, doors and walls, emerges incongruously from sofas, rises to ceilings to pool there before crashing down like a waterfall, and pools around victims as they die. Children are drowned in wells, bathtubs and fountains. Richard Morgan commits spectacular suicide by stepping into an overflowing bathtub and electrocuting himself. Faucets drip endlessly; everyday events like showers turn unsettling when the camera pans down to reveal a Hitchcockian vision of dark water swirling down the drain. Anna Morgan's suicide is shown partly from her POV: a static image from behind her showing her calmly flinging herself off the cliff is replaced by her POV as a falling body, agitated seawater rushing towards her (us) to swallow her (us) up. At the end of *2*, Rachel's re-enactment of Anna's suicide, which recap the same camera angles, constitutes her escape from Samara's world. But there is no escape from the encroaching water; like guilt, it gets in everywhere and soaks through everything. The ubiquity of water is more than the deliberate setting of a dystopian mood (although that is part of the point, too[11]); it is a metaphor for the prevalence and uncontainability of abuse.

This, then, is the final proclamation of the *Ring* films: because abuse is a global and universal problem, individual solutions are doomed to fail. This futility is expressed in a further metaphor, the mirror image, for which the tape and the TV stand as the most prominent examples. The inability of the visual image to express either a dependable reality or a trustworthy distinction between appearance and reality is a constant theme in both *Ring* films. The films glory in deceptive images, twice or thrice removed from "reality": reflections, usually of faces, in camera lenses, mirrors, windows, TV screens or water drops from a dripping faucet, or combinations of any of the above—a photograph of a reflection in a mirror, a film showing a reflection in a window. Things that are supposed to be there aren't: on the killer tape, a reflection in a mirror, although filmed from a straight angle, does not show the filming camera. Things that are not supposed to be there are: Samara's ghost, standing behind Aidan, is invisible in "reality" but clearly visible in photographs he takes of himself in front of a mirror. Photographs and video footage of Samara's future victims show their faces, which look perfectly normal in actual life, horribly distorted, similar to the deformed faces of her earlier prey. The point is not so much that images predict or turn into reality, it is that the very distinction becomes brittle. Just as Samara can burst through the TV screen into someone's living room, the tape's grainy footage and reality's sharp focus can easily trade places. In *2*, the POV on the first victim's death is Samara's from inside the television. As the victim falls to his knees and the inevitable girl witness behind him begins to scream, the living room turns a grainy black and white, pixelates and distorts, accompanied by a hissing sound. From inside the TV, we get a very bad reception of reality.

The dilemma is inescapable. On the one hand, no reality is ever safe. On the other, humans cannot function without an absolute reliance on the distinction between image and reality. Two further scenes demonstrate this most clearly. In *1*, as Noah watches the tape, Rachel steps out onto the balcony of her high-rise apartment, which offers a *Rear Window*-inspired vista of dozens of other apartments and their occupants going about their business, the TV in all apartments switched on in the background and blithely ignored by their owners, who imagine themselves safe. In *2*, the Happy Ending relies on the same illusion of safety: as Rachel, returned from Samara's reality, hugs her son in relief, she risks an anxious glance at the TV screen, which shows only a reflection of the two of them, embracing. But this, of course, does not really constitute a Happy Ending but merely an invitation to be fooled once more by the specious distinction between image and reality and the illusion of safety it offers.

As a Happy Ending, the reunion between Rachel and Aidan at the end of *2* is problematic in more ways than one. Not only is it undercut by its central reliance on an illusion that the film has dismantled all along, it also limits its dubious promise of future happiness to Aidan and Rachel and moreover implies an ending where there is only the beginning of a new cycle. For child abuse, a global problem, there can be no individual solution. This idea is most clearly expressed in the films' most central plot feature: to avoid death, you have to inflict it on someone else. Rachel's insight that she survived the curse by making a copy of the tape and passing it on to Noah stands for the ultimate denial of individual solutions, and also for a denial of endings. It is another one of those Orwellian paradoxes so

Fig. 20. "It will never stop": Rachel (Naomi Watts) watches the deadly tape in *The Ring* (2002) (Dreamworks SKG/Photofest).

abundant in the *Ring* films. Just as the evil child is the good child, child murder is also child rescue, and good mothering takes the form of rejecting the mother role, copying the tape represents simultaneously the individual's way out and the perpetuation of the larger problem. The continuous recreation of the problem, the killer tape, is yet another signal for the films' understanding of abuse as infinite and universal, also expressed in the endlessly recurring statement by several characters throughout both films: "It won't stop" (Fig. 20). *The Ring* ends with a brief dialogue between Rachel and Aidan as they copy the deadly tape:

*Aidan:* It's going to keep killing, isn't it? It'll never stop.
*Rachel:* Don't worry, sweetie. You're gonna be ok.
*Aidan:* What about the person we show it to? What happens to them?

To this, Rachel has no answer, not even something as feebly unconvincing as "it'll be ok." Manifestly, it won't be, since each individual escape exacerbates the global problem.[12] Saving oneself and one's family is pointless because abuse has long left the family behind; it has gone global and viral, "like a sickness"—a sentiment expressed in the title of yet another transnational remake of Nakata's original Japanese films, Kim Dong-bin's *The Ring Virus* (South Korea 1999). There is no "stop" button on the machine that plays the evil tape, only "copy." There is no solution, only buck-passing. Abuse is not resisted, merely recycled. True to *The Rings*' predilection for erasing distinctions, this ending does away with yet another one: that between abuser and abused. Yesterday's abuse victims become tomorrow's abusers. And this is why, as both films insistently proclaim, "it will never stop."

The idea of endlessly recycled abuse, perpetrated by abusers who were yesterday's victims, is also the central premise of Michael Haneke's 2009 black and white film *The White Ribbon* (*Das weiße Band: Eine deutsche Kindergeschichte*). The film is set in the Protestant hamlet of Eichwald ("oak forest") on the eve of the First World War. While the exact year of the action is not revealed until the final few minutes of the film, we do understand that the villagers live under a feudal regime, in subservience to a Baron (Ulrich Tukur) who owns everything from the land and the hamlet itself to the fish in the brook to the community's only bicycle. All villagers depend entirely on the Baron for their livelihood, either directly—his servants, tutor (Michael Kranz), nanny (Leonie Benesch), estate steward (Josef Bierbichler), and the farmers who bring in his harvest—or indirectly, like the village pastor (Burghart Klaußner), doctor (Rainer Bock), midwife (Susanne Lothar) and schoolteacher (Christian Friedel), who is also the film's voiceover narrator.

This rigidly regulated and sleepy community is disrupted by a series of crimes and unfortunate accidents. The village doctor, riding home on his horse, is wire-tripped and wounded severely enough to necessitate a two-month hospital stay. A farmer's wife dies when she breaks through rotten timbers in a hayloft floor. A window is left open in a baby boy's room in winter, bringing on a fever that nearly kills him. Both the Baron's son Sigi (Fion Mutert) and the midwife's mentally retarded son Karli (Eddy Grahl) are severely mistreated by a person or persons unknown. The village barn is set on fire. Farmer Felder (Branko Samarovski), whose wife died in the accident, hangs himself. The pastor finds his pet parakeet dead on his desk, speared with a pair of scissors to form a crucifix. One of the steward's sons steals Sigi's whistle and pushes him into the river, where he would have drowned had not the other steward's son, also present at the scene, dragged Sigi out in the nick of time. Finally, the village doctor and his children, as well as the midwife and her retarded child, disappear without a trace. Whenever a crime is committed (the trap set for the doctor, the window left open in the baby's room, the attacks on Sigi and Karli, and the firing of the barn), a group of children gather at or near the scene of the crime, exuding a dread that is difficult to quantify. When confronted by an adult, however, they salute politely, curtsey impeccably, and disperse as soon as told to do so. At long last, the schoolteacher begins to suspect that the crimes plaguing the village were committed by the children. When he shares his misgivings with the pastor, he is reviled, threatened with dismissal and forbidden to speak of it again. The film ends with a church service dedicated to blessing the village's first recruits about to be shipped off to fight in the First World War. The teacher leaves Eichwald, marries, serves briefly in the war, and becomes a tailor in a nearby town. The crimes committed in the village remain unsolved; the teacher's suspicion, while appearing plausible, is neither confirmed nor denied.

By withholding a solution, the film steers viewers in search of an explanation for the violence away from individual causes and toward the village's everyday normality. "Normality" is defined almost entirely by child abuse. The film contains numerous beating and caning scenes, the cane or fist wielded inevitably by the family father. To the nanny's horrified question after the attack on Sigi—"Who would do such a thing? ... Beat a child like that?"—the film offers an unequivocal response: nearly everyone. The steward brutally beats his son in retribution for stealing Sigi's whistle, kicks him in the ribs as he writhes on the floor, and then canes him to boot. The pastor's oldest children Klara (Maria-Victoria Dragus) and Martin (Leonard Proxauf) are caned behind a closed door on which the camera focuses unwaveringly as Martin screams behind it. When Farmer Felder's adult son Max (Sebastian Hülk), not unreasonably, accuses the Baron and his steward of negligence for sending his mother onto a floor with rotten floorboards, his father responds to this by boxing him hard on the head, in the presence of his wife and his other six children. The point of all this is not only to inflict pain but public humiliation. The pastor secures his children's explicit agreement to their own brutal punishment and then sends Martin to fetch the cane; both the children's coerced consent and the whipping are performed in front of the entire family. Public humiliation is also where the white ribbon of the film's title comes in[13]: a white ribbon—white, as the children are endlessly told, is the color of innocence—is a visible reminder of purity and righteousness for those lacking those virtues. Those forced to wear it are thus publicly defined as wicked and depraved. The white ribbon in Klara's hair and around Martin's arm is an exact parallel to the scarlet letter on Hester Prynne's chest.

Beatings and public humiliation in *The White Ribbon* are just one way of enforcing submission in a world where fathers lord it over their children in the manner of a Baron lording it over his vassals. Just as painful are the frequent scenes in which children are punished, often for very minor transgressions, by paternal guilt-tripping and the deliberate withholding of whatever scant affection is normally on offer. "I don't know what's worse, your absence or your return," says the pastor to Klara and Martin, who are shamed and caned for being late for dinner. After they have agreed to their punishment, he refuses to allow them, as is customary for children, to kiss his hand: "Don't touch me. Your mother and I will sleep badly tonight. I must beat you and the lashes will cause us more pain than you. Leave us alone and go to bed" (Fig. 21). A parallel scene involves the doctor, just returned from his two-month hospital stay, and his four-year-old son Rudi (Miljan Chatelain). Rudi has just understood that his mother, who he was told is travelling, is actually dead; his severe trauma is compounded by his father's illness and long absence. Clearly, this child fears nothing more than being abandoned. And abandonment is exactly what his father threatens him with when Rudi, so afraid to lose his father again that he cannot stand to welcome him back, locks himself in the toilet: "Fine. Then I don't want to see you, either. I'm going away now. … Farewell, Rudi,"[14] upon which he walks out the front door.

Finally, a third form of child abuse that is ever-present in the film is sexual abuse and sexual shaming, for instance the pastor's order that Martin's hands be tied each night to prevent masturbation (predictably, he first terrifies Martin with a horror story of another boy's dreadful death by masturbation), or the doctor's sexual abuse of his 14-year-old daughter Anna (Roxane Duran). The film's most heartbreaking scenes pile one form of abuse, for example sexual abuse, on another, for example the threat of abandonment. In one such double-whammy scene, little Rudi wakes up in the night. His sister Anna is not in the bed next to his, and so he wanders through the dark house, a tiny tearful ghost calling her name. He finds her in a room, weeping, her nightshirt hiked up to her hips, his father's fly unbuttoned. He cannot understand what he is seeing, but gets no reassurance from her explanation that her father pierced her earlobes so she can wear Mother's earrings for Pentecost. Asked why he's wandering around the house in the middle of the night, he offers the abandoned child's simplest reason: "I woke up and you weren't there."

One of the film's achievements is its proposition that the children respond to consistent abuse in different and sometimes contradictory ways. Three that the film highlights are

Fig. 21. "Don't touch me": Klara (Maria-Victoria Dragus) and Martin (Leonard Proxauf; both standing by the door) are forbidden to kiss the hand that will beat them in *The White Ribbon* (2009) (Sony Pictures Classics/Photofest).

the children's attacks on authority figures, their attacks on social outcasts (either society's weakest or those who break society's rules), and finally, a general absorption with death. The first response is encapsulated, among others, in the attack on the doctor, the pastor (it is his daughter Klara, viciously punished in an earlier scene, who stabs the parakeet and arranges it in crucifix form on his desk), the attack on Sigi, the Baron's son, and finally the firing of the barn. The second response is played out in the attack on Karli, the midwife's mentally disabled son, who is found in the woods with severe lacerations around his eyes and a note saying that God punishes "the children for the sins of the parents [as per the subtitles; in the German original: the sins of the fathers] down to the third and fourth generations." Finally, the children's morbid fascination with death and a corresponding contempt for life is central to several scenes throughout the film. The birth of the steward's latest offspring is greeted by his older siblings not with joy but with groans of disappointment; later, they open the window in the baby's room in mid-winter in an attempt to cause his death. Death, to the children, is something that one might inflict on others—the doctor, the village idiot, Father's parakeet, one's baby brother—but also something that is close to oneself, an ever-present threat that holds a dark appeal. In the wake of the revelation that his mother is not travelling but dead, Rudi insistently queries Anna on the nature of death—his father's, hers, and his own. Karli approaches the farmer's dead wife on her bier, scared but also utterly captivated, carefully lifting the lace handkerchief in order to look at her face. On the day of his caning, Martin precariously balances on the railing of a wooden bridge above a deep gorge. When angrily confronted by the schoolteacher, he explains: "I was giving God a chance to kill me. He didn't do it so he must be pleased with me. ... He doesn't want me to die." But when the teacher tells him that he will discuss this with his father, Martin panics, begging him not to tell.

That a boy could be far more terrified of an angry father who might cane him than of an angry God who might kill him is not only an implicit statement that abuse is a fate worse than death. It also showcases, once again, that in Eichwald abuse is normal and death is inconsequential, in the sense that nobody takes any note of it. Here is how Haneke's film plays out one of its most significant death scenes, the suicide of Farmer Felder. One of his sons, going about his daily chores, opens the barn door and sees his father hanging from the rafters. He walks off to one side, leaving the door open, his face full of shock. We hear children play happily in the snow as the camera focuses on him watching them. Without looking inside again, he returns and slowly closes the door. He enters the farm kitchen next to the barn, where his mother is cleaning vegetables for lunch, and disappears in the gloom of the badly lit room. Not a word is spoken. Cut. In the end, we don't know whether he then tells his mother or whether he simply leaves it to someone else to make the same discovery and alert the family. It is a scene that seems to demonstrate the utter uselessness of resistance[15]: death, like abuse, must simply be accepted. Mute endurance, the sign of such acceptance, is expressed several times in the film through the shoulder-shrugging line: "The world won't collapse." It is used whenever situations can't be changed and must simply be suffered through. When the nanny's father (Detlev Buck) informs the schoolteacher that he must wait for a year to marry her, he tells him, "A year goes by fast. The world won't collapse." When the doctor brutally rejects the midwife, with whom he has carried on a sexual affair for years, he tells the devastated woman: "The world won't collapse, not on you or on me." The same is implied when a son enters a barn to find his father swinging from the rafters. On the eve of the First World War, it is, to put it mildly, a scathing statement.

Haneke's film makes the same point as the *Ring* films: yesterday's abused become tomorrow's abusers. It makes the same point as Cohen's *Alive* films: abuse is a global matter, not a familial concern. What he adds to these points is a closer look at society's response to the universal problem of abuse. In *The White Ribbon,* that response amounts to downplaying the problem—the world won't collapse—and denial. The pastor fervently rejects the "repulsive" and "monstrous" suspicion that the children are at fault, although the idea can hardly be outlandish to a man who has recently found a parakeet impaled on scissors on his desk. Much like the pastor, the village has its own way of dealing with the unthinkable. After the doctor's and the midwife's disappearance, gossip runs rampant in the village. Ironically, the crime the doctor actually committed, that of child abuse and child rape, is just about the only one that does not come up in the village's catalogue of his misdeeds. The doctor and the midwife, now exposed as illicit lovers, are accused of having produced Karli while the doctor's wife was still alive, trying to abort him to hide their affair, and, in so doing, causing the child's mental disability. From there, it is a small step to accusing the pair of conspiring to murder the doctor's wife, who died—what could be more suggestive?—in childbirth. And from there, it is all but clear to the village gossips that the murderous couple committed *all* the crimes of the past year. Since the doctor himself and the midwife's own son are two of the most grievously hurt victims, this idea is manifestly absurd. It does, however, have the inestimable advantage of removing the problem along with its supposed perpetrators, leaving the village as pure and unspoiled as a white ribbon.

The film ends with the outbreak of the First World War and with two conflicting statements: on the one hand, "the world won't collapse"; on the other, in the narrator's words,

"Everything was about to change." "Everything" includes personal change for the narrator—from bachelorhood to marriage—historical change—from peace to war—and societal change, from the feudal system that ended with the German Emperor's abdication at the end of the First World War to Germany's first, and ill-fated, democracy, which in turn ended with Hitler's assumption of power in 1933. These markers provide a sinister historical dimension to the insight that yesterday's abused become tomorrow's abusers. It is not difficult to do the math and figure out that the abused children of the First World War will become the goose-stepping, Heil-screaming adults of the Second, "Hitler's Willing Executioners," as one historian has termed them.[16] Child abuse in Haneke's film begins in the family, but far transcends it. The point is made all too clearly by the film's insistent use of generics that refer to its adult characters not by name but by social position: Baron, Baroness, steward, schoolteacher, doctor, pastor, midwife, nanny, tutor, farmer. Abuse radiates outward from the family to swallow up the entire village of Eichwald, whose name, while evoking sentiments of *Heimat* through both *Eiche* (the oak tree, that most quintessentially German of all trees) and *Wald* (the Grimms' fairy tale forest), also alludes to two other, more sinister names: Eichmann and Buchenwald.[17] From Eichwald, abuse goes global, leaving 60 million dead in its wake. Haneke's timeline places child abuse squarely at the center of arguably the greatest horror that has befallen the world in the twentieth century. And as Haneke has made clear in many interviews, he really does mean "the world." *The White Ribbon* is not, according to him, a specifically German story. He insisted on the deletion of the German subtitle "Eine deutsche Kindergeschichte" (*A German Children's Story*) in foreign release versions of his film, arguing that he wants this film to be seen as a German film in Germany, an English film in England and a Arab film in Arab countries. To Haneke, the film's allusion to German fascism is merely a stand-in for "a broader theme.... Today, one could make a film about the same theme in other countries."[18] Yesterday's abused become tomorrow's abusers, the world over. Fascism is homegrown and can happen anywhere.

Other horror films draw viewers in, shoving blood and guts in their faces in glorious dripping red. Haneke's film does the opposite. It contains virtually no physical violence on screen—we hear it but don't see it. Most beating scenes of children, for example, take place off-screen, leaving the viewer alone with an indifferent image—of a door, for example—and an audio-only representation of what takes place behind that door, sharp whipping sounds followed by agonized screams. The film also contains no extra-diegetic sound at all and distances spectators through its black-and-white aesthetics, which simultaneously provide a more direct access to the historical period and "alienate" the audience—Haneke's term[19]—through stylization. A further means of viewer alienation is provided by the use of a narrator[20] who tells us the story from the hindsight of half a century, in an old man's tired voice. As a dark screen gradually gives way to the weak greyish illumination of the first scene showing the doctor riding towards his appointment with a wire strung between two trees, the narrator begins his tale with a series of equivocations:

> I don't know whether the story that I want to tell you corresponds to the truth in every detail. Much of it I only know from hearsay. Some of it I cannot fathom even now, after so many years. And innumerable questions remain unanswered. Nevertheless I believe that I must relate the strange events that occurred in our village, since they might possibly shine an illuminating light upon some occurrences in this country.

This rather stilted bureaucratese is only insufficiently rendered in the English subtitles.[21] Yet style clearly has its part to play in steering viewer reception of the story. For one thing, the passage is full of euphemisms. Crimes are downgraded to "strange events"; the horrors of the Nazi period, even more mincingly, to "some occurrences in our country." Worse, the narrator reveals himself, from the outset, to be an unreliable witness who does not know the whole story, or knows it only second-hand, and is at a loss to understand what happened even decades later. The film confirms this, for in fact, the narrator does *not* tell us the story, or at least not the whole story. Many of the most significant events occur in scenes he does not witness and cannot know about: the sex scenes between doctor and midwife; the caning of Klara and Martin; the conversation between Baron and Baroness (Ursina Lardi), in which she informs him that she will leave him; the young farmer's discovery of his father's dead body in the barn; the death conversation between Anna and Rudi; Martin being tied up in bed to prevent masturbation; Klara approaching the bird cage, scissors in hand. Most of the story does not come from the narrator, but from an outside perspective to which he has no access. The narrator, then, is not really a guarantor for the veracity of the story, but merely its first interpreter. He is the first person to state, falteringly, the significance of these events: "possibly," he says, we might wish to consider that "strange events" may result in "some occurrences." But in his inability to call a spade a spade, he is also the first to embody society's predictable response to the horror of child abuse and its dreadful and worldwide consequences: to ignore it and downplay it at all costs.

* * *

*"It's not what you look at that matters, it's what you see."*
—Henry David Thoreau

When we open a barn door and look into the darkness, it's not what we see that matters, it's whether we dare to look. Cohen's films, the *Ring* sequence, and *The White Ribbon* all define child abuse as a universal problem with global consequences, a self-perpetuating evil. The problem is stated baldly, plain for all to see. The question is: do we want to look? Cohen's films are full of talk about how to handle the symptom, the killer babies themselves, but equally full of a thundering silence about the disease. When it comes to the larger issues of global pollution, war and corruption, the society in his films looks away. Looking away also seems to be the answer advocated in the *Ring* series, where the best way to avoid death is not to look at the deadly tape in the first place, like the girl Emily at the beginning of *The Ring 2*, who condemns her friend Jake to death by covering her eyes as she plays the tape. This, of course, solves her individual problem, but it is tantamount to ignoring what happened to Samara. Following Jake's demise and Emily's survival, the virus that is the deadly tape is as potent as ever. Individuals may escape, but child abuse as a global problem cannot be addressed by looking away.

Looking away, closing one's eyes, and refusing to see also emerge as major concepts in Haneke's film. Suspicions are repressed, stories are invented, crimes ignored, and as the policemen investigating the various crimes point out in exasperation, nobody ever sees anything. Aesthetics mimic the plot; in Haneke's underlit interiors portraying a world before electricity, it is, in fact, difficult to see anything. His colorless characters move from over-lit exteriors defined by glaring summer sunshine or blinding white snow into pitch-dark rooms lit by a single candle. It is a merciless world of black sin and white innocence in which there are no grey zones of tolerance. Half of the time, one looks into the dark, and what one sees there is hard to fathom. When I first saw the film on a bad screen, I was bemused by the scene in which young Felder finds his father's corpse because I couldn't see the corpse, which appears—on a higher-resolution screen—as a darker shadow barely outlined against the dark wall of an unlit barn. What I saw initially was this: a young man opens a door, stares into black nothingness, goes off to one side, closes the door without looking inside again, and goes back to work. And perhaps missing the main detail, the corpse, is not the worst way to see the scene. If death—like the grievous injustice and despair that caused it, like subjugation, like abuse—is unremarkable, something to be simply endured and accepted, then it really doesn't matter what we see when we look into the dark.

Haneke himself once remarked that an ideal audience response to his films would be if viewers, unable to withstand the images he shows them, simply looked away,[22] like a son discovering his father's body. Looking away is a sign of both dismay and denial. Are they one and the same? One of Germany's premier writers, Martin Walser, famously outlined his response to a modern German's constant confrontation with the horrors of Auschwitz in a speech in which "looking away" is by far the most frequently used term:

> I close myself off from evils that I cannot help remedy. I have had to learn to look away. I have several visual sanctuaries to which my gaze flees as soon as the TV screen shows me an unbearable world. ... I have also practiced the art of thinking away. Without looking away and thinking away, I wouldn't make it through the day, let alone through the night. ... From the worst film sequences showing concentration camps I have looked away at least twenty times. Instead of being grateful for the incessant presentation of our shame, I begin to look away.[23]

And here is *The White Ribbon*'s narrator, in a scene from Haneke's screenplay that did not make it into the film, on the same theme but coming to the opposite conclusion:

> Today, more than a quarter of a century later, toward the end of my life, and several years after the end of a second war that was to change this world in a more cruel and radical way than the first one, the one we faced at the time, I wonder if the events of those days and our silence about them weren't the germ of the tragedy toward which we were heading. Didn't we all know secretly what had happened in our midst? Hadn't we, in a way, made it possible by closing our eyes? Didn't we keep our mouths shut because otherwise we would have had to wonder if the misdeeds of these children, of our children, weren't actually the result of what we'd been teaching them?[24]

Perhaps Walser's solution to the problem and the insistent questions of Haneke's narrator are not the opposites they appear to be. Perhaps there is only a short step from dismay to denial. Perhaps looking away from the horrors in order to make it through the night and enabling the horror by closing one's eyes to it are one and the same. It is this dilemma that also shines through the darkness of Cohen's films and the *Ring* series: solutions that work for the individual not only ignore the global problem, they enable it to continue. Looking away is an individual's entirely understandable response, but it saddles that individual with a truly global guilt. Cohen's films, the *Ring*s, and *The White Ribbon* don't state it, they merely imply it. They show us the problem, but they can't force us to look at it. To do so would be simultaneously beneficial and devastating. Perhaps this is what Haneke meant when he said that his films "rape" his viewers "into independence."[25]

## Guilt Trips

### LITTLE HORRORS

*Dark Water* (dir. Hideo Nakata, Japan 2002; remake dir. Walter Salles, USA 2005). The Japanese original tells the story of little Mitsuko, who drowned due to neglect and returns as a child ghost in search of a mother. She finds her target in Yoshimi, a single mother struggling to raise her little girl Ikuko. *Guilt trip:* Both the Japanese original and the American remake work extensively with the trauma of losing a mother, and with issues of child neglect. The Japanese version moreover implies that child neglect has consequences for future relationships. The first scene shows little Yoshimi all alone in front of a kindergarten, watching other children being picked up by their parents—nobody comes for her. The next scene shows her as an adult undergoing divorce. She, too, is too harried and overworked to take care of her child; there is a parallel scene where Yoshimi rushes from her job to Ikuko's kindergarten, only to find the facility already closed. The film is full of images of little Ikuko wandering around and getting into dangerous situations, and full of maternal promises that "I'll never leave you alone again," which are invariably broken in the following scene.

*Don't Look Now* (dir. Nicolas Roeg, UK/Italy 1973). Following the accidental drowning of their young daughter Christine, John and Laura, deep in grief, move to Venice (the water city), where they encounter two mysterious sisters who transmit beyond-the-grave messages from Christine. A small figure in a red coat that resembles their dead daughter's haunts their every step and finally kills John. *Guilt trip:* The film's main themes are grief peppered with a healthy dose of guilt, both over Christine's death by drowning, which is replayed in several scenes showing other victims or dolls being pulled from a river or canal, and over the couple's distance from their other child, a son who is in boarding school in England, where he is seriously injured in a fall.

*The Grudge* (*Ju-on*, dir. Takashi Shimizu, Japan 2002; remake dir. Takashi Shimizu, USA 2004). A brutally murdered mother and small son curse and kill everyone who lives in or visits the house where the murder occurred. Similarly to *The Ring*, the curse does not expire with the victim but is passed on from one to the next. *Guilt trip:* Unlike the Japanese versions, most of the American remakes (*The Grudge 1-3*, 1-2 dir. Shimizu, 3 dir. Toby Wilkins, USA 2004, 2006, 2009) struggle with the idea of individual solutions. All show a far greater investment in individual characters than the Japanese films; the detective in particular plays a much more central role, reviving the vain hope that someone in "authority" will come along and fix this (Director Wilkins described his film as "Sort of an American take on the story: there has to be a way to stop it"). In the American *Grudge 3*, the little boy Toshio, for the first time, becomes more of a threat than his mother; this is also the first *Grudge* film in which most victims are children.

*The Innocents* (dir. Jack Clayton, UK 1961). Two small orphans, Flora and Miles, are abandoned by their uncle, who declares: "I have no room for them. Neither mentally nor emotionally." As a result they are foisted on a series of governesses, the latest of whom, Miss Giddens, becomes convinced that the children are possessed by the evil spirits of two dead servants. Miss Giddens ends up killing the little boy in an effort to exorcise him. *Guilt trip:* The film leaves open whether the children are really possessed or merely the victims of the governess's overactive imagination. Child abuse (the killing of Miles) and neglect play a prominent, if understated, part in the film. The film constantly juxtaposes the governess's passionate declarations of love for the children ("More than anything, I love children") and the children's palpable fear of being abandoned again. Miles yells at Flora for her attention-grabbing (the unspoken question is: will they be able to share Miss Giddens?). In another scene, Miles unemotionally states that their uncle does not want anything to do with them: "It's a bit sad, though, when people don't have time for you."

*The Orphanage* (dir. J. A. Bayona, Spain 2007). Laura, an orphan and adopted child, returns to her old orphanage with her husband and her own adopted son Simón, planning to reopen it as a facility for disabled children. She discovers that social worker Benigna has killed several orphanage children in revenge for their part in the accidental drowning of Benigna's deformed son Tomás. Laura's own son Simón disappears. By contacting the dead children's spirits, Laura finds out that she herself caused his death by accidentally locking him in. Laura commits suicide, becoming the permanent caretaker of the murdered children. *Guilt trip:* Traditional families are replaced by more indirect carers such as adoptive parents or paid social workers; children fall victim to negligence (Simón, Tomás) and abuse (Benigna's victims). The murdered children haunting the orphanage and Tomás's accurate prediction of Simón's death by neglect symbolize the permanence and inescapability of abuse.

*Reincarnation* (dir. Takashi Shimizu, Japan 2005). Nagisa, a young actress, is cast in the lead role in a horror film about a real-life event that took place 35 years earlier, during which a college professor filmed himself on a rampage in a hotel, murdering 11 hotel guests and his own children. The most traumatic part of this horror is the murder of a little girl hiding in a cubbyhole and clutching a doll. Nagisa believes that she is the reincarnation of the little girl, but turns out to be the reincarnation of the murderous professor. *Guilt trip:* Aside from extensive POV shots from the killer's perspective showing various murders, the film is really about a person who fancies herself innocent but develops an awareness of guilt. As in *The Grudge* and *The Ring*, guilt does not die with the individual; like abuse, it is eternal; "it will never stop." Two things indicate this clearly: the murdered little girl's doll that haunts Nagisa with its eternal recording "Together forever," and the final scene, which shows Nagisa in a mental hospital, surrounded by the eternally vengeful ghosts of children she murdered in a previous incarnation.

*Shattered Lives* (dir. Carl Lindbergh, USA 2009). Little Rachel, whose mother cheats on her father and neglects Rachel completely, stabs her mother to death, manipulated by two evil clown dolls. In the end, Rachel embarks on a promising career as a serial killer. *Guilt trip:* Like so many other films on child abuse, the film makes the point that abused children are permanently damaged and pass on the abuse. Rachel is excruciatingly aware that her mother does not care about her: "I don't think you love me," she informs her mother. "Just because you're my mom doesn't mean you love me. You just think of me as someone you have to take care of." The idea that yesterday's abused become tomorrow's abusers is expressed not only through Rachel's ultimate career choice but also in an early scene showing her interpretation, at the age of five, of parenthood as she has experienced it. At a tea party with her stuffed animals, she rebukes her teddy Lelo for not drinking his tea, informing him that Mommy and Daddy don't love Lelo anymore and will now sell him to the circus. After the teddy is tossed aside, Rachel poses a threatening question to the other stuffed animals: "Now, does anyone *else* have a problem drinking their tea?"

*Village of the Damned* (dir. Wolf Rilla, UK 1960; remake dir. John Carpenter, USA 1995). A town is plagued by a horde of blonde children with eerily penetrating eyes, all born on the same day, who turn out to be hostile aliens endowed with unlimited powers, which they use to control and kill humans. *Guilt trip:* The film deals with a number of fears of the atomic age, often visualized in 1950s and 60s films through the themes of alien invasion, mad scientists, or nuclear fallout. Humanity's problems in dealing with the weird children are solved neatly by dropping an atomic bomb on them, a possible allusion to the American act of bombing the population (including the children) of Hiroshima and Nagasaki under the pretense of saving the human race.

*Wicked Little Things* (dir. J. S. Cardone, USA 2006). A widow moves with her two daughters, 16-year-old Sarah and 10-year-old Emma, to an old house in the Pennsylvania mountains, unaware that a nearby mine is haunted by zombie children with a taste for human flesh. Emma makes friends with a little girl named Mary, who used to live in her room. *Guilt trip:* As it turns out, the zombie kids, including Mary, were the victims of a cruel mine owner, who exploited and murdered immigrant children who would not be missed. While the theme of child abuse merely furnishes the background story and excuse for transgressive images of children feasting on the guts of their victims, the film does, in single scenes, address the theme of child neglect more seriously, if indirectly. As Emma explains her fondness for Mary: "I was playing with Mary. She hasn't had anyone to play with in a very, very long time."

*Would You Kill a Child?* (dir. Narciso Ibáñez Serrador, Spain 1976). The film is remarkable less for its actual story, in which the children on an island kill all of the island's adults, than for the prequel that motivates this story as a revenge flick. The prequel is essentially a global *guilt trip*, listing atrocities against children throughout the twentieth century in various countries.

## Teenage Wasteland

*Carrie* (dir. Brian de Palma, USA 1976; remake dir. Kimberly Peirce, USA 2013). Carrie's entire life outside of school is marked by egregious child abuse, both physical and psychological, at the hands her maniacally religious mother; it is ultimately this abuse that prevents Carrie from "fitting in" and that makes her the target of further abuse at school. *Guilt trip:* Viewers are far more likely to recognize themselves as members of a majority (in this case, the school bullies) rather than the exception that Carrie represents, a sadly abused outcast who develops deadly telekinetic powers.

*Dorothy Mills* (dir. Agnès Merlet, Ireland/France 2008) tells the story of a disturbed teenager under psychiatric observation in a devoutly religious Irish village on a remote island. Her psychiatrist, Jane Morton, who is brought in when Dorothy nearly kills a child, has lost her husband and child, and gradually discovers that Dorothy is being used by the entire village to channel their dead children. Dorothy, thus forced into dealing with multiple personalities, ends up channeling Jane's little boy, who accuses Jane of letting him drown. *Guilt trip:* The film is full of traumatic instances of abuse, including extensive scenes of mistreatment, woman hating, gang rape and murder, all of which are being covered up by the island community.

*Hard Candy* (dir. David Slade, USA 2005). Hayley, a 14-year-old girl, meets Jeff, a pedophile and child killer, online, acts seductively enough to get him to bring her home, dopes him and mistreats him severely (including a highly traumatic false castration scene) in order to get him to admit to the murder of another teen girl. Ultimately she forces him to confess and commit suicide. The entire film is an elaborate *guilt trip*. Extensive torture inflicted by the "innocent" (the girl and potential rape victim) on the guilty (the pedophile) make any kind of viewer identification impossible. The pedophile killer Jeff was himself severely abused as a child (he tells Hayley that his aunt sat him down on a hot burner when he was nine years old). The avenging angel of tortured and murdered girls is herself a serial killer (as the end of the film reveals, she has done this before). The film is a rarity: a revenge flick that withholds viewer satisfaction. Viewers are left with an urgent feeling that something has to be done about child abuse—but not that.

*The Hole* (dir. Joe Dante, USA 2009). Two brothers, Dane and Lucas, are moved to a small town by their single mother, where they befriend their next door neighbor Julie. In the basement of their new house the three stumble on a deep hole that leads to the darkest corridors of their worst fears. For the older brother, this turns out to be fear of his severely abusive father who used to beat him with a belt. *Guilt trip:* The worst fear turns out to be nothing but a symbol for guilt. Julie feels profoundly guilty about her role in the accidental death of her best friend; Dane feels guilty about his inability to protect Lucas from harm. What Dane needs to find out is not that he is afraid of his father, but that he has not inherited his father's abusive tendencies. In the surreal world on the other side of the hole, in which his father pursues Dane, Dane breaks the spell by stating his unwillingness to pass on the abuse he has experienced. "I'm nothing like you," he tells his father, throwing the belt, the symbol of child abuse, down on the floor on which his father is standing. The floor shatters like glass, plunging his father into darkness.

# 8

# Play
## *The Peter Pan Syndrome*

*"Day*
*Play*
*We play all day.*
*Night*
*Fight*
*We fight all night."*
—Dr. Seuss, *Hop On Pop* (1963)

## Psych(o) Games

Developmental psychology has had rather a lot to say about the question why, and how, children play: to expend superfluous energy (Herbert Spencer), to train for survival in the adult world (Karl Groos), to acquire new skills with the assistance of adults (Lee Vygotsky), or for experiential reasons of their own, also known as: having fun (David Elkind). Freud famously offered a more sinister description of the male child's development in *The Ego and the Id*, when he defined, under the heading "The Oedipus Complex," desires to remove (murder) the father as a normal part of the son's psychosexual development. Freud tempered this disturbing scenario with the good news that the potential killer is merely the son's *Id*, part of the child's unconscious mind, not the child himself. Normal development into adulthood mandates resolving the Oedipus complex in a process in which the purely instinctual Id, which wants to eliminate Father, is vanquished by the far more reasonable Ego. Like the Id, the Ego is part of the unconscious mind; unlike the Id, it recognizes the father's superiority, turning him from a potential victim into the object of idolization and identification. All of these assessments of child's play and child development are motivated not by the world of children but by that of adults. Developmental psychology commonly views childhood as a path, not a destination.

Can these ideas by the world's greatest thinkers on child development help us fathom a child's murder of an adult, which is, after all, hardly a rarity in horror films about evil children? If childhood is, as developmental psychology claims, merely the path to adulthood, and if the most significant steps on this path are taken, as Freud tells us, by the unconscious rather than the conscious mind, one explanation that readily springs to mind is the child's unconscious rejection of his or her own future, namely: adulthood. Experts on emotional disorders have called this the "Peter Pan Syndrome" and defined it as a psychological condition that affects people who do not wish or feel unable to grow up. And yet, when children kill adults, in the movies or in real life, the act is almost never assigned this or any symbolic meaning. Explanations for such acts emerging from reporters' pens and judges' benches range from revenge for or self-defense against child abuse to cult, gang and thrill killings, pathology, or violence on TV.[1] A child's killing of an adult is thus interpreted literally, as an attack on a specific adult, not figuratively, as an attack on the idea of adulthood. Doing so would be severely at odds with the psychological literature's positivistic view of adulthood as not only the inevitable but also the appropriate and desirable outcome of childhood. To assign a symbolic value to murder—or, for that matter, to child's play—means rethinking the act as an end in and of itself, rather than a means to an end, such as thrill-seeking (in the case of murder) or training for adulthood (in the case of child's play). Jean Piaget may have gone half-way down this disturbing path when he described children's play as "assimilation," the transformation of the environment to meet the requirements of the self, and contrasted it with work, which he defined as "accommodation" or the transformation of the self to meet the requirements of the environment.[2]

Many horror films cast a child's murder of adults both as a game and as a wholesale rejection of adulthood. Such killing games appear as "assimilation" in Piaget's sense, as a subordination of the environment to the self, and thus as an act of childish self-assertion. Murdering adults, particularly parents, is an expression of the Peter Pan Syndrome, an act defining childhood as intrinsic, not preparatory. Such films uncouple children from adults by denying that adulthood is the child's future. In so doing, they also deny that children and adults form part of the same race of humans. What these two distinct species have in common is that both play psych(o)-games. Children express what they think of adults through play. Adults express what they think of children through child psychology.

## Peopletoys *(USA 1974)*, Mikey *(USA 1992)*, Home Movie *(USA 2008)*

*Peopletoys*, a.k.a. *Devil Times Five*, a.k.a. *The Horrible House on the Hill* (dir. Sean MacGregor and David Sheldon [uncredited], USA 1974) features a team of killer children, including 15-year-old Sister Hannah (Gale Smale), so called because she appears in a nun's habit, 13-year-old vain and beautiful David (Leif Garrett), 12-year-old soldier boy Brian (Tierre Turner), pyromaniac Susan, who looks about 14 (Tia Thompson) and four-year-old cutie Moe (Dawn Lyn). The Fearsome Five are pitted against a group of adults snowed in in a holiday chalet: arrogant and overbearing patriarch Papa Doc (Gene Evans) and his entourage consisting of his daughters Julie (Joan McCall) and Lovely (Carolyn Stellar), Julie's partner and Lovely's ex Rick (Taylor Lacher), Papa Doc's disgruntled employee Harvey (Sorrell Brooke), Harvey's alcoholic wife Ruth (Shelley Morrison), and the mentally retarded Ralph (John Durren), who serves the guests as handyman, cook and general dogsbody. Once the children are taken in by the adults, the rest of the film is given over to a predictable series of gory slayings.

Two aspects stand out. The first is the film's rejection of the definition of childhood as a phase leading inexorably and appropriately to adulthood. The second is its explicit definition of all killings as communal child's play, visualized precisely as described by child psychologists from Spencer to Montessori: as a means to expend superfluous energy, to train for survival in the adult world, and to acquire new skills. The children entrap and kill Papa Doc with the help of an elaborate contraption such as only a child could devise, a chair swinging from the ceiling with a long sword-like stabbing instrument attached to its seat. Immediately after his death, David and Brian get into a fight over who deserves credit for rigging the murder weapon. The children then place Papa Doc outside in a sitting position and build a snowman around his corpse. Harvey is killed—presumably for beating David, an exquisitely sore loser, at chess—while showing David how to chop wood and belittling his swing, but as it turns out, David's swing is much improved when he chops through Harvey's neck. Pyromaniac Susan sets Ruth on fire after Brian and David have set the stage by pouring gas over her; afterwards all children dance merrily around the screaming and twisting bonfire that is Ruth. Little Moe, upbraided by Lovely for playing with her make-up, kills Lovely with Hannah's help as Lovely is taking a bath: Hannah holds Lovely's head under water, while Moe pours Papa Doc's pet piranhas into the tub, giggling gaily at Lovely's death throes (Fig. 22).

With the exception of Harvey's decapitation, all killings are collaborative, the result of elaborate contraptions and planning. The impression one is left with is that of childish problem-solving akin to building a Lego castle or a model ship. Spur-of-the-moment play, such as dances around burning people or snowmen built around corpses, develops spontaneously post-mortem. The final scene shows all kids and corpses, their "peopletoys," assembled in the living room, the corpses arranged in a circle the way a little girl might arrange dolls for a tea party. The children interact with them as a child interacts with dolls, with the child speaking both the lines assigned to the doll and his or her own. When finally the decision is made to move on—"Game's over," Susan announces bossily—little Moe cries inconsolably, wailing: "I don't want to leave Julie!," but Hannah soothes her with the timeless

Fig. 22. Child's play as "assimilation": Bathtime in *Peopletoys* (1974) (Barrister Productions).

parental classic: "We're gonna have some brand-new toys soon." Mollified, Moe pecks dead Lovely on the cheek with a cheery "Bye, Lovely!," exactly the way in which a little girl would kiss a favorite doll good-bye when Mommy puts her foot down: No, you can't take your doll into the bathtub. The play-theme is so elaborately enacted that it practically trumps the terror the scene seeks to create. There is an "Aaaawwwww, how cute" quality about it that contrasts absurdly with, but also quite overpowers, the visual reminders of the awful reality behind the game—gaping wounds, Ruth's charred face, blood everywhere.

Initially, most children are paired with an adult. Hannah latches onto Ralph; Susan willingly submits to Ruth's mothering; David plays chess with Harvey and wants to be his "friend"; Moe develops a very cuddly relationship with Lovely. But if this seems to imply a normal child-adult relationship, with the adult in authority over the child and the child in training to become an adult, the viewer is soon disabused of this idea. All men in the film are defined by careerism and greed. Papa Doc, the film's Alpha Male, brags tirelessly about his own "achievements" and riches. The other men are cast as little more than circling sharks, jockeying for position and hoping for offal from his table. Almost all adult relationships in the film are fraught and shallow. Harvey resents Papa Doc for withholding his promotion. Rick hates Papa Doc's overbearing nature. Julie and Lovely cat-fight for Rick's affections. Lovely tries to seduce retarded Ralph, who does not cooperate because he simply doesn't understand what she wants. Drunkard Ruth rejects Harvey's increasingly desperate sexual advances in favor of her love relationship with Jim Beam. All women are defined by sex: the wanton (Lovely), the willing (Julie), and the frigid lush who replaces sex with booze (Ruth). There are no adults in this film that could serve as role models for children. If these characters are as good as it gets, adulthood richly merits rejection.

Indeed, the natural link between children and adults, and adulthood as the inevitable future of childhood, is broken several times throughout the film. One such rift is shown in the inexplicable disproportionality between the normality of the child's problem—being upset at losing a game, for instance, or being forbidden to play with the adult's possessions—and the extremity of the child's response. Unless we feel moved to accept the insanity plea offered by the fact, mentioned once in passing and not referred to again, that the children have escaped from a mental institution, this rift remains unexplained. But there are also more principal differences made in the film between children and adults, differences that pertain not only to psychotic but to all children. When Julie, for example, comments on the children's "strange" behavior, Rick offers an explanation: "Kids today," he tells her, "are smoking pot at 10 and a bong at 12. So we're not gonna be expecting them to be normal like us." Kids, in other words, are *not* little adults-in-training; they are fundamentally different from adults, "strange" in the sense of alien.

Another aspect that the film leaves up in the air is the fact that some killings are cast as revenge for unexplained grievances, which are, as dialogue establishes, unrelated to the childish gripes of being beaten at a game or having a toy taken away. Hannah, while cutting Rick's throat, screams: "You killed it! You killed it!" Whom or what Rick has supposedly killed remains unclear. Similarly, Susan accuses Ruth immediately before setting her on fire: "You want to hurt me," a statement completely unsupported by evidence. None of this—the casting of some murders as avenging an imagined wrong, the collaborative nature of all killings, and the unbridgeable difference between child and adult—makes any *prima facie* sense. Yet all three aspects are strangely evocative of Piaget's ideas about how children construct a moral worldview. Children, he claims, arrive at ideas of justice in interaction with peers, not adults, who are swept aside in the process. Since adult authority and the child's desire for autonomy war with each other, the child's sense of justice not only develops independently from adult teaching but must be upheld in the face of adult opposition. The murders in *Peopletoys,* and worse, its reduction of people to toys, are a game not only in the literal filmic portrayal of child's play, but also in the sense of Piaget's definition of the child's game as "assimilation." By adjusting the environment to benefit the self, the children constitute and assert themselves at the adults' expense. Murder as a game does more than get rid of adults; it tears down the bridge between kids and grown-ups. No road leads from childhood to adulthood, for adults are fundamentally unrelated to children: creatures who can't be expected to be "normal like us," who play their gruesome games following their own mysterious and, to adults, utterly incomprehensible sense of justice.

Perhaps the best way to describe *Mikey* (dir. Dennis Dimster, USA 1992) is as a sort of *Omen* minus the Devil. At the age of nine, Mikey (Brian Bonsali) is an experienced killer of adults, most often using toys as murder weapons (Fig. 23). Part of the circumstance that enables his career as a serial murderer is the fact that he is adopted. This provides him with an unlimited supply of families to kill, a good cover story as a traumatized child, and a clean slate after each murder since the records of adopted children are commonly sealed. In the first five minutes of the film, he builds a bonfire on his bedroom floor, drowns his little sister in the swimming pool, electrocutes his adoptive mother in the bathtub and bashes his adoptive father's head in with a baseball bat after tripping him by throwing marbles on the floor. The police find Mikey cowering in the closet, the sole survivor of a horrible tragedy. Although Detective Reynolds (Mark Venturini) suspects him, it hardly matters: Mikey is taken in by Social Services, examined by a child psychologist, cleared for adoption, and assigned to Neil (John Diehl) and Rachel Trenton (Mimi Craven), who are delighted with their "perfect" new son. His new neighbors are his playmate Ben (Whitby Hertford) and Ben's older sister Jessie (Josie Bissett), on whom Mikey develops a crush. The only people who ever suspect Mikey, beyond the powerless detective investigating the first murder, are Jessie and Shawn (Ashley Laurence), Mikey's teacher, Rachel's best friend, and a trained child psychologist. Shawn presents Neil and Rachel with disturbing evidence, which is met with complete denial. Thus given a new lease on lunacy, Mikey murders Jessie's boyfriend David (David Rogge, using the old electrocution in the bath trick), Rachel (hammer and huge glass splinter), Mr. Jenkins (Lyman Ward), his head teacher and coach (bow and arrow), Shawn (marble and slingshot) and

Fig. 23. Child's play as "assimilation": Playtime in *Mikey* (1992) (Imperial Entertainment/Tapestry Films).

Neil (gas explosion). The film ends with a new start for Mikey: an agency worker tells a new set of adoptive parents that they found "Josh" on a highway with a bad case of amnesia and were unable to determine his origins. "Josh," impeccably scrubbed and looking like Sweet Innocence personified, delights his new parents with the line that he uses on each new set: "Are you gonna be my new Mommy and Daddy?"

Mikey is not a traumatized kid, but he plays one to perfection, fooling every shrink and every parent. Clearly, he's got the adults' numbers, but their own systems for the protection of children make it difficult for them to get his. How good he is at playing the victim is encapsulated in the scene in which he meets Jessie. As Jessie returns home, Ben and Mikey conspire to make him appear dead. Mikey is on the floor, not breathing, his pulse stopped. Jessie, panicked, administers mouth-to-mouth resuscitation. After enjoying this for a bit, Mikey sits up laughing and explains how one can fake a dead pulse by clutching a marble.

Part of what makes Mikey such a good con artist is his ability to exploit the adult tendency to psychoanalyze "disturbed" children. He also knows that child psychologists, whether pop or pro, are exceedingly easy to guilt-trip because they inevitably assume the child's innocence and the adults' guilt. Immediately before dispatching various parents he accuses them of not loving him anymore, a line delivered with all the despondency of the neglected child. Apparently, this is enough to throw parents into an emotional turmoil sufficient to blanket any awareness of the danger he poses, no matter how obvious he makes that danger. In two scenes, Mikey stands over a mother in the bathtub with a plugged-in electrical gadget, practically announcing his intentions: "If I threw this in the bathtub, it would work just like an electric chair." In a third, he threatens his adoptive mother with a hammer. Each time he is told that whatever he's got in his hand is not a toy, and to please put it down.

The film is essentially composed of a series of mismatched adult-child interactions. Mikey kills adults; adults try to figure him out. He plays games based on a fairly shrewd assessment of the adult psyche; they imitate childish games and play-acting in the service of child psychology. In both games and psychology, Mikey is way ahead of adults, although—as in the scene with the hairdryer—he constantly tells them what he is doing. Mikey likes nothing better than to re-enact and re-view his own crimes, an act of murderous gloating that adults misinterpret every single time. After the first murder, the police psychologist tries to help Mikey over his trauma by asking him to re-enact the killings with dolls, and Mikey does so in lurid detail, upon which the psychologist pronounces him cured and releases him for adoption. At his new home, Mikey paints a picture of his former adoptive sister drowning in the swimming pool. His new parents see a little girl swimming in a blue lake and respond with praise, followed by a lengthy psychoanalysis of what the motif of the swimming girl might say about Mikey's character. And he shoots video footage of each of his killings, which he then watches in his bedroom, telling his concerned parents, when they ask what on earth he is watching: "Just a horror film." None of this rings any alarm bells with the film's adults. It is enough to make viewers a little impatient: must he really paint them a picture? He does just that, time and again, but adults can only see what he shows them through the lens of standard child psychology, which turns out to be a very blunt tool.

Mikey's strategy is simple; he plays the perfect little child. Chirpily affectionate toward his parents, he dutifully does his chores and returns the lost handbags of little old ladies without accepting the offered reward. Whenever fleeting concerns arise due to his occasional weird behavior—for example, his abiding interest in horror films, his declared favorite being *Friday the 13th*—he turns on the trauma. "My real mom and dad, they were bad," he informs Mr. Jenkins, and treats him to an elaborate shivering and heavy-breathing response to the school skeleton, knowing that this will bring the psychologists running, and knowing also that they are the easiest adults to fool. He sticks thumbtacks in his arm, where Shawn is certain to find them. Shawn and Mr. Jenkins promptly call in Neil and Rachel to share their psychiatric evaluation: "We feel that Mikey maybe, just maybe, is suffering from an emotional disorder called Unattached Syndrome."[3] Neil sputters his denial but then is told that Mikey is way beyond disturbing pictures now:

*Jenkins:* Self-mutilation is an expression of a child crying out for help.
*Neil:* Hey, wait a minute. I've read all the books, too, okay, and I haven't seen a child crying out for help. This is such crap! He's a wonderful kid, he … he's perfect!
*Shawn:* Yeah, he's *too* perfect.
*Neil:* There is no such thing.
*Shawn:* Yeah, Neil, there is. In children with psychotic tendencies.
*Neil:* Psychotics. So now we have Ted Bundy Junior, is that it?

The scene reveals a real uncertainty among adults as to what constitutes a normal child. Parents want a perfect child; to them, there is no such thing as too perfect. But this same quality would raise the suspicions of psychiatrists, in whose experience an abused and traumatized child is the expected normality. Mikey's career as a miniature serial killer is enabled by his uncanny ability to answer both expectations.

The film spends most of its time refuting psychoanalyses of Mikey as delusional. It offers no explanation for Mikey's murderous character beyond the fact that it constitutes his version of normality. When Jessie tells him that she was kicked out of school for being a bad girl, he asks nonchalantly, "What did you do? Kill somebody?," as if this were a perfectly ordinary thing to do to irksome classmates. Although he usually accuses his parents of insufficient parenting right before dispatching them, it is clear that the murders are not reactive, motivated by revenge, or related in any way to his parents' behavior. His first parents are strict with him, and he kills them. His second parents are veritable push-overs, and he kills them. Several times throughout the film, he is defined as a sadist; he enjoys reliving his victims' awful deaths on tapes that he calls "Mikey's funniest home videos," and he clearly takes pride in his work. When Neil returns home from work and asks Mikey, who has just gruesomely murdered three people, whether he had a good day, Mikey answers with great satisfaction: "Yeah. Got a lot accomplished." He takes Neil into the dining room, promising him a surprise, and reveals with a flourish a scene taken straight from *Peopletoys*: the corpses of Mr. Jenkins, Shawn and Rachel seated around the table, with the school skeleton set up at the head of the table, ready to carve up the turkey. But this kind of gloating does as little to "explain" Mikey as does the label "psychotic." In child psychiatry, this may mean something; in horror, it is akin to the film throwing up its hands: *I don't know what's making him tick. You* tell *me.*

If *Mikey* can be said to have a point, it is simply that adults, when faced with the inexplicably evil child, are chronically incapable of this act of resignation. Because they see Mikey as a future adult, they cannot accept that his character and killings may be inexplicable in adult terms. Thus they exhaust themselves in chasing any number of spurious explanations, usually psychological ones, all of which turn out to be wrong. A more apropos title for the film might have been *Mikey's Parents, Teachers and Shrinks*: at the end of *Mikey*, we know everything about how adults see Mikey but nothing about Mikey, whose motivations remain obscure to the end.

*Home Movie* (dir. Christopher Denham, USA 2008) confronts viewers with two inexplicably evil children, ten-year-old twins Jack (Austin Williams) and Emily (Amber Joy Williams). Their parents, David (Adrian Pasdar), a pastor, and Clare (Cady McClain), a child psychiatrist, struggle in vain to achieve the Norman Rockwell family idyll.[4] The externals match that idyll rather well: Mr. and Mrs. Extremely Goodlooking produce the requisite two children, a boy and a girl, love them to bits, acquire assorted pets (dog, cat, frog and goldfish) and move to a peaceful rural location. But this blissful scenario is immediately undercut by hefty hints at the horror tradition. The family's last name is Poe (as in Edgar Allan); the children were born on Halloween; the house they live in is an upscale version of the proverbial cabin in the woods, and the woods look like they should be haunted by the Blair Witch.[5] As if that were not enough, all forms of interaction and fun in the Poe household evoke, play with, or caricature horror conventions. For Halloween, the parents enact an elaborate ghost story. Bedtime stories are tales of a sinister child-eating double-headed dragon who pretends to be a child, disguising his true identity with a paper mask. On their tenth wedding anniversary, David approaches Clare in the shower with a rose, and then humorously enacts *Psycho*'s famous shower scene by pretending to stab the shower curtain with the rose, mimicking the screechy string music that punctuates the stabbing motions in Hitchcock's original scene.

The home movie of the film's title consists of two parts: the personal—home movie footage shot initially by the parents and later the children—and the professional, Clare's video diaries of her psychiatric treatment of disturbed children. The home movie part constitutes the majority of the footage and is, as one would expect, dominated by holidays—Halloween, Thanksgiving, Christmas, Valentine's Day, Easter. Both parents exhibit an impish playfulness and sense of fun that would delight every child, or so one should think. David, ever full of beans, hams it up for the children on camera, where he dons a Santa suit at Christmas and a pink bunny overall for Easter. The children, however, stubbornly refuse to cooperate in their parents' cinematic fabrication of happy family life. Contrasting sharply with David's unrelenting chirpiness, the children are sullenly uncommunicative and aggressively uninterested in his silly games. The first sign of a rift between children and parents is Jack and Emily's Clubhouse, a shack in the woods with a big sign at the gate reading "No Parents Allowed." The first sign of hostility is Emily biting Clare and Jack throwing a rock at David's head while playing baseball in the yard. From there, matters deteriorate sharply. Jack puts the goldfish in his sandwich; Emily puts the frog in a vise. They crucify the family cat; they decapitate the family dog and put its head on a spike; they are caught eating raw meat. When they attack a boy at school by biting him severely, David and Clare finally admit that something is wrong with their children and embark on a search for solutions. Like a good churchman, David hits upon demonic possession and tries to exorcise his children; like a good shrink, Clare puts her faith in psychiatric testing and pills.

Fast-forward two months, and the children seem cured. Giggly, cute, communicative, and affectionate, they even befriend Christian (Lucian Maisel), the classmate they had savaged at school. It soon emerges, though, that they have merely learned how to act normal. At Easter, Jack and Emily come close to murdering Christian. David and Clare surprise them in the clubhouse, where they find Christian tied to the table, trussed up in a garbage bag. Jack and Emily sit at the table with paper masks over their heads and knives and forks in their hands, as if sitting down at dinner, ready to eat Christian alive. The children are charged with attempted murder and inexplicably left in their parents' custody while awaiting arraignment on the following day. During their final night in the house, they drug their parents, truss them up in garbage bags and rope, and place them on the dinner table. The final shot, before Emily covers the camera with her hand and turns it off, shows Jack and Emily with their paper masks at the dinner table, knives and forks in hand, ready to tuck into Mom and Dad.

*Home Movie* is not, as it appears to be, a Rockwellian idyll gone horribly wrong, but—from the outset—a tale of two dragons. The first time we see Jack and Emily is in the Halloween sequence filmed by David, where Jack and Emily appear sitting at the table wearing dragon masks, with David uttering a mock scream from behind the camera: "My children have been turned into fire-eating dragons!" Playing Hide and Seek with the children, the parents find a dragon puppet, shortly before one of the dragon-masked children runs towards a laughing Clare. As the camera goes dark, we hear her surprised voice: "Did you just bite me?" Dragons, masks, and biting recur in a bedtime story David reads to the children. The tale is that of a two-headed dragon (alluding to Jack and Emily, who are twins), who disguises his evil identity behind a paper mask in order to convince children that he is really a child (just as, in the earlier Halloween scene, Jack and Emily donned dragon masks, playing two children pretending to be dragons). The dragon in the bedtime story springs into action on Halloween (the children's birthday). The children in the tale ask him to prove that he's one of them by taking off his mask. He refuses, but "What I can do, he said, is talk like you. I can walk like you. Shoot, I can even dance like you." After this demonstration, the children trust him and invite him to eat with them, only to be gobbled up themselves. "The children started to scream, but their screams were soon swallowed inside the dragon's stomach."

This scene has been interpreted as not merely prefiguring, but actually inspiring Jack's and Emily's later taste for human flesh: in exposing the children to horror stimuli, or so the theory goes, the parents themselves are guilty of bringing about the children's deviance.[6] In fact, it is almost impossible to read the film in that way. The film does not offer a "before" and "after" scenario during which viewers see the children's gradual decline from normality to monstrosity. In fact, there is no pretense that Jack and Emily ever were anything other than that as which they appear from the very first scene: man-eating dragons playing children. The conflicting interpretations of the two-headed dragon story seem to hint at this already. Whereas Clare considers it "the most vastly inappropriate fairy tale I've ever heard," David defends it as "an allegory for the young: Don't trust strangers." The children, however, listen to the story with rapt attention. To them, its moral is neither pedagogical nor allegorical but literal: from the dragon, they learn to walk, talk and dance like children. They show off these skills in the Easter segment of the home video, in which they act all cute and cuddly, delighting their parents with hugs and I love you's. If such shows of affection and normality are their figurative version of the dragon's paper mask, Jack and Emily don actual paper masks in both cannibal scenes, thus outing themselves—like the tale's two-headed dragon—as dragons pretending to be children.

The problem is not that the parents cause the horror; the problem is that they play with it and refuse to take it seriously even when it stares them in the face. Following each domestic disaster, they simply go on to the next activity, usually involving costuming, child's play—in which the parents engage with a gusto that the children conspicuously lack—and another chapter in the home movie. Soon after Jack puts the goldfish in his sandwich and Emily squashes the frog in the vise, David rewards the children with ice cream cones. Clare gently points out the obvious: "You know, our kids don't deserve ice cream right now. They deserve a lecture from their father, because what they did was wrong." But instead of "lecturing" the children—a rather anemic response to the sadistic killing of three family pets—David jauntily returns to his cure for all ills: "Why don't we make a movie? Spend a little more family time together."

Like horror movies, David's home movie sequences are repetitive, following a formulaic and predictable pattern. In trying to construct familial bliss, David and Clare become children themselves, creating fun and games-scenarios which they film as a chronicle of their happy family life. They force their children's surly participation in activities ranging from bedtime stories, birthday parties, and baseball games in the yard to Easter egg hunts, cutting a Christmas tree, unwrapping Christmas presents, Thanksgiving dinners, and theatrical Halloween hauntings. Each scene cuts off abruptly when the children do something to disrupt the idyll by, for example, biting their parents, pelting them with rocks, pissing on the floor, throwing their Thanksgiving dinners onto the floor, or killing pets in ever more colorful ways. This is then followed by a new fun and games-snippet, as if nothing untoward had ever happened. This circular and repetitive structure expresses the level of denial on the part of the parents. Their business-as-usual attitude, the chipper tenacity with which they keep playing Happy Family, bespeaks a desperation that gives this fantasy the lie. Until the attempted murder of Christian, nothing the children do ever has real consequences.

Despite the recurring horror themes in the games the parents play, the film explicitly uncouples the children's behavior from the parents', much like *Mikey* does. David's and Clare's stubborn self-deception and other lapses in judgment notwithstanding, they are portrayed as solid parents. They love their children and each other, and they are moreover, between the two of them, professionally qualified—or so one should think—to handle all aberrations of the mind (Clare's expertise as a child psychiatrist) or the soul (David's vocation as a pastor). In one of the rare sweet segments of the film, the two muse what a psychiatrist and a pastor could possibly have in common, and conclude that it is faith. He doesn't believe in Freud; she doesn't believe in God, but both believe in their family—wrongly, as it turns out. In the end, it is David's and Clare's noblest quality, their faith, that leads to disaster. The children fool both of them easily by playing into their respective faith systems. They respond strongly to David's exorcism, writhing and screaming when he sprinkles them with holy water: it's not quite turning heads 360 degrees and spitting pea soup, but not terribly far from it, either. Based on this spirited performance from children who are usually about as lively as a potted plant, David would have every reason to believe that the exorcism worked, and he does. Conversely, Clare puts her faith in science; she diagnoses Jack and Emily with "conduct disorder, a precursor to adult ASP, or Anti-Social Personality Disorder" and puts them on a regime of pills. Like David, she is apparently rewarded with success and interprets the children's improvement as "proving once again that there is no good child, there is no bad child, there is only diagnosis, and with diagnosis, treatment. I have treated my children."

Just as the treatments represent opposite beliefs, David and Clare disagree about the cause of the problem. Clare suspects David, himself an abused child, of abusing his children in turn, leading to their aberrant behavior: "Abused children, as proven by Piaget, are predisposed, as adults, to abusing their own children," she lectures, and explains the children's actions as an "obvious revolt from two abused children." David, conversely, muses about the modern disbelief in the reality of demons: "We've somehow today deemed it more palatable to reduce John Wayne Gacy's 33 murders to the fact that he was abused as a child." Thus David and Clare are not presented as an ideal couple. Although they love each other, they do not cooperate in their attempts to heal the children, each stuck in his or her own inflexible beliefs in specific causes and possible cures. Neither are they portrayed as ideal parents; they ignore the problem for far too long for that. Yet the film offers no link between David's and Clare's faults of faith and denial and their failure to cure their children. There is no indication that an earlier response or greater cooperation on the parents' part would have resulted in a different outcome, no sign even that Jack and Emily can be healed. They can neither be won over by the adult imitation of children's games nor dissected by adult tools, such as child psychiatry. They are not, after all, actual children but dragons posing as children, and thus utterly unrelated to adults and their world.

Ultimately, David's and Clare's greatest act of denial is their refusal to realize this. To the very end, they hold on to the illusion that these are children and thus likely to respond like children. Shortly before being killed, David, tied up and helpless, decides that now might be the time to show them a firm hand: "Jack! Emily! Stop this shit. Right now! Listen to your father. Untie me." Similarly Clare, in what will turn out to be her last words to the children: "This is it. You are leaving this house." These belated and useless assertions of parental authority, delivered at a time when the children have them completely at their mercy, serve to underscore the parents' helplessness, but also the one aspect that has defined all of their parenting: profound denial.

Whereas Clare and David learn nothing about Jack and Emily, the children learn much from them. But while child psychology views a child's learning as training for adulthood, Jack and Emily store every bit of information carefully away for future use *against* their parents. When Jack rakes leaves in the yard and finds a dead bug, David tells him to put it in the trash bag because "dead things go in trash bags," little imagining that he and Clare will end up in one. David shows Jack how to pick a lock, which comes in handy when Jack picks the lock on his parents' bedroom door shortly before killing them. David shows Jack how to tie a bowline, an unbreakable knot of rope, which Jack later uses to tie up his parents. The final scene shows David and Clare struggling wildly but vainly in their garbage bags, unable to undo their bonds (Fig. 24). Even the most important object lesson for Jack and Emily comes from David, who reads them the tale of the double-headed dragon as a bedtime story: learning from the dragon how to pose as a child enables Jack and Emily to progress from killing pets to murdering parents.

The final lesson Jack and Emily learn from their parents is how to make a home movie. David's and Clare's loss of control is symbolized by their loss of the camera, which the children take over. Once they establish their directorship of the new home movie, which they

Fig. 24. "Dead things go in trashbags": Dinnertime in *Home Movie* (2008) (Moderncine).

call "The Jack and Emily Show," it becomes clear that everything we have seen thus far, while filmed by David or Clare, was overlaid by the children's vision. Throughout "The David and Clare Show," several scenes, usually scenes showing them in great anguish, are rewound and replayed, as if watched by someone who simply can't believe it, or—and this is far more likely—as if watched by someone who enjoys it so much that he wants another peek. That vision is now revealed as the POV of Jack and Emily, the viewers of the footage. This is ironically appropriate, since David and Clare shot all home movie footage for their children in the assumption that it "might be cool for you guys to look back at when you're older." Jack and Emily, on the other hand, are not filming for their parents, but for an unnamed viewer who is identified with our POV. Jack, speaking directly into the camera, issues a challenge to the viewer by way of introduction to the final sequence in which he and Emily subdue and cannibalize their parents: "You're quiet in there. I can't even hear you. But I know you're there. Let's have a staring contest. I dare you to stare until our movie's done. I bet you you can't."

This is, of course, the old horror trick of identifying the viewer with the perpetrator: both Jack and the viewer are staring, first at each other, then at David's and Clare's brutalization and murder. But Jack's introduction also feigns a moral test that the viewer will most likely fail. The reverse coin of Jack's nasty dare is the idea that an ethical viewer would, at some point, be unable to continue watching and turn away in horror, pity or fear. Finally, Jack's taunt guilt-trips the viewer by referencing the difference between staring, watching, and looking (or, as Clare suggested as the correct viewing mode for home movies, "looking back"). Staring can serve no moral purpose; it is a self-indulgence of the lowest order, like rubber-necking at car accidents, gawking at the guy on the 27th floor about to jump, or watching a horror movie. That we will ultimately win Jack's bet and outstare the dragon is the film's way of putting us in our moral place.

Like *Mikey*, *Home Movie* portrays evil in the form of a child without offering an explanation, psychological or otherwise, that would make sense to an adult. *Home Movie* goes a step further than *Mikey* by presenting us with a series of red herrings, playing expertly with the horror tradition of "explaining" the genre's evil children. It alludes to the haunted-house flick, the demonic-possession film, and the abused-child movie. In the end the film gleefully repudiates all of these explanations, offering nothing in their place. In an interview, Christopher Denham, *Home Movie*'s director and author of the screenplay, refused to offer a reason for the children's behavior. Instead he questioned the search for reasons: "There's this checklist that we have now for children where, whenever there's a problem, there's a solution."[7] The film essentially does the same; it attacks adult check-listing behavior and withholds solutions, leaving the viewer stumped and staring at nothing.

\* \* \*

All three films poke extensive fun at the adult science for the dissection of the evil child, child psychology and psychiatry. Murdering adults is a game (*Peopletoys*); the murder weapons are usually toys (*Mikey*). Children refuse to participate in their parents' games and ultimately substitute the parents' "show" with their own (*Home Movie*). Murderous games are centrally defined by the elaborate and playful rigging of kill contraptions. All this sits badly with developmental theories defining children's games as preparation for their future lives as adults, but might very well constitute a sort of horror shorthand for what psychologists have called the Peter Pan Syndrome. All three films portray the child's refusal to grow up or to grow up in the manner dictated by adults. All films at least hint at the possibility that the children are not "children" in the way in which adults commonly interpret the term. The films' children are not "normal like us" (Rick in *Peopletoys*); they are "unattached" to us (Shawn in *Mikey*), or, perhaps, not children at all but dragons (*Home Movie*). Whatever they are, they won't grow up to be a normal adult. Thus all three films break the natural link between children and adults, pointing out that this link, and its perception as "natural," is something in which only adults have any interest. So far, so obvious.

Less obvious, perhaps because it is even more disturbing, is another link that we might make between playing games and killing adults. In *The Power of Play: Learning What Comes Naturally*, David Elkind has offered the simplest answer of all to the question "Why do children play?": Because it comes naturally. Because it's fun.

Let us consider, for a moment, the scandalous consequences of applying Elkind's insight to horror films in which the murder of adults is visualized as child's play. Why do children murder adults? Because it comes naturally. Because it's fun.

There is, in fact, quite a bit of evidence for this. In *Peopletoys*, the children's joy is clearly visualized through cheery dances around burning people, happy giggles while building snowmen around corpses, or in the simple sense of achievement when a complicated murderous contraption turns out to work exactly as planned. But the idea that children experience the killing of adults as a fun game is not limited to the movies—not entirely. Time and again, filmmakers and adult actors involved in making horror films that feature a child's murder of an adult have described intense antagonism, to the point of physical violence, on the set, and linked this with the violence portrayed in the film. In 2006, *Peopletoys* producer Michael Blowitz reported that he and the film's first director Sean Mac-

Gregor clashed so badly at a production meeting that "he took a swing at me and I put him through a plate glass window."[8] Dawn Lyn, who played little Moe, remembered over 30 years later that according to her mother, she fought with her brother more than usual while making the film. Her mother attributed this increased aggression to "the negativity of the roles we were playing, being murderers." Lyn herself denied both fighting with her brother or being in the least disturbed by the role she was playing. For adults involved in making the film, the violence in the film was clearly traumatic to the point where it leaked out into the real world. But what of the children? Thirty-two years after the film first aired, they still remembered how much fun they had. "It was like a vacation for us," remembers Tierre Turner who played soldier boy Brian, "we were having a great time." Disturbingly, all the fun mentioned by the then-child actors is directly linked with the murders, seen either as a great lark or even, in Piaget's sense, as exercises in autonomy. Turner, for example, remembered that "I was the person who set out and devised all the murders; I was the person who made everyone else whack everybody else up, and I did this with great pleasure at 12 years old" (the film, interestingly, portrays all killings as communal efforts and assigns no such leadership role to the Brian-character). And Dawn Lyn described, her eyes shining, the truly Freudian situation of killing Lovely (played by her real-life mother, Carolyn Stellar) by pouring real (albeit dead, or presumed dead) piranhas into her bathtub, one of which actually latched onto her mother's leg, wounding her.

Such radically diverging perceptions of violence—distinctly traumatic for adults, a hoot for kids—permeate the interviews of cast and crew members of other horror films as well, including films separated considerably from *Peopletoys* by time, space and cultural context. Take the 2008 British film *The Children*, for example (dir. Tom Shankland), an authentic Isn't-this-fun kiddie slaughterfest of parents feebly trying to defend themselves (final score: kids 3, adults 3). Post-production interviews with adults reveal that they experienced severe trauma watching scenes in which the kids killed adults *and* presumed a similarly traumatic experience on the part of the children. Actor Jeremy Sheffield, who played the first father figure dispatched, described that considerable effort went into minimizing such trauma for the children: "We went through different games, exercises, play ... to make it very clear to the kids that it's a game, it's not real, whatever happens is not real, no matter how real it seems, it's not."[9] But Eva Birthistle, who played the last mother standing, seemed aware that such caution was unnecessary: "their confidence just grew, like in the first week, and then they were sort of ... delighted that they were gonna kill us all [*giggles*]." Tom Shankland claimed that "the kids loved it, stabbing eyeballs and seeing blood spurt out ... they were ... really getting kind of excited about this." Jane Karen, Child Wrangler on the set, confirmed this impression:

> We've got a little girl that has to stab her mother in the eye with a pencil, and she really likes it. She's been really ... good at that. They're just much better at that kind of bang-bang you're dead! kind of games than you imagine, they're quite gory in their playing, and so it's not a big leap for them, whereas as adults we get very sensitive about [*gasps*] "How would you, you know, explain this," and those kids go: "Oh yeah, yeah, I'm covered in blood, aren't I, because I just stabbed Mum Di..."

Similarly to the films themselves, the interviews document a strange rift between the verbal and the visual. While the statements themselves come very close to admitting the scary truth, the gasps and the giggles indicate that this is not a truth adults can live with. Horror films in which children kill adults turn child psychology on its head. They take the entire idea of "normalization" out of the hands of adults who, in the movies, uphold their fondest illusions of control by severely underestimating murderous children as "a little strange," and in real life are at a loss to explain why playing at killing adults is so much fun. The quite desperate-sounding incantations that these murders are "not real, whatever happens is not real" may be soothing for adults but are apparently completely wasted on kids. Adults need the distinction between the game and reality; children don't.

To be sure, horror films sometimes throw adults a bone of reassurance by "justifying" a child's murder of an adult by assigning to the act a logic that works in the adult world. The murdered adult may have "had it coming"; perhaps he is a child abuser, a pedophile, a child abductor, a home invader. Other films, however, are busily chipping away at such grown-up rationalizations, offering no motivation for the children's murderous impulses. *Peopletoys*, *Mikey* and *Home Movie* all fall into this category. The wound these films inflict to the adult self-image is threefold. The first cut is the sneaking suspicion that a child's development may be less influenced by adult modeling than by autonomous experience acquired through games. This is followed by the hammer blow of the realization that children don't need adults to develop, they only need to play. And then the final twist of the knife: not only are adults no help at all, they are often an actual hindrance to the child's development.

Once we accept these three premises of the horror film (gasp, giggle), we uncover its logic. Its objective is the elimination of adverse (and that means: adult) interference with the child's world. The device that achieves this is, cogently enough, the most fundamental means of child development: child's play. We tend to see horror films in which children off adults literally and narratively, as interesting insights into the games children apparently enjoy the most. But perhaps we should also see them figuratively and metaphorically, as repudiating a child psychology that, in a colossal inflation of adult self-importance, demotes the entire world of children to a boot camp for adulthood.

## Guilt Trips

### LITTLE HORRORS

*Case 39* (dir. Christian Alvart, USA 2009; see synopsis in the *Guilt Trips* section of Chapter 5) pits the unfathomable (religious possession) against scientific reasoning (a social worker's background and expertise as a child psychologist). Predictably, psychological approaches fail miserably.

*The Child* (dir. Robert Voskanian, USA 1977) may be the earliest Peter Pan Syndrome film on record. Little Rosalie refuses to grow up and expresses this refusal by murdering her entire family. *Fuller discussion in Chapter 3.*

*The Children* (dir. Tom Shankland, UK 2008). Two sets of parents with a total of five children converge in a house in the woods to celebrate New Year's. The children fall mysteriously ill and begin to murder parents, mostly by employing their own toys. Memorable murder or wounding scenes involve sleds, kiddie wagons, bloodied dolls, monkey bars, a Ken doll, and a toy space ship. *Guilt trip:* The film is an extensive portrait of adult denial. Unable to believe that the children are at fault, the adults begin to accuse each other of the killings, thus minimizing their survival chances.

## Teenage Wasteland

*Funny Games* (dir. Michael Haneke, Austria 1997; remake dir. Michael Haneke, USA 2007). Two young men take a family hostage in their holiday cabin, torture them for a day, and murder them. In answer to the father's desperate question why they're doing this, one of the two killers offers a series of excuses for his partner that every child psychiatrist would pounce on: "His father divorced his mother when he was this big [*indicating two feet from the ground*] for another woman.... Which is why he's gay and he's a criminal. Got it? The truth is … he's white trash. He comes from a filthy, deprived family. Five siblings, all of them on drugs. His father is an alcoholic. His mother, well, I mean, you can imagine. Truth is … he's fucking her. It's sad, but it's true" (U.S. version). *Guilt trip:* The "funny games" of the film's title are obviously games played with psychological assumptions, leading to naïve and prefabricated explanations for criminal behavior.

*Kiss of the Tarantula* (dir. Chris Munger, USA 1976) tells the story of a teen girl, a mortician's daughter, who unleashes her friends, deadly tarantulas, on her enemies, including her abusive mother, numerous teen boys who try to get into her pants and cross over into violence when she says no, and her uncle, who harasses her sexually. *Guilt trip:* Susan looks about 18 but acts very much like a little girl, playing with stuffed toys and teddy bears. She experiences all moves towards adulthood as severely traumatic. The film supports her in this: compliments that she is a fine cook and will "make a fine wife for someone" come from her slimily abusive uncle; all sexual activity is cast in the form of rape (three high school boys ganging up on her) or incestuous rape (by her uncle). In brief, Susan rejects life as a woman—for good reason, as the film shows. This rejection of "life" is also indicated by the fact that she feels entirely at home in the mortuary, vastly preferring the company of the dead to that of the living.

*The Little Girl Who Lives Down the Lane* (dir. Nicholas Gessner, Canada 1976). Thirteen-year-old Rynn, a brilliantly intelligent girl, lives all alone after her father, who is dying from an incurable disease, goes off into the woods to die after setting her up to live on her own. With the help of a friend, the disabled boy Mario who leads a difficult home life, she must then defend her freedom from an intrusive and abusive landlady, her landlady's son Frank, who turns out to be the pedophile next door, and her evil mother, all of whom she dispatches by poison. *Guilt trip:* The film essentially proposes that so long as there is shelter and some money for food, children do not feel any need for parents or have any use for them. The good parent of the film is the father who takes himself out of the child's life, who walks into the woods, never to return and never to be found. The bad parent is the one who barges in and sniffs around, like Rynn's mother and her landlady, who meddles incessantly, bosses Rynn around, and belittles her at every turn. Other parent figures do not fare better: Mario's polio is due to his mother neglecting to have him inoculated; the father figure Frank turns out to be a pedophile. The only thing that disturbs Rynn's peaceful and happy life on her own is the recurring need to keep adults off her body and out of her affairs.

*We Need to Talk About Kevin* (dir. Lynne Ramsay, UK/USA 2011). Kevin has a hostile relationship with his family and refuses to participate in family life; his mother struggles to love her weird child from the moment of his birth. That love, paradoxically, does not come into existence until Kevin murders his father, his younger sister, and 11 people at his school. The film is a massive parental *guilt trip* because it suggests that the lack of love on the part of Kevin's mother is at fault for his psychosis; both she and her husband do, in fact, believe this. The final scene, however, dismantles this facile pop psychology. Visiting Kevin in prison, his mother asks him why he did this. His answer: "I used to think I knew. Now I'm not so sure." Lionel Shriver's book, on which the film is based, has Kevin answer the question even more simply: "There is no why."

# Conclusions

## Innocence v. Evil, or: Looking for the Difference

One hundred years after evil children first appeared in film, they have come into their own. More than half of the films featuring the type were made since the year 2000.¹ Around the same time, the genre began to become mainstream. For long decades, no self-respecting studio would have financed a horror production. Only in the rarest of exceptions, if a horror indie, despite its ludicrously low budget, goes viral (like Romero's *Night of the Living Dead* or Raimi's *Evil Dead*), there may be, at long last, a Hollywood remake. Horror is commonly acknowledged to be a "cult" or indie genre, something that rose from the slime despite Hollywood, not because of it. The understanding that much of the horror scene happens "underground," without official backing by Hollywood studios—and with all the artistic, philosophical or political license that may entail—was common in writing about horror until very recently.²

All this changed radically at the outset of the twenty-first century. Hollywood may pretend to be all coy and facetious about its new money-spinner, as indicated by the many horror spoofs of recent years, like the *Scream* series or *The Cabin in the Woods*. Nevertheless, twenty-first century Hollywood is also now getting in on the straight-up, deadly serious horror act, either by financing expensive remakes of foreign horror films, like *The Ring* (2002), *The Grudge* (2004), or *Dark Water* (2005),³ or by producing their own. Taking on the starring role in a horror flick is no longer a career-killer even for name-brand actors like Ethan Hawke (*Sinister*, 2012), Donald Sutherland (*An American Haunting*, 2005), Nicole Kidman *(The Others,* 2001) or Scarlett Johansson (*Under the Skin*, 2014). The evil kids of horror have recently scaled new heights of visibility. Not only do they appear in more films, but they also appear—perhaps for the first time since *Rosemary's Baby* and *The Exorcist*— in blockbuster movies which, buoyed by Hollywood sponsorship, marketing, and star allure, reach viewer numbers that the low-budget schlock horror indie of the 1950s to the late 1990s could only dream about. Both developments indicate that cultural attitudes towards children and childhood that have been around since the 1950s have gained considerable traction in the new millennium.

The first fatality of these attitudes is the idea of innocence. Children, even babies, are not innocent (see Chapters 1 and 2), just as Nature is not pure (Chapter 3). Children no longer represent the hope for a better future (Chapter 4) but are beholden to a sinister past, where they pay for the faith of their parents unto the third and fourth generations (Chapter 5). Children are consumers-in-training, or consumer products themselves (Chapter 6). Children grow into abusive adults (Chapter 7), or they refuse to grow up at all (Chapter 8).

The explanations horror offers for these extraordinary departures from the way we think we see children are about a dime a dozen and about as phony as a three-dollar bill. They range from alien abduction, nuclear fallout, misguided scientific experiments, zombie bites and deadly spores to ancient amulets, psychopathy, possession, or the old catch-all—plain old insanity. On occasion—and this, too, has become more commonplace since the year 2000—films don't bother with reasons but depict children who, free from trauma or possession, are inexplicably at war with adults. Horror has begun to advance a fatalistic view of evil children; it has run out of excuses and given up on causes. In this new postrationalization era of horror, a mother might find herself sitting across from her imprisoned son and ask him why he murdered his father, his little sister, and 11 people at his school. And she would get a non-committal answer: "I used to think I knew…. Now I'm not so sure."[4]

The dismantling of the presumption of innocence, surely one of our most dearly held assumptions about children and childhood, raises a number of uncomfortable questions. Why do we assume that children are innocent? Who benefits from this assumption? What does the assumption say about the assumer? Such questions are now being asked with increasing urgency, and not just in horror films but, to cite just a few, by art historians, media specialists, social historians and philosophers writing in 2010 or later. Media specialist Catharine Lumby, for example, has examined the symbolic meaning of photographs taken of children for adults, ranging from family photos to pornographic images, and concluded that children's images are less about childhood than about societal self-definition: "If we think there is something amiss with childhood then we are prone to think that there is something deeply wrong with our society as a whole."[5] Political philosopher Joanne Faulkner has put her finger on what might be deeply wrong: "The unpalatable truth is that the value of a child's innocence depends upon their capacity to be protected. Children born to conditions of poverty or abuse, children who need to work—in short, children deprived of the privilege that would confer innocence upon them—unsettle the parameters of our self-understanding."[6] The child's innocence is merely an image for that of the community. Horror film proposes the exact opposite, but with the same consequences: as William Paul has put it, if the evil child is not a freak "but rather a member of a seemingly ordinary middle-class family, then we are directly implicated in the creation of the monster."[7]

If adults are wedded to the idea of childlike innocence because it provides an agreeable image of their society, then the reverse would also apply: as soon as you view children outside of a social context, there is no longer a need to define them as innocent. This is precisely what Terry Eagleton suggests when he wonders aloud about the public response to the case of James Bulger, murdered at the age of two by two ten-year-old boys: "why the public found this particular murder especially shocking is not entirely clear. Children, after all, are only semi-socialised creatures who can be expected to behave pretty savagely from time to time…. In this sense, it is surprising that such grisly events do not occur more often. Perhaps children murder each other all the time and are simply keeping quiet about it."[8] Like Lumby and Faulkner, Eagleton claims that childlike innocence is a myth. Unlike Lumby and Faulkner, though, he proposes that the myth survives not because children are part of society but precisely because they are not, or rather, not yet. Outside of society, children can be seen as opposites in terms—as innocent, as evil, or both at the same time.

When it comes to horror films, these ideas matter because unlike society, horror juxtaposes not guilt and innocence but evil and innocence. Innocence, as defined above, is a social term. Evil, on the other hand, is not, or not exclusively; its meaning encompasses the social, the religious, even the ontological. Evil is absolute, "without a cause," which can mean two things: without reason and without origin. Evil is thus placed on the same pedestal as the Almighty. "Apart from evil," Eagleton tells us, "only God is said to be the cause of himself."[9]

If evil has no cause, then evil children can have no control over what they are. Once removed from free choice, "evil" and "innocent" cease to be what they appear in horror film—opposites in terms—and become one and the same. Society is perpetually torn between seeing evil as a *state* that cannot be helped and thus also not punished—in which case the evil child would also be the innocent child—and seeing evil as an *act*, an expression of free will that can and should be punished. Horror films, on the other hand, do not even engage in the debate. Working with an apparent contrast between innocence and evil, they deny innocence and portray evil, but then refuse to comment on its nature. The difference between willful and inherent evil is irrelevant to horror, as are social causes, philosophical rationales, religious solace, legal redress, or simple revenge. Because Evil in horror is unfathomable, it remains a presence, for explaining evil is tantamount to explaining it away. As Eagleton sums up: "Either human actions are explicable, in which case they cannot be evil; or they are evil, in which case there is nothing more to be said about them."[10]

Horror generally defines the term "evil" more or less as philosophers do, as pleasure in hurting and lack of remorse.[11] As guilt trips, horror films zone in specifically on the second part of this definition, the "lack of remorse" bit. Horror films moreover show considerable awareness of evil as something that touches upon the metaphysical in a way that "bad," for example, does not. When we talk about "bad," we are asking who did it and why. When we talk about "evil," we are asking why the world is the way it is.[12] "For over three thousand years," philosopher Fred Alford declares, "evil has been understood as what men and women suffer, not just what they do."[13] What men and women suffer from the most is *guilt*, whether or not they respond to this with remorse. A soldier who helped liberate the concentration camp Dachau, when asked to define "evil," "remembers corpses laid out as far as he could see, but his leading example of evil is drowning some kittens as a kid."[14] Evil, in brief, is that which showcases one's own guilt. A relatively minor deed implicating the *self*, such as the memory of drowning kittens, causes considerably more distress than looking at thousands of people murdered by someone else. All feelings evoked in horror that do not implicate the self pale beside guilt. Fear, loathing, terror, disgust, the gag reflex response to gore—all of this is "bad" enough but leaves the self relatively unscathed. Horror does not even begin to get into the act until it hones in on evil and on the self, in a word: on guilt.

In the image of the evil child, horror unites two apparent extremes, evil and innocence, raising the question whether innocence and evil are the opposites they appear to be or rather one and the same. The answer to that question depends on the nature of evil. Specifically, it depends on the question whether evil is something one "does" or something one "is," for if the children cannot help being evil, then the fact is that they are innocent. Yet this question, whether evil is willed or inherent, is precisely the one horror refuses to answer. And there is a reason for this, because if it did, there would be nothing more to be said about it. Thus the horror film's portrayal of evil as a mystery is a sign of its determination to say something more about it, to raise further questions. And those questions tend to be social ones: in confronting us, time and again, with the horrors of childhood, and in implicating us in the creation of the little monster, horror films indicate, in Lumby's words, "that there is something deeply wrong with our society as a whole."

## Guilt Trips v. Fear Flicks, or: How Horror Plays on Your Guilt

The horror film's most basic element is simple exacerbation. Someone gets into trouble and does not back off. He then gets into worse trouble, but fails to back off. He then gets into catastrophic trouble, and far from backing off, he walks blithely on, straight into apocalyptic trouble. At this point, more often than not, his head comes off.

Are we scared yet?

Remember Kirk in *The Texas Chain Saw Massacre*? Why, if he's already weirded out by the heads of freshly dead animals mounted on the wall and the sounds of pigs screaming, does he walk up to Leatherface's metal door? Remember Darry in *Jeepers Creepers*? If he already strongly suspects that the Creeper has thrown a bloody corpse down the pipe, why does he have to go look instead of driving off and calling the cops? The point about horror and fear, and the main reason why fear is not the principal driver of horror films, is this: nobody is ever scared *enough*. This is, of course, why the characters of horror get into ever-greater trouble. But it also applies to the viewer. Nothing shows this more clearly than the jump scare, a ubiquitous horror feature that really isn't much more than a reminder to the viewer to be scared. The implication seems to be that the viewer actually *isn't* scared, or rather, like horror's characters, not scared enough, and certainly also not scared for long enough. Otherwise, why all the jump cuts, fright music and slamming doors? Does the need to shock the audience into an extra-terrifying split second not imply that fear is, by definition, fleeting? Does it not imply that outside of that brief injection of adrenalin or sometimes just sheer noise—bang, bang, you're deaf—the horror film isn't actually all that frightening? Screaming, vomiting, fainting, edge-of-the-seat-perching and nail biting can only be kept up for so long. Compared to guilt, fear doesn't have much of a shelf life.

There are other reasons, as well, to bid the fear theory farewell. If H. P. Lovecraft, undeniably the godfather of horror, was right in saying that "the oldest and strongest kind of fear is fear of the unknown,"[15] this would essentially disqualify horror films as vehicles of fear. Horror films do not deal with the unknown; on the contrary. They practically epitomize predictability and repetitiveness. They get the same kind of character into the same kind of trouble, over and over again. We *know* that Kirk will not stick with opening the door and calling down the hallway, but go into the house. We *know* that Darry will lean so far down the pipe that he'll eventually fall in. We know that evil can be vanquished only provisionally, that our satisfaction in seeing the Creeper run over, Michael Myers burned to a crisp, or Chucky melted into a puddle of plastic is temporary. We know they will all be back. We know these things whether we have seen the film or not. Horror reliably presents us with the worst-case scenario. Is it possible to fear it if we know it's coming, if we expect it, even rely on it?

The idea of repetition is expressed not only in the horror narrative, but also in its franchising. No cinematic genre is as prone to sequelitis as horror. There are now 12 *Friday the 13ths*, 10 *Halloweens*, 10 *Puppetmasters*, 9 *Nightmares on Elm Street*, 9 *Hellraisers*, and 7 *Saws*, to name only the most famous. As anyone who has ever seen one of these can attest, sequels of horror films are not actually different films but the same film all over again, and appropriately so, since all horror films are fundamentally predictable. The predictability is not perceived as boring; it is, in fact, expected and relied upon. Part of the pleasure of watching a horror film is that you know exactly what is coming, which, in other film genres, like the thriller or detective genres, spells the very opposite of suspense. Both the supreme predictability of the film and the eternal sameness of sequels point squarely at guilt, rather than fear, as the driver of the horror film. If our worst fears are, as Lovecraft has claimed, those of "the unknown, being likewise the unpredictable,"[16] why would we presume that they can best be expressed in a genre that is so utterly predictable? We might, in fact, conclude the opposite, namely, that few cinematic genres are *less* likely to evoke fear than horror.

Horror sequels are not about confronting viewers with the new and unknown but about sending viewers *back* to something they already know—back into the same dank cellar, the same haunted house, the same nightmare.[17] An old fear becomes less troubling as it becomes more familiar. Not so an old guilt, which becomes not less, but more tormenting with increased familiarity. Sequels that typically tell the same story all over again are a signal that guilt can only be repressed for so long, that like Michael Myers, the Blob, or the Thing, it keeps coming back, and that unlike fear, it cannot be overcome.

Another reason the fear theory falls short is in that it presupposes the viewer's identification with—in the sense of moral allegiance to—the victim. Aristotle described viewer identification with a dramatic character as centrally dependent on a linked experience of compassion and fear: compassion with the hero's misfortune leading to a fear that the same might happen to *us*. In fact, it is almost impossible to respond in this way to the victims in a horror film, a genre that breeds nothing but contempt for victims and does all it can to discourage compassion.[18] Without compassion, fear is not an option. Guilt, on the other hand, is horror's steady undercurrent, and the reason why the themes of horror—child abuse, pollution, consumerism, irresponsible science, religious mania, and so forth—point the finger straight back at the viewer. Guilt is universal in the sense that given the choice between enduring and inflicting doom, most of us will choose to inflict it, and the horror film is more than happy to rub our noses in this fact. Guilt is already prefigured in the fact that the horror film offers viewers a false choice between fear and guilt, fully aware that fear relies on compassion. And guilt is compounded by the fact that such compassion, the identification with the victim, is both ethically mandatory and realistically unattainable.

If horror films are, as I've argued all along, more about guilt than fear, the question arises: where is the pleasure in watching horror? We all understand the pleasures of fear, particularly vicarious fear experienced from a position of safety. But is there any fun to be had with guilt? Why would viewers expose themselves to something that is so manifestly unpleasant? In the introduction to this book, I have cited horror's tendency to guilt-trip viewers as one reason why the genre is so commonly vilified as nasty, sleazy and manipulative. "Nobody," I wrote then, "likes to be guilt-tripped." But perhaps it is time to rethink this: perhaps we *do* like it. Recent marketing research, for example, has firmly established that guilty pleasures are the best. Goldsmith, Cho and Dhar conducted six inter-related studies to prove that there is a fundamental cognitive association between guilt and pleasure. Their studies show not only that people primed with guilt experience greater pleasure than others, but also that the effect of heightening the enjoyment of pleasures is unique to guilt. Other negative emotions, in other words, do not result in the same enjoyment; *only* guilt works in this way. What is more, two of their studies show that the pleasurable guilt-trip is not limited to consumption of guilt-inducing foods, such as candy, but applies to other contexts as well. One of their examples for what they call "hedonic consumption," a form of consumption in which guilt enhances pleasure, is watching videos.

If marketing research gives us an idea of how we enjoy guilt, philosophy can perhaps get us a bit closer to the "why." This is the point where we need to ask whether the viewer's identification with a film character is wholly determined by ethical stances. The question of ethics and identification is a particularly hairy one in horror films. Evil is the real deal; the monster is horror's real hero. Good, as far as the genre is concerned, can take a hike in the woods, preferably on a dark and stormy night. So often, the struggle against Evil is against something undefined and indefinable (the Thing, the Blob, the Slime). Not having a concrete enemy deprives the struggler of nobility, of the ability to win, and of the *meaning* of victory: where is the dignity in escaping, temporarily, from encroaching slime? Good takes one of two guises: horror's many victims—for whom viewers can hardly even muster sympathy—or, more rarely, an antagonist, a "zero hero"[19] who, like the victims, is hapless, dimwitted, laughably inadequate to the task, and always at least ten steps behind Evil.

Nevertheless, there is reason to suspect that the horror film's (and viewers') greater interest in Evil is more than a default position arrived at by the exquisite boredom caused by Good: it is a matter of identification. Once we understand that horror is more about guilt than fear, it becomes possible to read viewer identification with Evil as a way to overcome fear. Identifying with Evil may result in guilt, but at least it propels the viewer from the place of Fear, the victim's position—always held by Good, in horror—and into a position of power. Some philosophers have, in fact, built a fundamental definition of Evil on this. Fred Alford, for example, has shown that if the desire to combat fear is a natural impulse, then identification with Evil is not an aberration but simply a human trait, a "psychopathic moment" that everyone experiences:

> The psychopathic moment is a virtually universal moment in all lives. When we are faced with intolerable, uncontainable dread, the natural tendency is to identify with the persecutor, becoming the agent of doom, as the only way of controlling it. Evil is the attempt to inflict one's doom on others, becoming doom, rather than living subject to it. In this sense evil is bad faith, the lie that one could escape one's fate by inflicting it on others.[20]

Transferring Alford's insights from the lofty heights of philosophy to the damp dungeons of horror shows us *why* horror films concern themselves more with guilt than with fear. Horror films are fictionalized "psychopathic moments" in which viewers are faced with the alternative between fear and guilt and the option to choose guilt as the safer route. To identify with the persecutor is the only way to avoid being terrified. We pay for our rejection of fear (the victim's position) in coin of guilt (by assuming the perp's position), and guilt, Alford declares, will not sway us: "most of us feel guilty, at least sometimes. Neither guilt nor empathy will change this tendency to inflict terror on others, however."[21] Terror as defined by Alford is not fear (of Evil) but guilt—the terror of recognizing *ourselves* as evil. "We do not feel terror and *then* identify with the aggressor, or at least that is not the whole story. The terror stems *from* the identification with the aggressor, his aggression suddenly our own, directed against those we care about and depend on, including ourselves and our values."[22] And that, I think, is the second central aspect of horror: not only does it showcase the "psychopathic moment" when the viewer may choose guilt over fear, it also digs its fingers into the gaping wound created by the viewer's simultaneous alignment with Evil and presumed allegiance to Good.

If Goldsmith, Cho and Dhar's conclusion that "Guilt Begets Pleasure" is right, we are looking at the perfect vicious circle. Not only does watching schlock horror, if we find that sort of thing pleasurable, cause guilt, the reverse also applies: guilt enhances the hedonistic pleasure of watching horror. If the main point of horror is not fear but guilt, it is simply because guilt works. It works for the horror film because fear is fleeting but guilt lasts. It works for the viewer because, paradoxically, guilt offers greater pleasures than fear. And if Alford's conclusion that we will always fall victim to the psychopathic moment is right, we can go a step further and say: horror films play on our guilt not only by enticing us to identify with the guilty party, but also by pointing out that this is our default position. It is not merely a trick of the I-camera (visual identification of killer and audience through the killer's POV), but identification in the sense of *allegiance*. It is not due to manipulation by the movie, or at least not entirely, but a decision made by the viewer who chooses guilt over fear. And it is *pleasurable*. It is precisely the kind of nasty secret that we shouldn't put past the genre. In the sober world of market research and in the airy palaces of philosophy, probing the pleasures of guilt may be new, unexpected, even controversial. But in the darker places where guilt links with the imagination—the Catholic confessional, the horror cinema—the pleasures of guilt may well have been familiar to wallowers all along.

This is how horror, and its evil children, play on your guilt: by proclaiming you guilty and by pointing out that you like it that way. Pleading mitigating circumstances or diminished culpability—after all, you didn't do it, you only watched—won't get you pronounced innocent. And if you now, as would be entirely understandable, ask the fallback question of the desperate: *Why Me?*, horror would answer: Nothing personal. You are just the one who showed up, just like some horny teens always show up at the cabin in the woods. Guilt is universal. It isn't just you, it is also, as the troubled little girl writes in *Knowing*, ƎE (Everyone Else).

## *Finally, a Question*

Finally, a speculative question: is it possible to view the extreme violence of many horror films as the genre's response to the fact that viewers tend to be understandably obtuse about their own guilty involvement? Of course, violence can simply be shrugged off by pointing at the obvious delights of titillation (not exactly a cheery view of the human race, that). But understanding horror films as guilt trips might give us a different perspective on violence. If the horror film as a genre attempts to make us aware of the guilt we should be feeling but aren't, it runs constantly counter to our persistent determination *not* to go there. Clearly, a gentle hint will not do, and so the horror film hits us over the head with a hammer. Or a chain saw. Or an axe. Or a machete. Or, in the classic kill-someone-else-

or-die ploy, with a timed iron-mask contraption that will rip your face open unless you unlock it with the key hidden in your cellmate's digestive tract[23]—and really, why stop there?

Violence may well be the horror film's way of hacking away at its audience to engage with guilt. Admit who you are. Admit what you did.

# Chapter Notes

## Preface

1. Gerald Graff has claimed that "Underlying the exaggerated perception of academic difficulty is the belief—found inside and outside academia—that academic communication is fundamentally different from everyday vernacular discourse," and that this "explains why 'reductive' is felt to be just about the worst charge—this side of an accusation of plagiarism or sexual harassment—that can be leveled at an academic author" ("Scholars and Sound Bites").

2. In this I'm in fairly good company: Gerald Graff, associate dean of curriculum and instruction in the College of Liberal Arts and Sciences at the University of Illinois, Chicago, has exploded "The Myth of Academic Difficulty"; Steven Pinker, psychology professor at Harvard, has wondered publicly "Why Academics Stink at Writing"; Daniel M. Oppenheimer, a psychologist at UCLA, has conducted repeated experiments showing the dire "Consequences of Erudite Vernacular Utilized Irrespective of Necessity"; writer Victoria Clayton has marveled at "The Needless Complexity of Academic Writing."

## Introduction

My thinking on the subject of guilt and evil has been most centrally influenced by Alford's *What Evil Means to Us*, Copjec's *Radical Evil*, Eagleton's *On Evil*, and Tangney's and Dearing's *Shame and Guilt*. Literature on children in horror films includes Karen Renner's *The "Evil Child" in Literature, Film, and Popular Culture*; Dominic Lennard's *Bad Seeds and Holy Terrors: The Child Villains of Horror Films*; from a queer theory angle: Andrew Scahill's *The Revolting Child*; Bohlman and Moreland's edited collection *Monstrous Children*, and Julian Petley's essay "The Monstrous Child." Karen Renner is currently working on a book tentatively titled *Evil Children in the Contemporary Imagination*, which will include analyses of literature, film, television shows, music videos, video games, and graphic novels, without a specific focus on horror. Benjamin Moldenhauer, Christoph Spehr and Jörg Windszus have mounted convincing arguments why "children need horror" in various works. Valuable ideas on how viewers identify when watching films are offered in Murray Smith's *Engaging Characters*, where he also coined the juxtaposing terms "alignment" and "allegiance." Edward Branigan has worked most extensively on the issue of point-of-view shots in film; see his "The Point of View Shot," *Point of View in the Cinema*, and "Point of View in the Fiction Film."

1. "Scary Kids from Horror Movies," http://www.youtube.com/watch?v=v7kgvOOweYo. Scary kids are now so common in horror that they've received their share of YouTube spoofing; see, for example, "Creepy British Child Syndrome," https://www.youtube.com/watch?v=eHFVq6UTU1Y.

2. Nakata made the remark in an interview with horror fan-magazine *Fangoria* (quoted by Woodend).

3. "Children Need Fairytales" (*Kinder brauchen Märchen*) is the German translation for Bruno Bettelheim's famous book *The Uses of Enchantment*; "Children need horror" because it functions as a "training camp for the psyche": see Benjamin Moldenhauer, Christoph Spehr and Jörg Windszus, "Law of the Dead."

4. Stephen King, *Danse Macabre* 124. Some neurological research has agreed: Joanne Cantor and Mary Beth Oliver, for instance, cite studies showing that children tend to have only mild reactions to horror, whereas adults are distressed more intensely and for a longer time period, to the point of requiring medical treatment. Overall, however, neurologists and psychiatrists tend to disagree. Research on the difference between adult and children's brains has shown that witnessing violence—fictional or real—changes adult brains to a far lesser degree than brain systems still in development, i.e., in childhood. In children's brains, traumatic experience becomes part of the brain's fundamental organization, "states become traits": brain cell death occurs when children are repeatedly exposed to violence, to the point where their hippocampus may look like that of an elderly person (see Bruce Perry et. al. and John P. Murray specifically for the impact of screen violence on children).

5. King, *Danse Macabre* 457.

6. James Twitchell 301.

7. See Julian Petley's long list of evil-kid films from 1900 to 1922 and Karen Renner's headcount of recent films in "Evil Children" 4.

8. Blair Davis and Kial Natale 38.

9. Gillespie's *I Know What You Did Last Summer* (1997), Cannon's *I Still Know What You Did Last Summer* (1998), and White's straight-to-video follow-up *I'll Always Know What You Did Last Summer* (2006) are all films about teens literally pursued by their guilt in the form of a fisherman whom they have accidentally run down in the car and then thrown into the river, as opposed to trying to save his life, calling the authorities, or facing up to what they have done. The films have become iconic enough to spawn their own little spoof subgenre, including Blanchard's *Shriek If You Know What I Did Last Friday the Thirteenth* (2000) and the *Being Ian* episode "Scream Because I Know What You Did to That Psycho Last Summer" (2004).

10. Noted, among others, by Hutchings, who, however, explains the withholding of the victim's POV-shot with the horror film's attempt to prolong the mystery of the killer's identity: "the fact that the reverse shot, the shot of the person looking which usually accompanies a point-of-view shot, is often withheld in slashers until near the end of the narrative merits further consideration. One reason for this withholding of the face of the killer is, quite simply, that a number of slashers have whodunit structures that are dependent on hiding the killer's identity [...]. From this perspective, the killer's point-of-view shot becomes not so much a focus for our identification as it does a lure, a focus for our curiosity as we ask ourselves 'Who is looking, who is the killer?'" (*The Horror Film* 196).

11. The terms "alignment" and "allegiance" (to replace "identity" and "identification") were coined by Murray Smith.

12. Scott McCloud 36, emphases original.

13. In "Her Body, Himself" 90–1.

14. King, *Danse Macabre* 30.

15. Murray Smith 229.

16. The quotation is taken from the publisher's description of Dominic Lennard's *Bad Seeds and Holy Terrors*, available at http://www.sunypress.edu/p-5921-bad-seeds-and-holy-terrors.aspx .

17. This is the essence of Kathy Merlock Jackson's reading of the original *Village of the Damned*, in *Images of Children* 139–40.

18. Terry Eagleton, *On Evil* 1.

19. Douglas Coupland, *Player One* 85 (emphasis original).

## Chapter 1

For relevant works on psychoanalysis and its possible application to literature, see Sigmund Freud, *A General Introduction to Psychoanalysis*; Julia Kristeva, *Powers of Horror*; Melanie Klein, *Love, Guilt and Reparation*; Jacques Lacan, *Écrits*; as well as the following interpretations: Terry Eagleton, "Psychoanalysis"; Elizabeth Grosz, *Jacques Lacan*; Schippers, *Julia Kristeva and Feminist Thought*; Peter Barry, "Psychoanalytic Criticism"; and Elizabeth Wright, "Modern Psychoanalytic Criticism." Barbara Creed has offered several psychoanalytic interpretations of horror films, including "Male Masochism in the Horror Film," "Horror and the Monstrous-Feminine: An Imaginary Abjection," "Phallic Panic," and *The Monstrous-Feminine: Film, Feminism, Psychoanalysis*. For ideas about the grotesque, see Edwards's and Graulund's *The Grotesque*; Geoffrey Harpham's *On the Grotesque*; Wolfgang Kayser's *The Grotesque in Art and Literature*; and Peter Stallybrass and Allon White's *The Politics and Poetics of Transgression*. I completed this chapter before the appearance of the excellent essays by Karen J. Renner, Brooke W. Edge and Kristine Larsen in Bohlmann and Moreland's collection *Monstrous Children and Childish Monsters* (2015); particularly Renner's essay "Monstrous Newborns and the Mothers Who Love Them" makes a similar point about "Critiques of Intensive Mothering" for twenty-first century films (including *Grace*) as I make in this chapter more generally.

1. Barbara Creed, *The Monstrous Feminine* 56.

2. This is the main idea in Julia Kristeva's work *Powers of Horror*; the citation and discussion in Cynthia Freeland 18.

3. Julia Kristeva's *Powers of Horror*, paraphrased in Elizabeth Grosz's book on Lacan, 161–2.

4. In her *Love, Guilt and Reparation*, paraphrased in Terry Eagleton, "Psychoanalysis" 164.

5. Freud, *A General Introduction to Psychoanalysis* 341 (more on the Oedipus Complex on 341–7).

6. Wieland 374.

7. Bakhtin 325.

8. The term is Geoffrey Harpham's (9).

9. I wrote this before I read Hantke's excellent essay, and am cheered that he came to the same conclusion: "The horror of the film lies not in the sight of a grotesquely anomalous infant body. It lies in this reversal—from having the infant be the adjunct to her own body as its grounding biological and ideological reality, to becoming an adjunct to the infant as *her* grounding reality, turning her from an autonomous person into 'the baby's mother'" ("My Baby Ate the Dingo" 34, emphasis original).

10. The interview in which Solet made these remarks is in the featurette "Family," *Grace: Extras* (supplementary DVD materials, 2009).

11. Solet in the featurette "Family," *Grace: Extras* (supplementary DVD materials, 2009).

12. All quotations in Bradbury 150.

## Chapter 2

The history of families and family feeling in Western culture is described, among others, in Diana Gittins, *The Child in Question* and *The Family in Question*; Numa Denis Fustel de Coulanges, *Family, Kin, and City-State*; and Anne Millard's *Family Life in Ancient Greece*. Karin Hausen's seminal essay "Family and Role-Division" is still the best-argued piece on the changes forced on ideas of the family by the Industrial Revolution. On the depiction of children in art, see the work of Robert Flynn Johnson.

1. Goethe to Jacobi: "die trübe Jahreszeit hat mir trübe Schicksale gebracht. Wir wollen die Wiederkehr der Sonne erwarten" (quoted in Damm 186). Unless otherwise noted, all translations throughout this book are mine.

2. Goethe to Charlotte Schiller, letter dated November 17, 1795: "Der arme Kleine hat uns gestern schon wieder verlassen, und wir müssen nun suchen durch Leben und Bewegung diese Lücke wieder auszufüllen" (quoted in Damm 206).

3. Goethe to Schiller in a letter dated December 19, 1802: "Bei uns geht es nicht gut, wie Sie mir vielleicht gestern in der Oper anmerkten. Der neue Gast wird wohl schwerlich lange verweilen und die Mutter, so gefaßt sie sonst ist, leidet an Körper und Gemüth. Sie empfiehlt sich Ihnen bestens und fühlt den Werth Ihres Antheils. Heute Abend hoffe ich doch zu kommen um die Lücken meines Wesens durch die Gegenwart der Freunde auszufüllen" (Goethe, *Briefwechsel zwischen Schiller und Goethe*, http://gutenberg.spiegel.de/buch/3683/6).

4. Schiller to Goethe in a letter dated November 20, 1795: "Den Verlust, den Sie erlitten, haben wir herzlich beklagt. Sie können sich aber damit trösten, daß er so früh erfolgt ist, und mehr Ihre Hoffnung trifft. Ich könnte mich schwer darein finden, wenn mir mit meinem Kleinen jetzt noch ein Unglück begegnete." (Goethe,

*Briefwechsel zwischen Schiller und Goethe,* http://gutenberg.spiegel.de/buch/3659/3).

5. In Karin Hausen's seminal essay.

6. In his review of "The Good Son" on September 24, 1993, from which all future quotations in this chapter are taken as well.

7. A forensic attitude towards death on a child's part as evidence of the child's 'evil' is a popular theme in child horror, particularly if the corpse in question is that of a family member. Consider the parallel scene in *Night Child*, where Marcus describes his drowned mother as follows: "She looked like a fish, a dead fish under the water, her mouth wide open. ... I laughed. She looked so surprised. So ridiculous. So vulnerable. ... When Paul came, he was sick."

8. The film grossed a mere $715,704 worldwide; see the data in http://www.the-numbers.com/movie/Joshua-(2007)#tab=box-office (accessed January 30, 2014).

9. For divorce rates in the U.S. up until 2011, see the *National Vital Statistics System* at http://www.cdc.gov/nchs/nvss/marriage_divorce_tables.htm. On familicides, see Adams and Campbell, whose research shows that while homicides have declined by nearly 40% since 1989, familicides spiked significantly between 1997 and 2006 and have experienced the highest levels in the past ten years since the early 1800s ("Understanding Familicide"). Of 909 cases of mass murder occurring in the U.S. between 1900 and 2000, more than half occurred within the immediate family, making familicide the most common form of mass murder (see Berton). A list of familicides in the U.S., with documentations of press coverage, is provided by Wikipedia: http://en.wikipedia.org/wiki/List_of_familicides_in_the_United_States .

10. Criminal courts also tend to view criminal children as "simply *non-children*" or "some kind of freaks, monsters and thus able to be treated as adult criminals" (Gittins, *The Child in Question* 39).

## Chapter 3

General works on nature and the rural in film include Anat Pick and Guinevere Narraway's *Screening Nature: Cinema Beyond the Human* and Bernice Murphy's *The Rural Gothic in American Popular Culture*. Among the many authors who have written on the links between fairy tale and horror, I have found the following the most helpful: Karen Lury's *The Child in Film*, Carol Clover's *Men, Women, and Chainsaws*, and particularly Walter Rankin, who has investigated fairy tale archetypes in eight modern horror and suspense films in his *Grimm Pictures*.

1. Pick and Narraway, *Screening Nature* 6–8.
2. Bernice Murphy, *The Rural Gothic* 15.
3. Carol Clover, *Men, Women, and Chainsaws* 124.
4. Stephen King, *Danse Macabre*, 206–7.
5. An example is Brent McKnight's review "Yup, Sometimes Dead IS Better." McKnight claims to have been so painfully aware of the emotional manipulation of Gage's death scene—the little boy looking up, the tanker growing huge in the screen, a tiny bloody shoe falling on the road—that he burst out laughing, only to be forcibly ejected from the room by the deeply moved female friends with whom he was watching the film. Yup, sometimes the soil of a man's heart IS stonier.
6. See Coder, "Cultural Aspects of Trees," and the entry "Significant Buddhist trees," *Dhamma Wheel: A Buddhist Discussion forum on the Dhamma of the Theravada*. On the acacia in Egyptian myth, see the entry "Ancient Egyptian plants: Acacia," at http://www.reshafim.org.il/ad/egypt/botany/acacia.htm (accessed February 27, 2014).
7. Unless we read this scene as a simple hallucination called forth by Mi-sook's guilty conscience, this is the only time that Jin-sung returns as a ghost. *Acacia* alludes here to the Asian tradition of murdered children returning as ghosts to wreak revenge, such as in *Ringu* (1998), *Ju-on* (2002) and *Dark Water* (2002). *Acacia* is, however, both more moralistic and more subtle than all of the above: more moralistic because revenge is visited only on the guilty (whereas in J-horror, innocents without number are wiped out by the vengeful ghosts); more subtle because it does not attribute the destruction at the end directly to Jin-sung, but leaves the adults, ravaged by guilt, to savage each other.
8. See reviews of the film on the IMDb site at http://www.imdb.com/title/tt0380164/reviews (accessed October 29, 2015).

## Chapter 4

Robert Lambourne, Michael Shallis and Michael Shortland's *Close Encounters?* offers a good overview of science in sci-fi. Colavito has made the link between science, technology and the horror genre in more general and philosophical terms. On Mad Scientist horror, see Verona Kuni's "Un-Ordnung schaffen," Sidney Perkowitz's *Hollywood Science*, David J. Skal's *Screams of Reason*, and Duchaney's *The Spark of Fear*. Good works on nuclear horror include Mick Broderick's "From Atoms to Apocalypse" and his filmography *Nuclear Movies*; Robert Jacobs's *Filling the Hole in the Nuclear Future*; Mark Osteen's "The Big Secret"; Spencer Weart's "Nuclear Fear 1987–2007"; and Toni A. Perrine's *Film and the Nuclear Age*.

1. See, for instance, Barriga, Shapiro and Fernandez 3. Strangely, given this verdict, several attempts have been made to teach science through science movies; see, among others, Borgwald and Schreiner; and Dubeck, Moshier and Boss.
2. Scientist Lorraine Schembri in her review of *Gattaca*, 6.
3. Point made by Weart 260–1.
4. The problem was identified in Susan Sontag's *Against Interpretation*, and by many writers in her wake.
5. In Michael Ortiz Hill's study of nuclear Armageddon dreams, children were the single most recurring theme, appearing in over a quarter of all dreams (see his *Dreaming the End of the World*, 58).
6. At the time the film was made, four countries, three of which appear in the film—the USA, the UK, and the Soviet Union—had a button to press. China became a nuclear power in 1964, the year of the film's release.
7. "Zwischen Töten und Sterben ist ein Drittes: Leben" (Wolf 134).
8. Yacowar has dissected "Somafree" as a combination of the real Somerhill, Huxley's pacifying drug (soma) in *Brave New World* and the eternal illusion that "some are free" (85).
9. The original experiment and its implications are described in Chabris's and Simons's book *The Invisible*

*Gorilla*, where they elaborate on the human predilection to fail to see things directly in front of their eyes due to a focus on other things. The original video is at http://www.theinvisiblegorilla.com/gorilla_experiment.html (accessed October 29, 2015).

10. This is, for example, the gist of the interview with David Cronenberg conducted by William Beard and Piers Handling, in which they describe Nola as "unredeemingly bad" (182).

11. The quotations exculpating Dr. Raglan are taken from Harkness 93 and Beard 35.

12. The portrayal of Candice as a victim is in Beard 33–4.

13. As claimed, among many others, by Campbell 317 and Petley 101.

14. If so, this would throw an entirely new light on Dr. Raglan's practice. If Candice's ability is independent of Raglan's therapy, Nola's might be as well; in fact, the story Juliana tells of Nola's welts during childhood suggests as much. Raglan's therapy would, in this case, appear to be completely ineffective since his patients would exhibit these symptoms with or without it; he would, in that case, appear to be taking credit for something that happens on its own.

15. William Paul 375–6.

16. As claimed, for example, by Toni Perrine: "continuity in the face of destruction is one of the primary ideological and psychological dynamics at work in nuclear disaster scenarios" (8).

## Chapter 5

This chapter owes a debt of gratitude to Richard Dawkins's eminently rational *The God Delusion*.

1. On the Devil as a film protagonist, see Charles P. Mitchell.

2. Douglas E. Cowan's *Sacred Terror*, Hansen's collection of essays *Roman Catholicism in Fantastic Film*, and Nikolas Schreck's *Satanic Screen* are still among the best books on religion in horror films to date. For a theological perspective on some horror films, including *The Exorcist*, see Fraser. Much has been written on *Rosemary's Baby*, *The Exorcist* and *The Omen* respectively; readers will find a good cross-section of this literature in the bibliography.

3. Blatty, who also authored the screenplay, describes this case in detail in his book *The Exorcist: From Novel to Film* 3–4.

4. Examples related in Cowan 177–84.

5. Quoted in Cowan 197.

6. Quoted in David J. Skal, *The Monster Show* 294.

7. Skal, *Monster Show* 293–5.

8. Blatty, *The Exorcist* 311.

9. After Columbia dropped the film for distribution, Allied Artists agreed to distribute it on the condition that the title be changed to *Alice, Sweet Alice*, "in fear that the public would perceive the film to be religious due to its title" (see the film's Wikipedia entry at http://en.wikipedia.org/wiki/Alice,_Sweet_Alice). *Communion* aka *Alice, Sweet Alice* was re-released in 1981 under yet another title: the rather more tongue-in-cheek *Holy Terror*.

10. Weirdly (and I presume accidentally), some reviewers have misspelled the director's last name as "Soul";  see, for instance, the review of *Alice, Sweet Alice*, posted by Kristen (no last name given) on October 5, 2012 (http://journeysinclassicfilm.com/2012/10/05/alice-sweet-alice-1976/, accessed June 22, 2014).

11. See the review of *Alice, Sweet Alice* posted by Kristen (no last name given) on October 5, 2012 (http://journeysinclassicfilm.com/2012/10/05/alice-sweet-alice-1976/).

12. On "in- and out-groups," see Richard Dawkins, *The God Delusion* 254–6.

13. The monster is the same as that in the original *Children of the Corn*, made on a shoestring budget of $800,000: a turned-over wheelbarrow covered with tarpaulin and earth and drawn by a rope. The whole set-up cost less than $100. See "Harvesting Horror: *Children of the Corn*," dir. Perry Martin, Supplementary DVD Materials, *Children of the Corn*, DVD (2004).

14. The bumper sticker of National Rifle Association supporters reads, "Guns don't kill people; people kill people." See *Urban Dictionary* http://www.urbandictionary.com/define.php?term=guns%20don%27t%20kill%20people%2C%20people%20kill%20people (accessed June 24, 2014).

15. Why, in fact, does poor old Frank have to pull double duty as Wise Indian in life and benevolent ghost in the afterlife? Why not have the evil Corn God counterbalanced by the benevolent Corn Goddess, the ancient symbol of fertility, who does, after all, play a significant role in most Native American creeds? Clearly, a movie in which the truth is ridiculed just because it issues from a woman's mouth could not go there. On the Corn Goddess, see the entry "Corn" in the *Encyclopedia of Myths* (http://www.mythencyclopedia.com/Ca-Cr/Corn.html#b, accessed June 24, 2014).

16. This could be read as an ominous statement, given that *In Cold Blood* was Capote's final book (although he lived, and tried to write, for a number of years after its publication) and is commonly considered to be the book that "finished" Capote.

17. See Tracy Rich, "Qorbanot: Sacrifices and Offerings."

18. Arthur Miller, "Looking for a Conscience" 13.

## Chapter 6

Some of the remarks and ideas in this introductory section are adapted from my chapter "Losers, Meritocracy, and Identification" in Kord and Krimmer, *Contemporary Hollywood Masculinities* 197–219. Tomáš Sedláček's book *Economics of Good and Evil* demonstrates that economics is not an ethically neutral science. Interesting takes on consumerism and its cultural expressions include Tralee Pearce's "Is Family Consumerism the Root of All Evil?"; the unattributed article "Relative Poverty or Consumerism: Choose Your Evil" in the *Economist at Large* (February 27, 2011); Constance L. Hays, "Preaching Against the 'Evil' of Consumerism"; and Will Self's "A Point of View: Are We All Suffering from Consumption?" in the *BBC News Magazine* (August 15, 2014).

1. The Unicef report is quoted in John Bingham's article; see also the comment on the study by Tralee Pearce.

2. The authors of the study, John Paul Wright, Francis Cullen, Robert Agnew and Timothy Brezina, compared adolescents with greater and lesser access to money and found that those with more money had a greater involve-

ment in drug use and other forms of delinquency," "showing that money and its pursuit are associated positively with misbehavior" (see their Abstract).

3. The line is quoted from Jan Crouch's TBN appeal, available on YouTube at http://www.youtube.com/watch?v=zD6j5ONIxkc (accessed October 29, 2015).

4. Alexis de Tocqueville is cited in Alain de Botton, *Status Anxiety* 53.

5. I am referring here to Michael North's book on the subject, *Material Delight and the Joy of Living*, published in the bank-crash year 2008.

6. The quotation is taken from Michael Young's book *The Rise of the Meritocracy*; citation and brief discussion in de Botton, *Status Anxiety* 91.

7. Anthony Robbins is cited in de Botton, *Status Anxiety* 60.

8. The definition of "status anxiety" is Alain de Botton's, *Status Anxiety* 12.

9. See, for example, Tony Williams's take on the film in *Hearths of Darkness* 88, the essays by Gurel, Chuck Jackson, and Liebrand, and Hendershot's "Cold War Horror Film."

10. While practically wallowing in Chucky-POVs, the series is otherwise exceedingly stingy with POV shots, with one notable exception: the extensive Glen-POV at the beginning of *Seed of Chucky* (dir. Don Mancini, 2004), the fifth and (so far) final sequel. The sequence begins with a little girl opening the Glen-box, her birthday present, only to toss him disgustedly into a chest. From there, he emerges to fetch a carving knife from the kitchen drawer, goes upstairs, is picked up by the little girl's father and stabs him. The father, still clutching him, falls down the stairs. Glen climbs the stairs again, goes into the bathroom, and threatens the mother, who is taking a shower behind a clear plastic shower curtain, with the knife. She screams, slips and falls to her death on the tile, with the shower curtain draped over her. The sequence, shot entirely from Glen's POV, is a direct homage of several horror classics, most obviously the POV-opening of Carpenter's *Halloween* (1978) and Hitchcock's *Psycho* (1960), directly quoting *Psycho*'s two most memorable death scenes: Detective Arbogast's stabbing and subsequent tumble down the stairs and Marion Crane's death in the shower.

11. The theme of emotional homelessness continues in *3*, where a teenaged Andy answers the question why he never settled in any one foster family: "I never felt comfortable with those people. They weren't family. They were strangers."

12. Vincenzo Natali, who not only directed the film but also co-wrote the screenplay, has come to very different conclusions about these characters as parents. To him, the family story—he called *Splice* a "family film"—takes precedence over both the abuse of science and the film's critique of corporate greed. "It's about taking responsibility for something that you've created. And in this case, Clive and Elsa have made Dren, and they've made her with the best of intentions, like any good couple, any good parents, they—they want the best for their child." The problem, according to Natali, is not Clive's and Elsa's shameful exploitation of a sentient being but that "Dren just doesn't belong in this world, there's no place for her, and both Clive and Elsa are not prepared for this" ("Interview with Director Vincenzo Natali," supplementary DVD materials, *Splice* DVD-release, 2010). I don't know what kind of film Natali wrote, but it's certainly not the one I saw.

13. This is Greil Marcus's definition of modernity, taken from his *Lipstick Traces: A Secret History of the Twentieth Century*, 122.

## Chapter 7

In "Biology, Childhood Trauma, and Murder," Kathleen M. Heide and Eldra P. Solomon offer a useful overview of literature in neurophysiology and forensics that draws a direct link between childhood trauma and violent crime, specifically murder. Nina Lakhani has established similar links in her article "What drives a child to commit sexual abuse?" E. Ann Kaplan has written persuasively on manifestations of individual and collective trauma in culture, including film. All films and sequels in this chapter (Cohen's series, the *Ring* series and Haneke's film) have attracted considerable academic attention (see bibliography).

1. The study was conducted in 2005 by Heather Mitchell and Michael G. Aamodt.

2. Of the seven parricides interviewed by Heide, six had been the victims of child abuse; see her essay "Why Kids Kill Parents."

3. Examples include the murder committed by a 12-year-old in Michigan, which rated a brief paragraph on the right-hand bottom of page A14 of the *New York Times* ("Michigan: Boy Faces Murder Charge") and the perfunctorily reported case of a 9-year-old girl who fatally stabbed a playmate in New York ("9-Year-Old Girl Accused of Killing Playmate"). In psychology, criminology and forensics, on the other hand, the problem of children who kill is thought to merit serious study; see, among others, the studies published by Heckel and Shumaker, and Butts and Snyder.

4. William Paul, *Laughing Screaming* 282–3.

5. "Unicef: Violence Kills Child Every Five Minutes," *BBC News World* (October 21, 2014), http://www.bbc.co.uk/news/world-29699189. The report itself is available at http://www.unicef.org.uk/Documents/Publications/Unicef_ChildreninDanger_ViolencereportW.pdf (accessed October 29, 2015).

6. The quotation is taken from Julian Petley's "The Monstrous Child" 102.

7. Kim Newman, *Nightmare Movies* 148.

8. Sadako is cast as part of the Japanese myth of Yūrei, female vengeful ghosts endowed with white clothing (signifying traditional burial kimonos) and long black disheveled hair, believed to be a facet inherited from the wigs used in kabuki theatre. In the American films, Samara's appearance—white dress and long black hair obscuring her face—imitates that of a Yūrei ghost, but it is unlikely that Western viewers would see her as such. To an audience unable to access the same cultural and religious connotations as Japanese audiences of the original films, Samara loses depth of association. Sadako alludes to a specific and centuries-old understanding of the afterlife; Samara is merely a visual reminder of Sadako. Divested of her Yūrei origins, the eerie dark-haired white-clad girl has by now become a type that appears regularly in the cinema of various countries (see, for example, Christophe Gans's *Silent Hill*, Canada 2006, and Pete Riski's *Dark Floors,* Finland/Iceland 2008). On Japanese ghosts and their cultural as-

sociations, see Michiko Iwasaka and Barre Toelken's book *Ghosts and the Japanese*.

9. One of the *Ring*-films' many paradoxes is that although practically obsessed with mothering, they seem to discount fathers entirely. Samara has no fewer than three mothers: her birth mother, her adoptive mother Anna Morgan, and finally Rachel. Conversely, fathers play a negligible role. Whereas there are two rather traumatic mother-child scenes, including that showing Samara's murder at her mother's hands, Samara's adoptive father Richard (Brian Cox) is never once shown with Samara; his main function in the film is to commit a memorable suicide (*1*). Other father figures, Noah (Martin Henderson) in *1* and Max (Simon Baker) in *2*, are summarily dispatched by Samara before they have a chance to grow into a paternal role.

10. This is the main theme of Nakata's own *Dark Water* (Japan 2002), from which his American *Ring 2* has borrowed heavily in terms of both plot and symbolism—another reason not to read Nakata's *Ring 2* (USA) as a straightforward remake of his *Ring 2* (Japan).

11. Another way in which the American films achieve this is by near-constant bad-luck warnings, just barely this side of camp. In *1*, Noah buys cigarettes and sees his distorted face in the shop's security monitor, indicating certain death-by-Samara, and is promptly informed by the shop clerk: "You're gonna die" (she means, of course, from smoking). In another scene, Rachel, disturbed by the image of a ladder on the deadly tape, walks under a ladder on the street and stops dead in her tracks. As she contemplates the ladder, a workman warns her facetiously: "Watch out, missy. Bad luck. You don't need that." At this point, Rachel is already under Samara's evil spell, the inescapability of which is visually indicated in yet another scene in which Rachel is shown descending in an old-fashioned elevator: the image is that of her perturbed face, imprisoned behind bars (the slats of the elevator cage) and going down.

12. The Japanese *Ringu* (1998) takes some of the sting out of this dire ending by turning the American *Ring*'s guilty secret into public knowledge, but still manifestly portrays this "solution" as both socially absurd and ethically intolerable. The film's final dialogue lines are taken from an earlier interview detailing the recipe for escape: "*Interviewee.* They say there's one way you can see it and not die. You have to copy it and show it to someone else within one week. *Interviewer.* And what happens to them? *Interviewee.* They have to do the same thing. *Interviewer.* So it never ends. *Interviewee.* That's right. It goes on and on. But if you don't want to die, you'll do it, won't you." Accompanying this voice-over is the film's final shot showing Reiko (Matsushima Nanako) in the car, a strange smile on her face and a copy of the deadly tape beside her, on her way to commit parricide by video in order to save her son.

13. Haneke claimed in an interview that he did not invent the white ribbon but read about it in a nineteenth-century education manual that advised parents to use it on their children (Grundmann, "Unsentimental Education" 604).

14. The English subtitles on the DVD release mitigate the extreme cruelty of this scene considerably by mistranslating the German "Leb wohl, Rudi"—an expression that, unlike "Auf Wiedersehen," implies a permanent parting—as "Take care."

15. The farmer's suicide was indirectly occasioned by his eldest son's rebellion in revenge for his mother's death, upon which the Baron dismissed the entire family from his service, ruining them financially. Other scenes of resistance in the film appear equally futile, for instance Klara's killing of the parakeet, or the episode in which the steward's son first ardently denies having taken Sigi's whistle, but then blows it loudly as soon as his father has left the room, knowing that his father will hear it and beat him again.

16. This is the title of Daniel Goldhagen's infamous and controversial book, in which he claims that anti-semitism was near universal in Germany not only during the Hitler era, but centuries before. The timeline and implied future of the village children have been pointed out by Haneke himself in interviews, for example in his interview with Alexander Horwath (see Horwath's "The Haneke Code," 28).

17. Adolf Eichmann (1906–62), SS Obersturmbannführer and one of the main organizers of the Holocaust; Buchenwald was a concentration camp near Weimar, one of the first and largest on German soil. The film's combining the first and last syllables of these notorious names to form the village name has been noted, among others, by Christian Buß in his 2009 review of the film.

18. The quotation is taken from Haneke's interview with Roy Grundmann (Grundmann, "Unsentimental Education" 595). Haneke has made this point many times elsewhere, claiming, for example, that "For Germans it can be a film about Germany, but for English people it can just as much be a film about England ... you could make a film about an Arab country today" ("Interview," *The White Ribbon*, DVD release, 2009). Or: "I also hope that it has validity for America, France, and Italy—wherever. It is not exclusively about Protestantism. The latter is meant as an example" (Grundmann, "Unsentimental Education" 600).

19. In Haneke's own words: "The use of black-and-white film is also in the service of alienation" (Grundmann, "Unsentimental Education" 600).

20. Haneke again: "Erzähler und Schwarzweiß tun das gleiche: Sie verweisen darauf, dass es sich um ein Artefakt handelt. Nicht um die Wirklichkeit" ("The narrator and black and white achieve the same thing: they point out that this is an artifact, not reality." My translation; German original quoted in Sannwald 8). See also Haneke's similar remark in his interview with Horwath (Horwath, "The Haneke Code" 29): "I decided on two things early on: to do the film in black and white and to have a narrator. Both are means to create distance and avoid any false naturalism."

21. The preceding quotation is given in my translation. The English subtitles (*The White Ribbon*, DVD release, 2009) render this speech as follows: "I don't know if the story I want to tell you is entirely true. Some of it I only know from hearsay. After so many years, a lot of it is still obscure, and many questions remain unanswered. But I feel I must talk about the strange events that occurred in our village. They could perhaps clarify certain things that happened in this country." While this covers content rather well, it does not remotely approach the original's wooden formality: "Ich weiß nicht, ob die Geschichte, die ich Ihnen erzählen will, in allen Details der Wahrheit entspricht. Vieles darin weiß ich nur vom Hörensagen. Und manches weiß ich auch heute, nach so

vielen Jahren, nicht zu enträtseln. Und auf unzählige Fragen gibt es keine Antwort. Aber dennoch glaube ich, dass ich die seltsamen Ereignisse, die sich in unserem Dorf zugetragen haben, erzählen muss, weil sie möglicherweise auf manche Vorgänge in diesem Land ein erhellendes Licht werfen können."

22. The remark is cited in Günter Krenn, "Michael und die Alpha-Kunst" 89.

23. "Ich verschließe mich Übeln, an deren Behebung ich nicht mitwirken kann. Ich habe lernen müssen, wegzuschauen. Ich habe mehrere Zufluchtwinkel, in die sich mein Blick sofort flüchtet, wenn mir der Bildschirm die Welt als eine unerträgliche vorführt.... Auch im Wegdenken bin ich geübt. Ich käme ohne Wegschauen und Wegdenken nicht durch den Tag und schon gar nicht durch die Nacht.... Von den schlimmsten Filmsequenzen aus Konzentrationslagern habe ich bestimmt schon zwanzigmal weggeschaut.... Anstatt dankbar zu sein für die unaufhörliche Präsentation unserer Schande, fange ich an wegzuschauen." Martin Walser, "Erfahrungen beim Verfassen einer Sonntagsrede" 9, 11, my translation. The speech was held in the Paulskirche in Frankfurt on the occasion of his receiving the *Friedenspreis des deutschen Buchhandels*, 11 October 1998. The full text is available on http://www.friedenspreis-desdeutschen-buchhandels.de/sixcms/media.php/1290/1998_walser.pdf, last accessed October 29, 2015.

24. The quotation from Haneke's screenplay is taken from Michael Haneke, *The White Ribbon* [screenplay], unpag. English text available at http://www.pages.drexel.edu/~ina22/splaylib/Screenplay-White_Ribbon,%20The.pdf (accessed October 29, 2015).

25. As stated by Haneke in an interview with Stefan Grissemann and Michael Omasta: "[S]ie vergewaltigt den Zuschauer zur Selbständigkeit" (Grissemann and Omasta 205).

## *Chapter 8*

Our ideas of how children develop and play have been most centrally influenced by the following works: Herbert Spencer, *Essays on Education and Kindred Subjects*; Karl Groos, *The Play of Man*; Lee Vygotsky, *Mind in Society*; Maria Montessori, *The Secret of Childhood*; and David Elkind, *The Power of Play*. Sigmund Freud's ideas on child development are paraphrased from his *The Ego and the Id*.

1. Good overviews of motivations assigned to children who kill in real life are offered, among many others, by Frank Jones, Carol Anne Davis, Mones, Patrick Wilson, and Gardiner.

2. Jean Piaget's theories on children's autonomy and their development of a sense of justice are developed in his book *The Moral Judgment of the Child*.

3. "Unattached Syndrome" may be modeled on Reactive Detachment Disorder, or RAD, commonly caused by child abuse (see Walter D. Buenning's work on this condition).

4. Norman Rockwell has become ironic shorthand for the film's family life. See, for example, the plot summary offered on IMDb by Moderncinéé Staff: "In the remote woods of upstate New York, the Poe family lives a Norman Rockwell life. Perfect house. Perfect marriage" (http://www.imdb.com/title/tt1267319/plotsummary?ref_=tt_ov_pl, accessed October 29, 2015). *Home Movie's* screenwriter and director Christopher Denham also cites this particular idyll: "I'm always more interested in the American Norman Rockwell dream and how that's more of a nightmare in most cases" ("The Making of 'Home Movie,'" *Home Movie*, DVD supplementary materials, 2009).

5. *The Blair Witch Project* is quoted explicitly several times, usually in POV shots from the perspective of someone running through the woods with a handheld camera.

6. See, among others, by Karen Renner ("Evil Children" 17) and William Wandless ("Spoil the Child" 81).

7. The interview with Christopher Denham is in "The Making of 'Home Movie,'" *Home Movie*, DVD supplementary materials, 2009.

8. The interview with Michael Blowitz and cast members of *Peopletoys* are in "Interviews," 2006, supplementary materials, *Peopletoys* DVD-release.

9. The interviews with cast members of *The Children* are in *The Making of* The Children, supplementary materials, DVD-release of *The Children* (2008), dir. and written by Tom Shankland.

## *Conclusions*

For this chapter, I have relied centrally on Fred C. Alford's *What Evil Means to Us* and Terry Eagleton's *On Evil*; other influences include Nancy Billias's *Promoting and Producing Evil*, Joan Copjec's anthology on *Radical Evil* and Wayne Cristaudo's *Power, Love and Evil*. A history of evil on celluloid has been offered by Martin F. Norden in *The Changing Face of Evil in Film and Television*.

1. The headcount was done by Karen Renner in "Evil Children" 4.

2. See, for example, Mendik and Schneider's 2002 collection *Underground USA: Filmmaking Beyond the Hollywood Canon*.

3. On the remake phenomenon, see James Francis's *Remaking Horror* and Holston and Winchester. Some horror remakes command impressive budgets. *The Ring* (Dreamworks 2002) cost $48 million to make; *The Ring 2* (Dreamworks 2005) $50 million—nearly half of the first *Lord of the Rings* films, made around the same time (2001) with a budget of $109 million. See *The Numbers,* http://www.the-numbers.com/movie/Ring-Two-The#tab=summary (accessed October 29, 2015).

4. Scenario and quotation are taken from Lionel Shriver's *We Need to Talk About Kevin* 397.

5. Lumby 70.

6. Faulkner, *Importance* 6.

7. Paul 270.

8. Eagleton, *On Evil* 1. Horror films portraying evil children have, on occasion, succeeded in raising similar specters: apparently, the greatest contemporary concern after the 1956 release of *The Bad Seed* was that children would start imitating little Rhoda's murderous activities (Paul 270-7).

9. Eagleton, *On Evil* 3-4.

10. Eagleton, *On Evil* 8.

11. This is the definition of evil offered by Fred Alford (21).

12. For the distinction between "bad" and "evil," see Alford 18-19.

13. Alford 19.
14. Story and quotation in Alford 11.
15. Lovecraft 12.
16. Lovecraft 13.
17. This may also be why horror films are so often compared with nightmares, which are also often manifestations of guilt or bad conscience.
18. Derry has elaborated that this contempt is centrally tied to horror's "lack of consequences. Horror-film violence too often has a make-believe quality; when someone dies, although there may be surprise and screaming, there is not particularly grief. Nor is there suffering that lasts beyond the momentary, nor survivors emotionally wrecked for life, nor hospital vigils, nor doctor bills, nor economic deprivations, nor lifelong disabilities. And though these films promote voyeurism, they too often lack, even discourage, compassion" (*Dark Dreams 2.0*, 6).
19. I owe Stephen King for the lovely term, coined in *Danse Macabre* (441).
20. Alford 58.
21. Alford 59.
22. Alford 59, emphases original.
23. I am quoting a plot snippet from James Wan's *Saw* (USA/Australia 2004).

# Bibliography

"Aaron Ross Guilty of Raping Girl, 12, in East Lothian." *BBC News Edinburgh, Fife & East Scotland* (October 22, 2013). http://www.bbc.co.uk/news/uk-scotland-edinburgh-east-fife-24625392 (accessed November 30, 2013).

Adams, David, and Jacqueline Campbell. "Understanding Familicide." http://www.jwi.org/document.doc?id=179 (accessed February 5, 2014).

Adams, Derek. "Is That a Carving Knife in Your Pocket or Are You Just Pleased to See Me?" [on *Halloween*, 1978]. *Time Out London*. http://www.timeout.com/london/feature/2435/halloween (accessed April 19, 2012).

Adams, Derek. "One Hell of a Parents' Evening" [on *The Omen*, 1976]. *Time Out London*. http://www.timeout.com/london/feature/2420/100-best-horror-films-the-list/9 (accessed April 19, 2012).

Adams, Derek. "See You on the Other Side" [on *Poltergeist*, 1982]. *Time Out London*. http://www.timeout.com/london/feature/2420/100-best-horror-films-the-list/9 (accessed April 19, 2012).

Adler, Renata. "The Screen: 'Rosemary's Baby,' a Story of Fantasy and Horror." *The New York Times* (13 June 1968): 57.

Alford, C. Fred. *What Evil Means to Us*. Ithaca: Cornell University Press, 1997.

Allen, Steven. "Choosing Torture Instead of Submission." *Cinema, Pain and Pleasure* (March 2013) Palgrave Macmillan. 169–92. http://www.palgraveconnect.com/pc/doifinder/10.1057/9781137306692.0010 (accessed December 12, 2013).

Allmer, Patricia, Emily Brick and David Huxley. *European Nightmares: Horror Cinema in Europe Since 1945*. London, New York: Wallflower Press, 2012.

"Ancient Egyptian Plants: Acacia." http://www.reshafim.org.il/ad/egypt/botany/acacia.htm (accessed February 27, 2014).

Aristotle. *The Rhetoric of Aristotle*. Ed. John Edwin Sandys, commentary by Edward Meredith Cope. Hildesheim, Zurich, New York: Olms, 2006.

Arnold, Sarah. *Maternal Horror Film: Melodrama and Motherhood*. New York: Palgrave Macmillan, 2013.

Arnzen, Michael. "'There Is Only One': The Restoration of the Repressed in *The Exorcist: The Version You've Never Seen!*" *Horror Film: Creating and Marketing Fear*. Ed. Steffen Hantke. Jackson: University Press of Mississippi, 2004. 99–116.

Ayscough, Susan. "The Sexual Politics of David Cronenberg." *Cinema Canada* 102 (December 1983): 15–18.

"Babadook, Scary Children, Nightcrawler, Lightsabers." *BBC 4 Radio: The Film Programme*. http://www.bbc.co.uk/programmes/b04lss81 (accessed October 27, 2014).

Babington, Bruce. "Twice a Victim: Carrie Meets the BFI." *Screen* 24/3 (1983): 4–18.

Badley, Linda. "Zombie Splatter Comedy from *Dawn* to *Shawn*: Cannibal Carnivalesque." *Zombie Culture: Autopsies of the Living Dead*. Ed. Shawn McIntosh and Marc Leverette. Lanham, MD: Scarecrow, 2008. 35–53.

Bakhtin, Mikhail. *Rabelais and His World*. Trans. Helene Iswolsky. Cambridge, MA: MIT Press, 1968.

Balmain, Colette. "The Enemy Within: The Child as Terrorist in the Contemporary American Horror Film." *Monsters and the Monstrous: Myths and Metaphors of Enduring Evil*. Ed. Niall Scott. Amsterdam, New York: Rodopi, 2007. 133–47.

Barnouw, Erik. *The Magician and the Cinema*. Oxford: Oxford University Press, 1981.

Barriga, Claudia A., Michael A. Shapiro, and Marissa L. Fernandez. "Science Information in Fictional Movies: Effects of Context and Gender." *Science Communication* 32.1 (March 2010): 3–24.

Barry, Peter. "Psychoanalytic Criticism." *Beginning Theory: An Introduction to Literary and Cultural Theory*. Manchester: Manchester University Press, 1995. 96–120.

Bathrick, Serafina Kent. "Ragtime: The Horror of Growing Up Female." *Jump Cut* 14 (1977): 9–10.

Baudrillard, Jean. *The Evil Demon of Images*. University of Sydney: Power Institute of Fine Arts, 1987–88.

Baudry, Jean-Louis. "The Apparatus." *Camera obscura* 1 (Fall 1976): 105–26.

Beard, William. "The Visceral Mind: The Major Films of David Cronenberg." *The Shape of Rage: The Films of David Cronenberg*. Ed. Piers Handling. Toronto: General Publishing/New York Zoetrope, 1983. 1–79.

Beard, William, and Piers Handling. "The Interview." *The Shape of Rage: The Films of David Cronenberg*. Ed. Piers Handling. Toronto: General Publishing/New York Zoetrope, 1983. 159–98.

Bell, Carl C., and Esther J. Jenkins. "Community Violence and Children on Chicago's South Side." *Psychiatry* 56 (February 1993): 46–54.

Bell-Metereau, Rebecca. "Woman: The Other Alien in *Alien*." *Women Worldwalkers: New Dimensions of Science Fiction and Fantasy*. Ed. Jane B. Weedman. Lubbock: Texas Tech Press, 1985. 9–24.

Bellin, Joshua David. *Framing Monsters: Fantasy Film and Social Alienation*. Carbondale: Southern Illinois University Press, 2005.

Berenstein, Rhona. *Attack of the Leading Ladies: Gender, Sexuality, and Spectatorship in Classic Horror Cinema*. New York: Columbia University Press, 1995.

Berenstein, Rhona. "Frightening Women: An Introduction to Classic Horror's Marketing Strategies." *Framework* 5/2–3 (Fall 1992): 337–49.

Berenstein, Rhona. "Mommie Dearest: *Aliens*, *Rosemary's Baby*, and Mothering." *Journal of Popular Culture* 24/2 (Fall 1990): 55–73.

Bernardini, Craig. "*Auteurdämmerung*: David Cronenberg, George A. Romero, and the Twilight of the (North) American Horror Auteur." *American Horror Film: The Genre at the Turn of the Millennium*. Ed. Steffen Hantke. Jackson: University Press of Mississippi, 2010. 161–92.

Berton, Justin. "Familicide: Experts Say Family Murder-Suicides, Though Rare, Are Most Common Mass Killing." *San Francisco Examiner* (June 20, 2007).

Bettelheim, Bruno. *Kinder brauchen Märchen*. Trans. Liselotte Mickel and Brigitte Weitbrecht. 5th ed. Stuttgart: Deutsche Verlags-Anstalt, 1990.

Bettelheim, Bruno. *The Uses of Enchantment: The Meaning and Importance of Fairy Tales*. Harmondsworth: Penguin, 1991.

Billias, Nancy, ed. *Promoting and Producing Evil*. Amsterdam: Rodopi, 2010.

Bingham, John. "Cycle of 'Compulsive Consumerism' Leaves British Family Life in Crisis, Unicef Study Finds." *The Telegraph* (September 14, 2011). http://www.telegraph.co.uk/news/politics/8760558/Cycle-of-compulsive-consumerism-leaves-British-family-life-in-crisis-Unicef-study-finds.html (accessed July 22, 2014).

Blake, Linnie. "Another One for the Fire: George A. Romero's American Trilogy of the Flesh." *Necronomicon Presents Shocking Cinema of the Seventies*. Ed. Xavier Mendik. Hereford: Noir, 2002. 151–65.

Blake, Linnie. "'Everyone will suffer': National Identity and the Spirit of Subaltern Vengeance in Nakata Hideo's *Ringu* and Gore Verbinski's *The Ring*." *On Rules and Monsters: Essays zu Horror, Film und Gesellschaft*. Ed. Benjamin Moldenhauer, Christoph Spehr, and Jörg Windszus. Hamburg: Argument, 2008. 146–70.

Blatty, William Peter. *The Exorcist*. New York: Harper & Row, 1971.

Blatty, William Peter. *The Exorcist: From Novel to Film*. New York: Bantam Books, 1974.

Blouin, Michael J. *Japan and the Cosmopolitan Gothic: Specters of Modernity*. New York: Palgrave Macmillan, 2013.

Boas, George. *The Cult of Childhood*. London: Warburgh Institute, 1966.

Bohlmann, Markus P.J., and Sean Moreland, eds. *Monstrous Children and Childish Monsters: Essays on Cinema's Holy Terrors*. Jefferson, NC: McFarland, 2015.

Boon, Kevin Alexander. "Ontological Anxiety Made Flesh: The Zombie in Literature, Film and Culture." *Monsters and the Monstrous: Myths and Metaphors of Enduring Evil*. Ed. Niall Scott. Amsterdam, New York: Rodopi, 2007. 33–43.

Borgwald, James M., and Serge Schreiner. "Science and the Movies: The Good, the Bad, and the Ugly." *Journal of College Science Teaching* 23.6 (May 1994): 367–71.

Boss, Peter John. "Death, Disintegration of the Body and Subjectivity in the Contemporary Horror Film." Diss. University of Warwick, 1989.

Botton, Alain de. *Status Anxiety*. London: Penguin, 2004.

"Boy, 12, Sought over Manchester Campus Sex Attacks." *BBC News Manchester* (October 18, 2013). http://www.bbc.co.uk/news/uk-england-manchester-24589477 (accessed November 30, 2013).

Bradbury, Ray. "A New Ending…" *Focus on the Horror Film*. Ed. Roy Huss and Theodore J. Ross. Englewood Cliffs: Prentice-Hall, 1972. 149–51.

Branigan, Edward. "The Cinematic Narrator: The Logic and Pragmatics of Impersonal Narration." *Journal of Film and Video* 42 (Spring 1990): 3–16.

Branigan, Edward. "Controversy and Correspondence: Narration Issues" [reply to Seymour Chatman]. *Film Quarterly* 41 (Fall 1987): 63.

Branigan, Edward. *Narrative Comprehension and Film*. London: Routledge, 1992.

Branigan, Edward. *Point of View in the Cinema: A Theory of Narration and Subjectivity in Classical Film*. New York: Mouton, 1984.

Branigan, Edward. "Point of View in the Fiction Film." *Wide Angle* 8 (1986): 4–7.

Branigan, Edward. "The Point of View Shot." *Movies and Methods: An Anthology*, vol. 2. Ed. Bill Nichols. Berkeley: University of California Press, 1985. 672–90.

Britton, Andrew. "The Devil, Probably: The Symbolism of Evil." *American Nightmare: Essays on the Horror Film*. Ed. Robin Wood and Richard Lippe. Toronto: Festival of Festivals, 1979. 34–42.

Britton, Andrew. "The Exorcist." *American Nightmare: Essays on the Horror Film*. Ed. Robin Wood and Richard Lippe. Toronto: Festival of Festivals, 1979. 50–53.

Brockmann, Stephen. *A Critical History of German Film*. Rochester: Camden House, 2010.

Broderick, Mick. "From Atoms to Apocalypse: Film and the Nuclear Issue." *Nuclear Movies: A Filmography*. Northcote: Post-Modern Publishing, 1988. 7–29.

Broderick, Mick. *Nuclear Movies: A Filmography*. Northcote: Post-Modern Publishing, 1988.

Brophy, Phil. "Horrality—The Textuality of Contemporary Horror Films." *Screen* 27 (1986): 2–13.

Brosnan, John. *The Horror People*. New York: St. Martin's Press, 1976.

Brottman, Mikita. *Hollywood Hex: Death and Destiny in the Dream Factory, An Illustrated History of Cursed Movies*. New York: Creation Books, 1998.

Brown, Noel. *The Hollywood Family Film: A History, from Shirley Temple to Harry Potter*. London: I.B. Tauris, 2012.

Brown, Royal S. "*Dressed to Kill*: Myth and Male Fantasy in the Horror/Suspense Drama." *Film/Psychology Review* 4/2 (Summer/Fall 1980): 169–82.

Brunette, Peter. *Michael Haneke*. Urbana: University of Illinois Press, 2010.

Buckingham, David. "New Media, New Childhoods? Children's Changing Cultural Environment in the Age of Digital Technology." *An Introduction to Childhood Studies*. Ed. Mary Jane Kehily. Maidenhead, England: Open University Press, 2004. 108–22.

Buenning, Walter D. "Reactive Detachment Disorder Treatment [RAD]: Healing with Love and Limits." http://www.reactiveattachmentdisordertreatment.com/ssi/article2.html (accessed September 28, 2014).

Buntzen, Linda K. "Monstrous Mothers: Medusa, Grendel, and Now *Alien*." *Film Quarterly* 40/3 (Spring 1987): 11–17.

Burns, Ronald, and Charles Crawford. "School Shootings, the Media, and Public Fear: Ingredients for a Moral Panic." *Crime, Law and Social Change* 32 (1999): 147–68.

Buß, Christian. "Oscar-Kandidat 'Das weiße Band': Monster im Dorf." *Spiegel Online Kultur*, October 14, 2009. http://www.spiegel.de/kultur/kino/oscar-kandidat-das-weisse-band-monster-im-dorf-a-654825.html (accessed September 24, 2014).

Büssing, Sabine. *Aliens in the Home: The Child in Horror Fiction*. New York: Greenwood, 1987.

Butler, Ivan. *The Horror Film*. London: Zwemmer; New York: A.S. Barnes, 1967.

Butler, Ivan. *Horror in the Cinema*. 2nd ed. New York: International Film Guide Series, 1970.

Butts, Jeffrey A., and Howard N. Snyder. *Arresting Children: Examining Recent Trends in Preteen Crime*. Chicago: Chapin Hall Center, 2008.

Byree, Carl, James D. Robinson and Joseph Turow. "The Effects of Television on Children: What the Experts Believe." *Annenberg School for Communications Departmental Papers* (1985): 149–55.

Calhoun, Dave. "The Hoof that Rocks the Cradle" [on *Rosemary's Baby*, 1968]. *Time Out London*. http://www.timeout.com/london/feature/2436/rosemarys-baby (accessed April 19, 2012).

Campbell, Mary B. "Biological Alchemy and the Films of David Cronenberg." *Planks of Reason: Essays on the Horror Film*. Ed. Barry Keith Grant. Metuchen, NJ: Scarecrow, 1984. 307–20.

Canini, Mikko, ed. *The Domination of Fear*. Amsterdam: Rodopi, 2010.

Cantor, Joanne, and Mary Beth Oliver. "Developmental Differences in Responses to Horror." *Horror Films: Current Research on Audience Preferences and Reactions*. Ed. James B. Weaver III and Ron Tamborini. Mahwah, NJ: Lawrence Erlbaum Associates, 1996. 63–80.

Carroll, Noël. "Nightmare and the Horror Film: The Symbolic Biology of Fantastic Beings." *Film Quarterly* 36.3 (Spring 1982): 51–81.

Carroll, Noël. *The Philosophy of Horror: Or, Paradoxes of the Heart*. New York: Routledge, 1990.

Carroll, Noël. "Toward a Theory of Point-of-View Editing: Communication, Emotion, and the Movies." *Poetics Today* 14/1 (Spring 1993): 123–41.

Castle, William. *Step Right Up! I'm Gonna Scare the Pants Off America*. New York: Putnam, 1978.

Cavanaugh, T.A. *Double-Effect Reasoning: Doing Good and Avoiding Evil*. Oxford: Clarendon, 2006.

Chabris, Christopher F., and Daniel J. Simons. *The Invisible Gorilla and Other Ways Our Intuitions Deceive Us*. New York: Crown, 2010.

Champlin, Charles. "Hypnotic Spell of 'Exorcist' Based on Fact." *Los Angeles Times* (30 December 1973): HI.

Champlin, Charles. "'Rosemary's Baby' on Crest Screen." *Los Angeles Times* (14 June 1968): HII.

Chappetta, Robert. "Rosemary's Baby." *Film Quarterly* 22/3 (1969): 35–38.

"Child-on-Child Abuse Shocking, Children's Commissioner Report Says." *BBC News UK* (26 November 2013). http://www.bbc.co.uk/news/uk-25090896 (accessed November 26, 2013).

Clarens, Carlos. "Horror for the Young, Horny and Mobile." *Soho Weekly News* (18 June 1980): 46.

Clarens, Carlos. *An Illustrated History of the Horror Film*. New York: Putnam, 1967.

Clark, Cath. "The Miracle of Birth" [on *Alien*, 1979]. *Time Out London*. http://www.timeout.com/london/feature/2439/alien (accessed April 19, 2012).

Clark, Cath. "Suffer the Little Children" [on *The Innocents*, 1961]. *Time Out London*. http://www.timeout.com/london/feature/2420/100-best-horror-films-the-list/9 (accessed April 19, 2012).

Clark, Cath. "Who's That Girl?" [on *Ringu*, 1998]. *Time Out London*. http://www.timeout.com/london/feature/2420/100-best-horror-films-the-list/4 (accessed April 19, 2012).

Clarke, Peter, and Tony Claydon, eds. *Saints and Sanctity*. Woodbridge, Suffolk: Boydell Press, 2011.

Clayton, Victoria. "The Needless Complexity of Academic Writing." *The Atlantic* (October 25, 2015). http://www.theatlantic.com/education/archive/2015/10/complex-academic-writing/412255/ (accessed November 3, 2015).

Clemens, Valdine. *The Return of the Repressed: Gothic Horror from The Castle of Otranto to Alien*. Albany: State University of New York Press, 1999.

Clover, Carol. "Her Body, Himself: Gender in the Slasher Film." *The Dread of Difference: Gender and the Horror Film*. Ed. Barry Keith Grant. Austin: University of Texas Press, 1996. 66–113.

Clover, Carol. *Men, Women, and Chain Saws: Gender in Modern Horror Film*. Princeton: Princeton University Press, 1992.

Cobbs, John L. "*Alien* as an Abortion Parable." *Literature/Film Quarterly* 18/3 (1990): 198–202.

Coder, Kim D. "Cultural Aspects of Trees: Traditions and Myths." November 1996. http://warnell.forestry.uga.edu/service/library/index.php3?docID=129&docHistory%5B%5D=2 (accessed February 27, 2014).

Colavito, Jason. *Knowing Fear: Science, Knowledge and the Development of the Horror Genre.* Jefferson, NC: McFarland, 2008.

Colman, Felicity. *Deleuze and Cinema: The Film Concepts.* Oxford: Berg, 2011.

Coltrane, Scott, and Randall Collins. *Sociology of Marriage & the Family: Gender, Love, and Property.* 5th ed. Belmont, CA: Wadsworth/Thomson Learning, 2001.

Copjec, Joan, ed. *Radical Evil.* London, New York: Verso, 1996.

Coupland, Douglas. *Player One: What Is to Become of Us. A Novel in Five Hours.* London: Heinemann, 2010.

Coveney, Peter. *The Image of Childhood: The Individual and Society. A Study of the Theme in English Literature.* Harmondsworth: Penguin, 1967.

Cowan, Douglas E. *Sacred Terror: Religion and Horror on the Silver Screen.* Waco, TX: Baylor University Press, 2008.

Craig, Pamela, and Martin Fradley. "Teenage Traumata: Youth, Affective Politics, and the Contemporary American Horror Film." *American Horror Film: The Genre at the Turn of the Millennium.* Ed. Steffen Hantke. Jackson: University Press of Mississippi, 2010. 77–102.

Crane, Jonathan. "A Body Apart: Cronenberg and Genre." *The Modern Fantastic: The Films of David Cronenberg.* Ed. Michael Grant. Westport, CT: Praeger, 2000. 50–68.

Crane, Jonathan. *Terror and Everyday Life: Singular Moments in the History of the Horror Film.* Thousand Oaks, CA: Sage Publications, 1994.

Creed, Barbara. "Dark Desires: Male Masochism in the Horror Film." *Screening the Male: Exploring Masculinities in Hollywood Cinema.* Ed. Steven Cohan and Ina Rae Hark. London: Routledge, 1993. 118–33.

Creed, Barbara. "Horror and the Monstrous-Feminine: An Imaginary Abjection." *The Dread of Difference: Gender and the Horror Film.* Ed. Barry Keith Grant. Austin: University of Texas Press, 1996. 35–65.

Creed, Barbara. *The Monstrous-Feminine: Film, Feminism, Psychoanalysis.* London: Routledge, 1993.

Creed, Barbara. *Phallic Panic: Film, Horror, and the Primal Uncanny.* Carlton, Vic.: Melbourne University Press, 2005.

Creed, Barbara. "Phallic Panic: Male Hysteria and *Dead Ringers.*" *Screen* 31/2 (Summer 1990): 125–46.

"Creepy British Child Syndrome." https://www.youtube.com/watch?v=eHFVq6UTU1Y (accessed October 27, 2014).

Crisp, Tony. "Historical Perspectives—On the Primary Connection Between Parents and Child." http://dreamhawk.com/pregnancy-childbirth/historical-perspectives-on-the-primary-connection-between-parents-and-child/ (accessed January 22, 2014).

Cristaudo, Wayne. *Power, Love and Evil: Contribution to a Philosophy of the Damaged.* Amsterdam: Rodopi, 2008.

Dadoun, Roger. "Fetishism in the Horror Film." *Enclitic* 1/2 (1979): 39–63.

Damm, Sigrid. *Christiane und Goethe: Eine Recherche.* Frankfurt/Main: Insel Verlag, 1998.

Davis, Blair, and Kial Natale. "'The Pound of Flesh Which I Demand': American Horror Cinema, Gore, and the Box Office, 1998–2007." *American Horror Film: The Genre at the Turn of the Millennium.* Ed. Steffen Hantke. Jackson: University Press of Mississippi, 2010. 35–57.

Davis, Carol Anne. *Children Who Kill: Profiles of Pre-Teen and Teenage Killers.* London: Allison & Busby, 2003.

Dawkins, Richard. *The God Delusion.* London: Bantam, 2006.

De Lauretis, Teresa, and Stephen Heath, eds. *The Cinematic Apparatus.* New York: St. Martin's, 1980.

Deleuze, Gilles. *Cinema 1: The Movement-Image.* Trans. H. Tomlinson and B. Habberjam. London: Athlone, 1986.

Deleuze, Gilles. *Cinema 2: The Time-Image.* Trans. H. Tomlinson and B. Habberjam. London: Athlone, 1989.

Dempsey, Michael. Review of *The Exorcist. Film Quarterly* 27/4 (1974): 61–62.

Dendle, Peter. "The Zombie as Barometer of Cultural Anxiety." *Monsters and the Monstrous: Myths and Metaphors of Enduring Evil.* Ed. Niall Scott. Amsterdam: Rodopi, 2007. 45–57.

Dendle, Peter. *The Zombie Movie Encyclopedia.* Jefferson, NC: McFarland, 2001.

Denne, John D. "Society and the Monster." *Focus on the Horror Film.* Ed. Roy Huss and Theodore J. Ross. Englewood Cliffs, NJ: Prentice-Hall, 1972. 125–31.

Derry, Charles. *Dark Dreams: A Psychological History of the Modern Horror Film.* London: Thomas Yoseloff, 1977.

Derry, Charles. *Dark Dreams 2.0: A Psychological History of the Modern Horror Film from the 1950s to the 21st Century.* Jefferson, NC: McFarland, 2009.

Derry, Charles. "More Dark Dreams: Some Notes on the Recent Horror Film." *American Horrors: Essays on the Modern American Horror Film.* Ed. Gregory A. Waller. Urbana: University of Illinois Press, 1987. 162–74.

Dickstein, Morris. "The Aesthetics of Fright." *Planks of Reason: Essays on the Horror Film.* Ed. Barry Keith Grant. Metuchen, NJ: Scarecrow, 1984. 50–62.

Dika, Vera. "From Dracula—With Love." *The Dread of Difference: Gender and the Horror Film.* Ed. Barry Keith Grant. Austin: University of Texas Press, 1996. 388–400.

Dika, Vera. *Games of Terror: Halloween, Friday the 13th, and the Films of the Stalker Cycle.* Cranbury, NJ: Associated University Presses, 1990.

Dika, Vera. "The Stalker Film, 1978–81." *American

*Horrors: Essays on the Modern American Horror Film.* Ed. Gregory A. Waller. Urbana: University of Illinois Press, 1987. 86–101.

Dillard, R.H.W. *Horror Films.* New York: Monarch Press, 1976.

Dillard, R.H.W. "*Night of the Living Dead*: It's Not Like Just a Wind That's Passing Through." *American Horrors: Essays on the Modern American Horror Film.* Ed. Gregory A. Waller. Urbana: University of Illinois Press, 1987. 14–29.

Dillard, R.H.W. "The Pageantry of Death." *Focus on the Horror Film.* Ed. Roy Huss and Theodore J. Ross. Englewood Cliffs, NJ: Prentice-Hall, 1972. 36–41.

Dixon, Wheeler Winston. "The Child as Demon in Films." *Films in Review* 37.2 (February 1986): 78–83.

Do Vale, Simone. "Trash Mob: Zombie Walks and the Positivity of Monsters in Western Popular Culture." *The Domination of Fear.* Ed. Mikko Canini. Amsterdam: Rodopi, 2010. 191–202.

Doherty, Thomas. "Genre, Gender, and the *Aliens* Trilogy." *The Dread of Difference: Gender and the Horror Film.* Ed. Barry Keith Grant. Austin: University of Texas Press, 1996. 181–99.

Douglas, Ann. "The Dream of the Wise-Child: Freud's Family Romance Revisited in Contemporary Narratives of Horror." *Prospects* 9 (1984): 293–348.

Dubeck, Leroy W., Suzanne E. Moshier, and Judith E. Boss. *Science in Cinema: Teaching Fact Through Science Fiction Films.* New York: Teachers College Press, 1988.

Duchaney, Brian N. *The Spark of Fear: Technology, Society and the Horror Film.* Jefferson, NC: McFarland, 2015.

Duell, Mark. "Teenager Obsessed with Dexter TV Series Stabbed 17-Year-Old Girlfriend to Death before Dismembering Her in His Bedroom." *MailOnline*, October 2, 2014. http://www.dailymail.co.uk/news/article-2777794/Teenager-obsessed-Dexter-TV-series-stabbed-17-year-old-girlfriend-death-dismembering-bedroom.html (accessed October 3, 2014).

Eagleton, Terry. *On Evil.* New Haven, CT: Yale University Press, 2010.

Eagleton, Terry. "Psychoanalysis." *Literary Theory: An Introduction.* Minneapolis: University of Minnesota Press, 1983. 151–93.

Ebert, Roger. "The Good Son." Review. September 24, 1993. http://www.rogerebert.com/reviews/the-good-son-1993 (accessed January 29, 2014).

Ebert, Roger. "Why Movie Audiences Aren't Safe Anymore." *American Film* 16/5 (March 1981): 54–56.

Edge, Brooke W. "'She Needs More': The Villainization of Infertile Women in Horror Films." *Monstrous Children and Childish Monsters: Essays on Cinema's Holy Terrors.* Ed. Markus P.J. Bohlmann and Sean Moreland. Jefferson, NC: McFarland, 2015. 42–60.

Edwards, Justin, and Rune Graulund. *The Grotesque.* London: Routledge, 2013.

Edwards, Leigh H. *The Triumph of Reality TV: The Revolution in American Television.* Santa Barbara, CA: Praeger, 2013.

Eisenstein, Alex. "*Alien* Dissected: Anatomy of a Monster Movie." *Fantastic Films* 13 (1980): 51–63.

Elias, Norbert. *The Civilizing Process: Sociogenetic and Psychogenetic Investigations.* Trans. Edmund Jephcott, ed. Eric Dunning, Johan Goudsblom and Stephen Mennell. 3rd ed. Oxford: Blackwell, 1994.

Elkind, David. *The Power of Play: Learning What Comes Naturally.* Philadelphia: Da Capo, 2007.

Elsaesser, Thomas. "Performative Self-Contradictions: Michael Haneke's Mind Games." *A Companion to Michael Haneke.* Ed. Roy Grundmann. Chichester: Blackwell, 2010. 53–74.

*Empire: The Greatest Horror Movies Ever, The Definitive Guide.* London: 2000.

*Encyclopedia of Children and Childhood in History and Society.* http://www.faqs.org/childhood/index.html (accessed January 22, 2014).

*Encyclopedia of Myths.* http://www.mythencyclopedia.com/index.html (accessed June 24, 2014).

Erens, Patricia Brett. "*The Stepfather*: Father as Monster in the Contemporary Horror Film." *The Dread of Difference: Gender and the Horror Film.* Ed. Barry Keith Grant. Austin: University of Texas Press, 1996. 352–63.

Erens, Patricia Brett, ed. *Sexual Stratagems.* New York: Horizon, 1979.

Evans, Walter. "Monster Movies: A Sexual Theory." *Planks of Reason: Essays on the Horror Film.* Ed. Barry Keith Grant. Metuchen, NJ: Scarecrow, 1984. 53–64.

Everman, Welch. "What Is a Cult Horror Film?" *The Cult Film Reader.* Ed. Ernest Mathijs and Xavier Mendik. Maidenhead, England: Open University Press, 2008. 212–15.

Everson, William K. *Classics of the Horror Film.* Secaucus, NJ: Citadel, 1974.

Everson, William K. *More Classics of the Horror Film: Fifty Years of Great Chillers.* Secaucus, NJ: Citadel, 1986.

Fahy, Thomas. "Introduction." *The Philosophy of Horror.* Ed. Thomas Fahy. Lexington: University Press of Kentucky, 2010. 1–13.

Fahy, Thomas, ed. *The Philosophy of Horror.* Lexington: University Press of Kentucky, 2010.

Farber, Stephen. "The New American Gothic." *Focus on the Horror Film.* Ed. Roy Huss and Theodore J. Ross. Englewood Cliffs, NJ: Prentice-Hall, 1972. 94–102.

Faulkner, Joanne. *The Importance of Being Innocent: Why We Worry About Children.* Cambridge: Cambridge University Press, 2011.

Faulkner, Joanne. "The Innocence Fetish: The Commodification and Sexualisation of Children in the Media and Popular Culture." *Media International Australia* 135 (May 2010): 106–17.

Fischer, Lucy. "Birth Traumas: Parturition and Horror in *Rosemary's Baby*." *The Dread of Difference: Gender and the Horror Film.* Ed. Barry Keith Grant. Austin: University of Texas Press, 1996. 412–31.

Fisher, Jaimey, ed. *Generic Histories of German Cinema: Genre and Its Deviations*. Rochester, NY: Camden House, 2013.

"The 5 Horror Trailer Trends That Always Work," *Celebuzz!* http://www.celebuzz.com/2013-08-26/the-5-horror-trailer-trends-that-always-work/ (accessed October 30, 2013).

Floyd, Nigel. "The Beginning of the End" [on *Night of the Living Dead*, 1968]. *Time Out London*. http://www.timeout.com/london/feature/2420/100-best-horror-films-the-list/9 (accessed April 19, 2012).

Forshaw, Barry. *British Gothic Cinema*. (October 2013) Palgrave Macmillan. http://www.palgraveconnect.com/pc/doifinder/10.1057/9781137300324 (accessed December 12, 2013).

Foucault, Michel. "Of Other Spaces, Heterotopias." http://foucault.info/documents/heterotopia/foucault.heterotopia.en.html (accessed November 24, 2013).

Fradley, Martin. "'Hell Is a Teenage Girl'? Postfeminism and Contemporary Teen Horror." *Postfeminism and Contemporary Hollywood Cinema*. Ed. Joel Gwynne and Nadine Muller. Palgrave Macmillan. 204-21. http://www.palgraveconnect.com/pc/doifinder/10.1057/9781137306845.0019 (accessed December 12, 2013).

Francis, James Jr. *Remaking Horror: Hollywood's New Reliance on Scares of Old*. Jefferson, NC: McFarland, 2013.

Frank, Marcie. "The Camera and the Speculum: David Cronenberg's *Dead Ringers*." *PMLA* 106/3 (May 1991): 459-70.

Franke-Penski, Udo. "Kettensägen, Lust und Toleranz: Zur Konsumierbarkeit von Horrorfilmen." *On Rules and Monsters: Essays zu Horror, Film und Gesellschaft*. Ed. Benjamin Moldenhauer, Christoph Spehr, and Jörg Windszus. Hamburg: Argument, 2008. 20-41.

Fraser, Peter. *A Christian Response to Horror Cinema: Ten Films in Theological Perspective*. Jefferson, NC: McFarland, 2015.

Frayling, Christopher. *Nightmare: The Birth of Horror*. London: BBC, 1996.

Freeland, Cynthia. *The Naked and the Undead: Evil and the Appeal of Horror*. Boulder, CO: Westview, 2000.

Freud, Sigmund. *The Ego and the Id*. Seattle: Pacific Publishing Studio, 2010.

Freud, Sigmund. *A General Introduction to Psychoanalysis*. Trans. Joan Riviere. New York: Permabooks, 1958.

Freud, Sigmund. *The Uncanny*. Trans. David Mclintock. New York: Penguin, 2003.

Fromholzer, Frank, Michael Preis and Bettina Wisiorek, eds. *Noch nie war das Böse so gut. Aktualität einer alten Differenz*. Heidelberg: Universitätsverlag Winter, 2011.

Fuchs, Cynthia. "'The Whole Fucking World Warped around Me': Bad Kids and Worse Contexts." *Bad: Infamy, Darkness, Evil, and Slime on Screen*. Ed. Murray Pomerance. Albany: State University of New York Press, 2004. 273-85.

Fustel de Coulanges, Numa Denis. *Family, Kin, and City-State: The Racial Underpinning of Ancient Greece and Rome*. Washington, D.C.: Scott-Townsend, 1999.

Galbraith, Stuart, IV. *Japanese Science Fiction, Fantasy and Horror Films: A Critical Analysis and Filmography of 103 Features Released in the United States, 1950-1992*. Jefferson, NC: McFarland, 2006.

Gans, Herbert J. "*The Exorcist*: A Devilish Attack on Women." *Social Policy* 5 (May-June 1974): 71-73.

Gardiner, Muriel. *The Deadly Innocents: Portraits of Children Who Kill*. New Haven, CT: Yale University Press, 1985.

Gershman, Boris. "The Economics of the Evil Eye Belief." June 2014. https://www.american.edu/cas/economics/research/upload/2013-14.pdf (accessed July 1, 2014).

Gifford, Denis. *Monsters of the Movies*. London: Carousel, 1977.

Giles, Dennis. "Conditions of Pleasure in Horror Cinema." *Planks of Reason: Essays on the Horror Film*. Ed. Barry Keith Grant. Metuchen, NJ: Scarecrow, 1984. 38-52.

Gillis, John. *Youth and History*. London: Academic Press, 1981.

Gittins, Diana. *The Child in Question*. Basingstoke: Macmillan, 1998.

Gittins, Diana. *The Family in Question: Changing Households and Familiar Ideologies*. Basingstoke: Macmillan, 1985.

Glazebrook, Philip. "The Anti-Heroes of Horror." *Films and Filming* 13/1 (October 1966): 36-7.

Goethe, Johann Wolfgang. *Briefwechsel zwischen Schiller und Goethe*. Digitized at http://gutenberg.spiegel.de/buch/3659/1. Handwritten: Goethe und Schiller Archiv, "Bestand 28: Goethe, Johann Wolfgang / Eingegangene Briefe—Verzeichnungseinheiten," http://ora-web.swkk.de/archiv_online/gsa.entry?b=28&vc=1046&source=gsa.archivalien (accessed January 22, 2014).

Goldhagen, Daniel. *Hitler's Willing Executioners: Ordinary Germans and the Holocaust*. London: Abacus, 1997.

Goldsmith, Kelly, Eunice Kim Cho, and Ravi Dhar. "When Guilt Begets Pleasure: The Positive Effect of a Negative Emotion." *Journal of Marketing Research* XLIX (December 2012): 872-81.

Goldstein, Ruth M., and Edith Zornow. *The Screen Image of Youth: Movies About Children and Adolescents*. Metuchen, NJ: Scarecrow, 1980.

Gomery, Douglas. "The Economics of the Horror Film." *Horror Films: Current Research on Audience Preferences and Reactions*. Ed. James B. Weaver III and Ron Tamborini. Mahwah, NJ: Lawrence Erlbaum Associates, 1996. 49-62.

Gonder, Patrick. "Race, Gender and Terror: The Primitive in 1950s Horror Films." *Genders* 40 (2004). http://www.genders.org/g40/g40_gondor.html (accessed April 19, 2012).

Gotto, Lisa. "Bösewerden. Mädchen, Macht und Medium in *The Exorcist* (William Friedkin, USA 1973)." *rebellisch verzweifelt infam: Das böse Mäd-*

*chen als ästhetische Figur.* Ed. Renate Möhrmann in collaboration with Nadja Urbani. Bielefeld: Aisthesis, 2012. 371–88.

Graafland, Johan. "Review of Tomáš Sedláček's Economics of Good and Evil: The Quest for Economic Meaning from Gilgamesh to Wall Street." *Erasmus Journal for Philosophy and Economics* 6/2 (Autumn 2013): 108–16.

Graff, Gerald. "Scholars and Sound Bites: The Myth of Academic Difficulty." *PMLA* 115.5 (October 2000): 1041–1052. http://courses.wcupa.edu/fletcher/special/graff.htm (accessed November 3, 2015).

Graham, Allison. "'The Fallen Wonder of the World': Brian De Palma's Horror Films." *American Horrors: Essays on the Modern American Horror Film.* Ed. Gregory A. Waller. Urbana: University of Illinois Press, 1987. 129–44.

Grant, Barry Keith. *Film Genre: From Iconography to Ideology.* London: Wallflower, 2007.

Grant, Barry Keith. "Introduction." *The Dread of Difference: Gender and the Horror Film.* Ed. Barry Keith Grant. Austin: University of Texas Press, 1996. 1–12.

Grant, Barry Keith. "Introduction." *Planks of Reason: Essays on the Horror Film.* Ed. Barry Keith Grant. Metuchen, NJ: Scarecrow, 1984. xi–xiv.

Grant, Barry Keith. "Taking Back the *Night of the Living Dead*: George Romero, Feminism, and the Horror Film." *The Dread of Difference: Gender and the Horror Film.* Ed. Barry Keith Grant. Austin: University of Texas Press, 1996. 200–12.

Grant, Barry Keith, ed. *The Dread of Difference: Gender and the Horror Film.* Austin: University of Texas Press, 1996.

Grant, Barry Keith, ed. *Film Genre: Theory and Criticism.* Metuchen, NJ: Scarecrow, 1977.

Grant, Barry Keith, ed. *Film Genre Reader II.* Austin: University of Texas Press, 1995.

Grant, Barry Keith, ed. *Planks of Reason: Essays on the Horror Film.* Metuchen, NJ: Scarecrow, 1984.

Grant, Michael, ed. *The Modern Fantastic: The Films of David Cronenberg.* Westport, CT: Praeger, 2000.

Greenberg, Harvey R., M.D. "Reimagining the Gargoyle: Psychoanalytic Notes on *Alien.*" *Camera Obscura* 15 (1986): 87–108.

Greven, David. *Representations of Femininity in American Genre Cinema: The Woman's Film, Film Noir, and Modern Horror.* Basingstoke: Palgrave Macmillan, 2011.

Grissemann, Stefan, and Michael Omasta. "Herr Haneke, wo bleibt das Positive? Ein Gespräch mit dem Regisseur." *Der siebente Kontinent: Michael Haneke und seine Filme.* Ed. Alexander Horwath. Vienna, Zurich: Europaverlag, 1991. 193–214.

Grixti, Joseph. *Terrors of Uncertainty: The Cultural Contexts of Horror Fiction.* London: Routledge, 1989.

Grodal, Torben. *Moving Pictures: A New Theory of Film Genres, Feelings and Cognition.* Oxford: Clarendon, 1997.

Groos, Karl. *The Play of Man.* Trans. Elizabeth L. Baldwin. New York: Appleton, 1901.

Grossman, Dave, and Gloria DeGaetano. *Stop Teaching Our Kids to Kill: A Call to Action Against TV, Movie, and Video Game Violence.* New York: Crown, 1999.

Grosz, Elizabeth. *Jacques Lacan: A Feminist Introduction.* London: Routledge, 1990.

Grundmann, Roy. "Introduction: Haneke's Anachronism." *A Companion to Michael Haneke.* Ed. Roy Grundmann. Chichester: Blackwell, 2010. 1–50.

Grundmann, Roy. "Unsentimental Education: An Interview with Michael Haneke." *A Companion to Michael Haneke.* Ed. Roy Grundmann. Chichester: Blackwell, 2010. 591–606.

Grundmann, Roy, ed. *A Companion to Michael Haneke.* Chichester: Blackwell, 2010.

Guerrero, Edward. "AIDS as Monster in Science Fiction and Horror Cinema." *Journal of Popular Film and Television* 18/3 (Fall 1990): 86–93.

Gunning, Tom. "Flickers: On Cinema's Power for Evil." *Bad: Infamy, Darkness, Evil, and Slime on Screen.* Ed. Murray Pomerance. Albany: State University of New York Press, 2004. 21–37.

Gurel, Perin. "A Natural Little Girl: Reproduction and Naturalism in *The Bad Seed* as Novel, Play, and Film." *Adaptation* 3/2 (2010): 132–54.

Halberstam, Judith. *Skin Shows: Gothic Horror and the Technology of Monsters.* Durham, NC: Duke University Press, 1995.

Hall, Stuart. "Encoding / Decoding." *Culture, Media, Language.* Ed. Stuart Hall, Dorothy Hobson, Andrew Lowe and Paul Willis. London: Hutchinson, 1980. 128–39.

Hanawalt, Barbara. *The Ties that Bound: Peasant Families in Medieval England.* Oxford: Oxford University Press, 1986.

Hand, Richard J., and Jay McRoy, eds. *Monstrous Adaptations: Generic and Thematic Mutations in Horror Film.* Manchester: Manchester University Press, 2007.

Handling, Piers. "A Canadian Cronenberg." *The Shape of Rage: The Films of David Cronenberg.* Ed. Piers Handling. Toronto: General Publishing/New York Zoetrope, 1983. 98–114.

Handling, Piers, ed. *The Shape of Rage.* Toronto: General Publishing/New York Zoetrope, 1983.

Haneke, Michael. *The White Ribbon* [screenplay]. Unpag. English text available at http://www.pages.drexel.edu/~ina22/splaylib/Screenplay-White_Ribbon,%20The.pdf (accessed September 24, 2014).

Hanich, Julian. *Cinematic Emotion in Horror Films and Thrillers: The Aesthetic Paradox of Pleasurable Fear.* New York: Routledge, 2010.

Hansen, Regina, ed. *Roman Catholicism in Fantastic Film: Essays on Belief, Spectacle, Ritual and Imagery.* Jefferson, NC: McFarland, 2011.

Hantke, Steffen. "My Baby Ate the Dingo: The Visual Construction of the Monstrous Infant in Horror Film." *The "Evil Child" in Literature, Film, and Popular Culture.* Ed. Karen J. Renner. New York: Routledge, 2013. 28–44.

Hantke, Steffen. "They Don't Make 'Em Like They Used To: On the Rhetoric of Crisis and the Current

State of American Horror Cinema." *American Horror Film: The Genre at the Turn of the Millennium*. Ed. Steffen Hantke. Jackson: University Press of Mississippi, 2010. vii–xxxii.

Hantke, Steffen, ed. *American Horror Film: The Genre at the Turn of the Millennium*. Jackson: University Press of Mississippi, 2010.

Hantke, Steffen, ed. *Horror Film: Creating and Marketing Fear*. Jackson: University Press of Mississippi, 2004.

Hardy, Phil. *The Encyclopedia of Horror Movies*. New York: Harper & Row, 1986.

Harkness, John. "The Word, the Flesh and David Cronenberg." *The Shape of Rage: The Films of David Cronenberg*. Ed. Piers Handling. Toronto: General Publishing/New York Zoetrope, 1983. 87–97.

Harper, Graeme, and Xavier Mendik. "Introduction: Several Theorists Ask 'How Was It for You Honey?' Or Why the Academy Needs Cult Cinema and Its Fans." *Unruly Pleasures: The Cult Film and its Critics*. Ed. Xavier Mendik and Graeme Harper. Guildford: FAB Press, 2000. 7–11.

Harper, Graeme, and Jonathan Rayner. "Introduction." *Cinema and Landscape*. Ed. Graeme Harper and Jonathan Rayner. Bristol: Intellect, 2010. 13–28.

Harper, Graeme, and Jonathan Rayner, eds. *Cinema and Landscape*. Bristol: Intellect, 2010.

Harpham, Geoffrey Galt. *On the Grotesque: Strategies of Contradiction in Art and Literature*. Princeton: Princeton University Press, 1982.

Hausen, Karin. "Family and Role-Division: The Polarization of Sexual Stereotypes in the Nineteenth Century—An Aspect of the Dissociation of Work and Family Life." *The German Family: Essays on the Social History of the Family in 19th- and 20th-century Germany*. Ed. Richard J. Evans and W.R. Lee. London: Barnes & Noble Books, 1981. 51–83.

Hawking, Stephen, and Leonard Mlodinow. *The Grand Design: New Answers to the Ultimate Questions of Life*. London: Bantam, 2010.

Hays, Constance L. "Preaching Against the 'Evil' of Consumerism." *The New York Times* (January 1, 2003). http://www.nytimes.com/2003/01/01/business/01BILL.html (accessed July 1, 2014).

Heckel, Robert V., and David M. Shumaker. *Children Who Murder: A Psychological Perspective*. Westport, CT: Praeger, 2001.

Heide, Kathleen M. "Why Kids Kill Parents." *Psychology Today* (September 1, 1992). http://www.psychologytoday.com/articles/200910/why-kids-kill-parents (accessed August 25, 2014).

Heide, Kathleen M., and Eldra P. Solomon. "Biology, Childhood Trauma, and Murder: Rethinking Justice." *International Journal of Law and Psychiatry* 29/3 (2006): 220–33.

Heldreth, Leonard G. "The Beast Within: Sexuality and Metamorphosis in Horror Films." *Eros in the Mind's Eye*. Ed. Donald Palumbo. Westport, CT: Greenwood, 1986. 117–25.

Hendershot, Cyndy. "The Cold War Horror Film: Taboo and Transgression in *The Bad Seed*, *The Fly*, and *Psycho*." *Journal of Popular Film and Television* 29/1 (Spring 2001): 20–31.

Hendershot, Cyndy. "Monster at the Soda Shop: Teenagers and Fifties Horror Films." *Images* 10 (September 2001). http://www.imagesjournal.com/issue10/features/monster/ (accessed April 19, 2012).

Hendershot, Cynthia. *I Was a Cold War Monster: Horror Films, Eroticism, and the Cold War Imagination*. Bowling Green, OH: Bowling Green State University Popular Press, 2001.

Hentschel, Frank. *Töne der Angst: Die Musik im Horrorfilm*. Berlin: Bertz & Fischer, 2011.

Hernandez, Vladimir. "The Country Where Exorcisms Are on the Rise." *BBC News Magazine* (November 26, 2013). http://www.bbc.co.uk/news/magazine-25032305 (accessed July 20, 2014).

Hill, Michael Ortiz. *Dreaming the End of the World: Apocalypse as a Rite of Passage*. Putnam, CT: Spring Publications, 1994.

Hipkins, Danielle, and Roger Pitts, eds. *New Visions of the Child in Italian Cinema*. Oxford: Peter Lang, 2014.

Hoffman, A. Robin. "How to See the Horror: The Hostile Foetus in *Rosemary's Baby* and *Alien*." *The "Evil Child" in Literature, Film, and Popular Culture*. Ed. Karen J. Renner. New York: Routledge, 2013. 150–72.

Hogan, David J. *Dark Romance: Sex and Death in the Horror Film*. Jefferson, NC: McFarland, 1986.

Holland, Patricia. *What Is a Child? Popular Images of Childhood*. London: Virago, 1992.

Holston, Kim R., and Tom Winchester. *Science Fiction, Fantasy and Horror Film Sequels, Series and Remakes*. Jefferson, NC: McFarland, 1997.

Horwath, Alexander. "The Haneke Code: Talking Shop, Theory, and Practice with the Director of *The White Ribbon*." *filmcomment* 45/6 (Nov./Dec. 2009): 26–31.

Horwath, Alexander. "Die ungeheuerliche Kränkung, die das Leben ist: Zu den Filmen von Michael Haneke." *Der siebente Kontinent: Michael Haneke und seine Filme*. Ed. Alexander Horwath. Vienna, Zurich: Europaverlag, 1991. 11–39.

Horwath, Alexander, ed. *Der siebente Kontinent: Michael Haneke und seine Filme*. Vienna, Zurich: Europaverlag, 1991.

Hoxter, Julian. "Taking Possession: Cult Learning in *The Exorcist*." *Unruly Pleasures: The Cult Film and its Critics*. Ed. Xavier Mendik and Graeme Harper. Guildford: FAB Press, 2000. 171–85.

Huddleston, Tom. "The Cabin in the Woods" [review]. *Time Out London* (April 12–18, 2012): 64.

Huddleston, Tom. "Father Knows Best" [on *Eraserhead*, 1977]. *Time Out London*. http://www.timeout.com/london/feature/2420/100-best-horror-films-the-list/4 (accessed April 19, 2012).

Huddleston, Tom. "The 100 Best Horror Films." *Time Out London*. http://www.timeout.com/london/feature/2494/best-horror-films (accessed April 19, 2012).

Huddleston, Tom. "Time Out's 100 best horror films." *Time Out London* (April 12–18, 2012): 62–63.

Huddleston, Tom. "William Friedkin Interview." *Time Out London.* http://www.timeout.com/london/feature/2508/william-friedkin-interview (accessed April 19, 2012).

Hunt, Thomas P. *The Book of Wealth: In Which It Is Proved from the Bible, That It Is the Duty of Every Man to Become Rich.* New York: Ezra Collier, 1836.

Huss, Roy, and T.J. Ross, eds. *Focus on the Horror Film.* Englewood Cliffs, NJ: Prentice-Hall, 1972.

Hutchings, Peter. *The Horror Film.* Harlow: Pearson, 2004.

Hutchings, Peter. "Masculinity and the Horror Film." *You Tarzan: Masculinity, Movies, and Men.* Ed. Pat Kirkham and Janet Thumim. London: Lawrence and Wishart, 1993. 84–94.

Hutchinson, Sharla, and Rebecca A. Brown, eds. *Monsters and Monstrosity from the Fin de Siècle to the Millennium: New Essays.* Jefferson, NC: McFarland, 2015.

Ingebretsen, Edward J. *At Stake: Monsters and the Rhetoric of Fear in Public Culture.* Chicago: University of Chicago Press, 2001.

Iwasaka, Michiko, and Barre Toelken. *Ghosts and the Japanese: Cultural Experience in Japanese Death Legends.* Logan: Utah State University Press, 1994.

Jackson, Chuck. "Little, Violent, White: The Bad Seed and the Matter of Children." *Journal of Popular Film and Television* 28/2 (2000): 64–73.

Jackson, Kathy Merlock. *Images of Children in American Film: A Sociocultural Analysis.* Metuchen, NJ: Scarecrow, 1986.

Jackson, Kimberly. "Metahorror and Simulation in the Scream Series and The Cabin in the Woods." *Technology, Monstrosity, and Reproduction in Twenty-first Century Horror.* (November 2013) Palgrave Macmillan. 11–30. http://www.palgraveconnect.com/pc/doifinder/10.1057/9781137360267.0006 (accessed December 12, 2013).

Jackson, Kimberly. *Technology, Monstrosity, and Reproduction in Twenty-first Century Horror.* (November 2013) Palgrave Macmillan. http://www.palgraveconnect.com/pc/doifinder/10.1057/9781137360267 (accessed December 12, 2013).

Jacobs, Robert, ed. *Filling the Hole in the Nuclear Future: Art and Popular Culture Respond to the Bomb.* Lanham, MD: Lexington Books, 2010.

Jancovich, Mark. "General Introduction." *Horror: The Film Reader.* Ed. Mark Jancovich. New York: Routledge, 2002. 1–19.

Jancovich, Mark. *Horror.* London: Batsford, 1992.

Jancovich, Mark, ed. *Horror: The Film Reader.* New York: Routledge, 2002.

Johnson, Robert Flynn. "Gottfried Helnwein: The Child." http://www.gottfried-helnwein-child.com/child_in_art.html (accessed January 22, 2014).

Johnston, David MacGregor. "Kitsch and Camp and Things That Go Bump in the Night; or, Sontag and Adorno at the (Horror) Movies." *The Philosophy of Horror.* Ed. Thomas Fahy. Lexington: University Press of Kentucky, 2010. 229–43.

Jones, Alan. *The Rough Guide to Horror Movies.* London: Penguin, 2005.

Jones, Darryl. *Horror: A Thematic History in Fiction and Film.* London: Arnold, 2002.

Jones, Ernest. "Nightmare of Bloodsucking." *Focus on the Horror Film.* Ed. Roy Huss and Theodore J. Ross. Englewood Cliffs, NJ: Prentice-Hall, 1972. 57–62.

Jones, Frank. *Murderous Innocents: True Stories of Children Who Kill.* London: Headline, 1994.

Jones, Steve. *Torture Porn: Popular Horror after* Saw. (July 2013) Palgrave Macmillan. http://www.palgraveconnect.com/pc/doifinder/10.1057/9781137317124 (accessed December 12, 2013).

Kalat, David. *J-Horror: The Definitive Guide to* The Ring, The Grudge *and Beyond.* New York: Vertical, 2007.

Kapczynski, Jennifer M., and Michael D. Richardson, eds. *A New History of German Cinema.* Rochester, NY: Camden House, 2012.

Kaplan, E. Ann. *Trauma Culture: The Politics of Terror and Loss in Media and Literature.* New Brunswick, NJ: Rutgers University Press, 2005.

Kaufman, Lloyd. "Foreword, I.A.: I-Won't-Suck-the-Mainstream-Art." *Underground USA: Filmmaking Beyond the Hollywood Canon.* Ed. Xavier Mendik and Steven Jay Schneider. London: Wallflower Press, 2002. xiii–xvii.

Kavanagh, James H. "'Son of a Bitch': Feminism, Humanism, and Science in *Alien.*" *October* 13 (Summer 1980): 91–100.

Kaveney, Roz. "Horror of Blood." *Times Literary Supplement* (9 December 2011). http://www.the-tls.co.uk/tls/public/tlssearch.do?querystring=Horror+of+Blood&x=54&y=13&sectionId=1797&p=tls (accessed November 19, 2013).

Kawin, Bruce F. *Horror and the Horror Film.* London: Anthem Press, 2012.

Kay, Glenn. "*The Child* (1977)." *Zombie Movies: The Ultimate Guide.* Chicago: Chicago Review Press, 2008. 88–89.

Kayser, Wolfgang. *The Grotesque in Art and Literature.* Trans. Ulrich Weisstein. New York: Columbia University Press, 1981.

Kehily, Mary Jane. "Understanding Childhood: An Introduction to Some Key Themes and Issues." *An Introduction to Childhood Studies.* Ed. Mary Jane Kehily. Maidenhead, England: Open University Press, 2004. 1–21.

Kehily, Mary Jane, ed. *An Introduction to Childhood Studies.* Maidenhead, England: Open University Press, 2004.

Kellerman, Jesse. *The Brutal Art.* London: Sphere, 2009.

Kempes, Maaike, Walter Matthys, Han de Vries and Herman van Engeland. "Reactive and Proactive Aggression in Children: A Review of Theory, Findings and the Relevance for Child and Adolescent Psychiatry." *European Child and Adolescent Psychiatry* 14/1 (2005): 11–19.

Kendrick, Walter. *The Thrill of Fear: 250 Years of Scary Entertainment.* New York: Grove, 1991.

Kennedy, Harlan. "Things That Go Howl in the Id." *Film Comment* 18 (1982): 37–39.

Kermode, Mark. *The Exorcist*. 2nd ed. London: BFI, 1998.

Kermode, Mark. "*The Exorcist*—Hype or Horror?" *BBC News* (November 2, 1998). http://news.bbc.co.uk/1/hi/entertainment/206337.stm (accessed July 20, 2014).

Kerswell, J.A. *Teenage Wasteland: The Slasher Movie Uncut*. London: New Holland, 2010.

Kinder, Marsha, and Beverle Houston. "Seeing Is Believing: *The Exorcist* and *Don't Look Now*." *American Horrors: Essays on the Modern American Horror Film*. Ed. Gregory A. Waller. Urbana: University of Illinois Press, 1987. 44–61.

King, C.M., and N. Hourani. "Don't Tease Me: Effects of Ending Type on Horror Film Enjoyment." *Media Psychology* 9/3 (2007): 473–492.

King, Geoff, and Tanya Krzywinska. *Science Fiction Cinema: From Outerspace to Cyberspace*. London: Wallflower, 2000.

King, Stephen. *Danse Macabre*. London: Warner Books, 1991.

King, Stephen. *The Dark Half*. New York: Viking, 1989.

King, Stephen. *Lisey's Story*. London: Hodder & Stoughton, 2006.

King, Stephen. *Night Shift*. London: Hodder & Stoughton, 2007.

King, Stephen. *Pet Sematary*. New York: Doubleday, 1983.

King, Stephen. *'Salem's Lot*. New York: Doubleday, 1976.

Klein, Christina. "The *American* Horror Film? Globalization and Transnational U.S.–Asian Genres." *American Horror Film: The Genre at the Turn of the Millennium*. Ed. Steffen Hantke. Jackson: University Press of Mississippi, 2010. 3–14.

Klein, Melanie. *Love, Guilt and Reparation and Other Works, 1921–45*. London: Vintage, 1975.

Knelman, Martin. "*The Exorcist*: Do You Have to Be Possessed to Dig It?" *The Globe and Mail* (31 December 1973): 10.

Kord, Susanne. "Bad Blood: The Cost of Sexual Curiosity in Archetypal Tales." *Oxford German Studies* 38.2 (2009): 203–17.

Kord, Susanne, and Elisabeth Krimmer. *Contemporary Hollywood Masculinities: Gender, Genre, and Politics*. New York: Palgrave Macmillan, 2011.

Krenn, Günter. "Michael und die Alpha-Kunst: Praktische Gedanken der Cutterin Monika Willi und des Kameramannes Christian Berger zu Michael Hanekes Modus Operandi." *Film-Konzepte 21: Michael Haneke* (February 2011): 76–91.

Kristeva, Julia. *Powers of Horror: An Essay on Abjection*. Trans. Leon S. Roudiez. New York: Columbia University Press, 1982.

Krzywinska, Tanya. *A Skin for Dancing In: Witchcraft, Possession and Voodoo in Film*. Trowbridge: Flicks Books, 2001.

Kuhn, Annette, ed. *Alien Zone: Cultural Theory and Contemporary Science Fiction Cinema*. London: Verso, 1990.

Kuhn, Reinhard. *Corruption in Paradise*. Hanover, NH: University Press of New England, 1982.

Kuni, Verena. "Un-Ordnung schaffen: Das Labor als Ort der Transgression." *On Rules and Monsters: Essays zu Horror, Film und Gesellschaft*. Ed. Benjamin Moldenhauer, Christoph Spehr, and Jörg Windszus. Hamburg: Argument, 2008. 100–20.

Lacan, Jacques. *Écrits: A Selection*. Trans. Alan Sheridan. London: Routledge, 2001.

Lakhani, Nina. "What Drives a Child to Commit Sexual Abuse?" *The Independent* (August 25, 2014), http://www.independent.co.uk/life-style/health-and-families/health-news/what-drives-a-child-to-commit-sexual-abuse-2114974.html (accessed August 25, 2014).

Lamberson, Gregory. *Cheap Scares! Low Budget Horror Filmmakers Share Their Secrets*. Jefferson, NC: McFarland, 2008.

Lambourne, Robert, Michael Shallis, and Michael Shortland. *Close Encounters? Science and Science Fiction*. Bristol: Hilger, 1990.

Larsen, Kristine. "When Procreation Becomes Perversion: Zombie Babies." *Monstrous Children and Childish Monsters: Essays on Cinema's Holy Terrors*. Ed. Markus P.J. Bohlmann and Sean Moreland. Jefferson, NC: McFarland, 2015. 61–78.

Lawrence, Patricia A., and Philip C. Palmgreen. "A Uses and Gratifications Analysis of Horror Film Preference." *Horror Films: Current Research on Audience Preferences and Reactions*. Ed. James B. Weaver III and Ron Tamborini. Mahwah, NJ: Lawrence Erlbaum Associates, 1996. 161–78.

Lazzeri, Antonella. "Robert Thompson Described Every Piece of James Bulger's Clothing…" *The Sun* (February 12, 2013). http://www.thesun.co.uk/sol/homepage/features/4790605/20-years-after-James-Bulger-ex-cop-describes-catching-Thompson-and-Venables.html (accessed August 25, 2014).

Lebeau, Vicky. *Childhood and Cinema*. London: Reaktion Books, 2008.

Lennard, Dominic. *Bad Seeds and Holy Terrors: The Child Villains of Horror Films*. Albany: State University of New York Press, 2014.

Lenne, Gerard. "Monster and Victim: Women in the Horror Film." *Sexual Stratagems*. Ed. Patricia Erens. New York: Horizon, 1979. 31–40.

Levine, Michael. "A Fun Night Out: Horror and Other Pleasures of the Cinema." *Senses of the Cinema* 15 (July–August 2001). http://sensesofcinema.com/contents/01/15/horror_fun.html (accessed April 18, 2012).

Liebrand, Claudia. "Gute Mädchen kommen in den Himmel, böse Mädchen trifft der Blitz. Mervyn LeRoy's *The Bad Seed* (USA 1956)." *Rebellisch verzweifelt infam: Das böse Mädchen als ästhetische Figur*. Ed. Renate Möhrmann in collaboration with Nadja Urbani. Bielefeld: Aisthesis, 2012. 349–70.

Lin, Zion Shyiren. "Divine Seeding: Reinterpreting Luke 1:35 in Light of Ancient Procreation Theories and Christological Developments." Diss. Fuller Theological Seminary (2008).

Lindsey, Shelley Stamp. "Horror, Femininity, and Carrie's Monstrous Puberty." *The Dread of Difference:*

*Gender and the Horror Film.* Ed. Barry Keith Grant. Austin: University of Texas Press, 1996. 279–95.

Lloyd, Blodwen, ed. *Science in Films.* London: Sampson Low, Marston & Co., 1948.

Lovecraft, Howard Phillips. *Supernatural Horror in Literature.* New York: Dover, 1973.

Lowe, Roy. "Childhood Through the Ages." *An Introduction to Early Childhood Studies.* Ed. Trisha Maynard and Nigel Thomas. 2nd ed. Los Angeles: SAGE, 2009. 21–32.

Lowenstein, Adam. *Shocking Representation: Historical Trauma, National Cinema, and the Modern Horror Film.* New York: Columbia University Press, 2005.

Lumby, Catharine. "Presumed Innocent: Picturing Childhood." *The Unacceptable.* Ed. John Potts and John Scannell. (November 2013) Palgrave Macmillan. 68–79. http://www.palgraveconnect.com/pc/doifinder/10.1057/9781137014573.0013 (accessed December 12, 2013).

Lury, Karen. *The Child in Film: Tears, Fears and Fairytales.* London: I.B. Tauris, 2010.

Lutz, John. "Zombies of the World, Unite: Class Struggle and Alienation in *Land of the Dead*." *The Philosophy of Horror.* Ed. Thomas Fahy. Lexington: University Press of Kentucky, 2010. 121–36.

MacLaird, Misha. "Coproduction and Transnationalism: National Cinema in a Global Market." *Aesthetics and Politics in the Mexican Film Industry.* (June 2013) Palgrave Macmillan. 163–88. http://www.palgraveconnect.com/pc/doifinder/10.1057/9781137319340.0012 (accessed December 12, 2013).

Maddrey, Joseph. *Nightmares in Red, White and Blue: The Evolution of the American Horror Film.* Jefferson, NC: McFarland, 2004.

Magistrate, Tony, ed. *The Films of Stephen King: From* Carrie *to* Secret Window. (February 2008) Palgrave Macmillan. http://www.palgraveconnect.com/pc/doifinder/10.1057/9780230610583 (accessed December 12, 2013).

Manchel, Frank. *Terrors of the Screen.* Englewood Cliffs, NJ: Prentice-Hall, 1970.

"Manchester Sex Attacks: Boy, 14, Admits Five Charges." *BBC News Manchester* (21 October 2013). http://www.bbc.co.uk/news/uk-england-manchester-24607544 (accessed November 30, 2013).

Mank, Gregory William. *It's Alive! The Classic Cinema Saga of Frankenstein.* San Diego: A.S. Barnes, 1981.

Marak, Katarzyna. *Japanese and American Horror: A Comparative Study of Film, Fiction, Graphic Novels and Video Games.* Jefferson, NC: McFarland, 2015.

Marcus, Greil. *Lipstick Traces: A Secret History of the Twentieth Century.* London: Faber and Faber, 2001.

Martin, Daniel. "Gaining Sympathy for Mr and Mrs Vengeance." *Times Higher Education* (Oct 25–31, 2012): 40–41.

Marx, Gary. "Young Killers Remain Well-Publicized Rarity." *Chicago Tribune* (February 11, 1998). http://articles.chicagotribune.com/1998-02-11/news/9802110044_1_juvenile-justice-experts-super predators-violent-juvenile-crime (accessed August 25, 2014).

Mathijs, Ernest, and Xavier Mendik. "The Concepts of Cult." *The Cult Film Reader.* Ed. Ernest Mathijs and Xavier Mendik. Maidenhead, England: Open University Press, 2008. 15–24.

Mathijs, Ernest, and Xavier Mendik. "Editorial Introduction: What Is Cult Film?" *The Cult Film Reader.* Ed. Ernest Mathijs and Xavier Mendik. Maidenhead, England: Open University Press, 2008. 1–11.

Mathijs, Ernest, and Xavier Mendik, eds. *The Cult Film Reader.* Maidenhead, England: Open University Press, 2008.

Mathijs, Ernest, and Xavier Mendik. *100 Cult Films.* London: BFI, 2011.

Matusa, Paula. "Corruption and Catastrophe: De Palma's *Carrie.*" *Film Quarterly* 31/1 (1977): 32–38.

Maynard, Joyce. "The Monster Children." *Newsweek* 26 (July 1976): 10–11.

Maynard, Trisha, and Nigel Thomas. *An Introduction to Early Childhood Studies.* 2nd ed. Los Angeles: SAGE, 2009.

Mazumdar, Tulip. "What Does It Feel Like to Be Airbrushed?" *BBC News Magazine*, October 15, 2013. http://www.bbc.co.uk/news/magazine-24522060 (accessed November 25, 2013).

McCabe, Bob. *The Exorcist: Out of the Shadows, The Full Story of the Film.* London: Omnibus, 1999.

McCann, Ben, and David Sorfa. "Introduction." *The Cinema of Michael Haneke.* Ed. Ben McCann and David Sorfa. New York: Wallflower, 2011. 1–9.

McCann, Ben, and David Sorfa, eds. *The Cinema of Michael Haneke.* New York: Wallflower, 2011.

McCarty, John. *The Modern Horror Film: 50 Contemporary Classics from "The Curse of Frankenstein" to "The Lair of the White Worm."* New York: Citadel, 1990.

McCarty, John. *Psychos: Eighty Years of Mad Movies, Maniacs, and Murderous Deeds.* New York: St. Martin's, 1986.

McCarty, John. *Splatter Movies.* New York: St. Martin's, 1981.

McCloud, Scott. *Understanding Comics: The Invisible Art.* New York: Harper Perennial, 1994.

McConnell, Frank. "Rough Beasts Slouching." *Focus on the Horror Film.* Ed. Roy Huss and Theodore J. Ross. Englewood Cliffs, NJ: Prentice-Hall, 1972. 24–35.

McCrae, Scooter. "The Best Horror Films That America Doesn't Want You to Know About." *Filmmaker Magazine* (Summer 2000). http://www.filmmakermagazine.com/issues/summer2000/features/best_horror.php (accessed April 18, 2012).

McIntosh, Shawn. "The Evolution of the Zombie: The Monster That Keeps Coming Back." *Zombie Culture: Autopsies of the Living Dead.* Ed. Shawn McIntosh and Marc Leverette. Lanham, MD: Scarecrow, 2008. 1–17.

McIntosh, Shawn, and Marc Leverette. "Introduction: Giving the Living Dead Their Due." *Zombie Culture: Autopsies of the Living Dead.* Ed. Shawn McIntosh and Marc Leverette. Lanham, MD: Scarecrow, 2008. vii–xiv.

McIntosh, Shawn, and Marc Leverette, eds. *Zombie Culture: Autopsies of the Living Dead*. Lanham, MD: Scarecrow, 2008.

McKnight, Brent. "Yup, Sometimes Dead IS Better: *Pet Sematary*." http://www.popmatters.com/review/164583-pet-sematary/. October 25, 2012 (accessed February 26, 2014).

McLarty, Lianne. "'Beyond the Veil of the Flesh': Cronenberg and the Disembodiment of Horror." *The Dread of Difference: Gender and the Horror Film*. Ed. Barry Keith Grant. Austin: University of Texas Press, 1996. 231–52.

Mendik, Xavier. "Part One: Hollywood on the Edge." *Necronomicon Presents Shocking Cinema of the Seventies*. Ed. Xavier Mendik. Hereford: Noir, 2002. 11–14.

Mendik, Xavier. "Part Three: Seventies Horror." *Necronomicon Presents Shocking Cinema of the Seventies*. Ed. Xavier Mendik. Hereford: Noir, 2002. 147–50.

Mendik, Xavier, ed. *Necronomicon Presents Shocking Cinema of the Seventies*. Hereford: Noir, 2002.

Mendik, Xavier, and Graeme Harper, eds. *Unruly Pleasures: The Cult Film and Its Critics*. Guildford: FAB Press, 2000.

Mendik, Xavier, and Steven Jay Schneider. "Introduction: Explorations Underground: American Film (Ad)Ventures Beneath the Hollywood Radar." *Underground USA: Filmmaking Beyond the Hollywood Canon*. Ed. Xavier Mendik and Steven Jay Schneider. London: Wallflower, 2002. 1–12.

Mendik, Xavier, and Steven Jay Schneider. "A Tasteless Art: Waters, Kaufman and the Pursuit of 'Pure' Gross-Out." *Underground USA: Filmmaking Beyond the Hollywood Canon*. Ed. Xavier Mendik and Steven Jay Schneider. London: Wallflower, 2002. 204–20.

Mendik, Xavier, and Steven Jay Schneider, eds. *Underground USA: Filmmaking Beyond the Hollywood Canon*. London: Wallflower, 2002.

Metelmann, Jörg. *Zur Kritik der Kino-Gewalt: Die Filme von Michael Haneke*. Munich: Wilhelm Fink, 2003.

Michel, Frann. "Life and Death and Something in Between: Reviewing Recent Horror Cinema." *Psychoanalysis, Culture & Society* 12 (December 2007): 390–97.

"Michigan: Boy Faces Murder Charge Over Stabbing at Playground." *The New York Times* (August 6, 2014). A14.

Millard, Anne. *Family Life in Ancient Greece*. London: Hodder Wayland, 2001.

Miller, Arthur. "Looking for a Conscience." *The New York Times* (Sunday, February 23, 2003): 1; 13.

Miller, Sam J. "Haunted House Films Are Really About the Nightmares of Gentrification." *AlterNet* (October 30, 2007). http://www.alternet.org/story/65512/haunted_house_films_are_really_about_the_nightmares_of_gentrification (accessed November 4, 2012).

Mitchell, Charles P. *The Devil on Screen: Feature Films Worldwide, 1913 through 2000*. Jefferson, NC: McFarland, 2010.

Mitchell, Heather, and Michael G. Aamodt. "The Incidence of Child Abuse in Serial Killers." *Journal of Police and Criminal Psychology* 20/1 (2005): 40–7.

Modleski, Tania. "The Terror of Pleasure: The Contemporary Horror Film and Postmodern Theory." *Studies in Entertainment: Critical Approaches to Mass Culture*. Ed. Tania Modleski. Bloomington: Indiana University Press, 1986. 155–56.

Modleski, Tania, ed. *Studies in Entertainment: Critical Approaches to Mass Culture*. Bloomington: Indiana University Press, 1986.

Möhrmann, Renate, ed., in collaboration with Nadja Urbani. *Rebellisch verzweifelt infam: Das böse Mädchen als ästhetische Figur*. Bielefeld: Aisthesis, 2012.

Moldenhauer, Benjamin. "Teenage Nightmares: Jugend und Gewalt im modernen Horrorfilm." *On Rules and Monsters: Essays zu Horror, Film und Gesellschaft*. Ed. Benjamin Moldenhauer, Christoph Spehr, and Jörg Windszus. Hamburg: Argument, 2008. 60–82.

Moldenhauer, Benjamin, Christoph Spehr, and Jörg Windszus. "Einleitung: Der Kongress der lebenden Toten." *On Rules and Monsters: Essays zu Horror, Film und Gesellschaft*. Ed. Benjamin Moldenhauer, Christoph Spehr, and Jörg Windszus. Hamburg: Argument, 2008. 4–5.

Moldenhauer, Benjamin, Christoph Spehr, and Jörg Windszus. "Law of the Dead: Zehn Thesen zum modernen Horrorfilm." *On Rules and Monsters: Essays zu Horror, Film und Gesellschaft*. Ed. Benjamin Moldenhauer, Christoph Spehr, and Jörg Windszus. Hamburg: Argument, 2008. 6–19.

Moldenhauer, Benjamin, Christoph Spehr, and Jörg Windszus, eds. *On Rules and Monsters: Essays zu Horror, Film und Gesellschaft*. Hamburg: Argument, 2008.

Monaco, James. "Aaaueeearrggh!! Horror Movies." *Sight and Sound* 49/2 (Spring 1980): 80–82.

Mones, Paul A. *When a Child Kills: Abused Children Who Kill Their Parents*. New York: Pocket Books, 1991.

Monk, Daniel. "Childhood and the Law: In Whose 'Best Interests'?" *An Introduction to Childhood Studies*. Maidenhead, England: Open University Press, 2004. 160–77.

Montessori, Maria. *The Secret of Childhood*. Chennai: Orient Longman, 2004.

Morris, Jeremy. "The Justification of Torture-Horror: Retribution and Sadism in *Saw*, *Hostel*, and *The Devil's Rejects*." *The Philosophy of Horror*. Ed. Thomas Fahy. Lexington: University Press of Kentucky, 2010. 42–56.

Moss, Robert. *Karloff and Company: The Horror Film*. New York: Pyramid Publications, 1973.

Muir, Kenneth. *Horror Films of the 1970s*. Jefferson, NC: McFarland, 2002.

Muir, Kenneth. *Horror Films of the 1980s*. Jefferson, NC: McFarland, 2007.

Muir, Kenneth. *Horror Films of the 1990s*. Jefferson, NC: McFarland, 2011.

Mulvey, Laura. "Afterthoughts on 'Visual Pleasure and

Narrative Cinema' Inspired by King Vidor's *Duel in the Sun* (1946)." *Framework* 15–17 (1981): 12–15.

Mulvey, Laura. *Visual and Other Pleasures.* Bloomington: Indiana University Press, 1981.

Mulvey, Laura. "Visual Pleasure and Narrative Cinema." *Screen* 16/3 (Autumn 1975): 6–18.

Murphy, Bernice M. *The Rural Gothic in American Popular Culture: Backwoods Horror and Terror in the Wilderness.* New York: Palgrave Macmillan, 2013.

Murray, John P. "TV Violence and Brainmapping in Children." *Psychiatric Times* XVIII (10): October 2001. http://www.psychiatrictimes.com/articles/tv-violence-and-brainmapping-children (accessed November 14, 2013).

Naha, Ed. *Horrors: From Screen to Scream.* New York: Avon, 1975.

Naureckas, Jim. "*Aliens*: Mother and the Teeming Hordes." *Jump Cut* 32 (1986): 1, 4.

Neale, Steve. "*Halloween*: Suspense, Aggression and the Look." *Planks of Reason: Essays on the Horror Film.* Ed. Barry Keith Grant. Metuchen, NJ: Scarecrow, 1984. 331–45.

Nelson, Andrew Patrick. "Traumatic Childhood Now Included: Todorov's Fantastic and the Uncanny Slasher Remake." *American Horror Film: The Genre at the Turn of the Millennium.* Ed. Steffen Hantke. Jackson: University Press of Mississippi, 2010. 103–18.

Newman, Kim. *Nightmare Movies.* 2nd ed. London: Bloomsbury Publishing, 2011.

Newman, Kim, ed. *The BFI Companion to Horror.* London: BFI, 1996.

Newton, Judith. "Feminism and Anxiety in *Alien*." *Science Fiction Studies* 7/3 (1980): 278–304.

Newton, Michael. *Savage Girls and Wild Boys: A History of Feral Children.* London: Faber & Faber, 2002.

Ng, Andrew Hock Soon, ed. *Asian Gothic: Essays on Literature, Film and Anime.* Jefferson, NC: McFarland, 2008.

Nichols, David B., and Bob Martin. "An Anatomy of Terror." *Fangoria* 10 (January 1981): 19–22, 48–49.

Niesel, Jeffrey. "The Horror of Everyday Life: Taxidermy, Aesthetics, and Consumption in Horror Films." *Journal of Criminal Justice and Popular Culture* 2.4 (1994): 61–80.

"9-Year-Old Girl Accused of Killing Playmate." *Fox News* (May 31, 2005). http://www.foxnews.com/story/2005/05/31/year-old-girl-accused-killing-playmate/ (accessed November 30, 2013).

Norden, Martin F., ed. *The Changing Face of Evil in Film and Television.* Amsterdam: Rodopi, 2007.

North, Michael. *Material Delight and the Joy of Living: Cultural Consumption in the Age of Enlightenment in Germany.* Trans. Pamela Selwyn. Aldershot, NH: Ashgate, 2008.

*The Numbers: Where Data and the Movie Business Meet.* http://www.the-numbers.com (accessed October 14, 2014).

Oppenheimer, Daniel M. "Consequences of Erudite Vernacular Utilized Irrespective of Necessity: Problems with Using Long Words Needlessly." *Cognitive Psychology* 20/2 (March 2006): 139–56.

Orr, John. "The White Ribbon in Michael Haneke's Cinema." *The Cinema of Michael Haneke.* Ed. Ben McCann and David Sorfa. New York: Wallflower, 2011. 259–64.

Osteen, Mark. "The Big Secret: *Film Noir* and Nuclear Fear." *Journal of Popular Film & Television* 22.2 (Summer 1994): 79–90.

O'Toole, Lawrence. "The Cult of Horror." *The Cult Film Reader.* Ed. Ernest Mathijs and Xavier Mendik. Maidenhead, England: Open University Press, 2008. 257–62.

"Overprotecting Parents Can Lead Children to Develop 'Peter Pan Syndrome.'" *Science Daily* (3 May 2007). http://www.sciencedaily.com/releases/2007/05/070501112023.htm (accessed October 1, 2014).

Paffenroth, Kim. *Gospel of the Living Dead: George Romero's Visions of Hell on Earth.* Waco, TX: Baylor University Press, 2006.

Page, Clarence. "6 Who Saw 'Exorcist' under Care." *Chicago Tribune* (18 January 1974): I.

Paszylk, Bartlomiej. *The Pleasure and Pain of Cult Horror Films: An Historical Survey.* Jefferson, NC: McFarland, 2009.

Patterson, Natasha. "Cannibalizing Gender and Genre: A Feminist Re-Vision of George Romero's Zombie Films." *Zombie Culture: Autopsies of the Living Dead.* Ed. Shawn McIntosh and Marc Leverette. Lanham, MD: Scarecrow, 2008. 103–18.

Paul, William. *Laughing Screaming: Modern Hollywood Horror and Comedy.* New York: Columbia University Press, 1994.

Pearce, Tralee. "Is Family Consumerism the Root of All Evil?" *The Globe and Mail* (Sept. 14, 2011). http://www.theglobeandmail.com/life/the-hot-button/is-family-consumerism-the-root-of-all-evil/article617351/ (accessed July 1, 2014).

Perkins, V.F. *Film as Film: Understanding and Judging Movies.* Harmondsworth: Penguin, 1972.

Perkowitz, Sidney. *Hollywood Science: Movies, Science, and the End of the World.* New York: Columbia University Press, 2007.

Perrine, Toni A. *Film and the Nuclear Age: Representing Cultural Anxiety.* New York, London: Garland Publishing, 1998.

Perry, Bruce D., Ronnie A. Pollard, Toi L. Blakley, William L. Baker, and Domenico Vigilante. "Childhood Trauma, the Neurobiology of Adaptation & Use-dependent Development of the Brain: How States become Traits." http://www.traumapages.com/a/perry96.php (accessed November 14, 2013).

Pessl, Marisha. *Night Film.* New York: Random House, 2013.

Petley, Julian. "The Monstrous Child." *The Body's Perilous Pleasures: Dangerous Desires and Contemporary Culture.* Ed. Michele Aaron. Edinburgh: Edinburgh University Press, 1999. 87–107.

Pevere, Geoff. "Cronenberg Tackles Dominant Videology." *The Shape of Rage.* Ed. Piers Handling.

Toronto: General Publishing/New York Zoetrope, 1983. 136–48.

Phillips, Kendall R. *Dark Directions: Romero, Craven, Carpenter, and the Modern Horror Film*. Carbondale: Southern Illinois University Press, 2012.

Phillips, Kendall R. *Projected Fears: Horror Films and American Culture*. Westport, CT: Praeger, 2005.

Piaget, Jean. *The Moral Judgment of the Child*. Trans. Marjorie Gabain. Glencoe, IL: The Free Press, 2004.

Pick, Anat, and Guinevere Narraway. "Introduction." *Screening Nature: Cinema Beyond the Human*. Ed. Anat Pick and Guinevere Narraway. Oxford, New York: Berghahn, 2013. 1–18.

Pick, Anat, and Guinevere Narraway, eds. *Screening Nature: Cinema Beyond the Human*. Oxford: Berghahn, 2013.

Pinedo, Isabel Christina. *Recreational Terror: Women and the Pleasures of Horror Film Viewing*. Albany: State University of New York Press, 1997.

Pinker, Steven. "Why Academics Stink at Writing." *The Chronicle of Higher Education* (September 26, 2014). http://chronicle.com/article/Why-Academics-Writing-Stinks/148989/ (accessed November 3, 2015).

Pirie, David. "Carrie." *Movie* 25 (1977–78): 20–24.

Pirie, David. *A Heritage of Horror*. London: Gordon Fraser, 1973.

Pomerance, Murray. "Introduction: From Bad to Worse." *Bad: Infamy, Darkness, Evil, and Slime on Screen*. Ed. Murray Pomerance. Albany: State University of New York Press, 2004. 1–18.

Pomerance, Murray, ed. *Bad: Infamy, Darkness, Evil, and Slime on Screen*. Albany: State University of New York Press, 2004.

Porton, Richard. "Blue Collar Monsters: An Interview with George Romero." *Filmhaftet* 119 (2002). http://www.filmint.nu/pdf/english/119/georgeromerointerview.pdf (accessed April 18, 2012).

Porton, Richard. "Collective Guilt and Individual Responsibility: An Interview with Michael Haneke." *Cineaste* XXXI (1): Winter 2005: 50–51.

Potts, John. "The Monstrous-Familial: Representations of the Unacceptable Family." *The Unacceptable*. Ed. John Potts and John Scannell. (November 2013) Palgrave Macmillan. 137–55. http://www.palgraveconnect.com/pc/doifinder/10.1057/9781137014573.0013 (accessed December 12, 2013).

Prawer, S.S. *Caligari's Children: The Film as Tale of Terror*. Oxford: Oxford University Press, 1980.

Price, Brian, and John David Rhodes, eds. *On Michael Haneke*. Detroit: Wayne State University Press, 2010.

Prudence, Allen. *The Concept of Woman: The Aristotelian Revolution 750 B.C.–A.D. 1250*. Montreal: Eden Press, 1985.

Ramsland, Katherine. "The Unthinkable: Children Who Kill." *Crime Library: Criminal Minds and Methods*. http://www.trutv.com/library/crime/serial_killers/weird/kids2/index_1.html (accessed October 1, 2014).

Rankin, Walter. *Grimm Pictures: Fairy Tale Archetypes in Eight Horror and Suspense Films*. Jefferson, NC: McFarland, 2007.

Rasmussen, Randy. *Children of the Night: The Six Archetypal Characters of Classic Horror Films*. Jefferson, NC: McFarland, 2006.

Reed, Rex. "The Horror of the Horror." *New York Sunday News* (October 19, 1980): 3, 18.

Reed, Rex. "Schlock and Shock: Horror Films Turn to Horror Show." *New York Post* (October 29, 1982): 45.

"Relative Poverty or Consumerism: Choose Your Evil." *Economist at Large* (February 27, 2011). http://economistatlarge.blogspot.co.uk/2011/02/relative-poverty-or-consumerism-choose.html (accessed July 1, 2014).

Renner, Karen J. "The Apocalypse Begins at Home: The Antichrist-as-Child Film." *Frame* 26.1 (May 2013): 47–59.

Renner, Karen J. "Evil Children in Film and Literature." *The "Evil Child" in Literature, Film, and Popular Culture*. Ed. Karen J. Renner. New York: Routledge, 2013. 1–27.

Renner, Karen J. "Monstrous Newborns and Mothers Who Love Them: Critiques of Intensive Mothering in Twenty-First Century Horror Films." *Monstrous Children and Childish Monsters: Essays on Cinema's Holy Terrors*. Ed. Markus P.J. Bohlmann and Sean Moreland. Jefferson, NC: McFarland, 2015. 27–41.

Renner, Karen J., ed. *The "Evil Child" in Literature, Film, and Popular Culture*. New York: Routledge, 2013.

Rhodes, Ron. *Alien Obsession*. Eugene, OR: Harvest House Publishers, 1998.

Rich, Tracy R. "Qorbanot: Sacrifices and Offerings." http://www.jewfaq.org/qorbanot.htm (accessed June 29, 2014).

Robbins, Anthony. *Awaken the Giant Within: How to Take Immediate Control of Your Mental, Emotional, Physical & Financial Destiny!* London: Simon & Schuster, 1992.

Robbins, Helen W. "'More Human Than I Am Alone': Womb Envy in David Cronenberg's *The Fly* and *Dead Ringers*." *Screening the Male: Exploring Masculinities in Hollywood Cinema*. Ed. Steven Cohan and Ina Rae Hark. London: Routledge, 1993. 134–47.

Robinson, John A.T. *In the End, God: A Study of the Christian Doctrine of the Last Things*. Cambridge: James Clarke & Co., 1950.

Rodley, Chris, ed. *Cronenberg on Cronenberg*. London: Faber & Faber, 1992.

Rodriguez, Richard. "The Coming Mayhem: Pre-Teens Today Are More Violent than Ever Before." *Los Angeles Times* (January 21, 1996). http://articles.latimes.com/1996-01-21/opinion/op-27205_1_adult-responsibility (accessed August 25, 2014).

Russell, David J. "Monster Roundup: Reintegrating the Horror Genre." *Refiguring American Film Genres: History and Theory*. Ed. Nick Browne. Berkeley: University of California Press, 1998. 233–54.

Russell, Jamie. *Book of the Dead: The Complete History of Zombie Cinema*. Godalming, UK: FAB Press, 2005.

Russell, Lorena. "Ideological Formations of the Nuclear Family in *The Hills Have Eyes*." *The Philosophy of Horror*. Ed. Thomas Fahy. Lexington: University Press of Kentucky, 2010. 102–20.

Saban, Stephen. "*Halloween* Horror, Dangerous Dummy." *Soho Weekly News* (9 November 1978): 58.

Samuel, J., and P. Bryant. "Asking Only One Question in the Conservation Experiment." *Journal of Child Psychology and Psychiatry* 25 (1984): 315–18.

Sanders, Bob. "Childhood in Different Cultures." *An Introduction to Early Childhood Studies*. Ed. Trisha Maynard and Nigel Thomas. 2nd ed. Los Angeles: SAGE, 2009. 9–20.

Sannwald, Daniela. "Vorwort oder: Schwarz und Weiß: Ästhetik und Moral in Michael Hanekes Werk." *Film-Konzepte 21: Michael Haneke* (February 2011): 3–15.

Sapolsky, Barry S., and Fred Molitor. "Content Trends in Contemporary Horror Films." *Horror Films: Current Research on Audience Preferences and Reactions*. Ed. James B. Weaver III and Ron Tamborini. Mahwah, NJ: Lawrence Erlbaum Associates, 1996. 33–48.

Sargeant, Jack. "The Baying of Pigs: Reflections on the New American Horror Film." *Senses of Cinema* 15 (July–August 2001). http://sensesofcinema.com/contents/festivals/01/15/biff_nightmare.html (accessed April 18, 2012).

Scahill, Andrew. *The Revolting Child in Horror Cinema: Youth Rebellion and Queer Spectatorship*. Basingstoke: Palgrave Macmillan, 2015.

"Scary Kids from Horror Movies." http://www.youtube.com/watch?v=v7kgvOOweYo (accessed October 30, 2013).

Schembri, Lorraine. "Science at the Movies—Future Perfect?" *Biomedical Scientist* 42.1 (January 1998): 6.

Schippers, Birgit. *Julia Kristeva and Feminist Thought*. Edinburgh: Edinburgh University Press, 2011.

Schmidt, Jakob. "Vom Entsetzen, einen Körper zu haben: Das bedrohte Ich in George A. Romeros Zombiefilmen." *On Rules and Monsters: Essays zu Horror, Film und Gesellschaft*. Ed. Benjamin Moldenhauer, Christoph Spehr, and Jörg Windszus. Hamburg: Argument, 2008. 84–99.

Schneider, Kirk J. "From Despair and Fanaticism to Awe: A Posttraumatic Growth Perspective on Cinematic Horror." *Death in Classic and Contemporary Film: Fade to Black*. Ed. Daniel Sullivan and Jeff Greenberg. (October 2013) Palgrave Macmillan. 217–30. http://www.palgraveconnect.com/pc/doifinder/10.1057/9781137276896.0020 (accessed December 12, 2013).

Schneider, Steven Jay. "The Essential Evil in/of *Eraserhead* (or, Lynch to the Contrary)." *The Cult Film Reader*. Ed. Ernest Mathijs and Xavier Mendik. Maidenhead, England: Open University Press, 2008. 250–56.

Schneider, Steven Jay. *Fear Without Frontiers: Horror Cinema Across the Globe*. Guildford: FAB Press, 2003.

Schneider, Steven Jay. "Introduction: Psychoanalysis in/and/of the Horror Film." *Senses of Cinema* 15 (July–August 2001). http://sensesofcinema.com/contents/01/15/horror_psych.html (accessed April 18, 2012).

Schneider, Steven Jay. "Murder as Art/The Art of Murder: Aestheticising Violence in Modern Cinematic Horror." *Necronomicon: The Journal of Horror and Erotic Cinema*. Book 4, ed. Andy Black. London: Noir Press, 2001. 65–85. Revised and extended version available at http://intensities.org/Essays/Schneider.pdf (accessed April 19, 2012).

Schneider, Steven Jay, ed. *Horror Film and Psychoanalysis: Freud's Worst Nightmare*. Cambridge: Cambridge University Press, 2004.

Schoell, William. *Stay Out of the Shower: Twenty-Five Years of Shocker Films Beginning with Psycho*. New York: December, 1985.

Schomacker, Tim. "Im Innern ein lebhaftes Bild: Über Inszenierungen von Angst—ein Brief." *On Rules and Monsters: Essays zu Horror, Film und Gesellschaft*. Ed. Benjamin Moldenhauer, Christoph Spehr, and Jörg Windszus. Hamburg: Argument, 2008. 122–34.

Schreck, Nikolas. *The Satanic Screen: An Illustrated History of the Devil in Cinema, 1869–1999*. New York: Creation Books, 2000.

Schuller, Alexander. "Gräßliche Hoffnung: Zur Hermeneutik des Horror-Films." *Die andere Kraft: Zur Renaissance des Bösen*. Ed. Alexander Schuller and Wulfert von Rahden. Berlin: Akademie-Verlag, 1993. 341–54.

Sconce, Jeffrey. "Spectacles of Death: Identification, Reflexivity, and Contemporary Horror." *Film Theory Goes to the Movies*. Ed. J. Collins, H. Radner, and A. Preacher Collins. New York, London: Routledge, 1993. 103–19.

Scott, Niall, ed. *Monsters and the Monstrous: Myths and Metaphors of Enduring Evil*. Amsterdam: Rodopi, 2007.

Scott, Vernon. "Mishaps, Tragedies Beset 'Exorcist' Cast." *Hartford Courant* (13 January 1974): 13F.

Sears, John. "The Boundaries of Horror in Wolf Rilla's *Village of the Damned*." *European Nightmares: Horror Cinema in Europe Since 1945*. Ed. Patricia Allmer, Emily Brick and David Huxley. London, New York: Wallflower, 2012.

Sedláček, Tomáš. *Economics of Good and Evil: The Quest for Economic Meaning from Gilgamesh to Wall Street*. Oxford: Oxford University Press, 2011.

Self, Will. "A Point of View: Are We All Suffering from Consumption?" *BBC News Magazine* (August 15, 2014). http://www.bbc.co.uk/news/magazine-28756372 (accessed August 27, 2014).

Sharrett, Christopher. "The Horror Film in Neoconservative Culture." *The Dread of Difference: Gender and the Horror Film*. Ed. Barry Keith Grant. Austin: University of Texas Press, 1996. 253–76.

Shavelson, Richard J., Gail P. Baxter, and Jerry Pine. "Performance Assessment: Political Rhetoric and Measurement Reality." *Educational Researcher* 21/4 (May 1992): 22–27.

Shome, Siddhartha. "Is Consumption Evil?" *The Breakthrough* (June 11, 2008). http://thebreakthrough.org/archive/is_consumption_evil (accessed July 1, 2014).

Shriver, Lionel. *We Need to Talk About Kevin*. London: Serpents Tail, 2005.

"Significant Buddhist Trees." *Dhamma Wheel: A Buddhist Discussion Forum on the Dhamma of the Theravada*. http://www.dhammawheel.com/viewtopic.php?f=27&t=16314&start=20 (accessed February 27, 2014).

Sipos, Thomas M. *Horror Film Aesthetics: Creating the Visual Language of Fear*. Jefferson, NC: McFarland, 2010.

Skal, David J. *The Monster Show: A Cultural History of Horror*. London: Plexus, 1993.

Skal, David J. *Screams of Reason: Mad Science and Modern Culture*. New York: Norton, 1998.

Smith, Angela M. *Hideous Progeny: Disability, Eugenics, and Classic Horror Cinema*. New York: Columbia University Press, 2011.

Smith, Murray. *Engaging Characters: Fiction, Emotion, and the Cinema*. Oxford: Clarendon, 1995.

Sobchack, Vivian. "Bringing It All Back Home: Family Economy and Generic Exchange." *The Dread of Difference: Gender and the Horror Film*. Ed. Barry Keith Grant. Austin: University of Texas Press, 1996. 143–63.

Sobchack, Vivian. "Child/Alien/Father: Patriarchal Crisis and Generic Exchange." *Camera Obscura* 15 (1986): 7–34.

Sobchack, Vivian. "Revenge of *The Leech Woman*: On the Dread of Aging in a Low-Budget Horror Film." *Uncontrollable Bodies: Testimonies of Identity and Culture*. Ed. Rodney Sappington and Tyler Stallings. Seattle: Bay Press, 1994. 79–91.

Sontag, Susan. *Against Interpretation*. New York: Farrar, Straus & Giroux, 1966.

Sontag, Susan. "The Imagination of Disaster." *Film Theory and Criticism*. New York: Oxford University Press, 1985. 451–65.

Soren, David. *The Rise and Fall of the Horror Film*. Baltimore, MD: Midnight Marquee, 1977.

Sparks, Glenn G. "An Activation-Arousal Analysis of Reactions to Horror." *Horror Films: Current Research on Audience Preferences and Reactions*. Ed. James B. Weaver III and Ron Tamborini. Mahwah, NJ: Lawrence Erlbaum Associates, 1996. 125–45.

Speck, Oliver. *Funny Frames: The Filmic Concepts of Michael Haneke*. New York: Continuum, 2010.

Speck, Oliver. "Thinking the Event: The Virtual in Michael Haneke's Films." *The Cinema of Michael Haneke*. Ed. Ben McCann and David Sorfa. New York: Wallflower, 2011. 49–64.

Spehr, Christoph. "Honeycomb World: Gesellschaft und Utopie im zeitgenössischen Horrorfilm." *On Rules and Monsters: Essays zu Horror, Film und Gesellschaft*. Ed. Benjamin Moldenhauer, Christoph Spehr, and Jörg Windszus. Hamburg: Argument, 2008. 174–86.

Spencer, Herbert. *Essays on Education and Kindred Subjects*. London: Dent, 1911.

Stacey, Jackie. "She Is Not Herself: The Deviant Relations of *Alien Resurrection*." *Screen* 44/3 (Autumn 2003): 251–76.

Stallybrass, Peter, and Allon White. *The Politics and Poetics of Transgression*. Ithaca: Cornell University Press, 1995.

Steakley, John. *Vampire$*. New York: ROC, 1990.

Stewen, Christian. *The Cinematic Child: Kindheit in filmischen und medienpädagogischen Diskursen*. Marburg: Schüren, 2011.

Stone, Bryan. "The Sanctification of Fear: Images of the Religious in Horror Films." *Journal of Religion and Film* 5/2 (2001); www.unomaha.edu/~wwwjrf/sanctifi.htm (accessed April 10, 2012).

Svehla, Gary J. "Introduction: What Is a Guilty Pleasure?" *Guilty Pleasures of the Horror Film*. Ed. Gary J. Svehla and Susan Svehla. Baltimore: Marquee, 1996. 7–9.

Svehla, Gary J., and Susan Svehla, eds. *Guilty Pleasures of the Horror Film*. Baltimore: Marquee, 1996.

Tallon, Philip. "Through a Mirror, Darkly: Art-Horror as a Medium for Moral Reflection." *The Philosophy of Horror*. Ed. Thomas Fahy. Lexington: University Press of Kentucky, 2010. 33–41.

Tamborini, Ron. "A Model of Empathy and Emotional Reactions to Horror." *Horror Films: Current Research on Audience Preferences and Reactions*. Ed. James B. Weaver III and Ron Tamborini. Mahwah, NJ: Lawrence Erlbaum Associates, 1996. 103–23.

Tamborini, Ron, and Kristen Salomonson. "Horror's Effect on Social Perceptions and Behaviors." *Horror Films: Current Research on Audience Preferences and Reactions*. Ed. James B. Weaver III and Ron Tamborini. Mahwah, NJ: Lawrence Erlbaum Associates, 1996. 179–97.

Tamborini, Ron, and James B. Weaver III. "Frightening Entertainment: A Historical Perspective of Fictional Horror." *Horror Films: Current Research on Audience Preferences and Reactions*. Ed. James B. Weaver III and Ron Tamborini. Mahwah, NJ: Lawrence Erlbaum Associates, 1996. 1–13.

Tangney, June Price, and Ronda L. Dearing. *Shame and Guilt*. 2nd ed. New York: Guildford, 2002.

Tangney, June Price, and Kurt W. Fischer, eds. *Self-Conscious Emotions: The Psychology of Shame, Guilt, Embarrassment and Pride*. London: Guildford, 1995.

Tarratt, Margaret. "Monsters from the Id." *Film Genre: Theory and Criticism*. Ed. Barry Keith Grant. Metuchen, NJ: Scarecrow, 1977. 161–81.

Tatar, Maria. *Grimm's Grimmest*. New York: W.W. Norton, 1997.

Telegraph Reporters. "One in 100 Children Are Psychopaths, Experts Believe." *The Telegraph* (August 31, 2012). http://www.telegraph.co.uk/health/children_shealth/9510937/One-in-100-children-are-psychopaths-experts-believe.html (accessed August 31, 2012).

Telotte, J.P. "Faith and Idolatry in the Horror Film." *Planks of Reason: Essays on the Horror Film*. Ed. Barry Keith Grant. Metuchen, NJ: Scarecrow, 1984. 21–37.

Telotte, J.P. "Through a Pumpkin's Eye: The Reflexive Nature of Horror." *American Horrors: Essays on the Modern American Horror Film*. Ed. Gregory A. Waller. Urbana: University of Illinois Press, 1987. 114–28.

Thacker, Eugene. *In The Dust of This Planet*. Winchester: Zero Books, 2011.

Thompson, Dennis, John D. Hogan, and Philip M. Clark. *Developmental Psychology in Historical Perspective*. Malden: Wiley-Blackwell, 2012.

Thomson, David. *The Alien Quartet*. London: Bloomsbury, 1998.

Thomson, David. *The Big Screen: The Story of the Movies and What They Did to Us*. London: Penguin, 2012.

Thuswaldner, Gregor. "'Mourning for the Gods Who Have Died': The Role of Religion in Michael Haneke's Glaciation Trilogy." *A Companion to Michael Haneke*. Ed. Roy Grundmann. Chichester: Blackwell, 2010. 187–201.

Tilmann, Christina. "'Du bist hässlich und ungepflegt': Frauenbilder und Frauenrollen im Filmschaffen Michael Hanekes." *Film-Konzepte 21: Michael Haneke* (February 2011): 39–51.

Toikkanen, Jarkko. *The Intermedial Experience of Horror*. (August 2013) Palgrave Macmillan. http://www.palgraveconnect.com/pc/doifinder/10.1057/9781137299093 (accessed December 12, 2013).

Torato, Donato. "The Final Girl: A Few Thoughts on Feminism and Horror." *Offscreen* (January 31, 2002). http://www.horschamp.qc.ca/new_offscreen/final_girl.html (accessed April 19, 2012).

Tropp, Martin. *Images of Fear: How Horror Stories Helped Shape Modern Culture (1818–1918)*. Jefferson, NC: McFarland, 1990.

Truffaut, François, with the collaboration of Helen G. Scott. *Hitchcock*. Revised Edition. New York: Simon & Schuster, 1983.

Tudor, Andrew. *Monsters and Mad Scientists: A Cultural History of the Horror Movie*. Oxford: Blackwell, 1989.

Tudor, Andrew. "Why Horror? The Peculiar Pleasures of a Popular Genre." *Cultural Studies* 11/3 (1997): 443–63.

Turner, Victor. *The Anthropology of Performance*. New York: PAJ, 1986.

"20 Most Iconic Horror Movie Scenes of All Time." *Moviefone*. http://news.moviefone.com/2010/10/12/best-iconic-horror-movie-scenes/ (accessed October 30, 2013).

Twitchell, James B. *Dreadful Pleasures: An Anatomy of Modern Horror*. Oxford: Oxford University Press, 1985.

Tydal, Fredrik. "Bringing Out Henry James's Little Monsters: Two Film Approaches to *The Turn of the Screw*." *Monstrous Children and Childish Monsters: Essays on Cinema's Holy Terrors*. Ed. Markus P.J. Bohlmann and Sean Moreland. Jefferson, NC: McFarland, 2015. 142–59.

"Unicef: Violence Kills Child Every Five Minutes." *BBC World News* (October 21, 2014). http://www.bbc.co.uk/news/world-29699189 (accessed October 21, 2014).

United Nations. "Conventions on the Rights of the Child." *United Nations Treaty Collection*. Text: http://treaties.un.org/doc/Publication/UNTS/Volume%201577/v1577.pdf; signatories' addenda: http://treaties.un.org/Pages/ViewDetails.aspx?src=TREATY&mtdsg_no=IV-11&chapter=4&lang=en (accessed October 30, 2013).

*Urban Dictionary*. http://www.urbandictionary.com/ (accessed June 24, 2014).

Ursini, James, and Alain Silver. *The Vampire Film*. South Brunswick: A.S. Barnes, 1975.

Valsiner, Jaan. *Culture and the Development of Children's Action: A Cultural-Historical Theory of Developmental Psychology*. Oxford: John Wiley & Sons, 1987.

Victor, Jeffrey S. *Satanic Panic: The Creation of a Contemporary Legend*. Chicago: Open Court, 1993.

Vieth, Errol. *Screening Science: Contexts, Texts, and Science in Fifties Science Fiction Film*. Lanham, MD: Scarecrow, 2001.

Vygotsky, Lev. *Mind in Society: The Development of Higher Psychological Processes*. Cambridge, MA: Harvard University Press, 1978.

Walker, Tim. "Is Ridley Scott the Most Macho Man in Movies?" *The Independent* (26 May 2012). http://www.independent.co.uk/news/people/profiles/is-ridley-scott-the-most-macho-man-in-movies-7782369.html (accessed May 26, 2012).

Waller, Gregory A. "Introduction." *American Horrors: Essays on the Modern American Horror Film*. Ed. Gregory A. Waller. Urbana: University of Illinois Press, 1987. 1–13.

Waller, Gregory A. *The Living and the Undead: From Stoker's Dracula to Romero's Night of the Living Dead*. Urbana: University of Illinois Press, 1986.

Waller, Gregory A. "Made-for-Television Horror Films." *American Horrors: Essays on the Modern American Horror Film*. Ed. Gregory A. Waller. Urbana: University of Illinois Press, 1987. 145–61.

Waller, Gregory A., ed. *American Horrors: Essays on the Modern American Horror Film*. Urbana: University of Illinois Press, 1987.

Walser, Martin. "Erfahrungen beim Verfassen einer Sonntagsrede." http://www.friedenspreis-des-deutschen-buchhandels.de/sixcms/media.php/1290/1998_walser.pdf (accessed September 24, 2014).

Wandless, William. "Spoil the Child: Unsettling Ethics and the Representation of Evil." *The "Evil Child" in Literature, Film, and Popular Culture*. Ed. Karen J. Renner. New York: Routledge, 2013. 66–86.

Weart, Spencer. "Nuclear Fear 1987–2007: Has Anything Changed? Has Everything Changed?" *Filling the Hole in the Nuclear Future: Art and Popular Culture Respond to the Bomb*. Ed. Robert Jacobs. Lanham, MD: Lexington Books, 2010. 229–65.

Weaver, James B., III, and Ron Tamborini, eds. *Horror Films: Current Research on Audience Preferences and Reactions*. Mahwah, NJ: Lawrence Erlbaum Associates, 1996.

Weaver, Tom. *It Came from Horrorwood: Interviews with Moviemakers in the SF and Horror Tradition*. Jefferson, NC: McFarland, 2004.

Wee, Valerie. *Japanese Horror Films and their American Remakes*. Abingdon: Routledge, 2014.

Weedman, Jane B., ed. *Women Worldwalkers: New Dimensions of Science Fiction and Fantasy*. Lubbock: Texas Tech Press, 1985.

Wertham, Frederic. "Battered Children and Baffled Adults." *Bulletin of the New York Academy of Medicine* 48/7 (August 1972): 888–98.

Wexman, Virginia Wright. "The Trauma of Infancy in Roman Polanski's *Rosemary's Baby*." *American Horrors: Essays on the Modern American Horror Film*. Ed. Gregory A. Waller. Urbana: University of Illinois Press, 1987. 30–43.

Wheatley, Catherine. "'Le Cineaste d'Horreur Ordinaire': Michael Haneke and the Horrors of Everyday Existence." *European Nightmares: Horror Cinema in Europe Since 1945*. Ed. Patricia Allmer, Emily Brick and David Huxley. London: Wallflower, 2012. Unpag.

Wheatley, Catherine. *Michael Haneke's Cinema: The Ethic of the Image*. New York: Berghahn Books, 2009.

White, D.L. "The Poetics of Horror: More Than Meets the Eye." *Film Genre: Theory and Criticism*. Ed. Barry Keith Grant. Metuchen, NJ: Scarecrow, 1977. 124–44.

Wieland, Christoph Martin. "Unterredungen mit dem Pfarrer von \*\*\*." *C.M. Wielands Sämmtliche Werke* vol. 30. Leipzig: Georg Joachim Göschen, 1797. 310–82.

*The Wilderness Act*. Public Law 88-577 (16 U.S. C. 1131–1136). http://wilderness.nps.gov/document/wildernessAct.pdf (accessed November 4, 2015).

Wilkinson, Simon A. *Hollywood Horror from the Director's Chair: Six Filmmakers in the Franchise of Fear*. Jefferson, NC: McFarland, 2008.

Williams, Evan Calder. *Combined and Uneven Apocalypse*. Ropley: Zero Books, 2011.

Williams, Linda. "Film Bodies: Gender, Genre, and Excess." *Film Genre Reader II*. Ed. Barry Keith Grant. Austin: University of Texas Press, 1995. 140–58.

Williams, Linda. *Hard Core: Power, Pleasure, and the Frenzy of the Visible*. Berkeley: University of California Press, 1989.

Williams, Linda. "When the Woman Looks." *The Dread of Difference: Gender and the Horror Film*. Ed. Barry Keith Grant. Austin: University of Texas Press, 1996. 15–34.

Williams, Linda. "When Women Look: A Sequel." *Senses of Cinema* 15 (July-August 2001). http://sensesofcinema.com/contents/01/15/horror_women.html (accessed April 19, 2012).

Williams, Sara. "'The Power of Christ Compels You': Holy Water, Hysteria, and the Oedipal Psychodrama in *The Exorcist*." *The "Evil Child" in Literature, Film, and Popular Culture*. Ed. Karen J. Renner. New York: Routledge, 2013. 129–49.

Williams, Tony. *Hearths of Darkness: The Family in the American Horror Film*. London: Associated University Presses, 1996.

Williams, Tony. "Trying to Survive on the Darker Side: 1980s Family Horror." *The Dread of Difference: Gender and the Horror Film*. Ed. Barry Keith Grant. Austin: University of Texas Press, 1996. 164–80.

Willis, Donald C. *Horror and Science Fiction Films*. Metuchen, NJ: Scarecrow, 1972.

Wilson, Emma. *Cinema's Missing Children*. London: Wallflower, 2003.

Wilson, Patrick. *Children Who Kill*. London: Joseph, 1973.

Winchell, James. "Century of the Uncanny: The Modest Terror of Theory." *The Return of the Uncanny: Special Issue of Paradox: Studies in World Literary Genres* 3/3-4 (1997): 515–20.

Wolf, Christa. *Kassandra*. Darmstadt: Luchterhand, 1983.

Wood, Robin. "Apocalypse Now: Notes on the Living Dead." *American Nightmare: Essays on the Horror Film*. Ed. Robin Wood and Richard Lippe. Toronto: Festival of Festivals, 1979. 91–97.

Wood, Robin. "Beauty Bests the Beast." *American Film* 8/10 (September 1983): 63–65.

Wood, Robin. "Cronenberg: A Dissenting View." *The Shape of Rage*. Ed. Piers Handling. Toronto: General Publishing/New York Zoetrope, 1983. 98–114.

Wood, Robin. *Hollywood from Vietnam to Reagan... and Beyond*. Expanded and Revised Edition. New York: Columbia University Press, 2003.

Wood, Robin. "Introduction." *American Nightmare: Essays on the Horror Film*. Ed. Robin Wood and Richard Lippe. Toronto: Festival of Festivals, 1979. 7–28.

Wood, Robin. "An Introduction to the American Horror Film." *Planks of Reason: Essays on the Horror Film*. Ed. Barry Keith Grant. Metuchen, NJ: Scarecrow, 1984. 164–200.

Wood, Robin. "Neglected Nightmares." *Film Comment* 16/2 (March-April 1980): 25–32.

Wood, Robin. "Return of the Repressed." *Film Comment* 14/4 (July-August 1978): 25–32.

Wood, Robin. "Returning the Look: *Eyes of a Stranger*." *American Horrors: Essays on the Modern American Horror Film*. Ed. Gregory A. Waller. Urbana: University of Illinois Press, 1987. 79–85.

Wood, Robin. "World of Gods & Monsters: The Films of Larry Cohen." *American Nightmare: Essays on the Horror Film*. Ed. Robin Wood and Richard Lippe. Toronto: Festival of Festivals, 1979. 75–86.

Wood, Robin, and Richard Lippe, eds. *American Nightmare: Essays on the Horror Film*. Toronto: Festival of Festivals, 1979.

Woodend, Dorothy. "World of Horror: In the Last Five Years the Public's Appetite for Horror Movies Has Increased Exponentially." *AlterNet* (February 2, 2004). http://www.alternet.org/movies/17729 (accessed April 19, 2012).

Wright, Elizabeth. "Modern Psychoanalytic Criticism." *Modern Literary Theory: A Comparative Introduc-

*tion*. Ed. Ann Jefferson and David Robey. 2nd ed. Totowa, NJ: Barnes & Noble Books, 1986. 145–65.

Wright, John Paul, Francis Cullen, Robert Agnew and Timothy Brezina. "'The Root of All Evil'? An Exploratory Study of Money and Delinquent Involvement." *Justice Quarterly* 18/2 (2001): 239–68.

Yacowar, Maurice. "The Comedy of Cronenberg." *The Shape of Rage: The Films of David Cronenberg*. Ed. Piers Handling. Toronto: General Publishing/New York Zoetrope, 1983. 80–86.

Young, Michael Dunlop. *The Rise of the Meritocracy: An Essay on Education and Equality*. London: Thames and Hudson, 1958.

Zillman, Dolf, and Rhonda Gibson. "Evolution of the Horror Genre." *Horror Films: Current Research on Audience Preferences and Reactions*. Ed. James B. Weaver III and Ron Tamborini. Mahwah, NJ: Lawrence Erlbaum Associates, 1996. 14–31.

Zillman, Dolf, and James B. Weaver III. "Gender-Socialization Theory of Reactions to Horror." *Horror Films: Current Research on Audience Preferences and Reactions*. Ed. James B. Weaver III and Ron Tamborini. Mahwah, NJ: Lawrence Erlbaum Associates, 1996. 81–101.

Zimmer, Catherine. "The Camera's Eye: *Peeping Tom* and Technological Perversion." *Horror Film: Creating and Marketing Fear*. Ed. Steffen Hantke. Jackson: University Press of Mississippi, 2004. 35–51.

Zimmerman, Bonnie. "*Daughters of Darkness*: The Lesbian Vampire on Film." *The Dread of Difference: Gender and the Horror Film*. Ed. Barry Keith Grant. Austin: University of Texas Press, 1996. 379–87.

Zolkos, Magdalena. "The Origins of European Fascism: Memory of Violence in Michael Haneke's *The White Ribbon*." *The European Legacy: Toward New Paradigms*, 20:3 (2015), 205–23. DOI: 10.1080/10848770.2015.1004913.

Zuckerman, Marvin. "Sensation Seeking and the Taste for Vicarious Horror." *Horror Films: Current Research on Audience Preferences and Reactions*. Ed. James B. Weaver III and Ron Tamborini. Mahwah, NJ: Lawrence Erlbaum Associates, 1996. 147–60.

# Index

Numbers in **_bold italics_** refer to pages with photographs.

*Abby* (film, 1974) 115
abortion, as portrayed in horror 21, 28, 29, 31
abuse, as portrayed in horror 29–30, 46–7, 50, 64–5, 73, 81–6, 99–100, 112–4, 116–7, 131–2, 136, 138–60, 171, 178, 182; links to violent crime 138, 162, 191*ch7gen.note*; 191*n*1, 191*ch7n*2; *see also* rape; sexual abuse
*Acacia* (film, 2003) 67–72, **_70_**; review 71, 189*ch3n*8
Adams, Brooke **_23_**
*The Addams Family* (TV series, 1964–66) 35
adoption, as portrayed in horror 48–9, 54–5, 67–71, 165–8
adulthood, as portrayed in horror 61, 71, 161–76, 178; *see also* Peter Pan Syndrome
aesthetic ranking 11
aesthetics *see* cinematography
Alford, Fred 180, 183–4, 187*Intro.gen.note*, 193*Concl.gen.note*, 193*n*11, 193*n*12, 194*n*13, 194*n*14, 194*n*20, 194*n*21, 194*n*22
*Alice, Sweet Alice* (film, 1976) 190*n*9; *see also* Communion
*Alien* (film, 1979) 10, 29, 130
*Alien Resurrection* (film, 1997) 10–1, 29
*Alien³* (film, 1992) 10, 29
*Aliens* (film, 1986) 10, 29, 77
aliens, as portrayed in horror 32, 159
alignment *see* point of view
allegiance *see* viewer identification
Allen, Sheila **_80_**
Alvart, Christian 113, 175
*An American Haunting* (film, 2005) 178
*The Amityville Horror* (film, 1979) 136

*The Amityville Horror* (film, 2005) 136
animal cruelty, as portrayed in horror 35–8, 47, 59, 113, 168, 170
animals, as portrayed in horror 63–7
apocalypse films 57, 77, 91
*Apocalypto* (film, 2006) 3
Aquinas, Thomas 97
Aristotle 4, 13, 182
*Awaken the Giant Within* (self-help book, 1992) 120
babies in horror 13–32, 93, 140–4, 178
*Baby Blues* (film, 2008) 29–30
Bács, Zsolt 113
*The Bad Seed* (film, 1956) 120–5, **_124_**, 127, 129–30, 135, 193*Concl.n*8
*The Bad Seed* (play, 1954) 120
Bakhtin, Mikhail 15, 28
*Barbe bleue* (film, 2009) 58
*Batoru rowaiaru* (film, 2000) *see* Battle Royale
Battle Royale (film, 2000) 74
Bayona, J.A. 158
Beckstrom, Ron 32
Bender, Jack 127
Berdejo, Luis 116
Berdejo, Luiso *see* Berdejo, Luis
Bernhard, Harvey 95
Bettelheim, Bruno 4, 187*n*3
*The Beverly Hillbillies* (TV series, 1962–71) 35
Bianchi, Andrea 35
*The Birds* (film, 1963) 57
birth, as portrayed in horror 13–32, 81–2, 85; *see also* babies
Birthistle, Eva 174
*Blade Runner* (film, 1982) 147
Blair, Linda 116
*The Blair Witch Project* (film, 1999) 57, 168, 193*ch8n*5

Blanchard, John 187*n*9
Blatty, William Peter 94, 190*n*3, 190*n*8
Blixen, Karen *see* Dinesen, Isak
*The Blob* (film, 1958) 182–3
Blowitz, Michael 173–4, 193*ch8n*8
*Bluebeard* (film, 2009) *see* Barbe bleue
body, human: in grotesque art 15; in horror 15, 18, 25–6, 28, 30, 32
Bong, Man-dae 58
*The Book of Eli* (film, 2010) 57
*The Book of Wealth* (treatise, 1836) 119
Botton, Alain de 120, 191*ch6n*4
Bradbury, Ray 31–2
*Brave New World* (novel, 1932) 189*ch4n*8
Breillat, Catherine 58
*Bride of Chucky* (film, 1998) 126, 129–30
Bright, Cameron **_88_**
Bright, Matthew 58
*The Brood* (film, 1979) 30, 81–6, **_83_**, 90–2, 189*ch4n*8
Brook, Peter 57, 72
The Brothers Grimm *see* Grimm, Jakob; Grimm, Wilhelm
Bulger, James 138, 179
*Bunhongsin* (film, 2005) 58
burial ground, Indian 57, 63–7, 116; *see also* Native Americans
Bush, George W. 76–7, 116

*Cabin Fever* (film, 2002) 74
*The Cabin in the Woods* (film, 2012) 6, 74, 178
camera angles *see* point of view
Cameron, James 29
Cammell, Donald 16, 92
cannibalism, as portrayed in horror 142–3, 159, 168–75
Cannon, Danny 187*n*9
Capote, Truman 190*ch5n*16

215

Cardone, J.S. 159
caricatures (in art) 14–5
Carpenter, John 7, 53, 159, 191n10
*Carrie* (film, 1976) 115, 139, 159
*Carrie* (film, 2013) 115, 159
cartoon theory 7–8
*Case 39* (film, 2009) 113, 175
Castle, William 95
Catholicism 94–5; as portrayed in horror 95–100
Chabris, Christopher 82, 189–90ch4n9
Chaneac, Delphine **133**
*The Child* (film, 1977) 59–63, **62**, 67, 68, 71–2, 175
*The Child* (film, 2012) 113
child abuse *see* abuse
child murder *see* infanticide
child murderers 138, 161–2, 179, 191n3, 193ch8n1; as portrayed in horror 162–77
child neglect *see* neglect
child psychology *see* psychology, developmental
childlessness, as portrayed in horror 32
*The Children* (film, 1980) 92
*The Children* (film, 2008) 174–5
children, as portrayed in art 34, 188ch2gen.note
*Children of the Corn* (film, 1984) 6, 57, 72, 100–1, 136, 190ch5n13
*Children of the Corn II: The Final Sacrifice* (film, 1992) 100–6, **105**, 111–3, 136, 190ch5n13
*Children of the Corn III: Urban Harvest* (film, 1995) 106, 136
*Children of the Damned* (film, 1964) 77–81, **80**, 87, 90–2
children's play *see* play
*Child's Play* (film, 1988) 6, 7, **126**, 126–30, 135, 181
*Child's Play 2* (film, 1990) 126, 128–9
*Child's Play 3* (film, 1991) 120, 126–9, 191n11
Cho, Eunice Kim 182–4
*The Chosen* (film, 2015) 115–6
Christie, Julie **18**
cinematography 24, 26, 36–9, 43–5, 51–2, 59–61, 63, 66, 77–8, 85–6, 91–2, 97, 102, 108, 148, 154–6, 192n19, 192n20
*City of Ember* (film, 2008) 57
Clark, Christie **105**
Clayton, Jack 37, 53, 157
Clinton, Mildred **100**
cloning, human, as portrayed in horror 86–90; *see also* gene manipulation
Clover, Carol 9, 58, 74
Cohen, Larry 19, 30, 93, 140, 142, 144, 153, 155–6
Cohn, Michael 58
Collet-Serra, Jaume 54

comedies (films) 11
*Communion* (film, 1976) 95–100, **100**, 111–3, 190ch5n9, 190ch5n10; reviews 190ch5n10, 190ch5n11
*The Company of Wolves* (film, 1984) 58
computers as horror film characters 16–9
consumerism, as a driver of criminality 118–9; as portrayed in horror 118–37, 178, 182
Corn Goddess 190ch5n15
*Could You Kill a Child?* (film, 1976) *see ¿Quién puede matar a un niño?*
Coupland, Douglas 12, 188n19
crime film 109
Cronenberg, David 13, 30, 77, 81, 85, 190ch4n10
Crouch, Jan 191ch6n3
*The Crucible* (drama, 1952) 116
*The Crucible* (film, 1996) 116
Culkin, Macaulay **41**

*Damien: Omen II* (film, 1978) 12
Dante, Joe 136–7, 160
*Dark Floors* (film, 2008) 190ch7n8
*Dark Water* (film, 2002) 146, 157, 189ch3n7, 192n10
*Dark Water* (film, 2005) 157, 178
Dawkins, Richard 98, 116, 190ch5gen.note, 190n12
*Dawn of the Dead* (film, 1978) 6
*The Day After Tomorrow* (film, 2004) 57, 91
DeCoteau, David 58
*Deep in the Woods* (film, 2000) *see Promenons-nous dans les bois*
Delplanque, Lionel 58
*Demon Seed* (film, 1977) 16–9, **18**, 21, 23, 28, 92
demonic possession *see* possession
demons *see* God; possession; religion
Denham, Christopher 168, 173, 193ch8n4, 193ch8n7
de Niro, Robert **88**
de Palma, Brian 115, 159
*The Departed* (film, 2006) 10
Derrickson, Scott 106, 108, 116
detective films 7, 109, 182
devil, as portrayed in horror 94–5, 112, 190ch5n1
*Devil Doll* (film, 1964) 136
*Devil Times Five* (film, 1974) *see Peopletoys*
*The Devil's Child* (film, 2009 DVD-release) 50; *see also Joshua*
Dhar, Ravi 182–4
Dimster, Dennis 165
Dimster-Denk, Dennis *see* Dimster, Dennis

Dinesen, Isak 56, 71
disaster movies 77, 91; *see also* apocalypse films; nuclear horror
divorce rates 51, 189ch2n9
dolls in horror 7, 40, 55, 97, 112, 126–30, 135–6, 157–8, 163–4, 166, 175
Donner, Richard 32, 94, 114
*Don't Be Afraid of the Dark* (film, 2010) 53
*Don't Look Now* (film, 1973) 157
*Dorothy Mills* (film, 2008) 159
Double Effect (Catholic doctrine) 97–8, 100, 104
Douglas, Andrew 136
Dragus, Maria-Victoria **152**
dreams 77, 189ch4n5, 194n17

Eagleton, Terry 179–80
Ebert, Roger 40, 43, 189ch2n6
economics 190ch6gen.note; *see also* consumerism
*Eden Lake* (film, 2008) 57, 74
*The Edge* (film, 1997) 56
Eichmann, Adolf 154, 192n17
Ekland, Britt **39**
*Elephant* (film, 2003) 3
Elkind, David 161, 173, 193ch8gen.note
*Embryo* (film, 1976) 93
endings of films 10
environment 118; as portrayed in horror 92–3, 141–4, 155; *see also* landscape; nature; wilderness
*Eraserhead* (film, 1977) 30
evil, as a philosophical concept 178–84, 193Concl.gen.note; societal view 180
*The Evil Dead* (film, 1981) 74, 178
*Evil Dead* (film, 2013) 178
Evil Eye 119
evolution, human, as portrayed in horror 16–23, 143–4
The exorcism 94, 114–6, 157, 168, 170, 190n3; *see also* devil; *Exorcist*; possession; religion
*The Exorcism of Emily Rose* (film, 2005) 116
*The Exorcist* (film, 1973) 5, 12, 53, 94–5, 104, 111–2, 114, 116, 139, 178
*The Exorcist* (novel, 1971) 94
extinction, human, as portrayed in horror 28–9, 31

*F* (film, 2010) 3
"Fable of the Bees " (poem, 1705) 118
fairy tale films 58
fairy tales 58, 189ch3gen.note; as horror motif 59–61, 71–2, 169–70
faith, as portrayed in horror *see* religion

familicide 51, 189*ch2n9*; as portrayed in horror 106–13
families in history 33–4, 188*ch2gen.note*; as portrayed in horror 35–55, 59–61, 63, 64–5, 67–71, 106–9, 123–4, 150–6, 161–77
Farmiga, Vera **46**
*Father Knows Best* (TV series, 1954–60) 35
fatherhood, as portrayed in horror 35–53, 150–3, 192*n9*, 192*n15*
Faulkner, Joanne 179
feminism, as portrayed in horror 20–3, 24, 28
film genres *see* genres
The Final Girl 74
*The Final Sacrifice* (film, 1992) *see Children of the Corn II: The Final Sacrifice*
Fincher, David 29
first-person POV *see* point of view
Flender, Rodman 19, 93
*Frailty* (film, 2002) 114
Frankenstein, Dr. (literary character) 18, 31, 82, 90, 93, 142
*Freeway* (film, 1996) 58
Freud, Sigmund 5, 14, 161, 170, 174, 193*ch8gen.note*
*Friday the 13th* (film, 1980) 167, 182
Friedkin, William 94, 114, 116
Fukasaku, Kenta 74
Fukasaku, Kinji 74
Fulci, Lucio 114
fundamentalism, religious *see* religious fundamentalism
*Funny Games* (film, 1997) 176
*Funny Games* (film, 2007) 176

Gacy, John Wayne 171
games *see* play
*The Gamma People* (film, 1956) 92
Gandhi, Mohandas Karamchand (Mahatma) 79
Gans, Christophe 191*ch7n8*
*Gattaca* (film, 1997) 189*ch4n2*
Geisel, Theodor *see* Dr. Seuss
gene manipulation, as portrayed in horror 86–93, 122, 130–6, 140–4
genres (of film) 10–1; *see also* apocalypse films; comedies; detective films; disaster movies; sci-fi films; suspense films; thrillers
Gessner, Nicholas *see* Gessner, Nicolas
Gessner, Nicolas 3, 176
ghosts 53, 73–4, 107–8, 114–5, 144–9, 157–9, 189*ch3n7*, 190*ch5n15*; in Japanese culture 191–2*ch7n8*

Gibson, Mel 3
Gillespie, Jim 187*n9*
Gilling, John 92
Girdler, William 31, 115
God/gods 180; as portrayed in horror 31, 87–8, 94–117
Goddard, Drew 74
*The Godfather* (film, 1972) 35
*Godsend* (film, 2004) 86–92, **88**
Goethe, Johann Wolfgang von 33–4, 188*n1*, 188*n2*, 188*n3*, 188*n4*
Goldhagen, Daniel 192*n16*
Goldsmith, Kelly 182–4
*The Good Son* (film, 1993) 40–5, **41**, 47, 51–3; reviews 40, 189*ch2n6*
gorilla, invisible 82, 189–90*ch4n9*
Goyer, David S. 114
*Grace* (film, 2009) 23–7, **26**, 28
greed, as portrayed in horror 102–4, 110–1, 118–37; *see also* consumerism
*Gremlins* (film, 1984) 136–7
*Gremlins 2: The New Batch* (film, 1990) 137
Grimm, Jakob 58, 60–1, 154
Grimm, Wilhelm 58, 60–1, 154
Groos, Karl 161, 193*ch8gen.note*
grotesque in art 14–5; in horror films 14–32
*The Grudge* (film, 2002) 157–8; *see also Ju-on*
*The Grudge* (film, 2004) 157, 178
*The Grudge 2* (film, 2006) 157
*The Grudge 3* (film, 2009) 157
Gunn, James 32

*Halloween* (film, 1978) 7, 10, 11, 53, 74, 181–2, 191*n10*
Hamm, Nick 86
Haneke, Michael 10, 150, 153–6, 176, 192*n13*, 192*n16*, 192*n18*, 192*n19*, 192*n20*, 193*n22*, 193*n24*, 193*n25*
*Hansel and Gretel* (film, 2008) *see Henjel gwa Geuretel*
*The Happening* (film, 2008) 57
*Hard Candy* (film, 2005) 159–60
Hardwicke, Catherine 58
Harrington, Curtis 116
haunted house film 109, 173
Hawke, Ethan **110**, 178
*Heavenly Creatures* (film, 1994) 3, 72
Heide, Kathleen 138
*Hellraiser* (film, 1987) 182
Hendler, Stewart 115
*Henjel gwa Geuretel* (film, 2008) 58
heredity theory, as portrayed in horror 121–5
*The Hills Have Eyes* (film, 1977) 35, 56
Hiltzig, Robert 75

Hinds, Cindy **83**
*A History of Violence* (film, 2005) 10
Hitchcock, Alfred 147, 168, 191*n10*
*The Hole* (film, 2009) 160
Holland, Tom 126
Hollywood 178
*Holy Terror* (film, 1976) 190*n9*; *see also Communion*
*Home Movie* (film, 2008) 168–75, **172**
home movies, as portrayed in horror 45, 106–13, 145–9, 167–75
*Honogurai mizu no soko kara* (film, 2002) *see Dark Water*
Hook, Harry 57, 72
Hooper, Tobe 4, 137
*The Horrible House on the Hill* (film, 1974) *see Peopletoys*
*Hostel* (film, 2005) 137
*Humanoids from the Deep* (film, 1980) 92
*Humanoids from the Deep* (film, 1996) 92
*The Hunger Games* (film, 2012) 74
Hunt, Thomas 119
Huxley, Aldous 189*ch4n8*
Hytner, Nicholas 116

*I Am Legend* (film, 2007) 57
*I Know What You Did Last Summer* (film, 1997) 6, 187*n9*
*I Spit on Your Grave* (film, 1978) 58
*I Still Know What You Did Last Summer* (film, 1998) 187*n9*
Ibáñez Serrador, Narciso 6, 139, 159
identification: with cinematic characters *see* viewer identification; with Father (in psychoanalytic theory) 14
*Identity* (film, 2003) 3–4
*I'll Always Know What You Did Last Summer* (film, 2006) 187*n9*
*In Cold Blood* (non-fiction novel, 1966) 110, 190*ch5n16*
*The Incredible Two-Headed Transplant* (film, 1971) 92–3
Indians *see* Native Americans
Industrial Revolution 34
infant mortality 33–4
infanticide 40–1, 45, 140–1, 144–9; *see also* abuse
infertility, as portrayed in horror 32
innocence 178–81
*The Innocents* (film, 1961) 37, 53–4, 157–8
*Insidious* (film, 2010) 4
*Interview with the Vampire* (film, 1994) 54

in-vitro fertilization, as portrayed in horror 20–21
*Island of the Alive* (film, 1987) 19, 30–1, 93, 140–4, **144**, 153, 155–6, 191*ch7gen.note*; reviews 140
*Island of the Damned* (film, 1976) see *¿Quién puede matar a un niño?*
*It Lives Again* (film, 1978) 19, 30–1, 93, 140–4, 153, 155–6, 191*ch7gen.note*; reviews 140
*It's Alive!* (film, 1974) 19, 30–1, 93, 140–4, 153, 155–6, 191*ch7gen.note*; reviews 140
*It's Alive* (film, 2008) 31

J-horror *see* Japanese horror film
Jackson, Peter 3, 72
Jacobson, Lars 29
Jacobson, Rick 19, 93
James, William 122
Japanese horror film 4
*Jaws* (film, 1975) 9, 11
*Jeepers Creepers* (film, 2001) 181
Jehoshua, Ben 115
Jeunet, Jean-Pierre 29
Johansson, Scarlett 178
Jones, Mark 58
Jordan, Neil 54, 58
*Joshua* (film, 2007) 45–53, **46**
jump scare 10, 181
*Ju-on* (film, 2002) 157, 189*ch3n7*
*Jurassic Park* (film, 1993) 57

Kaleka, Amardeep 29
Kalmanowicz, Max 92
Karen, Jane 174
*Kassandra* (novel, 1983) 81
Keating, David 115
Kelley, James 35
Kelly, Nancy **124**
Kelly, James *see* Kelley, James
Kennedy, John Fitzgerald 95
Kidman, Nicole 178
Kiersch, Fritz 72, 100
killer POV shots *see* point of view
Kim, Dong-bin 149
Kim, Yong-gyun 58
*Das Kind* (film, 2012) 113
King, Stephen 4–5, 10, 58, 194*n19*
*Kiss of the Tarantula* (film, 1976) 176
Klein, Melanie 14
*Knowing* (film, 2009) 3, 184
Kogan, Jacob **46**
Kristeva, Julia 14
Krüger, Hardy **39**
Kubrick, Stanley 30, 57, 115

Ladd, Jordan **26**
Ladman, Cathy 94
Lafia, John 126
Lakhani, Nina 138

Lambert, Mary 63
landscape in horror film 43–5, 52, 56, 59–61, 65; *see also* environment; nature; wilderness
Lanza, Anthony M. 92
Larson, Bob 94
Leader, Anton 77
*Leave It to Beaver* (TV series, 1957–63) 35, 121
legends as horror motifs 63–72
Lehman, Lew 73
LeRoy, Mervyn 120, 123
Lindbergh, Carl 158
*The Little Girl Who Lives Down the Lane* (film, 1976) 3, 176
Longfellow, Henry Wadsworth 58
*Lord of the Flies* (film, 1963) 57, 72–4
*Lord of the Flies* (film, 1990) 57, 72
*The Lord of the Rings* (film, 2001) 75, 193*Concl.n3*
love, familial, in history 33–4; as portrayed in horror 29, 35–53
Lovecraft, H.P. 181–2
Lumby, Catharine 179, 181
Lyn, Dawn 174
Lynch, David 30

MacGregor, Sean 55, 162, 173–4
*Mad Max* films (1979–85) 57
mad scientist *see* scientists in horror
*Mama* (film, 2013) 73
Mancini, Don 191*n10*
Mandeville, Bernard 118, 122
Mangold, James 3
*Manhattan Baby* (film, 1982) 114
Manifest Destiny 58
*The Manitou* (film, 1978) 31
Marcus, Greil 135, 191*n13*
marketing research 182–3
Martin, Malachi 94
Masonberg, Hal 31
materialism *see* consumerism
McCarthy, Joseph 116
McCloud, Scott 8
McCormack, Patty **124**
McKee, Lucky 73
meritocracy 119–20
Merlet, Agnès 159
Michel, Anneliese 116
*The Midwich Cuckoos* (novel, 1957) 77
*Mikey* (film, 1992) **165**, 165–8, 170, 173–5
Miller, Arthur 116, 190*n18*
Molyneux, Stefan 138
Monkey's Paw tale 63–5
Montessori, Maria 163, 193*ch8 gen.note*
motherhood, as portrayed in horror 13–55, 60, 75, 82, 93, 130–1, 145–9; in ideology 34; in psychoanalysis 13–4, 23, 28; in

*Rosemary's Baby* 5, 16, 114, 188*n9*; *see also* babies
Mulligan, Robert 55
Munger, Chris 176
Murphy, Bernice 57, 71, 95
Muschietti, Andrés 73
mutants 140–4
mythology *see* legends

Nakata, Hideo 4, 144, 146, 157, 187*n2*
narrative perspective *see* narrator; perspective
narrator 154–5, 192*n20*
Narraway, Guinevere 56
Natali, Vincenzo 93, 130, 191*n12*
National Rifle Association 190*ch5n14*
Native Americans, as portrayed in horror 31, 57, 101–6, 190*ch5n15*
nature, as portrayed in horror 56–75, 101–6, 178; *see also* environment; landscape; wilderness
nature religion 104–6; *see also* religion
neglect, as portrayed in horror 29–30, 38, 53, 55, 64, 67, 70, 73, 98–9, 113, 116, 145–9, 157–8, 166, 176
Nelson, Ralph 93
neurological research 187*n4*
*The New Daughter* (film, 2009) 116
Newman, Kim 143
Nietzsche, Friedrich 71
*Night Child* (film, 1971) 35–40, **39**, 51–3, 189*ch2n7*
*Night of the Living Dead* (film, 1968) 10, 54, 66, 178
*Night of the Living Dead* (film, 1990) 54, 178
*A Nightmare on Elm Street* (film, 1984) 182
Nixey, Troy 53
NRA *see* National Rifle Association
nuclear family *see* families, as portrayed in horror
nuclear horror 76–7, 79, 91–2, 159, 179, 189*ch4gen.note*, 190*ch4n16*
nuclear powers 189*ch4n6*

*Oblivion* (film, 2013) 57
Oedipus complex 13–4, 161; in horror 19
Ohrbin, Mun **70**
*The Omen* (film, 1976) 12, 32, 94–5, 98, 111–2, 114, 165
*Omen II* (film, 1978) *see* Damien
*El Orfanato* (film, 2007) *see* The Orphanage
*Orphan* (film, 2009) 54–5
*The Orphanage* (film, 2007) 158
Orwell, George 148

*The Other* (film, 1972) 55
*The Others* (film, 2001) 178

paedophelia *see* pedophelia
pagan gods 107–13; *see also* Corn Goddess; God/gods
Parental Responsibility Act (2005) 74
Park, Ki-hyeong 67
Parker, Honora 72
Paul, William 85, 139, 179
Paxton, Bill 114
pedophilia 98–9, 113–4, 160, 176; *see also* abuse
Peeters, Barbara 92
Peirce, Kimberly 115, 159
penis envy 14
*Peopletoys* (film, 1974) 55, 162–5, *163*, 167, 173–5
Personal Responsibility Act (1996) 120
perspective 36–8, 52–3, 61; *see also* cinematography; narrator; point of view; viewer identification
*Pet Sematary* (film, 1989) 63–7, *64*, 68, 71–2, 76; review 189*ch3n5*
Peter Pan Syndrome 61, 72, 161–2, 173–6
Philips, Lee 32
photography 179
Piaget, Jean 162, 164–5, 171, 174, 193*ch8n2*
Pick, Anat 56
*The Pit* (film, 1981) 73
*The Plague* (film, 2006) 31
play, children's, as portrayed in horror 161–77; in child psychology 161–3
Poe, Edgar Allan 168
point of view 7–9, 17, 21, 24, 30, 36–7, 52–3, 59, 61, 66, 69, 71, 73–5, 90, 102, 107–9, 126, 130, 135, 142, 147–8, 158, 172, 184, 188*Intro.n10*, 191*n10*, 193*ch8n5*
Polanski, Roman 5, 15–6, 31, 94, 114
Polley, Sarah **133**
pollution *see* environment
*Poltergeist* (film, 1982) 4, 5–6, 135, 137
*Possession* (film, 1981) 31
possession, as portrayed in horror 5, 31, 53, 94–5, 101–17, 126–30, 144–9, 157–8, 168, 173, 175, 179
*The Possession of Joel Delaney* (film, 1972) 112
Potts, John 35
POV *see* point of view
Powell, Clive **80**
*A Prairie Home Companion* (radio variety show, 1974–) 51
Price, David 100

*Promenons-nous dans les bois* (film, 2000) 58
*Prometheus* (film, 2012) 31
Proxauf, Leonard **152**
Proyas, Alex 3
psychiatry, as portrayed in horror 36–8, 42, 46, 51, 84, 96, 145–7, 159, 165–77
*Psycho* (film, 1960) 168, 191*n10*
psychoanalysis 13–4, 23, 28, 166–8, 188*ch1gen.note*
psychology, developmental 161–5, 171; as portrayed in horror 162–3, 166–8, 173–7
psychopathy, as portrayed in horror 47, 50, 55, 164–7, 173–7, 179
psychotheraphy, as portrayed in horror 81–6, 165–77, 190*ch4n14*
*Puppetmaster* (film, 1989) 7, 182

¿*Quién puede matar a un niño?* (film, 1976) 6, 57, 139, 159

RAD *see* Reactive Detachment Disorder
Raimi, Sam 74, 178
Ramsay, Lynne 3, 176
rape, as portrayed in horror 10, 16, 17–9, 29, 151, 153, 159–60, 176
Ratliff, George 45
Reactive Detachment Disorder 193*ch8n3*
Reagan, Ronald 76
*The Rear Window* (film, 1954) 148
*Red Riding Hood* (film, 2011) 58
*The Red Shoes* (film, 2005) *see* Bunhongsin
*Reincarnation* (film, 2005) 158
reincarnation, as portrayed in horror *see* ghosts
religion 119; as portrayed in horror 87–9, 94–117, 178, 182, 190*ch5n1*, 190*ch5n2*
religious fundamentalism 103–5, 115; *see also* religion
remakes 178, 193*Concl.n3*
resurrection, as portrayed in horror 115
Revere, Paul 58
Reverend Billy 119
Rilla, Wolf 77, 159
*The Ring* (film, 2002) 144–9, **149**, 153, 155–8, 178, 191*ch7gen.note*, 192*n9*, 192*n11*, 193*Concl.n3*
*The Ring 2* (film, 2005) 144–9, 153, 155–6, 191*ch7gen.note*, 192*n9*, 192*n10*, 193*Concl.n3*
*The Ring Virus* (film, 1999) 149
*Ringu* (film, 1998) 144, 189*ch3n7*, 192*n12*
*Ringu 2* (film, 1999) 144, 192*n10*
*The Rise of the Meritocracy* (treatise, 1958) 191*ch6n6*

Riski, Pete 191*ch7n8*
*The Road* (film, 2009) 57, 77
Robbins, Anthony 120
Roberts, Johannes 3
Rockwell, Norman 168–9, 193*ch8n4*
Roeg, Nicolas 157
Roman Catholic Church *see* Catholicism
Romero, George 6, 54, 178
*Rosemary's Baby* (film, 1968) 5, 12, 15–6, 31–2, 53, 94–5, 111–2, 114, 178
Rosenberg, Stuart 136
Roth, Eli 137
Rousseau, Jean-Jacques 57
Ruben, Joseph 40
*Ruby* (film, 1977) 116–7
*Rumpelstiltskin* (film, 1995) 58
Rusnak, Josef 31

sacrifice, human 100, 105–16; *see also* religion
sadism, as portrayed in horror 72–3, 102, 123, 137, 167–8, 170
Sagan, Carl 92
saints, as portrayed in horror 97–100; *see also* religion
Salles, Walter 157
*Sarah's Child* (film, 1994) 32
Sartre, Jean-Paul 39
satanism *see* devil
*Saw* (film, 2004) 182, 185, 194*n23*
*Scary Movie* (film, 2000) 7
Schiller, Friedrich 33–4
sci-fi films 10, 76–7, 91, 189*ch4gen.note*
science, as portrayed in horror 76–93, 130–6, 141, 179, 182, 189*ch4gen.note*; in disaster films 91; in sci-fi films 76–7, 91; *see also* scientists
scientists in horror 16–23, 28–9, 30, 76–93, 130–6, 141–2, 159, 170–1, 190*ch4n14*
Scott, Ridley 29, 31, 130
*Scream* (film, 1996) 178
*Scream 2* (film, 1997) 10, 178
*Scream 3* (film, 2000) 178
*Scream 4* (film, 2011) 178
*Scream Because I Know What You Did to That Psycho Last Summer* (TV episode, 2004) 187*n9*
*Seed of Chucky* (film, 2004) 126, 129–30, 191*n10*
self-help literature 119–20, 135
sequels 10, 11, 14, 58, 182
serial killers 138; as portrayed in horror 3–4, 113–4, 120–30, 158, 160, 165–8, 176–7
Serrador, Narciso Ibáñez *see* Ibáñez Serrador, Narciso
Seuss, Dr. 161
*Se7en* (film, 1995) 147

# Index

sex change, as portrayed in horror 75, 93, 131–4
sexual abuse 151; *see also* rape
Shankland, Tom 174–5, 193*ch8n9*
*Shattered Lives* (film, 2009) 158
Sheffield, Jeremy 174
Sheldon, David 55, 162
Shimizu, Takashi 157–8
*The Shining* (film, 1980) 3, 30, 57, 115
Shome, Siddharta 118
Shonteff, Lindsay 136
*Shriek If You Know What I Did Last Friday the Thirteenth* (film, 2000) 187*n*9
Shriver, Lionel 177, 193*Concl.n*4
sibling rivalry, as portrayed in horror 45–6, 49, 52
*Signs* (film, 2002) 91
*Silent Hill* (film, 2006) 191*ch7n*8
Simons, Daniel 82, 189–90*ch4n*9
sin *see* religion
*Sin-de-rel-la* (film, 2006) 58
*Sinister* (film, 2012) 106–13, **110**, 178
Skinner, B.F. 122
Slade, David 159
*Sleepaway Camp* (film, 1983) 75
*Slither* (film, 2006) 32
Smith, Murray 11, 188*n*15
*Snow White: A Deadly Summer* (film, 2012) 58
*Snow White: A Tale of Terror* (film, 1997) 58
*Snow White: The Fairest of Them All* (film, 2001) 58
Snyder, Zack 3
Sole, Alfred 95, 190*ch5n*10
Solet, Paul 23, 25, 27, 188*ch1n*10, 188*ch1n*11
Sontag, Susan 189*ch4n*4
Spencer, Herbert 161, 163, 193*ch8gen.note*
Spielberg, Steven 11
spirits *see* ghosts
*Splice* (film, 2009) 93, 130–6, **133**, 191*n*12
"Star Wars Program" *see* Strategic Defense Initiative
Stellar, Carolyn 174
*The Stranger Within* (film, 1974) 32
Strategic Defense Initiative 76
suspense films 10, 11
Sutherland, Donald 178

Tamahori, Lee 56
televangelism 119, 191*ch6n*3
television, as portrayed in horror 137, 144–9
*Terminator Salvation* (film, 2009) 57

*The Texas Chain Saw Massacre* (film, 1974) 4–5, 35, 56–7, 181
theology *see* religion
*The Thing* (film, 1982) 182–3
Thompson, Caroline 58
Thoreau, Henry David 56–7, 155
*300* (film, 2006) 3
thrillers 7, 11, 182
Tocqueville, Alexis de 119
trauma 84, 173–5, 191*ch7gen.note*; as portrayed in horror 166–7, 176; *see also* neurological research; violence
trees, as portrayed in horror films 67–71; in legend 68, 189*ch3n*6
Turner, Tierre 174
TV *see* television
Twitchell, James B. 140

*The Unborn* (film, 1991) 19–23, **23**, 28, 93
*The Unborn* (film, 2009) 114–5
*The Unborn II* (film, 1994) 19, 93
*Under the Skin* (film, 2014) 178
Unicef 118, 139, 190*ch6n*1, 191*ch7n*5

vampires 25–7, 54, 67
Van Sant, Gus 3
Velázquez, Diego 15
Verbinski, Gore 144
victims, in horror film 6–9, 82–6, 87, 113, 157, 182–3, 194*n*18
viewer alignment *see* point of view
viewer allegiance *see* viewer identification
viewer identification 7–10, 17, 22, 27, 28, 36–8, 53, 103–4, 160, 182–4
*Village of the Damned* (film, 1960) 12, 20, 77, 81, 159
*Village of the Damned* (film, 1995) 159
violence in horror 194*n*18; effect on children 109, 138, 162, 174; effect on film audiences 184–5; effect on filmmakers 173–5; *see also* abuse; neurological research
*Volcano* (film, 1997) 57, 91
Voskanian, Robert 59, 175
Vygotsky, Lee 161, 193*ch8gen.note*

*Wake Wood* (film, 2010) 115
*WALL-E* (film, 2008) 57
*Wall Street* (film, 1987) 118
Walser, Martin 156, 193*n*23
Wan, James 194*n*23
*War of the Worlds* (film, 2005) 91

Washington, George 58
water, as a horror motif 147–8, 192*n*10
*Waterworld* (film, 2005) 57
Watkins, James 74
Watson, John B. 122
Watts, Naomi **149**
*We Need to Talk About Kevin* (film, 2011) 3, 10, 176–7
*We Need to Talk About Kevin* (novel, 2003) 177, 193*Concl.n*4
*Das Weiße Band see The White Ribbon*
welfare reform *see* Personal Responsibility Act
*What the Peeper Saw* (film, 1971) 35–40, 39, 51–3, 189*ch2n*7
*Whisper* (film, 2007) 115
White, Andrew *see* Bianchi, Andrea
White, Sylvain 187*n*9
*The White Ribbon* (film, 2009) 10, 150–6, **152**, 191*ch7gen.note*; review 192*n*17
*The White Ribbon* (screenplay, 2007) 156, 193*n*24
*Who Can Kill a Child?* (film, 1976) *see ¿Quién puede matar a un niño?*
*Wicked Little Things* (film, 2006) 159
Wieland, Christoph Martin 14–5
Wilderness Act, U.S. 56
wilderness, as portrayed in horror 56–67; *see also* landscape; nature
Wilkins, Toby 157
*The Wizard of Oz* (film, 1939) 104
Wolf, Christa 81, 189*ch4n*7
Wood, Elijah **41**
*The Woods* (film, 2006) 73
*Would You Kill a Child?* (film, 1976) *see ¿Quién puede matar a un niño?*
Wyndham, John 77

*Yellowbrickroad* (film, 2010) 57, 59
Yim, Pil-sung 58
Yonis, Jeff 92
Young, Michael 119, 191*ch6n*6
Yu, Ronny 126
Yūrei ghosts *see* ghosts in Japanese culture

zombies 54, 59–61, 74, 92, 159, 179
Zulawski, Andrzej 31

www.ingramcontent.com/pod-product-compliance
Ingram Content Group UK Ltd.
Pitfield, Milton Keynes, MK11 3LW, UK
UKHW050529150426
5217IPUK00026B/1862